Discourse Analysis

Introducing Linguistics

This outstanding series is an indispensable resource for students and teachers – a concise and engaging introduction to the central subjects of contemporary linguistics. Presupposing no prior knowledge on the part of the reader, each volume sets out the fundamental skills and knowledge of the field, and so provides the ideal educational platform for further study in linguistics.

Discourse Analysis

SECOND EDITION

Barbara Johnstone

© 2008 by Barbara Johnstone

BLACKWELL PUBLISHING
350 Main Street, Malden, MA 02148-5020, USA
9600 Garsington Road, Oxford OX4 2DQ, UK
550 Swanston Street, Carlton, Victoria 3053, Australia

The right of Barbara Johnstone to be identified as the Author of
this Work has been asserted in accordance with the UK Copyright,
Designs, and Patents Act 1988.

All rights reserved. No part of this publication may be reproduced, stored in
a retrieval system, or transmitted, in any form or by any means, electronic,
mechanical, photocopying, recording or otherwise, except as permitted by
the UK Copyright, Designs, and Patents Act 1988, without the prior
permission of the publisher.

First edition published 2002 by Blackwell Publishing Ltd
Second edition published 2008 by Blackwell Publishing Ltd

1   2008

Library of Congress Cataloging-in-Publication Data

Johnstone, Barbara.
Discourse analysis / Barbara Johnstone. — 2nd ed.
p. cm. — (Introducing linguistics ; 3)
Includes bibliographical references and index.
ISBN 978-1-4051-4427-8 (pbk. : alk. paper)   1. Discourse analysis.   I. Title.

P302.J64 2007
401.41—dc22
2006103247

A catalogue record for this title is available from the British Library.

Set in 10.5/12pt Plantin
by Graphicraft Limited, Hong Kong
Printed and bound in Singapore
by Markono Print Media Pte Ltd

The publisher's policy is to use permanent paper from mills that operate
a sustainable forestry policy, and which has been manufactured from
pulp processed using acid-free and elementary chlorine-free practices.
Furthermore, the publisher ensures that the text paper and cover board
used have met acceptable environmental accreditation standards.

For further information on
Blackwell Publishing, visit our website:
www.blackwellpublishing.com

to my teachers

Contents

Figures

Preface to Second Edition

This new edition incorporates changes in every chapter. In chapter 1 there is now an extended discussion of the use of large corpora as data for discourse analysis. In chapter 2 the discussion of grammatical gender in French has been expanded and clarified. I am grateful to Maeve Conrick for pointing me to sources about the feminization of professional titles in Canadian French. There is also a new section on cognitive metaphor in this chapter. Chapter 4 has new sections on indexicality, stance and style, and social and personal identity. In chapter 5 the discussion of intertextuality has been broadened to include interdiscursivity, and in chapter 6 there is a new section on the analysis of multimodal discourse. Chapter 7 has new material on conversational implicature and an expanded discussion of critiques of speech act theory. I have made hundreds of smaller changes as well. There are added and updated theoretical overviews, examples, and citations throughout the book, and outdated discussion question texts have been removed or replaced.

In preparing this new edition I have benefited from comments and suggestions from students and colleagues at Carnegie Mellon University and elsewhere, as well as suggestions from a number of anonymous reviewers of the first edition. Since 1997, the English Department at Carnegie Mellon University has been a supportive place to work. I am grateful to all, and to the editors and other specialists at Blackwell Publishing who have made the process go as smoothly as possible. I am also grateful to the many people who have taken the time, at conferences and in emails, to tell me they liked the book. I would not have undertaken a revision without their encouragement.

Preface to First Edition

This book is intended to be a first-level text for undergraduates and beginning graduate students taking their first (or only) course about discourse. The subject matter of discourse analysis is vast – "language in use," as Brown and Yule (1983) put it, "utterances," according to Schiffrin (1994), "verbal communication" for Renkema (2004) – and most discourse analysts would be hard pressed to describe what, if anything, makes discourse analysis a discipline. Yet discourse analysis is implicitly treated as if it were a discipline in texts that are organized as a series of overviews of research topics (institutional discourse, discourse and gender, narrative, media discourse, and so on) or theories (pragmatics, Conversation Analysis, politeness theory, and so on). The approach I take in this book is different. I treat discourse analysis not as a discipline (or as a subdiscipline of linguistics) but as a systematic, rigorous way of suggesting answers to research questions posed in and across disciplines throughout the humanities and social sciences and beyond. In other words, I see discourse analysis as a research method that can be (and is being) used by scholars with a variety of academic and non-academic affiliations, coming from a variety of disciplines, to answer a variety of questions.

For this reason, this book is meant to encourage students not to think of discourse analysis as a collection of facts or canonical studies or as a body of theory. As we will see, discourse analysts set out to answer many kinds of questions about language, about speakers, and about society and culture. However, they all approach their tasks by paying close and systematic attention to particular situations and particular utterances or sets of utterances. This book attempts to separate the techniques of discourse analysis clearly from its results, trying to make sure that students understand and practice the former before concentrating on the latter. This will, I hope, help alleviate a problem I have had again and again in teaching discourse analysis – that of ending up with students who are fascinated by the results of sensitive analyses of discourse but unable themselves to perform analyses that go much beyond paraphrase. Discourse analysis, as I approach it here, is an open-ended heuristic, a research method consisting of a set of topics to consider in connection with any instance of discourse. This heuristic can help insure that discourse analysts are systematically paying attention to every possible element of the potential meaning of a stretch of talk or writing: every kind of context, every resource for creativity, and every source of limitation and constraint on creativity. My focus is thus less on providing detailed descriptions of the results of discourse analysts' work than on asking students to think systematically about a variety of sources of constraint on and creativity in discourse, a variety of reasons why spoken utterances and written texts have the meanings and uses they do. Discussion questions which in many cases ask readers to think about what they and other people in their field do or might do with discourse analysis, as well as ideas for small research projects using discourse analysis, are interspersed throughout the chapters.

Except for the first and the last, the chapters in this book are self contained, so they could be handled in any order. The order I have selected reflects a combination of what I have found students' interests and expectations to be. People often come to language study because their attention has been captured by the ways in which language, culture, and the world seem to be intertwined. (This can happen, for example, when one studies a foreign language or travels to a foreign place.) This is why I have put the chapter about discourse and world directly after the introduction. People expect language study to be about structures and rules, so the chapter about discourse and structure is also close to the beginning. No textbook author can expect to control how his or her book is used. I would like, however, to urge that readers of this book touch on every chapter in it. To pick and choose among the ways in which discourse is multiply constrained and enabled would be contrary to the overall purpose of the book, because it would encourage the kind of one-dimensional approach to explaining texts against which this book constitutes an argument.

Each chapter ends with a set of suggested supplementary readings. These are not intended as comprehensive bibliographies. Particularly in the areas in which most work is being done at the moment, it would be impossible to have included all the most recent sources, and such literature reviews would in any case have been outdated by the time the book was published. Instead, I have tried to make suggestions for one or two things a person might profitably read in connection with each section of the chapter. Some are particularly influential studies, often ones done relatively early on. Others are overviews and literature reviews. Instructors could use these lists to choose supplementary readings for the course, and students could use them as a way to get started with background reading in the areas they decide to focus on.

Although some are trained in departments of linguistics, most discourse analysts, at least in the US, do not teach in linguistics departments, but rather in departments of English, anthropology, communication, education, or foreign languages, among others. This means that most students in courses about discourse analysis are not linguistics majors or graduate students in linguistics. I have made every effort in designing this book not to lose sight of this fact. I have tried to avoid the temptation to write at such an advanced level and in such a discipline-specific way that students' frequent suspicions that linguistics is difficult and irrelevant to their other interests are simply confirmed. A course in discourse analysis is an ideal place to encourage interdisciplinary exploration, since discourse is a focus of study in most of the humanities and social sciences. Discourse analysis is practiced in one way or another by at least some people in most of the academic disciplines in which human life is the focus: anthropologists analyze discourse, as do communications scholars, rhetoricians, literary and cultural critics, sociologists, psychologists, geographers, and medical, legal, and educational researchers, among others. Non-linguists can be drawn into the study of language through discourse analysis, and linguists can be drawn into interdisciplinary work. I have written this book specifically with a non-specialist, interdisciplinary audience in mind. Although readers might benefit from having had a general introduction to linguistics first (particularly if the introduction was not limited to formal theories of semantics, syntax, and phonology), I assume that many readers will be newcomers to the field. In the text, I try to explain concepts from linguistics when they first arise. There is a glossary at the end of the book in which terms that may be unfamiliar, as well as specialized uses of familiar words, are briefly defined.

In order to make it possible for instructors to adapt the book to more specialized audiences, some of the discussion questions are geared to teachers and students in one field or another. For example, some discussion questions require students to produce translations or do detailed grammatical analysis. These will obviously not work for students who do not know foreign languages or who are unfamiliar with basic grammatical concepts and terms. Other discussion questions are on topics that will particularly interest people in one field or another: some deal with literary discourse, for example, others with technical genres; some deal with writing and some with spoken language. It is not intended, nor would it be possible, for a class to do all the discussion questions. Students and instructors are meant to develop a system for choosing among them.

Since many of the texts around which the questions revolve were selected and/or collected by my students, there is an inevitable North American bias. I have tried to counteract this to a certain extent in the body of the text by discussing and drawing examples from research done elsewhere. Unfortunately, it has simply not been practical to include anything approaching a representative sampling of work about languages other than English. Good discourse analysis usually cannot be done in translation (although good translation requires careful discourse analysis), and English is the only language all readers of this book will more or less share.

As will be obvious to anyone who knows his work, A. L. Becker has been a major influence on my approach to discourse analysis. I learned from him to think of discourse analysis in heuristic terms, as the systematic consideration of a set of broad analytical *topoi*. Becker has talked about the sources of constraint on discourse in a variety of ways, and the set of topics around which this book is based is not exactly the same as any of his. But the overall structure of this book reflects the way I structure my courses in discourse analysis, and that structure reflects the structure of a course called "Language and Culture" as Becker was teaching it at the University of Michigan in the late 1970s. I was fortunate enough to participate in that course twice, once as a student and once as a teaching assistant, and then to have Becker serve as my dissertation mentor. Since then I have learned more from him in many conversations, including discussions of my ideas for this book. Although I hope it is at least in a general way the sort of book he would write if he were to write a textbook, he of course bears no responsibility for its failings, nor do I claim to be speaking for him in this book. I am also grateful to everyone else whose work I have cited or discussed. I have learned from all of them and I hope not to have misrepresented any of them.

I have also learned from people I have worked with at Indiana University-Purdue University at Fort Wayne, Georgetown, Texas A&M, and Carnegie Mellon. Figuring out how to articulate my interests and skills with those of colleagues and students in anthropology, linguistics, literary studies, and rhetoric in four very different settings has encouraged me to learn to think and talk about the ways in which discourse analysis can be an interdisciplinary resource. Students at all four of these places have contributed to this book, both by letting me try out ideas on them in class and by contributing much of the data on which the discussion questions are based. (When the class is small enough, I have each of my discourse analysis students provide his or her own written text or transcript for analysis, and we work with the resulting corpus of student-selected materials all term. I have used many of these materials, with identifying details altered where necessary, in this book.) Since 1998, students at Carnegie Mellon have patiently put up with preliminary typescript iterations of this book as the primary text in my discourse analysis classes. Many have contributed suggestions and corrections, for which I thank them. I am particularly grateful to Denise Wittkofski, who identified the terms that needed to be included in the glossary.

I am also very grateful to the anonymous reviewers of the proposal for this book and, later, the manuscript, and to the editors with whom I have worked at Blackwell Publishers.

Text credits

The following permissions to reprint are gratefully acknowledged:

Chapter 1: "Pumpernickel," by Philip Schultz. From *New American Poets of the 90s*. Edited by Jack Myers and Roger Weingarten. Reprinted by permission of David R. Godine, Publisher, Inc. Copyright ©1991 Edited by Jack Myers and Roger Weingarten.

Chapter 2: "AIDS Drug Cocktails Fail 53% in Study," by Lisa M. Krieger. http://www.sfgate.com/cgi-bin/article.cgi?file=/examiner/archive/1997/09/29/ NEWS3491.dtl. Reprinted by permission of *The San Francisco Examiner*.

The publishers apologize for any errors or omissions in the above list and would be grateful to be notified of any corrections that should be incorporated in the next edition or reprint of this book.

chapter 1

Introduction

What is Discourse Analysis?

People in a variety of academic departments and disciplines use the term "discourse analysis" for what they do, how they do it, or both. Many of these people, though by no means all, have some training in general linguistics, and some would identify themselves primarily as linguists. Others, however, would identify themselves primarily with other fields of study, such as anthropology, communication, cultural studies, psychology, or education, to list just a few of the possibilities, and some situate their work in the interdisciplinary endeavor of discourse studies. Discourse analysts pose many different questions and propose many different sorts of answers. In one journal issue devoted to discourse analysis (Basham, Fiksdal, and Rounds, 1999), for example, there are papers by eleven people who all think of what they do as discourse analysis. One of these authors talks about the descriptive terms used of the African-American defendant in the media coverage of a murder trial. One talks about differences between English and Japanese. One describes newspaper coverage of a prison scandal in England. Another discusses metaphor, and another analyzes expressions of identity in Athabaskan (Native American) student writing. One talks about a poem, and there is a paper about the epitaph of the spiritual master of a sect of Muslims and one about whether the pronoun *I* should appear in formal writing. One paper is about the connection between personal pronouns and the human experience of selfhood, one is about political debate, one is about using case studies as a way of studying sociolinguistic variation. The papers make points such as these: media coverage of the murder trial was racist; the Japanese word *jinkaku*, used in Japan's new post-World War II constitution as an equivalent for the English expression *individual dignity*, both represented and shaped a particularly Japanese way of thinking and talking about the public person; female US college students describing seminars used metaphors of sharing whereas male students used metaphors of competing; poems by Gerard Manley Hopkins operate on numerous levels at once; a Bektashi Muslim community in the United States manages to maintain a sense of cultural continuity despite massive cultural and geographical changes and in several radically different languages; students need a voice with which to write in academia.

It might appear that the only thing all these projects have in common is that, in one way or another, they all involve studying language and its effects. Is discourse analysis, then, simply the study of language and its effects? It has been described that way. It has been suggested, for example, that "the name for the field 'discourse analysis' . . . says nothing more or other than the term 'linguistics': the study of language" (Tannen, 1989: 6). In a way, this is exactly correct: discourse analysis is the study of language, in the everyday sense in which most people use the term. What most people mean when they say "language" is talk, communication, discourse. (In formal language study, both descriptive and prescriptive, the term "language" is often used differently, to refer to structures or rules that are thought to underlie talk.) Even if discourse analysis is, basically, "the study of language," however, it is useful to try to specify what makes discourse analysis different from other approaches to language study. One way to do this is by asking ourselves what we can learn by thinking about what "discourse" is, and about what "analysis" is.

"Discourse"

To discourse analysts, "discourse" usually means actual instances of communicative action in the medium of language, although some define the term more broadly as "meaningful symbolic behavior" in any mode (Blommaert, 2005: 2). "Discourse" in this sense is usually a mass noun. Discourse analysts typically speak of *discourse* rather than *discourses*, the way we speak of other things for which we often use mass nouns, such as *music* ("some music" or "three pieces of music" rather than "three musics") or *information* ("the flow of information," "a great deal of information," rather than "thousands of informations"). Communication can of course involve other media besides language. Media such as photography, clothing, music, architecture, and dance can be meaningful, too, and discourse analysts often need to think about the connections between language and other such modes of semiosis, or meaning-making.

Not all linguistic communication is spoken or written: there are manual languages, such as American Sign Language, whose speakers use gesture rather than sound or graphic signs. (It is conventional to use the word "speaker" as a cover term for people who are writing or gesturally signing in addition to those who employ the aural–oral mode. Doing this is convenient, but it also can make it seem as if spoken language is more natural, neutral, or normal than signing or writing are. There are arguments to be made on all sides of this question, and we will return to it when we discuss media of communication in more detail in chapter 6.)

Calling what we do "*discourse* analysis" rather than "language analysis" underscores the fact that we are not centrally focused on language as an abstract system. We tend instead to be interested in what happens when people draw on the knowledge they have about language, knowledge based on their memories of things they have said, heard, seen, or written before, to do things in the world: exchange information, express feelings, make things happen, create beauty, entertain themselves and others, and so on. This knowledge – a set of generalizations, which can sometimes be stated as rules, about what words generally mean, about what goes where in a sentence, and so on – is what is often referred to as "language," when language is thought of as an abstract system of rules or structural relationships. Discourse is both the source of this knowledge (people's generalizations about language are made on the basis of the discourse they participate in) and the result of it (people apply what they already know in creating and interpreting new discourse).

Scholars influenced by Foucault (1972, 1980) sometimes use "discourse" in a related but somewhat different sense, as a count noun. "Discourses" in this sense can be enumerated and referred to in the plural. They are conventional ways of talking that both create and are created by conventional ways of thinking. These linked ways of talking and thinking constitute ideologies (sets of interrelated ideas) and serve to circulate power in society. In other words, "discourses" in this sense involve patterns of belief and habitual action as well as patterns of language. Discourses are ideas as well as ways of talking that influence and are influenced by the ideas. Discourses, in their linguistic aspect, are conventionalized sets of choices for discourse, or talk. Some discourse analysts distinguish the two meanings of "discourse" orthographically, using Discourse (with a capital D) for the former and discourse (with a lower-case d) for the latter (Gee, 2005). As we will see throughout this book (particularly in chapter 2), the two senses of the word "discourse," as mass noun ("discourse") and as count noun ("discourses"), are crucially connected.

"Analysis"

Why discourse *analysis* rather than "discourseology," on the analogy of "phonology," "discourseography," on the analogy of "ethnography," or "discourse criticism," on the analogy of "literary criticism" or "rhetorical criticism"? The answer has to do with the fact that discourse analysis typically focuses on the analytical process in a relatively explicit way. It is useful to think of discourse analysis as analogous to chemical analysis. Like chemical analysis, discourse analysis is a methodology that can be used in answering many kinds of questions. As we have already seen, discourse analysts start out with a variety of research questions, and these research questions are often not questions that only discourse analysts ask. Instead, they are often questions that discourse analysts share with other people, both in linguistics and in other fields. Some discourse analysts ask questions that are traditionally asked in linguistics: questions about linguistic structure, about language change, about meaning, about language acquisition. Other discourse analysts ask questions that are more interdisciplinary: questions about such things as social roles and relations, communication and identity. What distinguishes discourse analysis from other sorts of study that bear on human language and communication lies not in the questions discourse analysts ask but in the ways they try to answer them: by analyzing discourse – that is, by examining aspects of the structure and function of language in use.

Perhaps the most familiar use of the word "analysis" is for processes, mental or mechanical, for taking things apart. Chemical analysis, for example, involves using a variety of mechanical techniques for separating compounds into their elemental parts. Mental analysis is also involved, as the chemist thinks in advance about what the compound's parts are likely to be. Linguistic analysis is also sometimes a process of taking apart. Discourse analysts often find it useful to divide longer stretches of discourse into parts according to various criteria and then look at the particular characteristics of each part. Divisions can be made according to who is talking, for example, where the paragraph boundaries are, when a new topic arises, or where the subject ends and the predicate begins. Are grammatical patterns different when social superiors are talking than when their subordinates are? Does new information tend to come in the first sentence of a paragraph? Are topic changes signaled by special markers? Do sentence subjects tend to be slots in which events or actions or feelings can be presented as things? Discourse can be taken apart into individual words and phrases, and concordances of these – sets of statistics about where a particular word is likely to occur, how frequent it is, what words tend to be close to it – can be used to support claims about how grammar works or what words are used to mean.

But analysis can also involve taking apart less literally. One way of analyzing something is by looking at it in a variety of ways. An analysis in this sense might involve systematically asking a number of questions, systematically taking several theoretical perspectives, or systematically performing a variety of tests. Such an analysis could include a breaking-down into parts. It could also include a breaking-down into functions (What is persuasive discourse like? What is narrative like?), or according to participants (How do men talk in all-male groups? How do psychotherapists talk? What is newspaper writing like?), or settings (What goes on in classrooms? In workplaces? In sororities?), or processes (How do children learn to get the conversational floor? How do people create social categories like "girl" or "foreigner" or "old person" as they talk to and about each other?).

Discussion

1.1 One good way to begin to think about what discourse analysis involves is by thinking about, or, if you can, practicing translation. If you know another language well enough, try translating each of the following into it:

    a. All men are created equal.
    b. Don't count your chickens before they hatch.
    c. "We have also come to this hallowed spot to remind America of the fierce urgency of now." (Rev. Martin Luther King, Jr., "I Have a Dream" speech)

What decisions have to be made as you do this? What cultural resonances are lost as these sentences are taken out of the English (and, in the case of (a) and (c), United States) context? What resonances are added as they are articulated with another language and culture? Are there things you can do grammatically in English that can't be done in another language, and vice versa? What other kinds of texts or utterances does each sentence echo or draw on, in English and in other languages? Who would say things like these, to whom, in what circumstances, in each language? Why would these things be said? Are they usually said in writing, or orally, or in other media? Discuss whether it is ever possible to say the same thing in a different language, in a different style, in a different medium, or in a different situation.

1.2 In what other contexts have you analyzed written texts or conversations, systematically or unsystematically? Is the analysis of discourse ever involved in the study of literature? In history? In medicine or the law? What kinds of informal discourse analysis go on in homes and workplaces, when people try to figure out what written texts mean, how best to write or speak, what is going on in a conversation? What kinds of questions do people ask themselves and others as they do such analyses?

Some Uses of Discourse Analysis

As we have seen, discourse analysis has been used in answering many different kinds of questions. Some of these questions have to do with language.

What is involved in "knowing a language"? How do words, sentences, and utterances get associated with meanings? How does language change? How do children learn to talk and how do people learn new languages? Linguists have long been interested in the structure of words (morphology) and sentences (syntax). Discourse analysts have moved the description of structure up a level, looking at actual stretches of connected text or transcript of talk and providing descriptions of the structure of paragraphs, stories, and conversations. Language scholars also ask questions about meaning (semantics), and in a natural progression from work in semantics and syntax, discourse analysts have asked about what goes where in stretches of talk longer than words or phrases. Discourse analysis has shed light on how meaning can be created via the arrangement of chunks of information across a series of sentences or via the details of how a conversationalist takes up and responds to what has just been said. Discourse analysis sheds light on how speakers indicate their semantic intentions and how hearers interpret what they hear, and on the cognitive abilities that underlie human symbol use. In the field of pragmatics, discourse analysts looking at corpora of actual talk have helped to describe the culturally-shaped interpretive principles on which understanding is based and how people (and sometimes other entities) are thought to perform actions by means of utterances. Work on cohesion examines the meanings of utterances in their linguistic contexts.

Traditional approaches to questions about linguistic variation and language change involve examining internal causes of change (such as speakers' tendency to treat new words as analogous to old ones, adapting foreign sounds and words to the phonological and morphological patterns of the borrowing language) as well as external causes of change (such as geographical or social isolation of one group from another, which often leads to divergence in the ways they pronounce words and construct phrases and sentences). Discourse analysts have contributed to the study of variation and change from both perspectives. Looking at records of discourse over time, discourse analysts have described mechanisms of change having to do with what happens in talk. For example, forms that regularly serve useful functions in suggesting how speakers intend their words to be taken at a particular moment are sometimes "grammaticalized," changing over time into required elements of a language's grammar (Hopper and Traugott, 2003). Discourse analysts have also described external social and material influences that effect changes in patterns of language use, influences such as economic change, geographic mobility, and power relations, and they have studied patterns of variation in how people do things with talk such as making lists, constructing arguments, and telling stories.

Discourse analysts have also contributed to research on language acquisition. They have helped describe how speakers acquire new competence and what it is they are acquiring. In first language acquisition research, discourse analysis has a long history, dating back at least to important work by Charles Ferguson (1977) and others about the special simplified ways in which some people display the regularities of grammar as they talk to children. This research called into question the claim that innate linguistic knowledge was required for language learning to be possible. Work by discourse analysts on "foreigner talk" and "teacher talk" followed. Among the many discourse analysts who have added to our understanding of *what* language learners acquire are students of "contrastive rhetoric" and "contrastive pragmatics." They have shown that knowing a language means not just knowing its grammar and vocabulary but also knowing how to structure paragraphs and arguments and participate in conversations the way speakers of the language do, and it means understanding which sentence types can accomplish which purposes in social interaction: what might work as an apology, for example, or how to decline an invitation.

Discourse analysts also help answer questions about the roles of language in human cognition, art, and social life which have been asked for centuries. Students of literary style are discourse analysts (though they may not call themselves that) and they, along with folklorists and ethnographers of communication, have been exploring artistic uses of language, and the role of aesthetics and "performance" in all language use, for many years. Rhetorical study has always involved discourse analysis, explicit or not, as rhetoricians have analyzed relatively self-conscious, public, strategically designed talk and writing to see what makes it work. Discourse analysts have helped us understand why people tell stories, what the functions of "small talk" are, how people adapt language to specialized situations like teaching and psychotherapy, what persuasion is and how it works, how people negotiate the multiple roles and identities they may be called on to adopt.

Discourse analysis continues to be useful in answering questions that are posed in many fields that traditionally focus on human life and communication, such as anthropology, cultural studies, psychology, communications, and sociology, as well as in fields in which the details of discourse have not always been thought relevant, such as geography, psychology, human–computer interaction, medicine, law, public policy, and business. Anyone who wants to understand human beings has to understand discourse, so the potential uses of discourse analysis are almost innumerable. Discourse analysts help answer questions about social relations, such as dominance and oppression or solidarity. Discourse analysis is useful in the study of personal identity and social identification, as illustrated by work on discourse and gender or discourse and ethnicity. Discourse analysis has been used in the study of how people define and create lifespan processes such as aging and disability as they talk, how decisions are made, resources allocated, and social adaptation or conflict accomplished in public and private life. To the extent that discourse and discourses – meaning-making, in linguistic and other modes, and ways of acting, being, and envisioning self and environment – are at the center of human experience and activity, discourse analysis can help in answering any question that could be asked about humans in society.

Facets of Discourse Analysis

To introduce some of the kinds of questions discourse analysis can raise and help answer, and to lay out the analytical heuristic around which this book is organized, we begin with a set of brief examples. These exploratory analyses of small bits of text all deal with aspects of a familiar genre of discourse, the discourse directed to the public by an institution – in this case, an art museum. My purpose in presenting these mini-analyses is not to make any general point about the discourse and discourses of museums, or about how institutions construct and manipulate their publics, or about how ancient civilizations are commodified, exoticized, or made to seem threatening through the ways we talk about them, or about how condescending educational discourse can be – although all these angles are suggested in this analysis and would be worth pursuing further. My goal is simply to illustrate a few ways in which a systematic analysis of discourse can help illuminate facets of the communication process that are important and not immediately apparent.

The discourse to be analyzed here consists of what might be called popular Egyptology, in the form of advertising for and informational material about a museum exhibit called "Splendors of Ancient Egypt." (By "popular Egyptology" I mean non-academic talk, writing, and other representations of ideas about ancient Egypt, ranging from serious books about Egypt for general audiences to humorous uses of imagery involving mummies, hieroglyphic writing, body poses taken from Egyptian bas-reliefs and statuary, and so on.) The "Splendors of Ancient Egypt" exhibit traveled to several US museums, including the Museum of Fine Arts in Houston, Texas (MFAH). The exhibit consisted of over 200 artifacts from all phases of ancient Egyptian history, including coffins and mummy masks, statues, scrolls, and relief carvings in stone. The objects were on loan from the Pelizaeus Museum in Hildesheim, Germany, and the exhibit was jointly designed and mounted by Hildesheim curators and Houston ones. The material I will discuss comes from the Houston show, as well as from descriptions of and advertisements for the show and for related events.

The MFAH presented this exhibit as a "blockbuster," advertising it heavily and using it as a tool for raising museum attendance and increasing membership. This effort, and the show itself, gave rise to many texts, including magazine advertisements for the exhibit; articles about it in the bimonthly magazine sent to museum members, *MFA Today*; wall placards and labels in the exhibit; and some material that was available at the special "Splendors" gift shop outside the exhibit. (Because the exhibit took place in 1996–7, before the widespread use of the World Wide Web, there was no online advertising or educational material.) I present brief analyses of bits of this material to illustrate the approach to discourse analysis that will be taken in the chapters to follow. Let me stress again that the point of what

I will be doing here is illustrative. I will not be presenting a complete or coherent analysis of this popular-Egyptology data, just a few examples.

A heuristic for analysis

Before we start looking at this material, however, we need to consider our methodology. How are we going to proceed with these analyses? What questions should we ask, and how should we go about answering them? Discourse analysts work with material of many kinds, including transcripts of audio- or videorecorded interactions, written documents, texts transmitted via oral tradition such as proverbs, and printouts of online communication. Their material sometimes consists of words alone and sometimes includes pictures, gestures, gaze, and other modalities. But no matter what sort of discourse we consider – we discuss the "data" of discourse analysis later in the chapter – the basic question a discourse analyst asks is "Why is this stretch of discourse the way it is? Why is it no other way? Why these particular words in this particular order?"

To answer these questions, we obviously need to think about what our "text" is about, since clearly what a person is talking about has a bearing on what is said and how it is said. We also need to think about who said it, or who wrote it or signed it, who is thought, in its particular sociocultural context, to be responsible for what it says, who the intended audience was and who the actual hearers or readers were, because who the participants in a situation are and how their roles are defined clearly influences what gets said and how. We need to think about what motivated the text, about how it fits into the set of things people in its context conventionally do with discourse, and about what its medium (or media) of production has to do with what it is like. We need to think about the language it is in, what that language encourages speakers and writers to do and what it is relatively difficult to do in that language. We need to think about the text's structure, and how it fits into larger structures of sets of texts and sets of interactions.

We can divide the questions that need to be asked about a text into six broad categories. Each of these categories corresponds to one way in which contexts shape texts and texts shape contexts. Each of these aspects of text-building is both a source of constraint – a reason why texts are typically some ways and not others – and a resource for creativity, as speakers, signers, and writers express themselves by manipulating the patterns that have become conventional. As we explore pieces of the "Splendors of Ancient Egypt" exhibit we will touch briefly on each of these facets of discourse in turn. We will consider each aspect in more detail in the chapters to follow.

Figure 1.1 lists these six aspects of the shaping of texts. These constitute a *heuristic* for exploring, in a systematic way, what is potentially interesting and important about a text or a set of texts. A heuristic is a set of discovery procedures for systematic application or a set of topics for systematic

- Discourse is shaped by the world, and discourse shapes the world.
- Discourse is shaped by language, and discourse shapes language.
- Discourse is shaped by participants, and discourse shapes participants.
- Discourse is shaped by prior discourse, and discourse shapes the possibilities for future discourse.
- Discourse is shaped by its medium, and discourse shapes the possibilities of its medium.
- Discourse is shaped by purpose, and discourse shapes possible purposes.

Figure 1.1   How discourse is shaped by its context, and how discourse shapes its context

consideration. Unlike the procedures in a set of instructions (be they instructions for putting together a toy or instructions for analyzing a set of numerical data), the procedures of a heuristic do not need to be followed in any particular order, and there is no fixed way of following them. A heuristic is not a mechanical set of steps, and there is no guarantee that using it will result in a single definitive explanation. A heuristic can be compared to a set of exercises that constitute a whole-body physical workout, or to a set of tools for thinking with. A good heuristic draws on multiple theories rather than just one. The heuristic we use here forces us to think, for example, about how discourse is shaped by ideologies that circulate power in society, but it also forces us to think about how discourse is shaped by people's memories of previous discourse, along with other sources of creativity and constraint. We may end up deciding, in a particular project, that the most useful approach will be one that gives us ways of identifying how ideology circulates through discourse, or that the most useful approach will be one that helps us describe "intertextuality," or that the most useful approach will be one that helps uncover the relationships between the text and its medium, the language it is in, or its producers' goals or social relationships. The heuristic is a first step in analysis which may help you see what sorts of theory you need in order to connect the observations about discourse you make as you use the heuristic with general statements about language, human life, or society. It is a way to ground discourse analysis in discourse, rather than starting with a pre-chosen theory and using your texts to test or illustrate the theory.

Texts and interpretations of texts are shaped by the world, and they shape the world

Discourse arises out of the world or worlds that are presumed to exist outside of discourse, the worlds of the creators and interpreters of texts. Whether or not discourse is thought to be about something is relevant to how it is interpreted. Discourse that is thought not to refer to anything may be seen as nonsensical or crazy; it may be the result of a linguistic experiment like Dadaism in poetry; it may be required in ritual. The Western tradition of thought about language has tended to privilege referential discourse and to imagine that discourse (at least ideally) reflects the pre-existing world. But as twentieth-century philosophers (Foucault, 1980), rhetoricians (Burke, [1945]1969), and linguists (Sapir, 1921; Whorf, 1941) showed us again and again, the converse is also true, or perhaps truer: human worlds are shaped by discourse.

For example, advertisements for "The Splendors of Ancient Egypt" which the MFAH placed in the *Texas Monthly*, a general circulation magazine, involve choices about how to *describe* the ancient Egyptian world which have the effect of *creating* a particular image of this world. The ancient Egyptian world is seen through the lens of Western "orientalism" (Said, 1978), or habitual Western ways of talking about the East which create the Eastern world of our imagination. Figure 1.2 shows the written parts of two of these advertisements. (The advertisements also include pictures of some of the artifacts in the show, and a discourse analysis could also consider their visual design, which highlights the most exotic and anthropomorphic of the artifacts and makes strategic use of layout and typography.)

Egyptians are depicted in these advertisements as "full of mystery," "superstitious," "obsessed with living forever," "preoccupied with death." Ancient Egyptians needed "spells" and "curses" and "incantations" to

---

For a civilization obsessed with living forever, they sure had a peculiar preoccupation with death.

The ancient Egyptians felt so strongly about going to heaven, they spent their entire life on earth getting ready for life after death. Now, in the new exhibit, "Splendors of Ancient Egypt," you can see for the first time the awe-inspiring treasures they packed to take along for the trip. Everything from gilded mummy coffins and gold mummy masks to dazzling jewelry and the 18-foot-long Book of the Dead. Altogether, over 200 pieces have been assembled for this once in a lifetime exhibit. Why not make plans for a trip of your own?

(*Texas Monthly*)

If you doubt ancient Egyptian curses exist, be warned. This exhibit is full of them.

The ancient Egyptians were a superstitious bunch. They had spells for this. Incantations for that. And curses to protect them from harm. So it should come as no surprise to find the new exhibit, "Splendors of Ancient Egypt," full of mystery as well. You'll be captivated by the gilded mummy coffins covered with spells, the amulets to ward off evil spirits and the 18-foot-long Book of the Dead. Altogether, over 200 awe-inspiring artifacts have been assembled for this once in a lifetime exhibit. Let it cast its spell over you.

(*Texas Monthly*)

Figure 1.2 Two magazine advertisements for "Splendors of Ancient Egypt"

"protect them from harm." Repeated from one ad to the other are the expressions *the ancient Egyptians, awe-inspiring, gilded mummy coffins,* and *this once in a lifetime exhibit.* The effect of all this is (perhaps exactly as intended) to foreground the "otherness" of the ancient Egyptians, the ways in which they were different from us and both more primitive (their superstitions) and more splendid (their elaborate jewelry and golden sarcophagi). Only a systematically critical reader would be likely to wonder whether some of the advertisements' copy is not in fact equally descriptive of twenty-first-century Westerners. For example, "For a civilization obsessed with living forever, they sure [have] a peculiar preoccupation with death" could, in another context, be taken as an accurate description of the contemporary United States. In fact, even if not every society is interested in immortality, most human societies have rituals connected with death. In the context of the world that has been created in the advertisements, however, this sounds like a description of an exotic and unusual group of people.

In addition to being shaped by what *is* said, the worlds evoked and created in discourse also are shaped by silence: by what *cannot be* said or *is not* said. One source of silence in the "Splendors" exhibit was the silence of the Egyptian hieroglyphic writing. Egyptian writing appeared on a great many of the artifacts in the show. But there were almost no translations in any of the descriptive placards: the Egyptian writing was treated as decoration rather than as language. What the ancient Egyptians said in the many inscriptions was treated as irrelevant. Another interesting silence was evident in many of the informational wall placards, in phrases like these:

> *One assumes* that . . .
> *It is apparent*, therefore, that . . .
> His corpulence *is to be regarded* as . . .
> Such . . . works of art *are termed* "models" . . .

These phrases are not all grammatically the same, but all have in common a missing agent (the doer of the action) or experiencer. Who assumes? To whom is it apparent? Who decides how things are to be regarded? Who makes up or chooses terms for things? The use of expressions like these may have the effect of drawing attention to the fact that there are experts deciding how to explain things to the exhibit's viewers, and that these experts do not need to be identified, presumably because any expert would have come to the same conclusions. The stance taken here is that of someone who is entitled to describe and evaluate things and whose judgments are the correct ones, an art-historical Big Brother, we might say. More generally, making structural choices in which agents or experiencers are left out is one of the many ways people can create a sort of generic opinion (the opinion that "one" holds or that "is apparent") and thereby discourage others from challenging their claims. This sort of discourse tends to obviate the need for individual responsibility for meaning.

Discourse is shaped by the possibilities and limitations of language, and discourse shapes language

Texts and their interpretations are shaped by the structural resources that are available and the structural choices text-builders make. There are conventionalized ways of structuring texts on all levels. Speaking a language, such as English or Korean, means using conventional ways of structuring syllables (a new English word could start with the syllable *pri* but not with *ngi*), conventional ways of structuring words (the *-s* that shows that an English word is plural goes after the stem, not before), conventional ways of structuring sentences (in declarative English sentences, the subject typically precedes the predicate). Likewise, there are conventional ways of structuring longer chunks of discourse, some culturally specific and others resulting from what human cognition is like. They include ways of moving from familiar information to new information, for example, or moving from examples to general claim or from general claim to examples, or moving from question to response.

Striking uses of conventions of structuring can be found throughout the "Splendors of Ancient Egypt" material. For one example, a poster that was stapled into an issue of *MFA Today* a month or two before the exhibit made strategic use of the English possibility of presenting a claim as uncontestable by putting it in an embedded clause: "Thank you for *being a member of the Museum of Fine Arts, Houston.*" The poster makes rhetorical use of logical presupposition: it sounds as if the copywriter assumes that the reader of the poster is a member of the museum, just as the question "When did *John stop drinking?*" presupposes that John was once a drinker (and could thus be part of an indirect attack on John), or "I'm sorry that *you don't agree with me*" presupposes that we disagree (and could be used to position you in opposition to me). The poster, worded as it is, is a nice thank-you gift for people who have joined the museum, whose membership includes the magazine subscription. But the poster is also meant to be seen by other people, perhaps people who are not members of the museum and for whom the presupposition that they are will induce guilt and encourage them to join up too.

Just as the structure of sentences is always, to some extent, rhetorically motivated, so is the structure of larger blocks of discourse. The wall placards describing the artifacts in the "Splendors" show had an almost invariable form, as exemplified in this one:

Mummy Mask of Paser

New Kingdom, Dynasty 18, 1570–1320 B.C.
Cartonnage, which can be compared to papier maché,
painted and gilded, findspot not known

One assumes that the mummy of Paser, which has not survived to this day, was clad in a cartonnage ensemble, to which this mask belonged. The features are idealizing and are not to be regarded as a likeness, or portrait, of Paser. The mummy, once enveloped in that ensemble, was doubtless placed into Paser's anthropoid sarcophagus which is on display in this gallery as well. The gilding has a distinctly reddish hue and recalls contemporary ancient Egyptian texts from the New Kingdom which mention "the gold which bled." It is apparent, therefore, that the ancient Egyptians recognized this property of their gold and appreciated it.

(Informational wall placard)

The structure of this placard is like that of all the other placards in the show, as well as the structure of wall placards in other museum shows. One way to represent this structure is shown in figure 1.3.

This sort of artifact label probably seems natural to those of us who have seen it many times before – right down to some rather German-sounding elements in the prose. (*Findspot* sounds like a German word, for example, because it is formed out of two Germanic roots using the Germanic strategy of compounding nouns to form new words.) But note how the structure foregrounds some elements of the description and backgrounds others. The first thing, in large type, is a label, not in Egyptian but in English, and not in Egyptian hieroglyphic writing but in Roman letters. This label removes the object from its original context and puts it into a Western frame of reference. (It could be said that the label mimes the action of the archaeologist, the collector, or the grave-robber in this respect.) In the Western cultural context, naming something can be seen as a way of establishing dominion over it, as is represented in the Old Testament story in which God grants human beings control over other species by giving Adam the ability to name things. More generally, naming is like the glossing (interpreting words) and parsing (interpreting grammatical structures) that translators do. It requires fitting things from some other realm into the system of terms and ideas that goes with one's own language. And, like naming, "glossing is clearly a political process. How often do two languages meet as equals, with equal and reciprocal authority?" (Becker, 1995: 232). Note also the order in which facts about the artifact are presented on the wall placard, and what these facts are. History (kingdom, dynasty number, approximate dates) precedes craftsmanship (material, treatment). Place comes

Title

[kingdom] [dynasty # in Arabic numeral] [approx. dates]
[material] ([treatment]) ["findspot" = provenance]

Description

Figure 1.3 Structure of a "Splendors" artifact label

last: the Egyptian artifacts were taken out of their spatial context in their descriptions just as they are in Hildesheim (where they are usually on display) or Houston.

Discourse is shaped by interpersonal relations among participants, and discourse helps to shape interpersonal relations

The interpersonal relations connected with discourse include the relations among the speakers and writers, audiences, and overhearers who are represented in texts, as well as the relations among speakers and writers, audiences, and overhearers who are involved in producing and interpreting texts. For example, the explanatory material about Houston's "Splendors of Ancient Egypt" gives evidence of several sometimes conflicting visions of the relationships between museum staff and museum patrons. Sometimes the intended audience is clearly youthful, as in the *MFA Today* magazine's "Kaleidoscope for Kids" section, where Egyptian shabtis were depicted and explained in an article that appeared while the "Splendors" exhibit was on display:

SHABTIS

These small blue figures are called shabtis (pronounced shabtees). They are made of faience, a type of glazed pottery. Shabtis were believed to help people who died. They were placed in tombs to be servants in the afterlife, working for the dead. Hundreds of shabtis have been found in kings' tombs. These shabtis are holding hoes used by farmers for digging. They are standing like wrapped mummies, ready to work in the afterlife.

(*MFA Magazine*, "Kaleidoscope for Kids")

This is not children's language, but language by adults addressed to children. It represents, in other words, an adult's idea of how a child's mind might work. There is something jumpy about the paragraph; a reader has to work a bit to decide how each sentence is related to the previous one. This is in part because there are no explicit links between sentences. There are no conjunctions like *thus* or *so*, which might have clarified the causal relationship between "Shabtis were believed to help people who died" and "They were placed in tombs . . ." Adding a conjunction might also have helped with the unclear reference of the pronoun *they* in "They were placed in tombs . . ." Are *they* the "people who died" or the shabtis? It is not immediately clear. Using *and* might have helped smooth the flow and connect the events that are being represented in "These shabtis are holding hoes used by farmers for digging. They are standing . . ." The primary sentence-linking (or "cohesive") device is instead the repeated sentence subject: *these small blue figures, they, shabtis, they, hundreds of shabtis, these shabtis, they.*

Using repetition rather than conjunction to create cohesion is a feature of the speech of children themselves (Bennett-Kastor, 1994) and a feature of adults' "baby talk" to small children (Snow and Ferguson, 1977). We might wonder, however, about its usefulness in a text addressed to readers who are old enough to interpret conventional phonetic spelling such as "shabtees" (which may not actually reveal any more about how the word is to be pronounced than "shabtis" does) and who are able to understand (and need to know) what faience is. How old is this audience of imagined children? We could say that the text is designed for its readers, and that was no doubt the writer's explicit aim, but we could also say that it designs its readers, putting them in their place by talking to them the way older people talk to babies.

Discourse is shaped by expectations created by familiar discourse, and new instances of discourse help to shape our expectations about what future discourse will be like and how it should be interpreted

"Intertextual" relations between texts and other texts enable people to interpret new instances of discourse with reference to familiar activities and familiar categories of style and form. The uses of discourse are as varied as human cultures are. (For example, one important ceremonial genre for the Kuna of Panama is talk by a healer to small stick dolls, which none of the human participants except the healer understands or is even meant to understand (Sherzer, 1983), and one way of speaking in Tzeltal (a language of indigenous Mexicans) is called *lučul k'op*, which means "talk carried out while sitting on a tree branch" (Stross, 1974).) But often-repeated activities involving discourse give rise to relatively fixed ways of proceeding with the activities, and these ways of proceeding often include relatively fixed, routinized ways of talking and types of texts. For example, when the ads for the "Splendors" exhibit mention "The Book of the Dead," they call to mind expectations about books – what they look like, what they are about, what they are for, how they are produced and distributed and so on – that readers have formed in their own, Western contexts. Mentioning Egyptian "spells" calls to mind expectations about magical incantations, such as the expectation that spells contain Arabic-sounding "magic words" such as "shazzam" or "abracadabra." (This expectation could not, in fact, correspond to what Egyptian spells were like, since the ancient Egyptians were not Arabs and did not speak Arabic.) In these cases, the expectations created by intertextuality may predispose museumgoers to form misleading images of Egyptian "books" and "spells." But intertextuality is crucial for communicative successes, too. The fact that the show's wall placards are in a familiar format makes them relatively easy to read, for example. Museumgoers do not have to spend time and energy figuring out what kind of texts the placards are, what to expect them to contain, or how they are meant to be used.

Discourse is shaped by the limitations and possibilities of its media, and the possibilities of communications media are shaped by their uses in discourse

Strategic mixing of media is evident everywhere in the material about "The Splendors of Ancient Egypt." The magazine ads, for example, have a more spoken-like quality than do the magazine articles. For example, punctuation is used to represent the rhythm of speech, as in "They had spells for this. Incantations for that. And curses to protect them from harm." In all the materials, visual imagery is extremely prevalent and often repeated. It is not the history of Egypt that is on display and for sale, nor a set of lessons about culture or religion or mortuary practices, but a feast for the eyes. (The MFAH is, after all, an art museum; curators designing a display for a history museum might have done things differently.) This is especially clear in popular Egyptology's enthusiastic adoption of the Egyptian practice of using Egyptian writing as decoration. For the people who designed these texts and the audience they envision, the birds, cups, sphynx-like figures, human arms and legs, and abstract shapes that make up the hieroglyphic writing system are like figures in wallpaper borders. They are to be admired because they are unusual or delicate or colorful, not because they are meaningful. At the "Splendors of Ancient Egypt" gift shop, hieroglyph-themed gift wrapping paper and gold jewelery were for sale. For those who could not afford the popular "cartouche" jewelry, on which the buyer's name was supposedly spelled out in hieroglyphic characters, a "cartouche computer" would produce a paper one for a dollar, on a background of hieroglyphic decoration. (On these cartouches, names were spelled phonetically, as if the hieroglyphic writing system were an alphabet, with each character corresponding to a single language sound. In fact, the Egyptian hieroglyphic system did not work this way. This use of it suggests the Eurocentric attitude that the default writing system is an alphabet.) Decorative hieroglyphs were used in other ways, too. For example, the designers of a flyer circulated to museum members advertising the 1997 Houston BMW Group Fine Arts 5K footrace (an event with no connection whatsoever to ancient Egypt, except that runners' entry fees benefited the museum) used hieroglyphs as a decorative background for the heading and to fill in some unused space on the entry form. In all these uses of Egyptian writing, expectations associated with pictorial media (including expectations about visual harmony, beauty, and so on) were meant to override expectations associated with writing, such as the expectation that the symbols would be meaningful and that a reader would need to consider their meanings as a set rather than one by one.

Discourse is shaped by purpose, and discourse shapes possible purposes

The purposes of the "Splendors" show, and the purposes of the material about it, were several. As a result, many voices could be heard in the texts, voices that sometimes appeared to be in competition. For one thing, the exhibit was meant to be educational. In the American context in which the exhibit took place, certain language-use choices are associated with educators, including imperatives (more-powerful people can order less-powerful people around in direct ways), expressions of confidence in the evidence one has for one's claims (educators are often sure they know what they know, or are at least expected to act as if they were), various sorts of simplification, and various ways of speaking for other people that presuppose acknowledged expertise. This set of habits of speech reflects a set of habits of thought, both in educators and in others: educators are thought of as experts (whether or not they always are). As a result, Americans often accept their simplifying material and allow them to be spokespeople for truth.

This discourse of education was evident throughout the "Splendors" exhibit, as the curators spoke on the wall placards and artifact labels. The curators-as-educators told viewers how to think: "These objects, which *we admire* today for their intrinsic beauty . . ." and described what ordinary people like the viewers might have trouble thinking about: "*It is difficult for a contemporary audience to imagine* that . . ." They simplified, often by providing modern analogs. For example, mummified ibises (a kind of bird) were described as "'please' or 'thank-you' offerings," the clothing on the statue of a man was compared to a beach towel wrapped around his waist, administrative scribes in a granary were described as "ancient CPAs" (Certified Public Accountants), and an Egyptian offering tablet was said to resemble ". . . several halves of bread which have been sliced horizontally down the middle the way a modern prepare[s] bread for a hero sandwich . . ."

The curators used imperatives to tell museumgoers what to look at: "*Notice* how the laborers carry the grain in sacks and *pay particular attention* to the three figures . . ." The evidential certainty of educator discourse was created and represented on placards like that describing the Sarcophagus of Kaiemneferet: "the recessed panels recall the niches . . . *doubtless because* . . ." and the uncertainty or error of non-educators was contrasted with it in this description of a group of shabtis: "*Contrary to popular opinion*, shabtis were not placed in tombs in order to wait hand and foot on the deceased in the Hereafter." (This of course contradicts what the children were told in the magazine article about shabtis which was discussed above.)

But the curators who spoke on the "Splendors" placards also sometimes spoke as archivists. While some artifacts were described with reference to beach towels and hero sandwiches, other descriptions – and sometimes the same descriptions – included words like *anthropoid*, *polychromatic*, and *physiognomy*. The placard for one jug pointed out "the thick plasticity of its relief decoration." This is a different voice, one which did not always mesh smoothly with the educator voice. The exhibit information was also characterized by several other clashes of competing purposes which engendered competing discourses. The "Splendors" artifacts were, as mentioned, on loan from a museum in Hildesheim, and curators from Hildesheim helped mount the show. Throughout the exhibit, linguistic choices that sounded German (such as "findspot" in the "Mummy Mask of Paser" example above) competed with ones that sounded English, and sometimes a conflict between German and English ways of talking became evident, as on one somewhat whiny placard describing works of art that "are termed 'models' for lack of a better English word." Additionally, there was a clash between the discourse of high culture and that of commerce, as the MFAH tried to use this show as a way to make money, setting up a special shop directly outside the exit from the "Splendors" galleries that offered hieroglyph-themed coffee mugs and tote bags, tourist souvenirs from Egypt, made-to-order gold necklaces, and so on.

Discussion

1.3 As was pointed out, some of the curators of the "Splendors" exhibit were German. Is there further evidence of this in the "Mummy mask" placard? What would the English equivalents of the German-sounding phrases be? How do the German wordings create different audiences, different authors, different relationships among them?

1.4 Does the shabtis paragraph above remind you of other things addressed to children? Does it sound like a textbook? In what ways? On which other models do you think the authors of the "Kaleidoscope for Kids" page might have drawn?

1.5 Find a magazine advertisement that violates your expectations about what you will see in a magazine advertisement, and use that as the basis for discussing what magazine advertisements are usually like. Does the language of the "Splendors" advertisements reproduced above violate or play with your generic expectations for magazine advertisements in any way? If so, how? How have magazine advertisements changed since 1996, when these were published? How do they differ from country to country, from language to language?

1.6 In what ways, and why, would you expect a website about the "Splendors" exhibit to differ from the print-based modes of presentation we have been examining?

1.7   Look again at these examples from the "Splendors" exhibit of sentences with missing agents or experiencers.

> *One assumes* that . . .
> *It is apparent*, therefore, that . . .
> His corpulence *is to be regarded* as . . .
> Such . . . works of art *are termed* "models" . . .

In what other types of discourse do you find sentences like these? Why?

Data for Discourse Analysis

The material with which discourse analysts work consists of actual instances of discourse, which are sometimes referred to as "texts." With the exception of some scholarship in pragmatics, there is very little work in discourse analysis that relies entirely on non-empirical speculation about what discourse is like. Some "instances of discourse" seem easy to identify and collect. It would appear to make intuitive sense, for example, to treat a letter or an essay as a single, self-contained unit. These are the kinds of units that are traditionally referred to as "texts." Perhaps the prototypical text, in traditional literary and philological scholarship, is a book. A book is a physical object which stays the same (except for wear and tear) over time. Its beginning and ending are unmistakeable: the front cover and the back cover. It is written.

But many discourse analysts work with instances of discourse that do not have all – or any – of these characteristics. For one thing, many written texts, such as webpages, blogs, and wikis, are more fluid than printed discourse once was, co-created by many people, changing from minute to minute, and appearing different on different computer screens. Furthermore, a great deal of discourse analysis is about non-written discourse. Since we cannot analyze discourse in these modes in real time, as it is taking place – analysis requires much more time and distance than a single viewing or listening provides – we study *records* of discourse. For online discourse, these records may be in the form of printouts or screenshots. For oral discourse, they are often in the form of transcripts of audio- or videorecordings. By capturing changing written texts at a particular time or recording and transcribing non-written discourse, we give them some of the characteristics of books and other more prototypical texts: we make them into physical objects; we fix their structure; we convert them into writing, in the case of oral discourse; we give them boundaries. Texts of these kinds do not exist independently of discourse analysts' choices about how to "entextualize": how to select and delimit chunks out of the flow of talk or writing, make these chunks into texts, and treat them analytically in much the way we have traditionally treated written texts.

Every choice about what to count as a text for analysis is a choice not only about what to include but also about what to exclude. Such choices about what and how much to treat as a complete unit and where to draw its boundaries have important ramifications for the conclusions we draw. A text, in other words, might be one discussion or a whole series of television debates, a single email or an extended correspondence, one conversation or all the talk that constitutes a relationship. A dinner-table conversation might be defined as starting once everyone is seated at the table (and this might be a convenient way to define it, since it is much easier to record people when they are seated around a table than when they are on the move), but defining it this way would exclude the talk that occurred before that, which could be a vital part of the context. For that matter, even written texts of the most prototypical sort are the result of decisions about entextualization based on culture-specific expectations. A book is a complete text only if it is treated as relatively independent of other texts, independent of the rest of the author's oeuvre, for example, or independent of the ideas about what is natural and right that were circulating at the time the book was written. In order to be treated as a text, a wiki or a blog must be sampled at one or more discrete times – but one of the features of these forms of discourse that makes them different from other forms of writing is precisely that they change much faster and more continuously, so treating them as if they were analogous to writing on paper may obscure one of the things that is most interesting about how online discourse works.

Any analytical move that involves drawing boundaries, pulling out chunks from the flow of experience and treating them as wholes, is somewhat artificial. Nonetheless, such moves are the essential first step of any discourse analysis or any other approach to humanistic or social scientific research. The roots of discourse analysis are in the analysis of traditional texts – in classical philology, literary criticism, and hermeneutics – and the controlling metaphor behind this approach to research, explicit or not, has often been that analyzing human life is a matter of open-ended interpretation rather than fact-finding, more like reading than like identifying data points that bear on pre-formed hypotheses (Geertz, 1973). So it is especially important for us to be aware of the ways in which we may be tempted to treat all discourse as if it were like the writing in a book. It is crucial to be able to uncover the many ways in which texts are shaped by contexts and the many ways in which texts shape contexts. It is partly for this reason that this book is organized around the heuristic introduced above. A heuristic such as this is a good way to ensure that discourse analysis is systematic in its attempt to take multiple perspectives on texts, and thinking about analysis this way keeps reminding us that there are always many right answers to any question we ask about humans and language.

How many texts are enough? Discourse analysis typically starts with a relatively small amount of data. Many discourse analysts use this data to make qualitative claims. In other words, the claims they make on the basis of their analyses are not about how often something occurs in a language, in a genre, or in interaction in general, but about why or how it occurs in the data at hand, and any suggestions they make about the likelihood that the same thing will occur in other data are simply suggestions. The next step in such a project might be to ask the same questions of another body of data, to explore whether things work the same way there. Alternatively, the next step might be to focus in on a particular aspect of the findings of the qualitative analysis, one that can be defined in such a way as to be identified mechanically, and use a larger amount of data to make quantitative claims about it.

For example, research about language and aging by Coupland, Coupland, and Giles (1991) used detailed, multifaceted, qualitative analyses of conversations between older and younger adults to show that aging is not just a matter of getting older, wiser, or feebler, but is instead in part created in discourse, as people use some terms and not others to describe themselves and their interlocutors, talk about their lives and their abilities in some ways and not others, and so on. Starting from the observation made in such qualitative research that, in some conversations, words like *old* and *elderly* do not just refer to people's chronological age, but carry negative connotations as well, Gerlinde Mautner (2007) explored whether the term "elderly" has such connotations in English discourse more generally, and, if so, what the term suggests. To do this, Mautner used an electronic collection of 57 million words of written text in English, including British, American, and Australian newspapers, books, flyers, catalogues, unscripted speech, and radio broadcasts. Each word in this corpus has been labeled with its part of speech (noun, verb, adjective, and so on), so, using concordance software, Mautner was able to search for cases where *elderly* was part of a string of adjectives, or where it occurred together with the noun *people* and a verb. Whereas qualitative research like that of Coupland et al. justifies the qualitative claim that the meanings of words like *elderly* can be loaded, because people use such words to construct social identities in interaction, quantitative research like Mautner's justifies a different kind of claim, one about what *elderly* means in English. Qualitative, quantitative, and mixed approaches all have their place in discourse analysis. Researchers who choose to work with the large corpora of discourse that are increasingly available and easy to use need to make sure that their work is grounded in thorough qualitative analysis, though, so that choices about what to code and count, and how to do so, are well motivated, and people who do qualitative work need to be careful not to make unjustified generalizations about their findings.

Transcription: Representing Speech in Writing

Many examples throughout this book are taken from other scholars' work. In these examples, I have kept the original authors' transcription conventions, so that the examples appear exactly (or as nearly as possible) as they appeared in the articles and books from which they are taken. (In cases in which the meanings of special symbols and unconventional uses of punctuation, layout, capitalization, and so on are not obvious, I have explained them.)

Readers will thus quickly notice that there are almost as many ways to transcribe speech as there are researchers who do so. Although somewhat standardized transcription systems are used in some endeavors that involve discourse analysis (such as Conversation Analysis), there is no single generally accepted way to represent speech on the page. This sometimes surprises newcomers to discourse analysis, until they realize that any way of representing speech in writing is necessarily selective, and that different selections highlight (and disguise) different aspects of what speech is like. A transcript is by necessity a partial representation of talk, and transcribers' decisions about what to include and what to omit have practical and theoretical consequences (Ochs, 1979a; Bucholtz, 2000). For example, a transcription system that highlights interruption and simultaneous talk makes it relatively easy to think of conversation as collaborative, whereas a play-script transcript makes it look more as if each speaker had an independent conversational agenda. Practically speaking, highly detailed transcripts are often hard to read, whereas easy-to-read transcripts include less specific information. No transcription system could possibly be ideal for all purposes.

This is not to say that all systems are equally good: if the idea, for example, is (as it usually is) to include all the words that were spoken, a transcription in which a spell-checker has deleted repeated words will be inadequate. A transcription needs to be accurate in the sense that it includes what it claims to include. But it cannot include everything, and the most useful transcriptions in discourse analysis research are those which highlight what the researcher is interested in and do not include too much distracting extraneous detail. Very detailed transcripts may in fact include more information than people are able to process, and this may lead to high rates of error when such transcripts are reproduced (O'Connell and Kowal, 2000). Readers should compare and contrast the systems used in the examples as they go through the book, as a basis for deciding what sort of system they need for their own work.

Transcriptions of speech are representations of speakers as well as being representations of speech. The most literal way to represent a speaker's speech may not be the most desirable way to represent the speaker. For example, casual English, as spoken by almost anyone, is characterized by the pronunciation of "ing" as "in" ([ɪn] in the International Phonetic Alphabet) or "uhn" ([ən]), and English speakers almost invariably "drop" certain consonants in consonant clusters. When the letter "s" appears at the end of an English word, it often represents the sound [z]. When they are not stressed, English vowels often sound like "uh" ([ə]). So an accurate way to represent the sound of "I was cleaning out my desk," as casually spoken, might be something like this: "I wuhz cleanin' out muh des."

Notice, though, how the choice to represent sound accurately may have the effect of representing the speaker as stupid, uneducated, rural, or lower class. In general, realistic detail in the representation of speech in a transcription often comes at the expense of accuracy and fairness in how the speaker is represented, so some discourse analysts think it wise not to include any more detail about the sound of speech than is necessary to illustrate one's point. Others think fine detail is crucial because it encourages analysts not to take anything for granted about what particular utterances actually sounded like.

Discussion

1.8   Here are several written representations of oral discourse. For each, discuss what is added and what is lost in transforming talk into writing and deciding where to begin and end.

    a.   Transcript of a joke in a conversation. In this transcript, italics signal louder parts of the talk and capital letters even louder parts. Ellipses represent slight hesitations, their length relative to the number of dots.

        VIV: 'Member that time there was a mouse on our phone? on the . . . kitchen wall?
        RON: Um-hmm
        VIV: I went downstairs boy, and turned on the light, and there's this mouse sitting there, and he *jumps*, hits the table, and slides off, and of course I [sharp intake of breath] *"My* GOD LOOK *at that mouse!"* I said, "Ron there was a *mouse* sitting on *top* of the *telephone* this morning when I came downstairs." Ron said, "Well we'll have to check the bill, see if *he* made any *long distance calls!"* [imitating male voice]

    b.   Transcript (made according to somewhat different transcription conventions) of a telephone conversation between an emergency dispatcher (CT) and a caller (C). In the transcription system used in this example, equals signs indicate "latched" utterances, or utterances spoken one after the other without a pause; colons signal stretched-out sounds, as in "gu:ys"; a single period in parentheses signals a slight pause; words inside parentheses are guesses made on the basis of hard-to-decipher parts of the recording.

        1   CT: Mid-city emergency
        2   C: Yes sir uh go' uh couple gu:ys over here ma:n
        3   they thin' they bunch uh wi:se ((*background*
        4   *noise*))=
        5   CT: =Are they in your house? or is this uh business?

6 C: They're over here ah Quick Stop (.) They (fuckin) come over
        here
7   an pulled up at thuh Quick Stop slammin' their doors intuh my
8   truck.
9 CT: Quick Stop?=
10 C: =Yeah.
11 CT: Okay Uh- were you uh customer at that store?
12 C: Yeah.
13 CT: What thee address there or thee uhm: . . .

(Zimmerman, 1998: 100–1)

c. From a play script.

SCENE: An Island off the West of Ireland.
*(Cottage kitchen, with nets, oil-skins, spinning wheel, some new boards standing
by the wall, etc. Cathleen, a girl of about twenty, finishes kneading cake, and
puts it down in the pot-oven by the fire; then wipes her hands, and begins to spin
at the wheel. Nora, a young girl, puts her head in at the door.)*

NORA: *(in a low voice)*. Where is she?
CATHLEEN: She's lying down, God help her, and may be sleeping, if she's
            able.
            (Nora comes in softly, and takes a bundle from under her shawl.)
CATHLEEN: *(spinning the wheel rapidly)*. What is it you have?
NORA: The young priest is after bringing them. It's a shirt and a
            plain stocking were got off a drowned man in Donegal.
            *(Cathleen stops her wheel with a sudden movement, and leans out
            to listen.)*
NORA: We're to find out if it's Michael's they are, some time herself
            will be down looking by the sea.
CATHLEEN: How would they be Michael's, Nora. How would he go the
            length of that way to the far north?
NORA: The young priest says he's known the like of it. "If it's
            Michael's they are," says he, "you can tell herself he's got a
            clean burial by the grace of God, and if they're not his, let no
            one say a word about them, for she'll be getting her death,"
            says he, "with crying and lamenting."

(Synge, 1935: 83, *Riders to the Sea*, scene 1)

d. From a newspaper report. Note that speech is not only "reported" here
    but described indirectly, via "metalinguistic" verbs (that is, verbs that refer
    to linguistic actions) such as *say, insist, react, accuse, complain,* and *ask.*

Aboriginals must integrate, says Lib MP

THE "dysfunctional" Aboriginal community of Palm Island should be
abandoned and its residents moved to the mainland unless they integrate
into mainstream society, a federal Liberal MP has insisted.

Backbencher Peter Lindsay, whose north Queensland seat of Herbert includes the troubled island community, said that if Aboriginal people on Palm Island could not buy homes and generate jobs then "it would be better to move them back on to the mainland and integrate them that way".

Mr Lindsay said the same rule should be applied to remote Cape York communities such as Mornington Island, Lockhart River and Aurukun.

Local Aboriginal leaders reacted furiously, accusing Mr Lindsay and the federal Government of neglecting the island.

"He hasn't got a clue what he's talking about," Palm Island Deputy Mayor Zac Sam said. "The Government is always complaining to us about not doing anything. We have been asking about funding that is supposed to help us set up enterprise . . . but nothing has happened."

But Mr Lindsay said the Government was more than generous. "The fundamental issue that troubles me is that Palm Island is a hopeless dysfunctional community with almost no employment and no prospects of employment," the MP said.

(Ian Gerard, *The Australian*, January 6, 2006)

1.9   Use the heuristic with which we will be working (figure 1.1) to analyze the poem "Pumpernickel," which is reprinted below. You will need to ask yourself each of these questions:

- How is the text shaped by the world and how does it shape the world? (Would this poem make the same kind of sense to someone in Japan or Kenya as it does to someone in the US or England? What features of the world are most explicitly represented in the poem? Which are represented indirectly or not at all?)
- How is the text shaped by language – by the fact that it is in English, with English possibilities for sounds and juxtapositions of sounds, English grammar and conventions for structuring texts like this – and how does it shape future possibilities for saying things in English? Does the poet draw on the traditions of other languages as well?
- How is the text shaped by participants (writer, readers, editors, and any others you can think of) and how does it shape, position, define its participants? Is anyone excluded from participation?
- How is the text shaped by prior discourse like it and unlike it, and how does it shape future possibilities for such texts? (You might, for example, want to remind yourself what a sonnet is; you might want to think about other literary representations of Jewish life, prior representations of women's work, and so on.)
- How is the text shaped by its medium (writing in a book), and how does it shape the possibilities of the medium? (What would be gained and lost by reading the poem aloud? What would be gained and lost by illustrating it with a film or a still picture, or presenting it on a computer screen in moving letters? How does knowing that this poem appeared in a selective anthology affect your understanding of it? Would you interpret the poem differently if you came across it on a student's website?)
- How is the text shaped by purpose and how does it shape possible purposes? (Why do people write things like this: to persuade, to inform, to

request action, to make people laugh? How is your interpretation of the poem influenced by your guesses about what Schultz had in mind as he wrote it? What might Schultz have intended your intention to be in reading the poem: to learn something, to be moved, to complete this exercise?)

Pumpernickel

Monday mornings Grandma rose an hour early to make rye,
onion & challah, but it was pumpernickel she broke her hands for,
pumpernickel that demanded cornmeal, ripe caraway, mashed potatoes
& several Old Testament stories about patience & fortitude & for
which she cursed in five languages if it didn't pop out fat
as an apple-cheeked peasant bride. But bread, after all,
is only bread & who has time to fuss all day & end up
with a dead heart if it flops? Why bother? I'll tell you why.
For the moment when the steam curls off the black crust like a strip
of pure sunlight & the hard oily flesh breaks open like a poem
pulling out of its own stubborn complexity a single glistening truth
& who can help but wonder at the mystery of the human heart when you
hold a slice up to the light in all its absurd splendor & I tell you
we must risk everything for the raw recipe of our passion.

(Schultz, 1991)

"Descriptive" and "Critical" Goals

No matter what the overarching research question, all discourse analysis results in description: describing texts and how they work is always a goal along the way. In some discourse analysts' work, descriptions of texts are used in answering questions that arise in the service of what is traditionally known as "descriptive" research, particularly in linguistics. Work of this kind is based in the idea that the primary goal of scholarly research is to describe the world, or whatever bit of the world the researcher is interested in. (In linguistics, the prototypical descriptive project is the description of a language, resulting in the production of a grammar and a dictionary.) To aim to do purely descriptive work presupposes two beliefs: (1) that it is possible to describe the world – in other words, that there is not an infinite number of possible descriptions, any one of which would be valid in some situation, and (2) that the proper role of a scholar is to describe the status quo first, and only later, if at all, to apply scholarly findings in the solution of practical problems.

Some of the foundational work in discourse analysis took place in the context of descriptive linguistics. This includes, for example, work by Pike (1967), Grimes (1975), and other American linguists who attempted to describe the rules that determine the structure of texts in a variety of languages, as well as scholarship in the context of systemic-functional linguistics such as that of Halliday and Hasan (1976) on what makes English texts cohesive. Work such as this about discourse structure is discussed in detail in chapter 3. At the risk of some oversimplification, we can say that work in this tradition did not call into question either of the two beliefs under-lying descriptive research. Important early work by anthropologists (Hymes, 1972; Gumperz, 1982a) and sociologists (Sacks, Schegloff, and Jefferson, 1974) bearing on the nature of social interaction and the kinds of context that influence text did not overtly problematize the two beliefs, either. We also discuss these scholars' work later on. A great deal of work involving dis-course analysis continues to be based on the belief that pure description is possible and desirable. This is not to say that many descriptive linguists do not also have important practical goals for how they want to apply their findings in the world. For example, the descriptive work of Pike and Grimes was aimed, ultimately, at translating the Bible into previously unwritten languages, and much of Gumperz' research has taken place in the context of problem-solving work about intercultural communication.

Both of the beliefs that underlie pure descriptivism have, however, been called into question more and more urgently during the past several decades, under the influence of philosophical relativism and critical social theories such as Marxism. Relativism is the idea that different people live in different worlds, whether because they have different minds, different shared systems of beliefs and norms (this is "cultural relativism") or different languages ("linguistic relativism"). The three versions, all of which have been cur-rent in social and linguistic thought, have somewhat different implications for what it is thought possible to describe. A linguistic relativist such as B. L. Whorf (1941), could, for example, claim to describe the worldview of the Hopi as a group, whereas a philosopher for whom relativity was based in different minds would not be able to describe any more than one indi-vidual's world. Any version of relativism, however, leads to skepticism about the possibility of "scientific truth" and encourages researchers to take a critical, self-conscious (or "reflexive") stance vis-à-vis their own work and the claims they make. Critical social theory describes the human world not as a system in, or tending to, equilibrium, but as a system characterized by dominance, exploitation, struggle, oppression, and power. People whose grounding is in theory of this sort attempt to show what is wrong with the status quo. They tend to be interested in the dominated groups rather than in those who dominate them; their research about struggles over power is (at least in principle) meant to help empower the relatively powerless.

Discourse analysis has increasingly (though by no means exclusively) come to be used in the service of critical goals. This is to say that many researchers throughout the humanities and social sciences have come to be (1) critical of the possibility of producing a single, coherent, scientifically valid description, and (2) critical of the social status quo and concerned to have their work used in changing things for the better. Two groups of researchers who are particularly identified with this way of thinking (in part because they have been successful in appropriating and arguing for the use of the term "critical") have called their ways of working "Critical Linguistics," or CL (Fowler et al., 1979; Hodge and Kress, 1993) and "Critical Discourse Analysis," or CDA (Fairclough, 1985, 1992; van Dijk 1993a; Wodak 1996). We discuss their work in detail in chapter 2. It should be stressed, however, that there is far more research using discourse analysis that is critical in this sense than just the work explicitly associated with these two schools. Critical approaches to texts have a long tradition in American anthropology and linguistics (Adams, 1999), and these approaches have had considerable influence. More generally, discourse analysis is, at root, a highly systematic, thorough approach to critical reading (and listening), and critical reading almost inevitably leads to questioning the status quo and often leads to questions about power and inequality. In other words, sensitive discourse analysts should always be casting critical eyes on their own process of analysis and on the situation they study, whether or not methodological or social critique is the end goal.

Discussion

1.10   The words "critical" and "criticism" are used in several ways. "Criticism" can be evaluative. It can mean negative commentary (as in "She is too critical of her children"), or it can mean evaluative commentary whether negative or positive (like much literature, film, music, or theater criticism). "Criticism" can also be non-evaluative (at least in theory): "critical thinking" is careful, systematic, self-conscious thinking, without any necessary evaluative goals, and the goal of academic literary criticism is not always overtly evaluative, either. Would you say it is just a historical accident that the same set of words should be used to refer to description and evaluation, or is there a necessary connection between description and evaluation? Is it possible to describe without evaluating?

1.11   What are your goals as a discourse analyst? How do you imagine being able to use discourse analysis to help answer the questions you are asking? Are your goals descriptive, critical, or both?

Summary

People in many fields, with very diverse research projects, make use of discourse analysis. Although there is no universally agreed-on definition of discourse analysis, most practitioners use "discourse" to mean any actual talk, writing, or signing. To those who use the term, "discourses," in the plural, are conventional ways of talking that create and perpetuate systems of ideology, sets of beliefs about how the world works and what is natural.

"Analysis" involves various ways of systematically taking things apart or looking at them from multiple perspectives or in multiple ways. Discourse analysis is thus a methodology that is useful in answering many kinds of questions, both questions that linguists traditionally ask and questions asked by people in other humanistic and social-scientific disciplines. All uses of discourse analysis result in descriptions, but the end goal of discourse analysis is not always simply description of the status quo but social critique and, sometimes, intervention. For example, the exploratory analyses of various texts from a museum exhibit that were used in this chapter as examples of some of the things discourse analysis can uncover resulted both in explanations of how a museum's talk to the public can be designed and how it can be effective, and in critiques of some aspects of how the museum chose to represent itself and its audiences.

Discourse analysts work with "texts," pieces of discourse that have or are given boundaries and treated as wholes. Discourse analysts work outward from texts to an understanding of their contexts, trying to uncover the multiple reasons why the texts they study are the way they are and no other way. To insure that systematic attention is paid to all the possible reasons for a text's having the form and function it does, it is useful to refer to an analytical heuristic: a set of broad questions to ask about the texts with which we work. This helps insure that we do not just find out what we hope or plan to find out, and it results in analyses that are multidimensional and as sensitive as possible to all the many reasons why human languaging sounds, looks, and works in the ways it does. The chapters that follow are organized around one such heuristic.

Further Reading

This analytical heuristic described here is based on the work of A. L. Becker (1995). General overviews of discourse analysis, in addition to the present one, include Blommaert (2005), Brown and Yule (1983), Gee (2005), Mills (2004), Renkema (2004), Schiffrin (1994), Stubbs (1983), and Titscher et al. (2000). Each delimits the field differently, and only Schiffrin and Titscher et al. treat discourse analysis primarily as a set of methods, as I do here. Van Dijk (1997) is a collection of articles by experts about a wide variety of uses of discourse analysis. A reader edited by Jaworski and Coupland (1999) brings together some of the foundational work in the field, much of which is referred to or discussed in the chapters to follow, although some of the selections are so truncated that readers would do well to locate the originals instead. Van Dijk (1985) is an extensive though somewhat dated handbook of discourse analysis; a more recent handbook is Schiffrin, Tannen, and Hamilton (2001). General handbooks of linguistics include Bright (1992), Asher and Simpson (1994), and Malmkjaer and Anderson (1995). (More recent handbooks dealing with subfields of linguistics and other relevant areas will be mentioned in subsequent chapters.) Fairclough (1985) introduced the distinction between descriptive and critical discourse analysis and summarizes the goals of the latter. Recent overviews include Fairclough and Wodak (1997) and Blommaert and Bulcaen (2000). An interesting collection of papers about the problems and possibilities associated with entextualization, as practiced both by discourse analysts and by the people they study, is Silverstein and Urban (1996). On transcription, see Ochs (1979a), Edwards and Lampert (1993), and Bucholtz (2000). The metaphor of culture as text and humanistic research as hermeneutic interpretation is associated particularly with Clifford Geertz (1973). On corpus analysis, see Sinclair (1991) and Stubbs (1996). Interdisciplinary journals that specialize in work by discourse analysts include *Text*, *Discourse in Society*, *Discourse & Communication*, *Discourse Processes*, *Discourse Studies*, and *Critical Discourse Studies*; many other journals, associated with various disciplines, also include reports of discourse analytical research.

chapter 2

Discourse and World

We begin our exploration of the facets of discourse by thinking about paraphrase. Paraphrasing – saying what a text is "about" – is a kind of text analysis we often perform informally in everyday life. Think, for example, about reading a new novel and telling a friend about it, perhaps in answer to a question like "How's that book?" You might begin with an evaluation: "It's pretty good," or "I'm enjoying it so far." The next step would probably be some sort of description of what the book is about such as "It's about a boy who falls in love with an older woman," "It's about Europe during the Second World War," or "It's about nature."

To say that a novel, or any other text, is "about" something presupposes that there is a world outside of the text to which the text refers. It presupposes that there are young boys and older women in what we sometimes refer to as the "real world," for example, and that novels represent this real world in words, so that when we read the words we imagine real boys and women. To say that a novel is "about Europe during World War II" or "about nature" presupposes that there is a previously existing geographical area to which we point when we use the word "Europe," a historical event to which we point with the phrase "World War II," and a category and style of life to which we point when we say "nature." We often act as if language simply mirrored the world "out there," external to discourse, so that if there is a real thing in the world there is a way of referring to it in discourse. In this picture, the world is the cause, the text is the effect. Discourse imitates the world.

But the relationship between discourse and the world we think of as outside of and independent of discourse is not this simple. Debate over this relationship has been a recurring theme throughout the history of philosophy, and describing how language and thought, language and culture, or discourse and society are interrelated has been one of the major goals for theorists of language throughout the past century. The consensus among discourse analysts is that discourse is both shaped by and helps to shape the human lifeworld, or the world as we experience it. In other words, discourse both reflects and creates human beings' "worldviews." People bring worlds into being by talking, writing, and signing. Young boys fall in love with older women in part because there are novels about young boys falling in love with older women. "Falling in love" is the experience it is partly because of the expectations created by the fact that we use the image of "falling" when we talk about it. "Europe" became a place when people needed a name for it. Wars stop being "conflicts" or "military actions" and acquire dated beginnings and endings, as well as historical significance, partly through acquiring proper names such as World War II or the Seven Years' War. The category "nature" is not really "natural," either. Does nature include humans? (If it does, then perhaps public land should be open for recreational use; if not, perhaps it should be conserved for other species.) Can human activity that involves commerce be natural? (If so, then commercial logging on public land can be described as part of an ecologically sound method of forest management; if not, logging seems to violate natural law.) The interest groups that acquire the right to decide what "nature" is, what counts as "nature" and what does not, get to help shape the future of the environment. Like other words, "nature" is not "just a word" that refers to something that already exists in the world, but rather an idea which is created and contested as people name it and talk about it. Using one word or another, or arguing for one definition or another, can in itself be a way of staking a claim in a debate. (Think, for example, about the rhetorical force of merely using the word "life" or the word "choice" in the context of debate about abortion.) If words simply referred to real things, we would not have "fighting words," and we would never need to fight over definitions.

One of the best ways to see how words and world are related is to think about – or, better, practice – translation. People who have to learn a new language sometimes find that the experience feels like discovering or building a new world. Eva Hoffman (1989), who moved, as an adolescent, from Poland to Canada, entitled her memoir of this period in her life *Lost in Translation: Life in a New Language*. She describes the terrifying difficulty not just of talking but of thinking, seeing, knowing, even living when one's "interior language" has to change:

I have no interior language, and without it, interior images – those images
through which we assimilate the external world, through which we take it
in, love it, make it our own – become blurred too. . . . The verbal blur covers
these people's faces, their gestures with a sort of fog. I can't translate them
into my mind's eye. The small event, instead of being added to the mosaic
of consciousness and memory, falls through some black hole, and I fall with
it. What has happened to me in this new world? I don't know. I don't see
what I've seen, don't comprehend what's in front of me. I'm not filled
with language anymore, and I have only a memory of fullness to anguish me
with the knowledge that, in this dark and empty state, I don't really exist.
(1989: 108)

As Hoffman learns to talk (in English) the way people do around her, she
becomes better at seeing things the way they do. She becomes able to trace
the outlines of things in the Canadian world in which she now lives. English
gives her verbal categories that function as frames and boxes into which to
fit people, objects, and events and thereby differentiate them and give them
edges and shapes. Hoffman's lack of language when she first comes to
Canada does not just limit her access to the world. Instead, not having
a language means that she does not have a world at all and thus doesn't
"really exist," and acquiring a language means acquiring a world. In philosopher Ludwig Wittgenstein's enigmatic and intriguing terms, "The limits
of my language mean the limits of my world" (1955, section 5.6).

Translating between distant languages highlights the "exuberance" and
"deficiency" of any paraphrase (Ortega y Gasset, 1959): the reasons why
any attempt to say something a different way requires adding elements of
meaning that were not there in the original (here the original is deficient
and the paraphrase or translation exuberant) and omitting things in the
translation or paraphrase that were present in the original (here the original
is exuberant and the new version deficient). Thus paraphrase is not really a
process of "saying something a different way" but of evoking and creating a
different "something" in a different world. Different groups of speakers and
ways of speaking make available different grammatical strategies, different
vocabularies, and different prior instances of discourse for people to adapt
as they create new ones. Thus translation can never be exact. In the same
way, alternate phrasings in the same language can never mean exactly the
same thing, and habits of speaking reflected in customary choices of structure and wording lead to the habitual ways of imagining the world that
come to seem natural and uncontestable.

In this chapter we explore some of the ways in which discourse and
world are related. We begin by thinking about relatively fixed, conventional
habits of structure and wording of the kind that are often referred to as
facts about the grammars and lexicons of languages. Thinking first about
cross-linguistic differences, we explore how various classification systems for
nouns may predispose speakers to imagine things as naturally belonging
in sets as well as reflecting the ways in which speakers customarily group

things. We discuss versions of the hypothesis that the categories of language influence the categories of perception. We then look at how conventional habits of discourse and strategic choices of phrasing can sediment into the relatively fixed sets of words and structures which we call languages and into systems of belief about how the world works, systems which sometimes work in the interests of the powerful. We pay particular attention to the effects of linguistic ideologies – sets of beliefs about what language is and how it works – on social life and on language itself. Finally, in the context of another look at translation, we explore ways of thinking about and un-covering silence, the things that cannot be talked about and may hence be hard to imagine in a particular language, and the things that systematically go unsaid either because they are assumed to be true or because they are for social reasons unthinkable or unmentionable.

Discussion

2.1   Have you ever been in a situation in which you did not know the language of people around you? If so, to what extent does Hoffman's description of her experience with English ring true?

2.2   If you are able to, translate a paragraph of a novel or a stanza of a poem written in another language into English. What are the situations in which English is "exuberant": when a choice has to be made in English that does not have to be made in the original language? When is English "deficient": when does a distinction in the original have to be collapsed in English? Is there such a thing as a perfect translation for a text like this? By what criteria should a literary translation be judged?

2.3   Do bilinguals "think differently" in their different languages? Do they express different personalities? Act differently? See the world differently, or live in a different world? If you use more than one language, discuss this on the basis of your own experience. If you do not, talk to someone who does.

2.4   Can we conceive of things we cannot talk about?

2.5   Consider the following passage from a magazine article meant for a general readership, and discuss the questions below:

> Language is as vital to the physician's art as the stethoscope or the scalpel. A doctor begins by examining the words of his patient to determine their clinical significance. He than translates the words into medical language, describing how the condition came to be, what it means, and how it may evolve. Of all the words a doctor uses, the name he gives the illness has the greatest weight. It forms the foundation of all subsequent discussion, not only between doctor and patient but also between doctor and doctor and between patient and patient. With a name, the patient can construct an explanation of his illness not only for others but for

himself. The name of the illness becomes part of the identity of the sufferer –
"P.W.A." (person with AIDS), or "cancer survivor" – and indicates the status
the person has gained from his experience; it is shorthand for his odyssey, akin to
"veteran of foreign wars" or, in Muslim lands, "hajji," for one who has made the
hajj. The name can also provide an instant community.

(Groopman, 2000: 82)

a. What are some other situations in which the labels people use for them-
    selves and others "become part of [their] identity" or "provide an instant
    community"?

b. In the situation described in the passage, the actor with the most power
    in the interaction at hand (the doctor) labels the less powerful one (the
    patient). Does the process ever work the other way, with the less powerful
    actor labeling the more powerful one? Discuss the relationship between
    labeling and power in a situation you are familiar with.

c. What are the potential effects of the author's and/or editors' choice to use
    he (rather than *he or she* or *they*) to refer to any doctor or any patient ("*He*
    [the doctor] then translates . . ."; ". . . the patient can then construct an
    explanation of *his* illness")?

Linguistic Categories, Minds, and Worldviews

One way in which language and thought might be related is that the possibility of human cognition and human experience might depend on the fact
that humans are language-users. "Thought," "language," and "being human" might, in other words, all be aspects of a single activity. For example,
the existence of words might be responsible for our expectation that categories of things can be defined in terms of features shared by all members
of a set. It could be, as Wittgenstein (1958: 17–18) suggested, that the only
reason we expect all leaves to have some feature or set of features in common is that we use the same word, "leaf," for them all. The resemblances
among the members of the set of things we use "leaf" for may in fact be
more like the resemblances in a human family: there may not be any one
particular trait of appearance that all family members have in common.
Or, as the French linguist Benveniste suggested (1986[1971]), the fact that
humans experience themselves as individuals, separate from other beings,
may have to do with the fact that all human languages have systems
of grammatical person in which "I" is distinct from "you" and "she/he/it/
they."

Another way in which language and thought might be connected is that
the ways in which a specific language categorizes things might influence
how speakers of that language are forced to – or at least tend to – conceive

of things. For example, in English, experiencing something is sometimes treated, grammatically, as if it were the same as possessing something: a person can *have* a hat (a possession) or *have* a headache (an experience). Because of this, people who speak English might tend to think of, and maybe treat, headaches and other illnesses as if they were possessions. (We *give* diseases to other people, for example, and talk about *getting rid of* headaches as if they were objects that could be thrown in the trash.) Or the fact that English has an unusually complex grammatical tense-aspect system for classifying actions by time and manner might contribute to English speakers' often-noted concern with time.

The idea that categories of thought are determined, or at least influenced, by categories of language is often referred to as "linguistic relativism" or the "Sapir-Whorf hypothesis," although the idea was originally proposed as a theoretical postulate rather than as a testable hypothesis (Hill and Mannheim, 1992), and it can actually be traced back to earlier linguists and anthropologists such as Boas, Herder, and von Humboldt (Foley, 1997: 192–6). Edward Sapir was one of the pre-eminent American linguists of the twentieth century. Benjamin Lee Whorf, an independent scholar of Native American languages who made his living as an insurance claim adjuster, was a student of Sapir's. The Sapir-Whorf hypothesis holds that the ways in which people categorize things in the world are affected by the ways in which their language categorizes things grammatically. In Sapir's words (1949: 162), "the fact of the matter is that the 'real world' is to a large extent unconsciously built up on the language habits of the group." The extreme version of this idea, sometimes referred to as "linguistic determinism," is that categories of language *determine* categories of perception, so that a person would not be able to imagine things in any other than the way dictated by his or her language. Most scholars interested in the issue have not taken this strong position, pointing out that people are, after all, able to recategorize things and to create new ways of talking that reflect their recategorizations. For example, Whorf (1941) suggests that speakers of European languages such as English tend to analyze reality into objects, whereas Hopi speakers tend to talk about events. But it is possible, if perhaps difficult, for an English speaker to shift from thinking of something as an object to thinking of it as an event. Thinking about a mountain from the perspective of geological history (as a slowly unfolding geological event) requires this sort of shift, for example. So does thinking about the environment as an ecological system rather than as an inventory of resources. The more widely held version of the Sapir-Whorf hypothesis is that categories of language influence, but do not necessarily determine, how people construe the world. Under this version, a person would tend to categorize things the way his or her language did, but categorization systems, and languages, could change.

Since the Sapir-Whorf hypothesis is primarily a claim about classification – how languages and speakers group things into categories – one way to explore the idea is to look at noun classification, a feature of many languages, to see whether, and to what extent, categories of nouns and pronouns reflect or create categories of objects for speakers of the languages in question. In English, the grammatical marking of nouns is fairly minimal. When a speaker uses a noun in English, he or she must decide whether to mark it as singular or plural ("book" or "books"), definite ("the book") or indefinite ("a book," "some books"), and, for some nouns, whether to use it as a mass noun or a count noun ("two glasses of water" or "two waters"). But many other Indo-European languages also use differential grammatical marking to classify nouns into categories traditionally called "masculine" and "feminine" (or, in languages like German, "masculine," "feminine," and "neuter"). This type of noun marking is known as grammatical "gender." English nouns are not classified by grammatical gender, but third-person singular pronouns are: *she* is feminine, *he* is masculine.

In French, "masculine" nouns take the article *le*, "feminine" nouns take *la*, and adjectives must be marked so as to agree with the gender of the noun they modify. (Both *le* and *la* are shortened to *l'* when the noun begins with a vowel, and in the plural all nouns take *les*, but the nouns are still in one category or the other.) Here are some French nouns with their grammatical gender indicated.

MASCULINE NOUNS		FEMININE NOUNS	
le lait	'milk'	*la bouteille*	'bottle'
le bras	'arm'	*la jambe*	'leg'
le table	'table'	*la chaise*	'chair'
le pain	'bread'	*la viande*	'meat'
le garçon	'boy'	*la fille*	'girl'
le chanteur	'singer' (male)	*la chanteuse*	'singer' (female)
le soldat	'soldier' (male or female)	*la sentinelle*	'guard,' 'sentry' (male or female)

Does French grammatical gender correspond to how French speakers categorize things by their meaning? Does it predispose them to think about things in a certain way? The answer is not straightforward. For one thing, grammatical gender does not usually map onto semantic or sociological gender: "masculine" in grammatical terminology does not necessarily mean male or masculine in the sense of male-like. The French grammatical gender system derives from that of Latin, where the gender of a noun is based on its form rather than its meaning. In Latin, words ending in *-a* are usually feminine, words ending in *-us* usually masculine. Most linguists, along with most French speakers, would deny that milk seems more male or masculine to French speakers, bottles more female or feminine; legs more feminine than arms; or tables more masculine than chairs. But what of the use of masculine nouns for boys and male singers, feminine nouns for girls and female singers? Here the choice can seem to be motivated by meaning, with grammatically masculine *le* for males and grammatically feminine *la* for females. It could be argued that dividing the world up in this manner, into two categories associated with a supposedly two-way distinction, is one of the ways in which languages' categorization systems encourage speakers to view biological sexes and cultural sex roles as categorical and binary. It could be argued, in other words, that systems like this predispose speakers to imagine that people are either essentially male or essentially female and that there is one prototypical male way of acting and one female way of acting, rather than imagining, for example, that maleness and femaleness are matters of degree or that a person's maleness or femaleness could fluctuate and change. And what of the French use of the masculine for "soldier" or the feminine for "guard"? We will return to this question shortly.

Burmese has a quite different noun classification system. A person using a noun in Burmese must not only indicate its number but also choose from among a set of accompanying particles which are called "classifiers" in English. For example (Burling, 1970: 58–62), the noun phrase that means "two dogs" is *kwêi* 'dog' *hnakáun* 'two + classifier'; "four cows" is *nwâ* 'cow' *laikáun* 'four + classifier'. The nouns for "dog" and "cow" can take the same classifier, *káun*, but not all nouns can go with *káun*. Each noun has a default classifier, and if you were learning Burmese, you might simply try to memorize which classifier goes with each noun, just as students memorize whether each French noun they learn is masculine or feminine. But some nouns can in fact be found with multiple classifiers. For example, several different classifiers can be used with *ŋapyóθî* 'banana', and *ta* or 'one', including these:

ŋapyóθî ta<u>lôun</u>	one banana
ŋapyóθî ta<u>myôu</u>	one kind of banana
ŋapyóθî ta<u>weʔ</u>	one half of a banana
ŋapyóθî ta<u>tweʔ</u>	one bunch of bananas
ŋapyóθî ta<u>thân</u>	one shoulder-pole load of bananas

Each new classifier invites hearers to take a new perspective on the head noun of the noun phrase (which is *banana* in these examples). In these examples, the work done by the classifiers is fairly easy to duplicate in English, though English is exuberant here, requiring whole phrases to approximate meanings which Burmese expresses in one-syllable suffixes. In some cases, however, the shift in perspective produced by a change of classifier is more difficult to translate:

lôunji ta<u>thé</u>	sarong one + classifier for articles of clothing
lôunji ta<u>kwîn</u>	sarong one + classifier for things that encircle
lôunji ta<u>ouʔ</u>	sarong one + classifier for pairs ('one pair of sarongs')

The Burmese word for "shirt" can go with *thé*, the article-of-clothing classifier:

êinji tathé   shirt one + classifier for articles of clothing

However, *êinji* 'shirt' is typically not used with the things-that-encircle classifier or with the pair classifier the way *lôunji* 'sarong' can be.

This seems complex, at least from the perspective of English. But the meanings of many of the classifiers are helpful. The classifier *káun* means 'animal' and can be used with the noun for any animal but not with nouns that do not refer to animals. The classifier *twê* means 'bunch', and is sometimes used with bananas (which grow in bunches) but not with sarongs (which do not). The classifier *šîn* means 'pair of animals', so it can be used with oxen and buffalos, but not with mosquitos – or with horses, since in Southeast Asia oxen and buffalos are used in agriculture in yoked pairs, while horses are not. Sarongs are sold in sets of two, so the classifier for pairs is sometimes used, but shirts are not. Burmese classifiers create a "linguistic image of nature," highlighting certain aspects of the referent of the noun in question and inviting hearers to think about it in one way rather than another. They are not arbitrary, and linguists such as A. L. Becker (1975, 1995[1986]) have in fact investigated aspects of Burmese culture by investigating the Burmese noun classification system.

Is the difference between French (in which the grammatical noun classifiers we looked at appear to be arbitrary in many cases) and Burmese (in which the grammatical noun classifiers we looked at appear to be meaningful in most cases) a difference between two different kinds of classifier systems, or is the difference possibly that we are looking at the same phenomenon at different stages in its development? Exploring this question for a moment may help us see how facts about grammar are related to habits of perception. Bits of language like noun classifiers typically originate as bits of meaning, like Burmese classifiers as I have described them. But with repeated use, their meaning may become "bleached," and they may come to serve purely grammatical functions. That is, they may come to be used to connect parts of sentences and phrases and to show how words in various places in discourse are related. Via this process, called "grammaticalization" (Hopper and Traugott, 2003), meanings in discourse come, over time, to be the source of structures in grammar.

The process of grammaticalization is always underway, so that a linguistic form may be somewhere in between the two poles. Furthermore, speakers can call attention to a form which usually serves a structural function in such a way as to highlight its potential to be meaningful. For example, French speakers may use the "generic" masculine of *le soldat* for male and female soldiers alike, or the feminine *la sentinelle* for male and female sentries alike, without attending to the potential meaning of *le* and *la*, just as they use *le* for *bras* 'arm' and *la* for *jambe* 'leg' without associating these articles with the meanings male and female. But, as we noted above, the potential for the article to signal sociological gender (maleness or femaleness) is always present. *Le soldat* can, in other words, sound as if it encodes the claim that the "normal" soldier is male.

Since at least the sixteenth century, French writers have experimented with non-conventional uses of definite articles *le* and *la*, using the unexpected form to comment on a character's non-conventional sexuality. Because they are grammatically marked as masculine or feminine, nouns, too, can easily become invested with semantic, rather than just grammatical, gender. In a study of literary uses of noun and pronoun gender, Livia (2001) cites an example, taken from research by Houbedine-Gravaud (1988), of the tendency in the media to talk about the Eiffel Tower as if "she" were an "old lady." This semantically gendered personification of an inanimate object is encouraged by the feminine grammatical gender of the noun *la tour*, 'tower'. Livia suggests that as grammatical gender marking is becoming less and less obligatory in spoken French, the arbitrary grammatical gender-marking system is coming to be reanalyzed as a way of expressing semantic contrasts.

Interesting evidence for this reanalysis comes from the province of Quebec, Canada. By law, official communication in Canada must be published in French and English. Between 1979 and 1984, three policy recommendations were issued by the province's government suggesting that professional titles in French should be "feminized," or given grammatically feminine forms and treated as grammatically feminine, in contexts where the use of masculine forms was once conventional in Canada and is still conventional in other parts of the Francophone world (Conrick, 1998). For example, the use of gramamatically masculine designations such as *l'avocat* (the [m.] lawyer) or *le directeur* (the [m.] director) in generic contexts such as job advertisements ("We are searching for *un*[m.] *directeur*") is no longer condoned, and where feminine versions of these designations did not already exist, rules for creating them were proposed. The recommendations were widely adopted, and detailed guidelines can be found in handbooks for Canadian professional communicators (cf. Guilloton and Cajolet-Laganière, 2005). While conservative language purists in France maintain that the generic use of masculine professional titles is simply an arbitrary convention, Quebec's policy recognizes the potential for arbitrary grammatical facts to spring into meaningful life and reflects the fact that this has already happened in Canada.

Discussion

2.6 Compare the French and Burmese examples above with one of the ways in which English classifies nouns, into what is known as "mass nouns" and "count nouns":

MASS NOUNS	COUNT NOUNS
water	shoe
snow	book
ice	ice cube
milk	chair
information	page
research	term paper
music	chord
email?	email?

Nouns in these two categories behave differently in a number of ways. Count nouns are typically used with cardinal numbers, as in "two shoes," or "seven books," whereas, at least when they are used in their "mass noun" senses, mass nouns typically do not have cardinals before them, so that "two informations" or "seven musics" sound unusual. Count nouns are quantified with "some" only when plural – "some shoes," not "*some shoe" – whereas mass nouns can be used with "some" when singular – "some snow," "some music." Portions of mass nouns are usually talked about via "an x of y" ("a glass of milk," "a piece of ice"); count nouns do not usually work in this pattern ("*a volume of book," "*a beat of chord"). Count nouns typically take "many" + plural ("many pages," not "*much page"); mass nouns take "much" + singular ("much research," not "*many researches"). Does the grammatical distinction between mass and count nouns correspond to a distinction in the worlds of speakers of English? In other words, are we talking here about a way of segmenting reality that is specifically English? Does it reflect English speakers' perceptual tendencies in some way you could clearly describe? How could you tell?

2.7 Now say you are a teacher of English as a Second Language. How would you deal with sentences like these produced by your students?

a. I made a big research for my term paper.
b. She bought some shoe.
c. The newspaper gives many informations on that topic.
d. This book has too much page to read.

How would you explain to non-English speakers how to learn about mass and count nouns? Are people learning this distinction learning to categorize things differently? Or are they just learning two lists of nouns?

2.8 Merlin Donald (1993) describes a study by Lecours and Joanette (1980) of "Brother John," a monk who suffered from epileptic seizures that resulted in temporary aphasia, or loss of language. During these seizures, Brother John continued to be able to function quite normally. Here is Donald's description of one such occurrence:

> One episode, while [Brother John] was traveling in Switzerland, was particularly striking. He found himself at the peak of one of his seizures as he arrived at his destination, a town he had never seen before. He took his baggage and managed

to disembark. Although he could not read or speak, he managed to find a hotel and show his medic-alert bracelet to the concierge, only to be sent away. He then found another hotel, received a more sympathetic reception, communicated by mime, and was given a room. He was able to execute various procedures which formed a framework for linguistic operations; for example, he was able to point out to the desk clerk where in his passport to find the information required to fill out his registration slip, while not being able to read it himself. Finding himself too hungry and miserable to sleep, he went to the hotel restaurant. He could not read the menu, but he pointed to a line which he thought might be the hors d'oeuvres and randomly chose an item, hoping he would like it. In fact, it was a dish he detested, but he ate it, returned to his room, and slept for the remainder of his paroxysmal attack. When he awoke, he went to the hotel desk and explained the episode in detail. (pp. 84–5)

Does the case of Brother John have any bearing on the connections between language and thought which we have been discussing, or on any possible connections between language and thought? Is it a challenge to the Sapir-Whorf hypothesis that Brother John should have been able to function as well as he did without being able to speak or understand, read or write? Is it surprising that he should have been able to compensate by communicating in other ways?

2.9   Look at UNESCO's guidelines for gender-neutral language in English and French (http://unesdoc.unesco.org/images/0011/001149/114950mo.pdf). What ideas about the relationship between language and perception underlie these guidelines? Do you agree with the authors of this document that "If words and expressions that imply that women are inferior to men are constantly used, the assumption of inferiority tends to become part of our mindset" (p. 4)? Do "words and expressions" imply inequality, or is it speakers and writers who imply inequality through their choices of words and expressions? Does this make a difference, in your opinion?

Discourse, Culture, and Ideology

Three key terms in the formulation of the Sapir-Whorf hypothesis are "language," "thought," and "reality." One of the difficulties in determining exactly what the Sapir-Whorf hypothesis should be taken to mean, and how to study it, is that none of these terms is easy to define. To talk about "languages" is to assume that there are self-contained sets of syntactic rules and words which exist before and outside of talk, which groups of people share completely, and which everyone in a group accesses and uses in the same way as they talk. But languages in this sense are found only in dictionaries and grammar books, and then incompletely. It could be, in fact, that we think of languages as autonomous and shared precisely because we are used to grammars and dictionaries, because the experiences with language we are most self-conscious about (school experiences, for example) tend to involve the standardized written varieties that are codified in grammars and dictionaries. We cannot observe languages, nor can we study them without making the untenable assumption that our own intuitions about grammar and meaning are exactly the same as those of anyone else who speaks "the same language." In fact, the only thing we can really observe is discourse. Each individual makes a different set of generalizations, over a lifetime, based on a different set of experiences with discourse, about what the possibilities are for shaping and adapting to the world via language. Each individual's knowledge about language is different, and each individual's actual utterances are different.

"Thought" can refer to a variety of processes. Many studies of the Sapir-Whorf hypothesis have involved visual perception and memory, assuming that visual perception and memory were in some sense equivalent to "thought." For example, if you have a short, simple, "basic" word for a color, is it easier to remember having seen that color in an array of experimental stimuli (Hardin and Maffi, 1996)? Other studies have involved categorization. For example, if you ask people to separate pictures into piles, will the piles correspond to a way their language divides things up (Carroll and Casagrande, 1958; Lucy, 1992)? Still other studies bearing on "language and thought" have operationalized "thought" as the performance of logical operations, such as coming to the correct conclusion about the validity of a syllogism (Lévi-Bruhl, 1926). Each of these ways of defining thought is incomplete and to some extent inaccurate.

Whorf himself apparently assumed that there is a level of "reality" that is independent of language, so that while one's "worldview" might depend on features of one's language, the reality described by physics would be independent of language. Aspects of worldviews could thus be wrong, for Whorf. To use his example, the fact that, in English, we can describe a barrel that once contained gasoline as "empty" when it still (in "reality") contains highly combustible fumes might predispose an English speaker to make the dangerous mistake of lighting a cigarette next to such a barrel. To a thorough-going philosophical relativist, reality itself is relative; to a solipcist, we simply cannot know whether or not we share anything with anyone else. So the difficulty of answering questions about "language, thought, and reality" has a lot to do with the difficulty of deciding on a definition for any of these terms.

A way to think about the relationship between language and world that avoids some of these problems is to think about discourse rather than about language: to study actual instances of talk, signing, and writing rather than an idealized description of the knowledge that people draw on as they talk, sign, or write. In other words, instead of asking how the grammar and vocabulary of a language affect, and are affected by, the ways speakers of that language conceive of the world, we could ask about how the things people do when they talk, sign, or write influence, and are influenced by, their knowledge about language and the world as they experience it. For example, consider the first two sentences of "Sun and Moon," a short story by Katherine Mansfield (1923). (Mansfield was born in New Zealand and lived there until she was 20, then moved to England.)

> In the afternoon the chairs came, a whole big cart full of little gold ones with their legs in the air. And then the flowers came.

Like all writers of fiction – and like all speakers and writers in all situations – Mansfield has chosen one of a number of options. Among many possibilities for one part of the first sentence are, for example "the chairs were delivered," "they brought the chairs," "the caterers delivered some chairs," "some people arrived with 100 chairs." Because this is carefully planned, highly edited literature, we expect every choice the author has made to be significant (Pratt, 1977), not simply a mistake or the first available result of a quick mental processing search. In this case, Mansfield's choices for the first two sentences encourage the guess that the narrator of the story is a young child (a hypothesis which is confirmed in the rest of the story).

We come to this conclusion because every grammatical choice Mansfield makes is a choice about a world she is creating in the story. Every grammatical choice reflects the narrator's world as Mansfield imagines it, and every grammatical choice creates this world for the reader. Choices about the modification of nouns, for example, echo the ways British children are often encouraged to classify and describe things, by size ("a whole big cart") and color ("little gold ones"). An adult narrator in the pretentious, high-toned world of this story might be represented as someone who classifies by style or period: one of the adults might talk about "Louis XIV side chairs," for example rather than "little gold ones." Choices about cohesion – how the semantic connections among sentences are signaled – help create a world in which things happen one after another ("And then the flowers came") with no explicit logical relationship to one another. The shortness of the second sentence, and its close similarity to the beginning of the first sentence ("the chairs came"; "the flowers came") sounds like a children's book, in which there is often a great deal of syntactic parallelism like this. Saying "the chairs came" rather than one of the other alternatives listed above, or some other, presents the chairs as subjects of the verb *come*, which is often – though not exclusively – used of animate objects. It presents the chairs almost as if they had shown up of their own volition. This inexplicitness about agency (who originated the action or is responsible for it) creates the sense that the narrator does not know, or does not need to know, how such things get accomplished. This sort of language is "non-transactive" (Hodge and Kress, 1993: 43). In other words, it creates a world in which things happen rather than being caused to happen. It represents a non-analyzed, "pre-theoretical" (Hodge and Kress) model of the world like that of a child. (As we will see, this sort of language has other uses as well.) Finally, the representation of the objects in the two sentences suggests a child's perspective: the chairs are personified, with "their legs in the air." This is a world, in short, in which unconnected things happen for no obvious reasons, involving semi-animate characters (the chairs and the flowers) whose most salient features are their size and color.

We see, then, that Mansfield's choices are much more complex and meaningful than is at first apparent. They have several effects. For one thing, as mentioned, fiction writers such as Mansfield explicitly set out to create one or more "points of view" or worldviews for narrators and characters. They do this via choices of what to say and via choices of how to say things. They thus use language to create fictional worlds – which, to various extents, may be meant to mirror one or more non-fictional worlds. For another thing, each time a particular choice is made, the possibility of making that choice is highlighted. In other words, each use of an element of grammar in one text makes it more salient, more available for another use, or a slightly different use, in another text, and each use of one choice makes the whole range of potential alternatives – the grammatical paradigm – more salient. In the same way, each time a world is created in discourse it becomes easier to create that world again in subsequent discourse. Particular choices can come to stand for whole ways of seeing things, whole ways of being, and those ways of seeing things can come to seem natural, unchallengable, and right.

Three influential approaches to discourse and world have focused on aspects of this process. One of these theories, an important strand of cognitive linguistics, links the ways meaning is encoded with abstract mental metaphors that structure the process. Another, with its roots in Prague School linguistics, ethnography of communication, and literary theory, focuses on the ways in which particular speech events and reusable "ways of speaking" create and reinforce one another through patterns of parallelism. The third, rooted in neo-Marxist and Foucauldian social theory and systemic-functional linguistics, focuses on how discourse and ideological "discourses" are interrelated. Although not all designed for this purpose, all three approaches suggest ways in which close attention to the details of discourse can reveal how the relatively fixed, unchanging aspects of languages and social reality constantly sediment out of and serve as resources for discourse and other kinds of social activity, in a constant cyclical process.

Cognitive metaphors

Cognitive metaphor theory sees all language use as figurative. In literary metphors like "You are my sunshine," an item from one conceptual field ("sunshine") is overlain on an item from another ("you"), so that meanings from the two fields are blended. George Lakoff, Mark Johnson (Lakoff and Johnson, 1980; Lakoff, 1990) and other cognitive linguists claim that this process also accounts for everyday sentences like "His argument collapsed" or "What is the foundation of this theory?" This is because concepts are structured by complex cognitive metaphors that are reflected in everyday "literal" language. One such metaphor, for English speakers, is THEORIES (and ARGUMENTS) ARE BUILDINGS (Lakoff and Johnson, 1980: 46). The existence of this cognitive metaphor is reflected in how we customarily talk about theories and arguments, using expressions such as these:

- Is that the *foundation* for your theory?
- The theory needs *support*.
- The argument is *shaky*.
- We need some more facts or the argument will *fall apart*.
- We need to *construct* a *strong* argument for that.
- I haven't figured out yet what the *form* of the argument will be.
- Here are some more facts to *shore up* the theory.
- We need to *buttress* the theory with *solid* arguments.
- The theory will *stand or fall* on the *strength* of that argument.
- The argument *collapsed*.
- They *exploded* his latest theory.
- We will show that theory to be *without foundation*.
- So far we have put together only the *framework* of the theory.

Elements of the "source domain" (here, BUILDINGS) are mapped onto the "target domain" (THEORIES, ARGUMENTS) in two ways. "Ontological correspondences" mean that things in the target domain correspond to things in the source domain: theories correspond to buildings, and arguments correspond to structural elements of buildings. "Epistemic correspondences" mean that relationships between elements in the source domain are parallel with relationships between elements in the target domain: If a building that is not buttressed well can collapse, then a theory that is not butressed well can collapse.

Cognitive metaphor theory has been criticized because its practitioners sometimes appear to assume that cognitive structures shape linguistic structures, and not the other way around. It draws on a theory of cognition that privileges the ways in which cognition is "embodied," or shaped by human biology, rather than exploring how cognition is socioculturally shaped – for example, through the things people repeatedly do with language. But some discourse analysts have found cognitive metaphor theory to be a fruitful framework for exploring how concepts and relationships among concepts are not only reflected in discourse but also created and reinforced. For example, Koller (2005) shows how magazine articles about business mergers and acquisitions build on and enrich metaphors of evolutionary struggle: fighting ("a company that is being bought will too often feel like a **defeated army** in an **occupied land**, and will wage **guerilla warfare** against a deal"), mating ("**suitors** in the telecoms industry now need fat chequebooks and **a bunch of flowers**": "When a company merges to escape a threat, it often imports its problems into the **marriage**"), and feeding ("Bayrische Vereinsbank sought a merger . . . because its management was scared of being **gobbled up** by Deutsche Bank").

Metaphors that are repeatedly deployed in the same ways can result in idioms, and an idiom's origin in a metaphor can, over time, be lost, as people come to use the idiom without citation and in contexts where there is a notable lack of conceptual fit between the details of the metaphor and those of the target domain. For example, as Billig and MacMillan (2005) show, the phrase "smoking gun," meaning an uncontrovertible piece of evidence, is now used in ways that do not reflect the ephemeral nature of the evidence provided by a gun seen just after it has been fired, but before the smoke has cleared; metaphorical "smoking guns" can now be durable. But "dead" metaphors can be revivified and used in new ways, as in this example from Billig and MacMillan (2005: 475). In a 2003 interview, US television journalist Dan Rather asked US Secretary of State Colin Powell about the recent United Nations weapons inspector's report that no "smoking gun" had been found to prove that Iraq possessed weapons of mass destruction:

> *Dan Rather*: And to those who say, "Well, there's no smoking gun," would you argue with that?
>
> *Colin Powell*: What do you mean by a smoking gun? How about lots of smoke? I think I put forward a case today that said there's lots of smoke. There are many smoking guns. When we say that he has had thousands of litres of anthrax, and we know it – he's admitted it, it's a matter of record, there's evidence, there's no question about it – is that a smoking gun? Is it a smoking gun that he has this horrible material somewhere in that country and he's not accounted for it? And the very fact that he has not accounted for it, I say could be a smoking gun. It's a gun that's been smoking for years.

What Powell does here is "to contest the appropriateness of the idiom by contesting its meaning" (Billig and MacMillan, 2005: 475). He does this by suggesting that the phrase "smoking gun" could have multiple interpretations ("What do you mean by a smoking gun?") and by using the metaphor in a novel way, in which "smoke" refers not to evidence of a gun's having been fired but to obscurity caused by concealment. Anthrax is a "smoking gun" because Saddam Hussein "has not accounted for it."

Discussion

2.10   Here are some cognitive metaphors that have been claimed to underlie concepts in English and to be reflected in English idioms (Lakoff and Johnson, 1980: 46–51). Each is followed by two sentences that illustrate how the metaphor plays out in the ways English speakers talk. See if you can add more examples under each metaphor. Is there linguistic evidence of the same cognitive metaphors in other languages you are familiar with? What other metaphors for ideas, understanding, love, emotion, and life, in English and other languages, can you think of?

a. IDEAS ARE FOOD
    What he said *left a bad taste in my mouth.*
    All this paper has in it are *raw facts, half-baked ideas, and warmed-over theories.*

b. IDEAS ARE PEOPLE
    The theory of relativity *gave birth to* an enormous number of ideas in physics.
    He is the *father* of modern biology.

c. UNDERSTANDING IS SEEING
    I *see* what you're saying.
    It *looks* different *from my point of view.*

d. LOVE IS A PHYSICAL FORCE
    I could feel the *electricity* between us.
    They are uncontrollably *attracted* to each other.

e. LOVE IS A PATIENT
    This is a *sick* relationship.
    The marriage is *dead* – it can't be *revived.*

f. EMOTIONAL EFFECT IS PHYSICAL CONTACT
    His mother's death *hit him hard.*
    I was *touched* by his remark.

g. LIFE IS A CONTAINER
    I've had a *full* life.
    Her life is *crammed* with activities.

Poetics, grammar, and culture

Another approach to the study of how discourse, language, and world are connected traces its roots to Roman Jakobson's (1960, 1968) work on verbal art and poetics (see chapter 7). Whether or not this is its primary focus, discourse always has the potential to call attention to the way it is structured and the words it contains. For example, when two words or phrases occur near each other in the same or similar grammatical contexts or are structurally linked in some other way, we are led to wonder, consciously or unconsciously, about the relationship between the two. We make practical use of this predictable cognitive strategy when we employ grammatical parallelism in lists, highlighting the fact (or the claim) that listed items belong together in the world by putting them in identical contexts in

the text. Practices of verbal art and ritual in many societies involve sometimes elaborate patterns of parallelism that both create and highlight relationships among the items that vary in the patterns. As Joel Sherzer puts it:

> it is discourse which creates, recreates, modifies, and fine tunes both culture
> and language and their intersection, and it is especially in verbally artistic
> discourse such as poetry, magic, verbal dueling, and political rhetoric that the
> potentials and resources provided by grammar, as well as cultural meanings
> and symbols, are exploited to the fullest and the essence of language–culture
> relations becomes salient. (1987: 296)

As people construct discourse, they draw on the resources provided by
language and on the resources provided by culture, "patterned organizations of, perceptions of, and beliefs about the world in symbolic terms"
(Sherzer, 1987: 195). But acts of discourse are creative; discourse is not just
the automatic result of the application of language and culture. Each instance of discourse is another instance of the laying out of a grammatical
pattern or the expression of a belief, so each instance of discourse reinforces
the patterns of language and the beliefs associated with culture. Furthermore,
people do things in discourse in new ways, which suggest new patterns, new
ways of thinking about the world.

One of Sherzer's examples has to do with an optional marker which can
be used at the ends of verbs in the language of the Kuna of Panama. This
suffix indicates the body position in which the action of the verb was performed: *-mai* (lying, in a horizontal position), *-nai* (perched, in a hanging
position), *-kwici* (standing, in a vertical position), or *-sii* (sitting). Since the
marker is optional, a choice to use it is likely to seem especially meaningful.
Sherzer describes a magical chant, addressed to the spirit of a dangerous
snake, which is used to lift an actual snake into the air. In the chant, a vine
(a euphemism for snake) is described via two of these particles first as
horizontal and then as hanging, in two sets of parallel lines. In between is a
magical formula to raise the snake:

*kali mokimakke**mai**ye*
*kali piknimakkekwa**mai**ye*
The vine (euphemism for snake) is dragging *-mai* (in horizontal
position).
The vine is turning over *-mai* (in horizontal position).

"'unni na pe onakko' anti sokekwiciye"
"'Simply indeed I raise you' I am saying."

*kali mokimakke**nai**ye*
*kali piknimakke**nai**kusaye*
The vine is dragging *-nai* (in hanging position).
The vine is turning over *-nai* (in hanging position).

The shift from -*mai* to -*nai* symbolizes and reinforces the effectiveness of the magical formula. The fact that it is possible for a Kuna chanter to use -*mai* and -*nai* in this way has to do with the fact that previous Kuna chanters have done so, and that doing so was effective. The effectiveness of the current instance of the chant means that -*mai* and -*nai* are likely to continue to be used to symbolize what discourse can do in the world (the world of real snakes, the world of snake spirits that can be addressed in chants, the Kuna world). If the difference between being in a horizontal position and being in a hanging position is salient in this chant, it must be a relevant and important distinction in the world. Since language is brought to the fore in this way – made to serve as a condensed symbol of a whole set of beliefs – particularly in more self-conscious, "performed" (Bauman, 1977) instances of discourse, verbal art is, in this view, a good place to see how discourse mediates between language and culture. (We return to the topic of verbal art in chapter 7.)

But less self-conscious discourse is also the site of the kinds of juxtapositions Jakobson and Sherzer describe. Angela Reyes (2002) studied a panel discussion about culture and identity presented at a school district conference for Asian-American teenagers who had been involved in an after-school arts program together. A member of the audience (AF3) asked where the teens had been born. (Angie was the panel's moderator; Cham, Tha, Heng, Phila, and Phal were panelists.)

346 AF3:   what happens to families as- if- if you're in Americ- a- are
            y- w- all of y- were born- in-
347   your countries? or

Reyes notes that "America" and "your countries" are set in parallel, or at least partly parallel, contexts: "you're in America" and "you were born in your countries." As the students respond to the question, they adopt the binary opposition set up by the parallelism:

348 Cham: I was born in Thailand
349 AF3:   How about you?
350 Tha: I was born here
351 Heng: I was born here
352 Phila: I was born in Cambodia but I came here when I was young
353   so I don't know anything much (.) if I came here older I
            would have experienced more? but I don't even
354 Angie: Phal?
355 Phal: born here
356 Angie: okay

Reyes points out that the structure of AF3's question "presupposes that . . . even if the teens were born in America, it cannot be their country" (p. 189). That the teens by and large fit themselves into this scheme rather than challenging it speaks to the power of grammar to create as well as presuppose ideas about how the world is organized.

Discussion

2.11 How does parallelism (the repeated use of the same structure) serve to lay out (and make a claim about) the structure of a family in this traditional English folk ballad? Describe how the differences in structure and wording in the final stanza serve to position the lover as outside of and opposed to the family. (This song is discussed in Sherzer, 1975: 287–9.)

The Gallows Tree

Slack your rope, hangs-a-man;
 O slack it for a while;
I think I see my father coming,
 Riding many a mile.

O Father, have you brought me gold,
 Or have you paid my fee?
Or have you come to see me hanging
 On the gallows tree?

I have not brought you gold;
 I have not paid your fee,
But I have come to see you hanging
 On the gallows tree.

Slack your rope, hangs-a-man;
 O slack it for a while;
I think I see my mother coming,
 Riding many a mile.

O Mother, have you brought me gold,
 Or have you paid my fee?
Or have you come to see me hanging
 On the gallows tree?

I have not brought you gold;
 I have not paid your fee,
But I have come to see you hanging
 On the gallows tree.

Slack your rope, hangs-a-man;
 O slack it for a while;
I think I see my brother coming,
 Riding many a mile.

O Brother, have you brought me gold,
 Or have you paid my fee?
Or have you come to see me hanging
 On the gallows tree?

I have not brought you gold;
 I have not paid your fee,
But I have come to see you hanging
 On the gallows tree.

Slack your rope, hangs-a-man;
    O slack it for a while;
I think I see my sister coming,
    Riding many a mile.

O Sister, have you brought me gold,
    Or have you paid my fee?
Or have you come to see me hanging
    On the gallows tree?

I have not brought you gold;
    I have not paid your fee,
But I have come to see you hanging
    On the gallows tree.

Slack your rope, hangs-a-man;
    O slack it for a while;
I think I see my lover coming,
    Riding many a mile.

O Lover, have you brought me gold,
    Or have you paid my fee?
Or have you come to see me hanging
    On the gallows tree?

Yes, I have brought you gold;
    Yes, I have paid your fee,
Nor have I come to see you hanging
    On the gallows tree.
               (Brewster, 1940)

2.12 When the poet e.e. cummings, in the poem "anyone lived in a pretty how town," uses *how* as an adjective ("a pretty how town") or *didn't* as a noun ("he sang his didn't"), he creates a meaning that is possible only because *how* is not usually used as an adjective and *didn't* is not usually used as a noun. But cummings is not just violating the rules of English. He is intervening (if fleetingly) in the grammar of English, restructuring English to fit his purposes. Describe other examples of this in the poem (which you can find in many anthologies of twentieth-century American poetry and collections of e.e. cummings' work). Then see if you can find examples of the same sort of manipulation of the grammar of English in less self-consciously artistic discourse, such as everyday conversation.

Discourse and ideology

The umbrella term "Critical Discourse Analysis" (CDA) refers to a variety of overlapping methodologies associated with a somewhat different approach to discourse and world (see Fairclough and Wodak, 1997 for an overview). The controlling theoretical idea behind CDA is that texts, embedded in recurring "discursive practices" for their production, circulation, and reception which are themselves embedded in "social practice," are among the principal ways in which ideology is circulated and reproduced. The goal of

CDA is thus to uncover the ways in which discourse and ideology are inter-twined. Ways of talking produce and reproduce ways of thinking, and ways of thinking can be manipulated via choices about grammar, style, wording, and every other aspect of discourse. Ideologies – systems of belief – are like "culture" in Sherzer's formulation, except that ideologies tend to be seen as inevitably selective and potentially misleading. Ideologies are thus well suited for use by the dominant to make oppressive social systems seem natural and desirable and to mask the mechanisms of oppression. The goal of CDA is often explicitly political. Acknowledging that science is never value-free, critical discourse analysts begin as advocates of social justice and social change (most often from a leftist perspective).

CDA has its origins in versions of Marxism like those of Gramsci and Habermas that stress the cultural aspects of social relations in addition to the economic ones. In this view, social power results not just from economic or political coercion but more subtly, through "hegemonic" (Althusser, 1971) ideas about the naturalness of the status quo to which people assent without realizing it. These ideas circulate via recurring activities (or "practices") that include both discourse and actions and artifacts that are coordinated through discourse, such as systems of education or styles of architecture. Historical ("archaeological" or "genealogical") exploration of these practices and the "discourses" that emerge from them was popularized through the work of Michel Foucault (1972). By exploring the linguistic details of texts and, particularly in the "social semiotic" tradition (Hodge and Kress, 1988), semiotic media like pictures, CDA can add detail and rigor to somewhat abstract Foucauldian ways of describing practices of speaking and thinking. As mentioned above, CDA is also explicitly concerned with the discursive and social practices in which texts are embedded. However, because of its origins in linguistics, CDA is particularly well suited to the study of texts or transcripts, and it often articulates well with work by rhetoricians, linguistic anthropologists, and interactional sociolinguists, who bring to the table sys-tematic approaches to the study of interactional and sociocultural contexts.

As we have seen, every linguistic choice – every choice about how to produce discourse, but also every choice about how to interpret it – is a choice about how the world is to be divided up and explained. Every choice is strategic, in the sense that every utterance has an epistemological agenda, that is, a way of seeing the world that is favored via that choice and not via others. The following are among the many things discourse producers make choices about.

Choices about the representation of actions, actors, and events. Who or what is presented as an agent? Who or what is acted on? One domain in which such distinctions can be made, in English and many other linguistic traditions, is in the choice between active and passive voice. Contrast, for example, how rapists and victims of rape are represented in these sentences (Henley, Miller, and Beazley, 1995: 61):

In the US a man rapes a woman every six minutes.
In the US a woman is raped by a man every six minutes.
In the US a woman is raped every six minutes.

The passive voice is often used to portray the agents of an action as unknown ("I've been robbed"), obvious ("The suspect was arrested"), or unimportant ("Several experiments were conducted"). The passive can also be used to hide an agent who is known, or downplay the fact that an agent was involved.

The choice between passive and active voice is one of a set of choices which speakers inevitably make in representing actions and events having to do with how semantic roles are mapped onto grammatical structures. For example, the role of agent (the doer, or the source of the action) in an active sentence is mapped onto the position of sentence subject, and the role of patient (acted-upon) is mapped onto the position of grammatical object: **A man** (semantic agent/grammatical subject) *rapes* **a woman** (semantic patient/grammatical object) *every six minutes*. This sentence is "transactive," because an action is represented as having an origin and a receiver, an agent and a patient. Other sentence types are "non-transactive." For example, the same entity that is represented as the semantic patient in the transactive sentence "A man rapes a woman every six minutes" can be represented as the semantic experiencer: **A woman** (semantic experiencer/grammatical subject) *suffers a rape every six minutes*. Note that the agent is not represented in this way of wording the sentence. There is no place in this sentence structure for the semantic role of agent, which means that a reader or hearer might not notice the absence of the filler of that slot, *a man*. Rape can be used as the grammatical subject, too, as in "A rape occurs every six minutes." Here, the semantic agent and patient are both absent.

Choices about agency and transactiveness may help distinguish science writing from other types. Hodge and Kress (1993: 41–7) show how non-transactive choices in the writing of Francis Bacon (the seventeenth-century English philosopher who is sometimes credited with leading the scientific revolution of the renaissance) reflect Bacon's empirical, non-theoretical view of the world and of the scientist. For example, Bacon writes:

. . . many substances in nature which are solid do putrify and corrupt into worms.

Another option would have been

. . . something putrifies and corrupts solid substances into worms.

Bacon's use of *putrify* and *corrupt* as intransitive verbs, with *substances in nature* as the subject rather than the object, highlights what the observer sees rather than its underlying cause. Like the world of Mansfield's narrator, described above, this is a world in which things happen rather than being caused to happen. Passive-voice sentences, in which the agents and experiencers who might otherwise occupy the grammatical subject slot are omitted, are one of the ways in which science writers can highlight the belief that scientific activities and observations would be the same no matter who performed them (Tarone, Dwyer, and Icke, 1988).

Nominalization is another way in which the representation of events, actions, and actors, can be manipulated. Nominalization means using as nouns words that can also be used as verbs, adjectives, or adverbs, either with or without the addition of noun markers like the English *-tion*. In the examples above, *rape* was used both as a verb ("A man rapes a woman," "A woman is raped") and as a noun ("A woman suffers a rape," "A rape occurs"). Choices such as these are choices about whether to represent rape as an event (by making it a noun) or as as an action (by making it a verb). To give another example, members of the design staff in some advertising firms are referred to as "creatives." (Nouns can also be turned into verbs: "creatives" can say "I'm concepting" when they are at work.)

Choices involving the assignment of semantic roles and nominalization can represent people as being out of control of their destinies in the most fundamental ways, as in this sentence from a newspaper article about AIDS drugs (Krieger, 1997):

> "About half of our patients will see a long-term, possibly permanent, response to these drugs while the other half may begin to exhibit disease progression again," Deeks said.

In the first clause, AIDS patients are semantic experiencers who "see responses" to drugs. Here the patients are represented as observers of their bodies. In the second clause, patients "exhibit disease progression." The perspective here is that of the doctor looking at the patient, with the patient represented as the site of "disease progression." The patient is the object of observation. In neither case is the patient involved with his or her body or disease as an agent, someone who could be doing something. "Disease progression," a nominalization, treats the disease as having a goal toward which it "progresses." The perspective here is that of the disease; the patient would be unlikely, after all, to think of "progress" in this context.

Choices about the representation of knowledge status. Many languages provide ways for speakers to represent their relationships to the claims they make. Adverbials such as *clearly* or *without a doubt* are "evidential" or "epistemic" in this sense, as are ones such as *possibly* or *maybe*. Using *be* in the simple present tense is a way of presenting a claim as universally and hence incontrovertibly true. ("Global warming is the result of industrialization," "Allah is great.") Verbs such as *know*, *suspect*, *claim*, or *think* can indicate the level of confidence about the truth of a claim. The use of epistemic forms that indicate certainty can be a way of discouraging debate; epistemics that indicate uncertainty can make speakers appear to lack intelligence or confidence. Speakers can present themselves as knowers or merely supposers, their claims as known, believed, possible, or unlikely.

One way in which a claim about what the world is like can be made to seem natural is via syntactic claims to certainty. The effects of choices about how to present the writer's evidential stance can be subtle. For example, the second paragraph of the US Declaration of Independence begins with an explicit claim of complete certainty ("We hold these truths to be self-evident"), and evidential certainty is also conveyed by the uses of the verb *be* in the simple present tense (as in "among these *are* life, liberty, and the pursuit of happiness"):

> We hold these truths to be self-evident, that all men are created equal, that they are endowed by their Creator with certain inalienable Rights, that among these are Life, Liberty and the pursuit of Happiness. That to secure these rights, Governments are instituted among Men . . .

The simple present also conveys certainty in the following formulations of truths supposed to be self-evident, from George Orwell's (1949) dystopian novel *1984*:

> War is peace.
> Freedom is slavery.
> Ignorance is strength.

But the absence of an explicit claim to certainty ("we hold these truths to be self-evident") means that the possibility of disagreeing – of *not* seeing these claims as self-evident – is not raised in the way it is in the Declaration of Independence. Thomas Jefferson, the author of the Declaration of Independence, suggests that alternative views are possible (if not, in Jefferson's view, rational); for Big Brother, the leader of *1984*'s Ingsoc Party, alternatives are, literally, meant to be unthinkable.

Speakers can also be *represented*, via descriptions or reconstructions of their speech, as making knowledge claims. One way in which people can be positioned as relatively powerless, for example, is by being forced or expected to express uncertainty about the claims they make (this is known as "hedging"), or by being represented by others as doing this. For example, Patricia Dunmire (2005) explored how future events were discursively constructed in a 2002 speech by US President George W. Bush arguing for the invasion of Iraq. Dunmire shows how the speech uses contrasts in modality (the expression of possibility or certainty through modal verbs like *should* or *might* and choices in verb tense, among other things) to set up a contrast between an "oppositional future" associated with the public's voice and a "privileged future" associated with the Bush Administration. The contrast was often represented in the speech in a question-answer structure in which

Bush's voice responded to the (imagined) voice of the public. In these imaginary exchanges, the public is represented as unsure, questioning, Bush as certain, stating facts in the simple present tense (p. 502):

> Oppositional future: First, **I'm asked** why Iraq is different from other countries and regions that also have terrible weapons.

> Privileged future: While there **are** many dangers in the world, the threat from Iraq **stands** alone because it **gathers** the most serious dangers of our age in one place.

> Oppositional future: **Some ask** how urgent this danger is to America.

> Privileged future: The danger **is** already significant and it only **grows** worse with time.

In this example, the public "believes" in a possible ("can") but not certain course of action, wheras Bush is certain and draws on history as the source of his certainty (p. 503):

> Oppositional future: Some people **believe** that we **can** address this danger by simply resuming the old approach . . .

> Privileged future: Yet this **is precisely** what the world **has tried to do since 1991**.

"Throughout the speech," Dunmire claims, "the oppositional future of 'no military action against Iraq' is consistently projected through mental and verbal process clauses of the outsider-citizen which encode that future within a modality of 'hope', 'wonder', 'worry', and 'argument'. The privileged future, however, is presented though the 'absolute modality' of 'is' and 'will be', a modality that derives from evidence, history, and reason" (p. 502).

Choices about naming and wording.   Deciding what to call something can constitute a claim about it. For example, people who sell clothing through catalogs or over the internet make highly strategic choices of names for the colors of items, since buyers can only see them in pictures. One effect of these choices may be to suggest that women and men have different pre-occupations. One US catalog lists the colors of a casual dress for women as "butter," "pale aqua," "pale lilac," "watermelon," "cornflower," and "navy." Only one of these terms, "navy," is traditional in descriptions of the colors of cloth. Others are borrowed from the realm of flowers (lilac and corn-flower) and food (butter and watermelon), realms traditionally associated with women. In contrast, a dress shirt for men is available in "white," "ecru," "yellow," "classic green," "blue," and "French blue." All but "French blue" are standard (even in one case "classic") color terms. Note that the explanation for this difference cannot be simply that men do not know what colors such as butter or watermelon look like, since women do much of the purchasing of men's clothes and women's clothes alike in the US.

Choices from among existing terms also reflect claims about the world. Euphemism, the use of a supposedly less objectionable variant for a word with negative connotations, is a frequent kind of "rewording." The military uses "casualties" for "deaths"; the US Forest Service refers to logging as "vegetation management activity"; stockbrokers call falling prices "corrections" or "profit taking"; garbage is collected by the "Department of Environmental Services." "Tests" or "examinations" in school become "evaluations" or "skills assessments." Dysphemism is the opposite of euphemism. Choices between "genocide," "ethnic cleansing," and "murder" are choices on a euphemism–dysphemism scale. "Overwording" (Fairclough, 1992: 193) refers to the use of many different synonyms or near synonyms. The use of many words for something suggests its ideological significance. Fairclough describes a report on the teaching of English in British schools that refers to "competence," "effectiveness," "mastery," "facility," "expertise," and "skill," making clear to a critical analyst the authors' interest in defining the goals of English education in terms of lists of discrete, testable activities. Likewise, choices about the metaphorical representation of people and events both reflect and create ways of imagining what is normal. For example, debate, in politics and in academia, is often characterized metaphorically as war (Lakoff and Johnson, 1980; Tannen, 1999): you *marshall* your evidence, put up a *fight*, and *win* the argument, thereby *defeating* your *opponents*.

In a study of websites describing 51 major airlines' frequent flier programs, Crispin Thurlow and Adam Jaworski (2006) explore how these "loyalty programs" build and then draw on an image of the "global elite" by appealing to travelers' anxiety about status and creating an "illusion of distinction" to counteract it. While such programs do have some material benefits to offer (shorter check-in lines, special menus, and such), most of the "capital" they offer is not material, but symbolic (Bourdieu, 1991). Among other things, Thurlow and Jaworski explore the words and phrases used to describe the programs' benefits. Here is a partial list (p. 109):

- more legroom and space,
- better seating,
- escorts/chauffeurs,
- greater baggage allowance,
- special menus,
- upgrades,
- comfort,
- priority check-in,
- more/direct access,
- exemption from restrictions,
- special assistance/attention,
- greater choice,

- luxury,
- recognition.

"What is noticeable here," the authors point out, "is how these incentives slide between the more obvious materiality of greater baggage allowance and the kind of semiotic subjectivity of incentives such as 'comfort', 'special assistance/attention', 'luxury', and 'recognition'. In the latter cases, marketers are again peddling in the unmeasurable and the deliberately intangible, and the framework of loyalty is further secured by semiosis – by the connotative cachet of words and ideas, rather than the denotative materiality of 'things'" (pp. 109–10).

Choices about incorporating and representing other voices. As pointed out by the Russian linguist Mikhail Bakhtin (Bakhtin, 1981[1953]), all discourse is "heteroglossic" or multi-voiced. In other words, discourses incorporate, or are constructed from, bits and pieces of other discourses, other styles, other voices. We discuss the general idea of "intertextuality" in more detail in chapter 5. Here let us look briefly at relatively explicit representations of other voices in the form of quotations and descriptions of others' speech.

What we call "reported" speech is never simply a report of what someone said. For this reason, it is perhaps better referred to as "constructed dialogue" (Tannen, 1986a). Sometimes people "report" speech that quite explicitly *wasn't* said: "You can't say, 'Well Daddy I didn't HEAR you'" (Tannen, 1989: 111). In the following example, a woman represents her mother's reaction to the suggestion that she go to a rock concert, in English and then in Spanish (Ferrara and Bell, 1995: 285):

> I'm like, "Mom, let's go." Mom's like, "Well, no, I'm not gonna go without your dad." Nahhhh [laugh] It's like, "No voy sin él [I'm not going without him]."

In addition to representing the import of what her mother said (she didn't want to go to the concert without the narrator's father), the narrator suggests something about how she said it (in Spanish) by requoting in Spanish (the language of the mother's represented voice) after the quote in English (the language of the narrator's representing voice). The two formulations together create a sense of what happened and how, but neither is likely to be exactly what the mother actually said: the first is not in Spanish, and the second includes a personal pronoun, *él*, which refers back to the first and which would be very unlikely to have been used if the Spanish "version" had been the only one. Every representation of speech involves choices like these: choices that have to do with indicating what was said and how – if anything was actually said at all – but also choices about how to create a representation of another voice that fits the purposes of the present discourse.

Any choice about what to say or how to say it can function strategically, or can be interpreted as having a strategic goal. The only way to discover what aspects of discourse are in ideological service in a given instance is by looking at particular texts; there can be no complete inventory of all the possibilities. Here are just a few areas, in addition to those that have been discussed in detail, in which strategic choices are possible.

- How do pronouns help "position" speakers, addressees, characters in discourse?
- What are the effects of negation?
- What are the effects of questions?
- How do choices about tense and modality work?
- How do adjectives, adverbs, and other modifiers create systems of classification?
- What are the effects of choices about cohesion (see ch. 3)?
- How do choices about information flow work (see ch. 3)?
- What is suggested by patterns of turn-taking, turn allocation, repair (see ch. 3)?
- How is ethos (as social identity, and as personal authority) created (see ch. 4)?
- What is suggested by choices about politeness, forms of address, honorifics, indirectness (see ch. 4)?
- What other texts and ways of talking are alluded to or used (see ch. 5)?
- What are the ideological effects of manipulating expectations about genre (see ch. 5) and medium (see ch. 6)?
- How are explicit purposes and implicit ones related (see ch. 7)?

Figure 2.1 Some other areas of choice

Another facet of choice about represented speech has to do with "quotatives," words or particles that signal that what follows is to be taken as a report of speech. Among the choices in English are *say* and, less formally, *go*, *be like*, and *be all*, in addition to a large number of expressions that characterize constructed dialogue in more detail, such as *yell*, *aver*, *respond*, *whisper*, and so on. Or speakers can simply alter their voices, writers their styles, to suggest voices from outside. Speech may be "quoted," which, again, could mean anything from a literal transcription from tape to a fictional construction. ("She said, 'That's not the way I'd put it.'") Quotation takes the perspective of the reported voice. Alternatively, other voices can be described, from the perspective of the reporting voice. ("She disagreed with his formulation of the problem.") And there are mixed possibilities (sometimes referred to as "Free Indirect Discourse") in which the perspective shifts.

Such choices are clearly choices about how to represent other people or groups of people and the worlds they inhabit. The following excerpt, from a story that arose in a conversation among female friends, shows how a person can evoke and create an image of a foreigner as erotic, dangerous, and laughable, all via choices of ways to represent how he talks and what he says. Ruby is talking about an occasion during her childhood on which she and some friends filled a box with disgusting trash, gift wrapped it, and put it in the road to lure a passerby, while the girls hid and watched the reaction.

RUBY: And at this time also,
          there was these Mexicans that lived down the road from Ellen.
          And she kind of looked Mexican herself and his name was Javier,
              [laughs lightly]
          and he was you know really such a lover, [laughs lightly]
          and *he'd go, go by "Mu mu mu" [kissing noise] to that Ellen you know,*
              [laughing]
          "Eh baby eh baby" [imitating Javier; laughing] always to her.
          Well who would pull up in that van but Javier.
          [laughs]
          We about lost it you know. [laughs]
          We about gave ourselves away from laughing so hard. [laughs]
          And here he comes you know,
          "Aeee aeee," [imitating Javier]
          talking in this Spanish as fast as he could seeing that box there. [laughs
              lightly]
          Him and this other . . . Sancho . . . [was with him. [laughs]
FRED, SAMMIE: [laugh]
RUBY: You know and here they come,
          and stuff and they get out buddy and grab that box,
          you know excited as can be, [laughs]
          you know thinking they've really found something here. [laughs]
          Well . . . [laughing] they get that thing in the van and the van stops,
          and we're laughing so hard we can't hardly control it,
          and all of a sudden man *we hear them start this loudest Spanish talking
              ever,*
          growing louder and louder and all of a sudden, [laughing]
          this box comes a-flying out of that van all,
          they're *a-cussing in Spanish,* [laughs]
          and that stuff is scattered all over the road. [laughs]

Javier is depicted here as making suggestive invitations with kissing noises ("mu mu mu") and simplified "foreigner talk" English ("Eh baby eh baby"). His Spanish is represented as sounding something like "Aeee aeee" and as being "fast" and "loud," and he is said to be "cussing" when he discovers the trick. The voice that is created in this story is not just a particular voice, that of Javier, but a generic, inarticulate "Mexican" or "Spanish" voice, belonging to a stereotypical foreigner who is animal-like and gullible.

This excerpt illustrates some of the ways in which racism can be "enacted" in discourse which is not on the face of it "about" race at all (van Dijk, 1987, 1993b; Reisigl and Wodak, 2000). In the course of a story about individual people and a particular event, without making any overt generalizations about Mexicans, Ruby both alludes to and re-creates a racist picture of the typical Mexican man. Ruby's way of talking about Mexicans, in this case mainly by alluding to and representing what they sound like, is not Ruby's creation; it consists of bits and pieces of language that circulate constantly as Americans talk to one another about each other. The aspects of racism (as well as sexism and any other tendency to think of individuals as automatically representative of stigmatized groups) that are embedded in familiar ways of talking are in a sense the most pernicious ones, more dangerous than overtly racist generalizations are, because they are relatively invisible and they are deniable. People can be unaware of the ways their talk may be racist even if their explicit beliefs are not.

Discussion

2.13 In a book entitled *Talking Culture*, Michael Moerman (1988: 102) says that "for ethnographers and conversation analysts, 'the world out there' is a verb, not a noun; a social activity, not a pre-formed thing." What might it mean to say that the world is a social activity?

2.14 Here is the whole of the article about AIDS drugs discussed above. Explore how ideas about science and medicine are represented through linguistic choices in this article. For example, how are patients represented via choices of words and grammatical structures? How is AIDS represented? How are drugs represented? How are doctors represented? How are research and researchers represented? Look at the grammatical roles into which each of these "characters" is placed, at the words chosen to refer to them, at the verbs predicated of them (What are the verbs? Are they active or passive? Transitive or intransitive?), at the modifers used of them, at quotations attributed to them, and at anything else that seems potentially relevant. What are the relationships among disease, patient, drugs, doctors, and researchers in the world the article reflects, creates, and helps to "naturalize"?

For a shorter exercise, you might want to choose part of the article to talk about. As you do this, think about how to ensure that the part of the article you have chosen is representative of the language of the whole article.

AIDS drug cocktails fail 53% in study
Lisa M. Krieger
EXAMINER MEDICAL WRITER

Results of highly touted therapy disappointing in S.F. General trial on "real world" patients
There is disappointing new evidence that the highly acclaimed potent AIDS medicines are failing those who need them most.

Slightly more than half of the patients in a San Francisco General Hospital-based study developed evidence of drug failure after six months of treatment, and saw their AIDS virus levels rise, according to a study released Monday.

More optimistic are the results from the rest of the patients in the study: One year after the initiation of treatment, their virus remains persistently undetectable, suggesting long-term good health.

"In our clinics, we appear to be seeing the epidemic split in two," said Dr. Steven Deeks, assistant professor of medicine at UC-San Francisco, who is presenting his findings at the annual Interscience Conference on Antimicrobial Agents and Chemotherapy in Toronto.

"About half of our patients will see a long-term, possibly permanent, response to these drugs while the other half may begin to exhibit disease progression again," said Deeks.

The 53 percent of patients who had evidence of failure after at least six months of therapy tended to be people who already had very advanced HIV disease, defined by researchers as a low immune system CD4 cell count and high levels of virus. Most had tried multiple anti-viral drugs in the past.

The 47 percent of patients who obtained lasting benefit from the drugs, called protease inhibitors and often used in combination with one or more other anti-viral agents, were those who were more recently infected and who had not been treated with earlier generations of anti-viral medicines.

Until this S.F. General-based study, no one knew what proportion of "average" patients taking the drug combination was benefiting from it. Doctors generally do not track a therapy's success the way researchers do in the clinical studies that first document its results.

Clinical trials showed unqualified success with the drugs, which offered bright hope in a dark time. The often-disappointed AIDS community was told that things were different now – that the triple-drug combinations might turn AIDS into a chronic, manageable disease, a lifelong affliction rather than a fatal illness.

The news was so compelling that people at all stages of disease rushed to seek treatment.

But these latest findings show that for some people, lasting benefit is as elusive as ever. While drug combinations can delay disease and death, they have serious limitations. Keeping HIV at bay, even with the most potent three-drug cocktails now available, is not always possible.

For many patients, combination therapy is another in a long list of bitter disappointments.

The irony is that those less likely to be helped by the new drugs tend to be highly educated and engaged patients – often AIDS activists – who were infected long ago and conscientiously tried each of the AIDS drugs individually as they were introduced over the years. Now, this early conscientiousness may have worked against them, because they are resistant to the entire combination.

The failure of current therapies demands new and better drugs, said Deeks. "The pharmaceutical industry, the government and all researchers need to remain vigilant and continue to develop new therapeutic options for HIV-positive patients."

Unlike the patients selected for well-controlled, industry-sponsored clinical trials, "real world" San Francisco AIDS patients, particularly those treated in a public clinic like that at S.F. General Hospital, arrive with the odds stacked against them.

They tend to have been infected a long time, have tried a litany of other agents, and may have trouble complying with the complicated treatment regimen. So while clinical trials show a success rate of 80 to 90 percent, the more typical patient population may have only a 50-50 chance of enduring benefit.

"Clinical trials tend to enroll patients who are healthy, who haven't been on much therapy in the past and who are highly motivated; they are not the typical patient," explained Deeks.

The 136 patients in the study had, on average, a low CD4 count of 169. A normal CD4 count ranges from 500 to 1,000 and AIDS is defined by a CD4 count of under 200. They had a high viral load of 70,000 copies of HIV per milliliter of blood. They were treated with a protease inhibitor, such as indinavir or ritonavir, in combination with at least one and often two other anti-viral drugs, such as AZT and 3TC.

There is a biological basis for the problems encountered by this population: A virus that is exposed to sub-optimal doses of inferior drugs learns to side-step treatment. Because early treatments offered only partial suppression of the virus, HIV survived and rebounded, with a genetic diversity that then made it resistant to all available agents.

A companion paper, also presented by Deeks, offers the disappointing news that people who fail one treatment with a protease inhibitor have only limited success with a second. In this second study, 16 patients who failed one protease inhibitor were treated with an aggressive combination of two powerful protease inhibitors and two other anti-viral drugs. Most of the 16 had a limited and short-lived response to the drugs, Deeks said.

"This finding suggests that there is cross-resistance among protease inhibitors and that patients may have only one shot at achieving long-term viral suppression," he said.

But those patients who succeed in combination treatment may have a bright future.

"For those who made it past six months and have stayed undetectable for as long as they continue to take drugs, I predict they will stay undetectable," said Deeks. "If people fail (treatment), failure comes early," usually within six months.

Researchers at the conference await results from a trial by Dr. Roy Gulick of New York University, which is expected to show that the same 27 out of 30 people whose viral levels were undetectable after six months of three-drug therapy remained undetectable two years later.

Also anticipated is a study from France suggesting a dramatic new approach to treatment: "Maintenance therapy" for patients in whom the virus is consistently undetectable. Rather than keeping patients on three drugs for many years, perhaps decades, researchers there say they have had success in withdrawing the potent protease inhibitor, while maintaining anti-viral benefit.

Most researchers have abandoned the idea, at least for now, of attempting to stop treatment entirely, said Deeks. The terms undetectable and eradication may be chimera. Just because HIV can't be found doesn't mean the virus isn't there – or that it isn't replicating. HIV insinuates itself into the DNA of the body's cells and when treatment stops, the virus surges back without so much as a pause, experts now believe.

(*San Francisco Examiner*, September 29, 1997, p. A1. URL: http://www.sfgate.com/cgi-bin/article.cgi?file=/examiner/archive/1997/09/29/NEWS3491.dtl)

2.15 In his well-known 1946 essay "Politics and the English Language," English writer George Orwell (1968: 137) claimed that "if thought corrupts language, language can also corrupt thought." Newspeak, the artificial language described in Orwell's *1984* (1949), could be seen as an attempt to show how language could be used to "corrupt thought." How is Newspeak supposed to work? Does it work the way it is supposed to? Are you aware of any real-world attempts to control people's beliefs by controlling how they are allowed to talk and write? (You might think, for example, about editorial policies concerning non-sexist language like the Quebec recommendations discussed above: are these attempts to control how people think?) Do such attempts succeed? Are all such attempts undesirable, or do some result in change for the better?

2.16 Select an advertisement in any medium and analyze how the language of the advertisement depicts or "positions" the product, and seller, and the consumer. Consider the copy-writers' choices about (1) the representation of actions, actors, and events; (2) the representation of knowledge claims; (3) naming and wording; and (4) the representation and incorporation of other voices. Are any of these choices manipulative or deceptive? Since people make choices in these areas any time they say anything, how would you go about drawing the line between acceptable and unacceptable (deceptive, unacceptably manipulative) choices?

2.17 Are there situations in which there are no choices about how something has to be said? Are there times, in other words, when choices are not strategic, not ideological, not rhetorical?

Language Ideology

One set of beliefs about what is "natural" consists of "language ideology," or ideas about what language is and how it works. Students of language ideology explore the ways in which language is conceived of and thought to articulate with other aspects of social life, sometimes comparing these conceptions across sociocultural settings. Beliefs about how "language" and "reality" are related, beliefs about how communication works, and beliefs about linguistic correctness, goodness and badness, articulateness and inarticulateness all are aspects of language ideology, as are beliefs about the role of language in a person's identity, beliefs about how languages are learned, and beliefs about what the functions of language should be, who the authorities on language are, whether and how usage should be legislated, and so on. Such beliefs can be studied by asking people about them or eliciting them experimentally (Niedzielski and Preston, 1999), or by observing discourse and other modes of behavior more indirectly (Silverstein, 1979; Joseph and Taylor, 1990; Schieffelin, Woolard, and Kroskrity, 1998). Language ideology is of interest to students of language and to students of social life alike, because beliefs about what language is and how it works can affect languages as well as social relations among speakers. Language ideology has thus been examined in the context of linguistic anthropology, and sociolinguists have also been concerned with how beliefs about language are related to the choices speakers make. Work on language ideology shows how linguistic choices and language change are affected by how people conceive of language and its use and explores the circulation of and struggles over dominant conceptualizations of language and its functions.

For example, a powerful image of the communication process in the Western tradition has been shaped by the "conduit metaphor" (Reddy, 1993). In this view ideas are seen as objects. Speakers pack idea-objects into words and sentences and send the verbal packages, as if through a tube, to addressees. Addressees then unpack the containers, removing the ideas from the packaging of words. This view of the communication process is apparent in the metaphors used to talk about it: speakers "put ideas into words" and meanings "come across" to their interlocutors, who "discover" or "unpack" the meaning or "pull out the main ideas." Some ideas are difficult to "put into" words, and some words "don't fit" ideas well enough. Ineffective communicators are people who do not "come across" clearly.

Thinking about interaction in this way predisposes people to other beliefs about language and discourse. For example, the conduit metaphor privileges referential uses of language – uses of language to convey information – so that the non-referential functions of language (the uses of language for creating objects of beauty, for strengthening interpersonal rapport, for asserting control or struggling against it, for circulating ideas about morality, and so on) are difficult to keep in sight. In interpersonal relationships, people accuse each other of not being clear or not saying what they mean (i.e., not packaging their ideas correctly), when the real problems are often to be found elsewhere in the process of interaction (Gumperz, 1982a; Tannen, 1986b). In the world of information technology, the separation of words from ideas and the notion that words are packages for ideas suggest that communication can be "designed" by one person while another provides the "content." Technical writers in the corporate world are hired to take researchers' ideas and "put them into words." If words and sentences are seen as packages for ideas, then it should be possible to say "the same thing" in different ways, since the same object can come in a variety of packages (giftwrap, plain brown paper, newsprint, plastic). It means that educators can suggest to students that discarding their home dialects for school is like putting on their school uniforms (since, according to this way of thinking, you can say the same things in different dialects, just as the same person can wear different clothes). It means, in other words, that we are predisposed to see different ways of speaking as different social costumes or packages rather than different ways of being, different "forms of life" (Wittgenstein, 1953).

Language ideologies impact many areas of public and private life. In education, beliefs about correctness, standardness, and appropriateness influence how curricula are designed and students evaluated. For example, the British Education Reform Act of 1988, introducing a "National Curriculum," gave rise to furious public debate about the role of "grammar" in English education, pitting people who equated "English" with conscious knowledge of prescriptive rules for usage or mechanically flawless writing skill against people who saw "English" as a flexible set of strategies for dealing with the world in various contexts (Cameron, 1995: 78–115). Arguments about "political correctness," in the UK and in North America, can be rephrased as arguments about the relationships between words and "meanings." The Western concept of the author – the creator of ideas and texts who is responsible for what they mean and whose property they are – can be contrasted with the various ways in which speaking roles and relationships to discourse are assigned in other settings, where texts may be seen as joint constructions or communal property (Hill and Irvine, 1992).

Scholarly descriptions of languages are also colored by assumptions about the relationships between ways of talking and social and political differences (Gal and Irvine, 1995). For example, European linguists and ethnographers in Africa brought with them the idea that languages are linked to nation-states in an ideally one-to-one correspondence (so that each nation has a language and each language a nation). While this idea is central to the ideology underlying the nineteenth-century European nation-state, it had little relevance in Africa, where multiple languages coexisted (and continue to coexist) within the boundaries of post-colonial states and the same language could be spoken in multiple countries. However, the one-nation-one-language idea led European linguists to conclude that the coexistence of three languages in Senegal must be the result of migration or military conquest from elsewhere, and, since they thought black Africans were "primitive" and "simple," they assumed that the outsiders must have been from the lighter-skinned north. They thus decided that Fula, the language most concentrated in the northern part of Senegal, should be classified with Arabic as a Semitic language, despite abundant evidence (had they been in a position to see it) that Fula is in fact historically related to the other non-Semitic languages spoken in Senegal.

"Dialects" and "varieties" are likewise shaped by ideology. The meanings attached to speaking with "an accent" can function in the service of dominant ideologies about who has the right to political and economic power (Lippi-Green, 1997), and particular details of ways of sounding can acquire new ideological significance in defining self and community in the context of global economic and cultural change. Beliefs about what it means to sound like one is "from here" may, for example, have a bearing on the trajectory of change in regional varieties of speech, in places where mass media and social and geographical mobility might be expected to lead people to sound more like people elsewhere. Natives of Okracoke, a once isolated island fishing community off the Atlantic coast of the US, repeatedly perform for tourists one phrase which they think encapsulates what real "Okracokers" sound like (Schilling-Estes, 1998). This phrase, "Hoi toid on the south soid," and the local-sounding [oi] variant of the diphthong /ay/ which it highlights, comes to symbolize and, perhaps, eventually to constitute the Okracoke "dialect."

Another example comes from Pittsburgh, a de-industrializing city in the northeastern US. The idea that there is a dialect unique to the city (people call it "Pittsburghese") is both drawn on and reinforced in nostalgic online discussions among former Pittsburghers who have had to move elsewhere to find work (Johnstone and Baumgardt, 2004). For these people, showing that one is an "authentic" Pittsburgher, entitled to participate in the discussion, means showing that one knows "Pittsburghese," and people show this by citing and defining words that are thought of as unique to the city. Since people often do this in the context of talking about childhood memories, the words they mention and the ones used as examples of local pronunciations are words that resonate with their nostalgia and sense of place. As this set of words associated with "Pittsburghese" gets "enregistered" (Agha, 2003) in the local imagination as a unique, unchanging "dialect," it is not so much how people actually speak in Pittsburgh that is captured in local language ideology, but how people think authentic Pittsburghers speak, and this set of ideas is colored by the details of the situations in which people talk about localness.

Discussion

2.18 How do university curriculum committees (and the institutions that oversee them) view the role of language in higher education? How are their ideas circulated via such things as required courses in foreign languages and in writing? Does language ideology play a role in the division of scholarly labor into disciplines and departments?

2.19 A study by Rosina Lippi-Green (1997: 79–103) shows that the accents of Disney cartoon characters conform to persistent stereotypes. Characters who sound Middle Eastern are bad guys, male characters with French accents are lovers or cooks, and "good" foreigners do not have foreign accents. How are foreigners and foreign accents depicted in films for adults? What about regionally-marked accents?

2.20 What does this classified advertisement suggest about how having a foreign accent is perceived in the US?

> SPEECH & LANGUAGE PATHOLOGISTS
>
> COLETON REHABILITATION ASSOCIATES INC
> Treating Speech-Language, Stuttering
> Foreign Dialect And All
> Communication Problems
> Children and Adults
> Qualified Insurance Accepted

2.21 What are "bad words"? Who decides which words are acceptable and which are not? How are these decisions made and how and when are they enforced?

How does the "conduit metaphor" sometimes underlie debates about "good" and "bad" language?

2.22   Under what circumstances, in your sociocultural milieu, are speakers thought not to be responsible for the words they utter? For example, are speakers thought to be responsible for words they speak while asleep? For words they speak immediately after a traumatic event? For words they use to interpret the meaning of a divination ritual like reading someone's Tarot cards? Can you think of cases in which responsibility for the *form* of an utterance is thought to be separate from responsibility for the *effect* of the utterance?

Silence

The worlds that shape and are shaped in discourse involve absences as well as presences. Noticing silences, things that are not present, is more difficult than noticing things that are present, but it is equally important. Foregrounds are only possible in the context of backgrounds; what is not said or cannot be said is the background without which what is said could not be heard. Silence sometimes becomes the foreground, as, for example, when a pause in a conversation lasts too long, a comment is made about what someone failed to say, or we notice that something that is easy to talk about in one language seems impossible to talk about in another. Only when silence becomes the foreground and discourse the background – in a Quaker meeting, for example (Bauman, 1983; Davies, 1982) – do we routinely notice silence and its roles in discourse and world.

One source of silence in discourse is "implicature." In many situations, people can expect their interlocutors to share expectations about the relevance of what is said to what has already been said and to other elements of the context. Thus, logical connections and connections with contextual facts that people assume they share do not always have to be made explicit. For example, it may be possible, or even preferable, to say

Open the door.

rather than

Walk up to the door, turn the door handle clockwise as far as it will go, then pull gently towards you.

if the hearer is expecting the speaker to say no more than is necessary, and if both assume that the hearer knows how to operate a door. (This example is from Levinson, 1983: 108.) Note, however, that the silence of "Open the door" in comparison to "Walk up to the door, turn the door handle..."

may be a source of confusion or misunderstanding if the speaker and hearer do not, in fact, share this procedural knowledge. (In the US, door "handles" are often knobs that must be turned clockwise.) People who don't know basic culinary techniques may find that even a very explicit procedural text such as a recipe involves implicature. Other types of implicature, as well as related pragmatic principles such as presupposition, also create silences that can save communicative effort or cause communicative difficulty. We will return to this topic in more depth in chapter 7.

Translation, if practiced with care, often highlights silences, things that are unsaid or unsayable in one language world and not in another. Silences may have to do with words: it is often noted, for example, that there is no easy way to talk in English about "Gemütlichkeit" (a German word that can be used to refer to the ambience of a comfortable social group). Silences may have to do with how languages group things in grammar: Arabic second-person pronouns differentiate between female and male addressees (*ʔanti* 'you-feminine' versus *ʔanta* 'you-masculine'), whereas English speakers can do this only with some difficulty, and usually only in the plural (*you girls*, for example) and so may be less likely to do it at all. In English, silence about the agents of actions can be created through the use of passive voice ("Mistakes were made") or passive adjectives ("the well-established fact that . . ."). Translation can create silences, because it requires fitting one language into the categories of another. As A. L. Becker points out (1995: 211), this begins in the process of glossing, assigning words and labels in the translator's language to words in the translated language: ". . . a particular glossing, a deceptively simple form of translation, determines the parsing to a large degree. To gloss, say, a Burmese sentence into English is to anticipate an analysis using English categories." In this sense, says Becker, glossing is "a political process" (p. 232).

Political processes, and the discursive practices that enact these processes, often involve the creation of silences. Struggles over power and control are often struggles over whose words get used and whose do not and over who gets to speak and who does not. This can be relatively obvious (at least once you think about it), as, for example, when the one-page agenda for a public meeting about the conduct of the police in a US city announces three times that audience members should be more or less silent: they may speak only if there is time, only for three minutes, and only if acknowledged by the chair (Zawodny-Wetzel, 1999). Anthropologist Laura Graham (2005) provides another compelling example of how procedural rules set by the more powerful can silence the less powerful, even in a situation meant explicitly to elicit powerless voices. Hiparidi Top'tiro is a Xavante from central Brazil who has been active in debate about the risks and benefits of large-scale agribusiness in his area. Top'tiro attended the 2005 United Nations Permanent Forum on Indigenous Issues, where he decided to make a formal statement. It turned out, however, that in order to do this he would have to present it in one of the UN's official languages, none of which he could speak; that he could speak for no longer than five minutes; and that his statement would have to be typed and submitted in advance in many copies. These policies reflected a way of doing business that was foreign to Top'tiro, who, Graham says, is "most articulate and powerful as a Xavante spokesperson when he speaks spontaneously," and Top'tiro changed his mind about making a statement.

Silences can be very difficult to notice. One study of American couples found, for instance, that the women tended to suggest conversational topics, but the men determined which topics were taken up (Fishman, 1978), so while the women may have talked more they were heard less. Debate over what is sayable at all and what is not is, likewise, often hidden and some-times itself hard to talk about. Who can say "no" to a sexual overture, and how can having to say "no" bring to the fore sexual identifications that are usually repressed (Kulick, 2005)? How do doctors and patients talk about death (Coupland and Coupland, 1997)?

Like all others, the discourses that shape and are shaped by science and technology are loud in some ways and silent in others. It has often been noted, for example, that scientists are expected to efface themselves from reports of their research (Bazerman, 1988), for example via passive con-structions ("It was observed that . . . ," "Titration was performed"), and academic writing may require other kinds of "strategic vagueness" as well (Myers, 1996). Silences are built into the code that constitutes computer software. For example, an experimental computer program called "Julia," designed to pass as a woman in online chat, was programmed to respond to sexually provocative remarks only by saying things like "Thank you." The software did not allow responses like "Your behavior is unacceptable" (Zdenek, 1999).

Learning to notice silence means learning to "de-familiarize." It requires learning to imagine alternative worlds and alternative ways of being, think-ing, and talking. Making a point of noticing silence means making a point of asking questions like these: What else could have happened? How could you say this another way? How would you say it in another language? How would this have looked in another setting?

Discussion

2.23 What are some of the roles of silence in "conflict talk" in the settings with which you are familiar? What meanings are attributed to a person's silence? When does silence signal interactional weakness and when does it signal interactional strength, for example? Are there silences having to do with topics and tactics for talk? (For example, in debate in the Western tradition certain "lines of argument" are considered inappropriate or fallacious.) Are there strategies that depend on violating expectations about silences of these kinds?

2.24 John Lofty (1999) points out that high-school and college students are often taught to distance themselves from the texts they study, to approach what they read analytically, to make statements about the text rather than about how the text affects them, "not to use 'I'." Lofty suggests that this makes it difficult for students to develop their own voice, their own authority for meaning. What do you think?

2.25 In an analysis of graffiti by Hispanic gangs in Phoenix, Arizona, Adams and Winter (1997) show that one of the most powerful rhetorical moves a gang member can make is to cross out parts of the graffiti of a member of another gang. Why is this such a powerful move? In what other discourse contexts do people make analogous "crossing-out" moves?

2.26 A woman once told me a story about a time when a strange man offered her a ride, which she foolishly accepted, and took her to a motel room, from which she escaped through the bathroom window. Although the story was highly detailed and dramatically performed, the woman never mentioned the reason for which the man took her to the motel: to rape her. Perhaps the reason she didn't mention rape was because she assumed the man's purpose would be obvious to me (as it was). Or perhaps she didn't mention rape because "rape" feels like a dirty word, or because the topic is taboo, or because she didn't have an easy, familiar way to formulate that part of the story. Using this story as a starting point, discuss the relationship between things that *are not* talked about and things that *cannot be* talked about. Is it a relationship of cause and effect, for example? Is the relationship always the same?

Summary

Discourse is shaped by the world, by what it is "about." What we talk about and how we talk about it is related to our "worldview" – the world we think of as natural and independent of language. But discourse shapes the phenomenal (experienced) world in turn, as people bring worlds into being by talking. It is possible to imagine that entities would not exist without language, since it is through language that we come to imagine ourselves as separate from "the world out there," and it is through language that we come to categorize. The Sapir-Whorf hypothesis, starting from the realist assumption that there *is* a physical world independent of human cognition, suggests that the categories into which grammars group entities massively influence the categories to which speakers imagine things "naturally" belong. An approach to the topic which avoids some of the difficulties of the Sapir-Whorf hypothesis involves examining how discourse and ideology create and perpetuate one another. The chapter explored several of the many ways in which choices about how to talk function as ideological choices, choices rooted in and constitutive of beliefs about what is natural and right. One area of particular interest to linguistically-minded discourse analysts has been language ideology, the sets of assumptions, beliefs, and ways of talking about language that help shape what language is like and how it functions in society. Studies of language and world usually focus on the import of what *is* said, in general or in a particular text, but it is equally important to find ways to notice what *is not* said or cannot be said. Silence is the background against which discourse is interpreted. Noticing silence involves doing the sort of work a translator does.

We began this chapter by considering the role of paraphrase in the kind of informal discourse analysis we practice every day. We observed that one of the first things people tend to do, when asked to talk about a conversation or something they read, is to say something about what the talk or the text was about. This led into our discussion of what it means to say that discourse is "about" a world outside of the discourse.

Saying what a book is about is not, however, the end of an analysis of it. If the hypothetical friend we started with were sincere in wondering about the book you had just read, you might eventually talk about the author's style, mentioning details about the language. You might talk about what the novel had to say about social relationship in general, about power and control, for example, or about love. You might talk about how the book compared to other novels by the same author, or what other novels or novelists it reminded you of. You might talk about whether the book would make a good movie. You might wonder why someone would write such a book – about which details were autobiographical, about what audience the author had in mind. In the chapters to follow we ask analogous questions about discourse in general.

Further Reading

On the difficulty of translation, see Hatim and Mason (1990), Becker (1995). Malmkjaer (2005) is an introduction to translation studies, and Hatim (1998) discusses discourse analysis in the context of translation. The Sapir-Whorf hypothesis was presented in articles by Sapir (1929), reprinted in Sapir (1949), and by Whorf (1941), reprinted in Carroll (1956). Benveniste (1986[1971]) formulated a similar set of ideas in the context of French structuralism. Recent discussions of the Sapir-Whorf hypothesis and its repercussions are Hill and Mannheim (1992), Foley (1997, chs 8–12), and Lucy (1997). Reformulations of the idea which focus on the effects of aspects of language other than reference are Silverstein (1979) and Friedrich (1986). A fairly recent collection of papers on the topic of linguistic relativity is Gumperz and Levinson (1996). On grammatical gender and its literary uses in English and French see Livia (2001).

On the role of metaphor in language and cognition, see Lakoff and Johnson (1980); Lakoff (1987). Overviews of cognitive linguistics include Croft and Cruse (2004) and Evans and Green (2006). Sherzer (1987) discusses how discourse mediates between language and culture, particularly in artistic genres. This approach is particularly influenced by the work of Dell Hymes (1981b) on Native American ethnopoetics, and much of the work in this framework has been about Native North and South American groups. It includes Mannheim (1986) and Urban (1991, 1996), as well as collections of papers edited by Sherzer and Woodbury (1987) and Sherzer and Urban (1986). A good short overview of Critical Discourse Analysis is Fairclough and Wodak (1997). There are a number of longer overviews of work in this vein. One of the earliest, focused mainly on how grammatical choices serve ideological ends, is Hodge and Kress (1993), the first edition of which was published in 1979. Fairclough (1989, 1992) discusses a broader set of ways in which discourse and ideology inform one another. Bolinger (1980) is an informal treatment of some of the ways in which language can be used deceptively. Scholarship about evidentiality in discourse is represented in Chafe and Nichols (1986); see also references in chapter 4 on stance. On representations of speech, see Tannen (1989: 98–133), Coulmas (1986), and, with particular reference to literary discourse, Fludernik (1993).

An overview of theory and scholarship about language ideology is Woolard and Schieffelin 1994. Silverstein (1979) is an important early formulation of the idea. Collections of papers reporting language ideology research include Schieffelin, Woolard, and Kroskrity (1998) and Joseph and Taylor (1990). On the conduit metaphor, see Reddy (1993). Various ideologies about responsibility for meaning, the production of knowledge, authority, and authorship are contrasted in the papers in Hill and Irvine (1992). Very accessible discussions of language ideology in public life in the US and the UK respectively are Lippi-Green (1997) and Cameron (1995); Milroy and Milroy (1985) explore prescription and standardization in depth.

Two collections of articles about silence are Tannen and Saville-Troike (1985) and Jaworski (1997).

chapter 3

Discourse Structure: Parts and Sequences

Speakers tend to do what language makes it easy to do. Whether or not there is a specifically human "language instinct" hard-wired into the human mind (Pinker, 1994), it seems clear from comparative observation that there are general human tendencies to create and deploy words and structures in similar ways. Humans invent words, associating sets of sounds or gestures with referents or functions, and we use the same words repeatedly for the same or similar purposes. Out of words and collocations of words we build phrases and clauses which typically have certain kinds of structures and not others. We find ways to signal the beginnings, internal parts, and endings of conversational turns and moves, stories, paragraphs, and arguments. We use certain repeated sequences of conversational turns and moves to perform certain speech acts.

Conventions are created as people repeatedly create and interpret words and structures in similar ways. As this happens, some ways of building and understanding discourse become more easily available than others. Linguists and prescriptive "language guardians" use the term "grammars" to refer to sets of conventions for constructing phrases, clauses, and sentences that are relatively codified (that is, written down or otherwise fixed in place and time). We speak of "the grammar of English," for example, or "the grammar of Yoruba," even though in fact each speaker's grammar is somewhat different, since each speaker has different linguistic experiences and necessarily makes somewhat different generalizations about them. It is also possible to talk about the "grammar" of larger units of discourse, in the same sense, and some discourse analysts have done so.

This chapter is about how discourse is shaped by various kinds of structural conventions, and how structural conventions are influenced by what speakers use discourse for. We will explore two ways in which "grammar" and discourse intersect. For one thing, we will think about how the sentence-level grammar of a language, the set of generalizations that describe how speakers form phrases, clauses, and sentences, influences and is influenced by the ways in which phrases, clauses, and sentences are deployed in discourse. For example, research about where "given" and "new" information tends to be found (Prince, 1981, 1992) explores how the structure of sentences arises in part out of requirements of "information flow" from one sentence to another. Work on cohesion (Halliday and Hasan, 1976) also examines the meanings of utterances in their linguistic contexts. As we examine the role of structure in discourse, we will touch on the findings of these and other studies.

For another thing, we will look at the ways in which utterances that are longer than a sentence – conversations, paragraphs, stories, and arguments – can be described as having "discourse-level" grammars of their own. Linguists have long asked and answered questions about linguistic competence, or what is involved in knowing a language. This competence is typically described as consisting of knowledge about phonology (how sounds are categorized and combined in a language), morphology (the structure of words), syntax (the structure of sentences), and semantics (the interpretation or computation of meaning). Discourse analysis moves the description of competence up a level, providing models of the knowledge that enables people to produce and interpret paragraphs, stories, conversations, and arguments, and exploring the ways in which interlocutors both draw on and jointly create structure as they interact.

The idea that the structure of sentences reflects their roles in discourse dates at least to work by Prague School linguists of the 1930s (Firbas, 1992), and the idea of studying the syntax of units larger than the sentence is often dated to the early 1950s (Harris, 1952). But intensive work on discourse structure began in the 1960s and 1970s. Some of the earliest was about the structure of English paragraphs (Christensen et al., 1966). Also in the 1960s, William Labov and Joshua Waletzky (Labov and Waletzky, 1967, 1997) described the structure of spontaneous personal-experience narrative in a way that is still compelling, as we will see. Linguists associated with the Summer Institute of Linguistics, often drawing on a model of language known as Tagmemics (Pike, 1967), began to propose general models of what the parameters of discourse structure might be across the world's languages (Longacre, 1976; Grimes, 1975). Work on what distinguishes a cohesive text from a set of unrelated sentences (Halliday and Hasan, 1976), in the framework of Systemic-Functional linguistics, also dates from the 1970s, as does work by Li (1976), Givón (1979) and others about how the communicative function of a clause shapes its grammar. Schegloff and Sacks (1973) and others described the structure of parts of conversations, such as openings and closings, in the context of work by sociologists interested in how humans use conversation to organize themselves socially as they interact (Sacks, Schegloff, and Jefferson, 1974; Sacks, 1995). Models of discourse structure analogous to the abstract models of word and sentence structure developed by morphologists and syntacticians have included those of Polanyi (1988), who models coherence by means of branching trees representing hierarchies of structure, and of Mann and Thompson (1988; Mann, Mattheissen, and Thompson, 1992), "Rhetorical Structure Theory."

What do we mean by saying that discourse is structured? We mean that on the basis of internal patterns and regularities we can formulate generalizations about which kinds of units precede and follow which other kinds of units, both in single-sentence utterances and in longer texts and conversations. We can formulate generalizations about what kinds of units come where and what it means that a unit appears in one place or another. We can break discourse, or at least records of discourse (written texts and transcripts), into parts and the parts into parts. We may be able to explain what actually happens in talk, at least partially, by saying that when people produce discourse or interpret it they may make use of generalizations they have made about what the parts tend to be and how they tend to be arranged.

It is important to note that we can make these claims about structure without insisting that structural rules are innate (or based on innate sets of syntactic principles and parameters) and without positing a discourse-generating machine in the mind that operates only by applying structural rules. It may be the case, for example, that utterances and texts are sometimes not the result of structural rules at all, but rather the result of the repetition of partly or completely unanalyzed chunks of previous discourse (see chapter 5). Since humans can categorize and generalize, however, we can develop and use generalizations about structure, in other words grammar, and grammar is useful, both in the process of creating and interpreting discourse and in the process of analyzing it in retrospect the way discourse analysts do. It is useful, then, to think about the ways in which discourse can be said to be built out of units that are built out of smaller units, and to consider how people interpret discourse, at least sometimes and at least in part, by looking to see what the units are and how they relate to one another. At the end of the chapter we will return to a more detailed consideration of the status of grammar as a theoretical concept and of the role of grammar – rules, conventions, constraints – in discourse.

Some aspects of the grammar of written discourse are familiar to us because we have been taught, in school, something about recognizing and producing them, particularly in written texts. We have been taught to think of certain units as basic and have learned rules for combining them. In many writing systems, for example, words are separated by blank spaces; in traditional uses of the Roman alphabetic system, sentences begin with capital letters and end with periods, question marks, or exclamation points; paragraphs are often separated by blank lines or marked with indentations. Printed documents are also divided into units defined typographically – pages – or thematically – chapters, books. Different genres of writing involve the use of different units: in plays there are "lines," scenes, and acts; in poems there are "lines" (of a different sort), verses, and stanzas. New media for writing give rise to new units, such as screenfuls on a computer and web "pages" (which are different from print pages in some important ways). Although the boundaries of the units of written discourse may seem relatively easy to identify, even in this relatively fixed, rule-governed medium people do not always know or agree about where words, sentences, paragraphs, and chapters ought to begin and end. Different people, in other words, can and do make different generalizations about what the conventions are, the conventions change, and new conventions emerge. This gives rise to the need for instruction in spelling, prescriptive grammar, and style, in settings in which it is important for writing to remain relatively standardized.

It is often thought that oral discourse – in particular, unplanned oral discourse, such as casual conversation – is fairly chaotic, "random," or unstructured. The units of oral discourse are indeed different in some ways from those of written discourse. Unless they are reading aloud, people do not speak in paragraphs, for example. But a spoken utterance is not a random set of words, and a conversation is not a random set of utterances. The fact that we expect utterances and conversations to adhere to familiar patterns of structure becomes particularly clear in situations in which things do not work in the usual way. For example, certain cases of aphasia, a set of language disorders that can result from brain damage, impair their victims' ability to produce sentences structured in the expected ways, as in these examples (Lenneberg, 1967: 194):

He is speeching it, there and then, straight away for me, there.

. . . that I shall have lesson with the lungage [*sic*] of the hear itself.

That is a dark.

Well, I thought thing I am going to the . . . tell is about my operation . . .

Conversations also sound odd if our expectations about their structure are violated. For example, a telephone conversation which does not begin or end in the way we expect it to can lead to confusion and a feeling that order has been violated. If telephone interlocutors are cut off before they get to the expected conversation-closing turns, the original caller will sometimes call back to renew the connection, even if the business of the call has already been completed. (This can of course lead to awkwardness too, since we expect callers to have reasons for calling other than simply to say goodbye!)

These examples highlight the fact that we need to ask questions about the structure of oral discourse, too. What is talk made of, and how? What kind of information needs to go where in an utterance, if the utterance is to fit in the context of unfolding knowledge and unfolding social relations? We begin by considering relatively small parts of discourse – words – and then move to larger and larger chunks. After exploring how we might talk about parts of texts, we turn to questions about what goes where inside the parts, and why.

Words and Lines

It may seem uncontroversial to claim that people speak in words, but words are considerably easier to delimit in written text than in the stream of speech. Spoken words are not always surrounded by silence; in fact, pronouncing each word in a phrase with a silence before and after it may make the phrase sound more like a list of words than an attempt to produce a meaning. Casual spellings such as "alot" (for "a lot") and "gonna" (for "going to") suggest that word boundaries are not always audible. (And word boundaries can in fact change over time: *apron*, which has the same root as *napkin*, was once *napron*, until people who heard *a napron* as *an apron* began to spell it without the initial *n*.) Single words may not always be the basic semantic building blocks, either: a morpheme (the smallest unit of meaning in language) is often just one part of a word, and, conversely, people often remember and use sets of words as single units. *Blueberry* is one unit or two depending on whether one counts major stresses (of which there is one) or minimal semantic units (of which there are two). When American children say *trick or treat* on Hallowe'en, they may be expressing what to them is an indivisible unit of meaning. This is evidenced by their use of the verb *to trick-or-treat* in expressions like *going trick-or-treating*. Lexical formulas that function as building blocks for utterances can be even longer than this, and some start out as whole clauses. *God be with you* is an example of this. With time, the clause became so formulaic at partings and thus so unitary in meaning that its pronunciation was shortened to *goodbye*.

On the next level, discourse analysts have found it useful to talk about multiword units which they call "phrases," "lines," or "utterances," among other things. A unit of this size can be defined grammatically, acoustically, semantically, or via some combination of grammatical, acoustic, and semantic criteria. One grammatically-delineated unit is the clause, which can be defined as a unit consisting of subject, a finite verb (that is, a "main" verb, inflected for tense and person, or in whatever other ways are required in the language in question), and the complements of the verb (that is, the elements required to complete the predicate, such as objects and certain adverbials). There are also other ways of defining clauses. T-, or "thematic," units (Hunt, 1966) have proven especially useful in comparing styles of writing and studying the development of writing skill. Like clauses, t-units are defined structurally, as one main clause together with any subordinate clauses that are embedded in it or dependent to it. (A t-unit is thus roughly equivalent to a complete sentence in standard written English.) Noun phrases and verb phrases are also structurally defined units, consisting of a head word and its complements and/or modifiers. One acoustically-defined unit is the "tone group" (Crystal and Quirk, 1964; Crystal, 1969). A unit of prosody, a tone group is a stretch of speech consisting of one prominent pitch "nucleus" and one or more other syllables that trail off from it. Tone units are set off by slight pauses and other markers of juncture. A unit which is defined both acoustically and semantically is the "utterance" (Scollon, 1976; Crookes and Rulon, 1985). An utterance, in this technical sense, is a stream of speech which has a single intonation contour, is bounded by pauses, and/or constitutes a single unit of meaning.

There is also a variety of ways of explaining why talk almost always occurs in units of several words at a time, whether these units are best thought of as phrases, lines, utterances, or something else. Scholars such as Wallace Chafe (1980a, 1986, 1994) relate the "chunking" of oral discourse to cognitive constraints. Chafe describes how both monologue and conversation emerge in short bursts of talk, using as data narratives based on a short film (1980b) and conversations among friends (1994). Chafe relates this spurt-like nature of talk to the jerky way human consciousness scans the information banks of memory. Each "focus of consciousness" gives rise to a burst of talk, or "intonation unit," surrounded by very brief pauses. These bursts often consist of a single grammatical phrase or clause and end with a slight rise or fall in intonation. Within them, speakers often accelerate and then decelerate. Each intonation unit expresses what can roughly be seen as a new concept, though different speakers tend to produce different types of units. In the English-language data Chafe has studied, substantive idea units tend to be about four words long; fragmentary false starts and "regulatory" units that serve various cohesive and responsive functions are shorter. This excerpt illustrates both what intonation units can consist of and Chafe's system for transcribing talk. A and B are the speakers; lines are labeled with small letters; ellipses and the numbers in parentheses measure pauses (Chafe, 1994: 63).

a(A)   . . . (0.4) Have the . . . ánimals,
b(A)   . . . (0.1) ever attacked anyone ín a car?
c(B)   . . . (1.2) Well I
d(B)   well Í hèard of an élephant,
e(B)   . . . that sát down on a vw one time.

On the next level, groups of intonation units form what Chafe calls "centers of interest," or chunks of information larger than consciousness can be aware of at one time. Centers of interest are expressed in sentence-like form and end with sentence-final falling intonation. At this intermediate level, between the idea unit and the "island of memory" which underlies a narrative as a whole, speakers express roughly one predication (or, roughly speaking, a single claim about a single topic) at a time. Although the contents of centers of interest vary from speaker to speaker, there is some tendency, says Chafe, for settings, introductions of people, and events in the core of a narrative to be expressed as separate centers of interest. When changes in scene, participants, or other sorts of background information are necessary, breaks between centers of interest tend to be longer. Underlying Chafe's explanations of discourse chunks is the claim that universal facts about human mental processes – "the essentially scenic and musical nature of thought, experience, and discourse," in Tannen's (1989) words – interact with specific facts about languages to create the rhythm of talk.

Taking a less cognitive, more comparative perspective on chunking in oral discourse, a number of linguistic anthropologists studying Native American languages and language use have adopted terms traditionally used to talk about verbal art (Hymes, 1981b; Sherzer, 1982; Tedlock, 1983; Woodbury, 1987). They note the crucial importance of transcribing talk in "lines" which reflect the sound and internal organization of speech. For example, Sherzer notes that, for the Kuna of Panama, the same rhythmical and musical pattern occurs across a wide variety of speech genres, ranging from spontaneous casual conversation to memorized ritual chants. This pattern consists of a line uttered by one speaker, often marked at the beginning or end with one of a number of special particles similar to "see" or "indeed" and uttered with slowly falling intonation, followed by a response sound or word from a second speaker. Lines as Sherzer delineates them are longer than Chafe's intonation units. This example (slightly adapted from Sherzer, 1982: 374) is from a chant, performed during a public village meeting, by two village leaders. One of the "chiefs" is the chanter; the other responds after each oral line. The responding chief's utterances are indented in the transcript.

Chanting chief:	*we yalase papa anparmialimarye soke ittole.*
	(To this mountain Father sent us, say listen.)
	eka masmu akkwekarye oparye.
	(To care for banana roots for him, pronounce.)
Responding chief:	*teki*
	(Indeed.)
Chanting chief:	*eka inso tarkwarmu akkwekarye soke ittolete sunna ipiti oparye.*
	(In order to care for taro roots for him, say listen in truth pronounce.)
Responding chief:	*teki*
	(Indeed.)

Like Chafe's, this way of delimiting units in discourse highlights the rhythmical, musical quality of talk. As Sherzer and others point out (Sherzer and Woodbury, 1987; Sherzer and Urban, 1986), characteristic musical patterns of oral discourse are as much part of and reflective of the aesthetic expectations that make culture coherent as are characteristic patterns in visual art and in music itself.

Dell Hymes (1981b) also discusses larger units of oral discourse called "verses," "stanzas," "scenes," and "acts." These are delimited differently from group to group, according to Hymes. In many Native American societies, for example, groups of three or five lines tend to form larger units; in others, groups of two or four lines are more typical (p. 319). Units are marked by speakers and identified by audiences in various ways, such as by particles that signal their beginnings and ends and via internal consistency (for example, there is often more syntactic parallelism – that is, repeated use of the same structural pattern – within a unit than across units). Here, for example, is the first "scene" of a Clackamas myth that was told to ethnographer Melville Jacobs in 1959. (Clackamas was a Chinookan language spoken by natives of the northwest coast of the United States.) Jacobs translated the myth into English and transcribed it in prose paragraphs. It was reanalyzed, labeled, and laid out in this new way by Hymes (1981b: 310, 312), who sees it as poetry. The story is about a man who infiltrates Seal's home by posing as a woman, first sleeping with and then murdering Seal's brother. In this scene, Seal's daughter voices her suspicions about her uncle's "wife," but her mother shushes her. (For an orthographic key to the Clackamas transcription, see Hymes, 1981b: 25–6.)

>### *Wálxayu iCámxix gaLxílayt*
>### **Seal and her younger brother lived there**
>[i. The "wife" comes]

(A) (1) *GaLXílayt, Wálxayu, wagáxan, iCámxix*
          They lived there, Seal, her daughter, her younger brother.
          Lhúxwan qánCíxbÉt, aGa iLGagílak gaLigúqam Wálxayu iCámxix.
          After some time, now a woman got to Seal's younger brother.

(B) (2) *GaLXílayt.*
          They lived there.
               Alúya tLáXnix xábixix
               They would 'go out' [i.e., urinate] outside in the evening.

    (3) *Wak'áSkaS alagíma,*
          The girl would say,
               agulxáma wákaq:
               she would tell her mother:
               "Áqu! Dángi iXlúwidix wiCLm ayágikal.
               "Mother! Something is different about my uncle's wife.
               "TL'á wiLÉkala-díwi alubáya."
               "It sounds just like a man when she 'goes out.'"

(4)   *"Ák'wáSka! IwímiLm ayágikal!"*
       "Shush! Your uncle's wife!"
(C)   (5)   *Í::yatLqdix k'wátLqí gaLXílayt.*
       A long time they lived there like that
             Xábixix aLubáywa.
       In the evening they would each 'go out.'
(6)   *AGa agulxáma:*
       Now she would tell her:
             "Áqu! Dáng(i) iXlúwida wíCLm ayágikal.
       "Mother! Something is different about my uncle's wife.
             "Alubáya tL'a wiLÉkala díwi."
       "When she 'goes out' it sounds just like a man."
(7)   *"Ák'wáSka!"*
       "Shush!"

According to Hymes, it is characteristic of texts like this for verses to be constructed out of three lines, whose three verbs describe an *onset*, an *ongoing*, and an *outcome*, for stanzas to consist of three verses, and for scenes to consist of three stanzas. In the excerpt, we see this pattern in the stanzas marked (B) and (C), which have three verses each, (2, 3, 4) and (5, 6, 7) respectively, as well as in the structure of this scene as a whole, which has three stanzas (A, B, C).

Discussion

3.1   One unit of discourse which we have not discussed here is the sentence. In traditional pedagogical treatments of English grammar, a sentence is sometimes defined as "the expression of a complete thought." How would you go about identifying the sentences in a written text? Could you use the same criteria to identify sentences in oral discourse? If not, what criteria could you use? How useful is it to talk about speech (as opposed to written discourse) in terms of sentences? In an encyclopedia or a history of rhetoric, look up the history of the written sentence and report on it.

3.2   Audio-record a few minutes of a conversation and transcribe it in several ways: as a "playscript" with each speaker's turn starting on a new line, in t-units or clauses, and in intonation units or "lines." Which transcription is easiest to read and why? Which do you think captures the sound of the conversation best? Is any of the systems more "accurate" than the others? Experiment with other ways of representing the conversation on paper. Could you use musical notation, for example? A variety of fonts, type sizes, and colors?

3.3   Different ways of chunking oral discourse – into units of sound, units of structure, and units of meaning – sometimes coincide. As Chafe notes, for example, an intonation unit representing a cognitive focus often consists of one grammatical phrase; as Sherzer notes, a "line" is an acoustic unit as well as a grammatical one. You may have found in doing exercise 3.2 that there are other overlaps between transcription systems. Is it surprising that sound, grammar, and meaning coincide in ways like these? Which reason for discourse chunking (sound, grammar, or meaning), if any, do you think is the most basic or important?

3.4   How could the ideas presented in this section be used to critique the claim that people who are illiterate or poorly educated (or looked down on for some other reason) "don't speak in complete thoughts"? Does anyone "speak in complete thoughts"?

Paragraphs and Episodes

As was pointed out at the beginning of this chapter, it is often thought that "structure" belongs to smaller units such as phrases and sentences. Although we may be used to thinking of written paragraphs as being unified in content (i.e., as having a "topic" expressed in a "topic sentence" and, at least in some writing traditions, developed in other sentences), we do not as readily think of them as having structure – except to the extent that we may know that a safe place to put the topic sentence is at the beginning. The writer of an English paragraph may, in fact, be more free to decide what will go where than is the writer of an English sentence, and paragraph length and structure certainly vary across written media. (Paragraphs in newspaper columns and on web pages are usually shorter than paragraphs in books, for example, partly because narrow newspaper columns and computer screens wider than they are long make paragraphs look longer in these media.) But it is possible to make useful generalizations about the structure of paragraphs, and it is possible that writers at least sometimes make use of such generalizations, either formed unconsciously or taught explicitly.

One structural analysis of English expository paragraphs is that of A. L. Becker (1965), who suggests that there are two main patterns, each describable as a set of structural/semantic slots which can be filled with one or more sentences. One pattern involves a *Topic* (T) slot followed by a *Restriction* (R) slot, then an *Illustration* (I) slot, each more specific than the preceding. The other starts with a *Problem* (P) slot and proceeds with one or more *Solutions* (S). In some paragraphs, the S slot is filled with an embedded TRI structure. Operations similar to sentence-level grammatical transformations – deletion, reordering, additions, combination – can model how paragraphs may vary. Here is one of Becker's examples. This paragraph begins with a Problem slot, which is filled with a question ("How obsolete is Hearn's judgment?"). Two contrasting answers fill two Solution slots. Embedded in each of the S slots is a TRI structure. The paragraph is from a study of post-World War II Japan (Gibney, 1953).

There are a number of ways of "chunking" the flow of oral discourse into units. Each option has the effect of highlighting certain facts about talk; accordingly, different systems for dividing up talk in transcripts are associated with different theories of discourse structure and are used for different purposes. As you will see, many of these ways of describing the basic units of talk overlap with one another.

NAME OF UNIT	DEFINITION OF UNIT	WHICH ASPECTS OF TEXT FUNCTION AS CRITERIA IN DEFINITION?	WHAT ARE THE EFFECTS OF DIVIDING ORAL TRANSCRIPTS THIS WAY?
sentence (in traditional grammar)	"the expression of a complete thought," containing a subject and a predicate	semantic, structural	highlights similarities and differences between oral and written discourse
clause	subject + finite verb + verbal complements	structural	highlights similarities and differences between oral and written discourse
t-unit (Hunt, 1966)	main clause + embedded or dependent clauses	structural	highlights structural similarities of units with written sentences, even in the absence of capitalization and punctuation
line (Sherzer, Hymes, Tedlock)	differs across discourse traditions; marked by such things as intonation contour, syntactic completeness, conventional line-initial markers or responses by others. Sets of lines may constitute "verses," "scenes," "acts," "stanzas."	acoustic, semantic, structural, functional/ aesthetic	highlights aesthetic, musical, rhythmic quality of talk and people's responses to talk; highlights cross-cultural differences in discourse structure
intonation unit (Chafe)	a set of words that expresses a single cognitive "focus of consciousness"; surrounded by pause; acceleration then deceleration, final rising or falling intonation, often a single grammatical clause or phrase	cognitive; acoustic, structural	highlights presumably universal cognitive reasons for chunking
center of interest (Chafe)	a set of intonation units corresponding to roughly one predication each; often have sentence-like form and final intonation	cognitive, structural	highlights presumably universal cognitive reasons for chunking
utterance (Crookes and Roulon)	a stretch of speech with a single intonation contour, bounded by pauses and/or constituting a single unit of meaning	acoustic and/or semantic	highlights connections between sound and meaning, not structure
tone group (Crystal)	a stretch of speech consisting of one prominent pitch nucleus and one or more other syllables; set off by slight pauses, other juncture markers	acoustic	highlights the sound of speech

Figure 3.1 Units of discourse

(P) How obsolete is Hearn's judgment? **(S1) (T)** On the surface the five gentlemen of Japan do not themselves seem to be throttled by this rigid society of their ancestors. **(R)** Their world is in fact far looser in its demands upon them than it once was. **(I)** Industrialization and the influence of the West have progressively softened the texture of the web. Defeat in war badly strained it. A military occupation, committed to producing a democratic Japan, pulled and tore at it. **(S2) (T)** But it has not disappeared. **(R)** It is still the invisible adhesive that seals the nationhood of the Japanese. **(I)** Shimizu, Sanada, Yamazaki, Kisei and Hirohito were all bound within its bounds. Despite their individual work, surroundings and opinions, they have lived most of their lives as cogs geared into a group society. Literally as well as figuratively speaking, none of them has a lock on his house door. **[transition]** In 1948, long after Hearn had gone to his grave, a Japanese sociologist, Takegi Kawashima, could write with much justice about the behavior of his contemporaries: [A long quotation follows, beginning a new paragraph.]

Laying the paragraph out a different way makes it look less like a paragraph but highlights its internal structure:

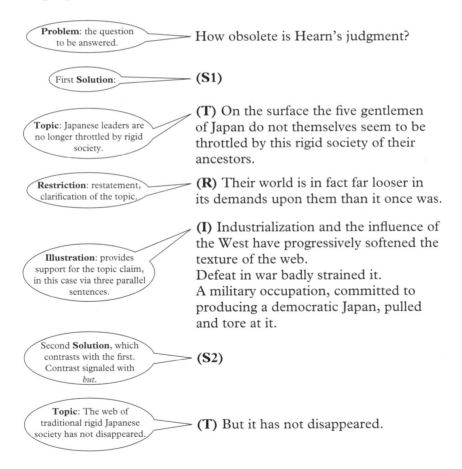

Restriction: Restatement, here by means of metaphorical image.

(R) It is still the invisible adhesive that seals the nationhood of the Japanese.

Illustration, again consisting of three sentences. This time support for the topic is provided by exemplification. The three sentences are tied together with pronouns, among other things: *their, they, their, them, his,* all of which refer back to the names in the first of the three sentences.

(I) *Shimizu, Sanada, Yamazaki, Kisei and Hirohito* were all bound within its bounds.
Despite *their* individual work, surroundings and opinions, *they* have lived most of *their* lives as cogs geared into a group society.
Literally as well as figuratively speaking, none of *them* has a lock on *his* house door.

Just as parts of sentences are formally marked – nouns via markers of number, gender, and case; verbs via markers of tense and aspect, and so on – parts of paragraphs are often formally marked. Markers can be graphic (indentation or line spacing signals beginnings and ends of paragraphs), lexical (a head word in the paragraph's first slot can be referred back to in subsequent slots), or grammatical (syntactic parallelism can signal that sets of sentences belong in the same part). A shift in verb form can signal a shift to a new slot, as can transition words such as *but* (as in the example) or *for example*.

While Becker's focus is on written paragraphs, discourse analysts have also found it useful to talk about paragraph-size units in oral discourse. Van Dijk (1980, 1981) uses the term "episode" to describe semantic units, intermediate in size between sentences and whole texts (however defined), which can be realized as written or oral paragraphs. An episode consists of a sequence of propositions that develops a single semantic "macroproposition" and is internally coherent. Beginnings of new episodes can be signaled, in speech, by pauses and hesitation phenomena, which can be seen as functionally equivalent to indentation and/or line spacing in written text; by markers of a shift in time (such as *meanwhile*), place (such as *in the other room*), participants, or perspective (such as a change in verbal tense/aspect or a change in style), among other things. Shifts in gesture may also accompany shifts from one oral "paragraph" to another (Kendon, 1972). For Dell Hymes (1981a), describing Native American narrative, "scenes" are similar to van Dijk's "episodes."

Discussion

3.5 What prescriptive rules are you familiar with for writing paragraphs? (Look in a writers' handbook if you do not remember.) How are paragraphs in expository essays different from paragraphs in novels, technical reports, or web pages? Are there general cognitive reasons, do you suppose, for the way paragraphs are organized? Would you expect there to be cross-cultural and cross-linguistic differences in paragraph structure?

3.6 What was the original order of sentences in these paragraphs? What cues do you use in deciding which sentence belongs where?

a. From Eudora Welty, *One Writer's Beginnings* (1984):

1 SILENCE in big black letters was on signs tacked up everywhere.
2 She ran the Library absolutely by herself, from the desk where she sat with her back to the books and facing the stairs, her dragon eye on the front door, where who knew what kind of person might come in from the public?
3 I never knew anyone who'd grown up in Jackson without being afraid of Mrs. Calloway, our librarian.
4 She herself spoke in her normally commanding voice; every word could be heard all over the library above a steady seething sound coming from her electric fan; it was the only fan in the Library and stood on her desk, turned directly onto her streaming face.

b. From Andrea Lunsford and Robert Connors, *The Saint Martin's Handbook* (1992: 113):

1 All of these changes helped transform shopping from serious requirement to psychological recreation.
2 Instead of visiting several market stalls or small shops, customers could now buy a variety of merchandise under the same roof; instead of feeling expected to buy, they were welcome just to look; and instead of bargaining with several merchants, they paid a fixed price for each item.
3 Before the Industrial Revolution, most consumer goods were sold in open-air markets, customers who went into an actual shop were expected to buy something, and shoppers were always expected to bargain for the best possible price.
4 Over the centuries, shopping has changed in function as well as in style.
5 In the nineteenth century, however, the development of the department store changed the relationship between buyers and sellers.
6 In addition, they could return an item to the store and exchange it for a different one or get their money back.

3.7 Here is a paragraph from a textbook chapter (Coulthard, 1985: 45) about the ethnography of communication. Try to use Becker's observations about paragraph strucure (described above) to analyze the paragraph. Does it have a TRI or a PS structure, or one embedded in the other? Identify the sentence or sentences which fill each slot. What signals the shift from one slot to another? What signals continuation of the same slot? Is there a noun or noun phrase in the first sentence that acts as the "head word" of the paragraph? How is it referred back to later?

> Traditionally speech has been described in terms of two participants, a speaker who transmits a message and a listener who receives it. However, while in the majority of situations the person who is speaking is also the addressor or the author of the "sentiments that are being expressed and the words in which they are encoded" (Goffman, 1981[1979]: 144), the labels "spokesman" and "porta voz" witness that there are times when *speakers* act as mouthpieces for others. Similarly, although there are no parallel labels like "listenman" or "porta ouvido," reports like "the Soviet ambassador was summoned to the Foreign Office to hear the views of . . ." recognize the role.

3.8   Below are (a) the first four sentences of a chapter from an essay written by a distinguished Arab political theorist and author, and (b) the beginning of an essay written in English by an advanced student of English as a Second Language whose native language was Arabic. Compare the al-Husari passage with paragraphs in expository essays in English. How many sentences are there in a paragraph? Could you make the argument that a sentence in this text does what a paragraph sometimes does in English? What are the semantic relationships among the sentences? Does the second, for example, express a restriction of the idea in the first? How do the third and fourth sentences relate to the second, and to each other? Do you see any similarities between the Arabic text and the ESL writer's text that might indicate that he has used Arabic discourse-structuring strategies in his English writing?

a.   From Saatiʕ al-Husari, 1959, *"Al-waqaa'iʕu wa-al-aHdaaθ: naZaraatun ʕamma,"* in *Maa hiya al-qawmiyya?* ("The Facts and the Events: General Observations" in *What is Nationalism?*) (For a key to this way of trans-literating Arabic into the International Phonetic Alphabet, see Johnstone, 1991b: ii.)

> [¶₁] [S₁] *wa-mimmaa   huwa jadiirun bi-al-ðikri*
> and among which it worthy of the mentioning
>
> *wa-al-mulaaHa-Dati: 'anna jamiiʕa al-'aaraa'i   allatii*
> and the noting   that all   the opinions which
>
> *'ubdiyat,   wa-al-'abHaaθi   allatii nuširat*
> they-were-produced and the researches which they-were-published
>
> *fii "fikrati al-qawmiyyati" wa-fii "mabda'i Huquuqi al-qawmiyyaati,"*
> on idea   the nationalism and on principle rights   the nationalities
>
> *xilaala al-qarni   al-taasiʕa ʕašara, kaanat tanHaSiru bi-al-šuʕuubi*
> during the century the nineteenth   were   confined   to the peoples
>
> *al-'urubbiyyati wa-furuuʕi-haa   wa-lam   tašmal   al-šuʕuuba*
> the European and branches their and NEG included the peoples
>
> *al-'asyawiyyata wa-al-'ifriiqiyyata.*
> the Asian   and the African

[¶₂][S₂] *li'anna jamiiʕa al-mufakkiriina al-'urubbiyyiina kaanuu*
because all the intellectuals the European were

yazʕumuuna 'anna tilka al-šuʕuubu laysat "muta'axxiratan"
claim that these the peoples are-not backward

fa-Hasbu, bal hiya "maHruumatun min qaabiliyyati
only rather they deprived of capacity

al-taqaddumi wa-al-tamadduni" 'ayDan.
the progress and the civilization as well

[S₃] *wa-li-ðaalika fa-hiya laa tastaHiqqu al-Huquuqa allatii*
and for that so they NEG deserve the rights which

tastaHiqqu-haa al-šuʕuubu al-'urubbiyyatu.
deserve them the peoples the European

[¶₃][S₄] *Hattaa al-kuttaabu allaðiina kaanuu 'iltazamuu mabda'a*
even the writers who were adhered to principle

"Huquuqi al- qawmiyyaati" 'ašadda al-'iltizaami,
rights the nationalities strongest the adherence

wa-taHammasuu la-hu 'ašadda al-taHammusi, lam yaxrujuu
and advocated it strongest the advocacy NEG go out

bi-'aaraa'i-him fii ðaalika xaarija niTaaqi al-'urubbiyyiina, wa-lam
in opinions their in that outside sphere the Europeans and NEG

yusallimuu bi-mieli tilka al-Huquuqi li-al-šuʕuubi al-'asyawiyyati
conceded such those the rights to the peoples the Asian

wa-al-'ifriiqiyyati.
and the African

And among that which is worthy of mentioning and noting: that all the opinions which were produced and the research which was published on "the idea of nationalism" and on "the principle of the rights of nationalities" during the nineteenth century, were confined to the European peoples and their branches and did not include the Asian and African peoples.

Because all the European intellectuals claimed that these peoples are not only "backward," but rather they are "deprived of the capacity for progress and civilization" as well. And so therefore they do not deserve the rights which the European peoples deserve.

Even the writers who had adhered to the principle of the rights of nationalities with the strongest adherence, and had advocated it with the strongest advocacy, did not go out, in their opinions about that, outside the sphere of the Europeans, and did not concede such rights to the Asian and African peoples.

b.   From the introduction to a research proposal, written in English by an Arabic-speaking graduate student.

(S₁) The nature of the desert played a role in creating linguistic differences between the dialects of the various desert tribes. (S₂) The vast desert land of the Peninsula and the lack of proper communication among the inhabitants led to the emergence of several tribes, each developing a dialect of its own. (S₃) The different customs and traditions of each tribe coupled with the long distances that separated them from one another led to the emergence of pre-Islamic dialects.

Discourse Schemata and the Structure of Narrative

We can also make useful generalizations about the structure of even larger units of discourse. Van Dijk (1986) shows, for example, that print news stories can be described in terms of a sequence of structural slots, starting with "summary" in the headline and lead, moving to the main story (organized as one or more episodes, each consisting of the report of events, followed by consequences and/or reactions), and ending with evaluative or predictive comments. This "macrostructure," according to van Dijk, reflects and realizes writers' and readers' cognitive "schema" for such articles, a set of pre-formed expectations about structure and content that simplifies information processing.

One of the first discourse genres to be analyzed as having a recurring set of structural/functional slots was oral narrative. The most influential model of the structural schema underlying spontaneous conversational narrative has been the one developed by William Labov (Labov and Waletzky, 1967, 1997; Labov, 1972b, 1981). According to Labov, any narrative, by definition, includes at least two "narrative clauses." A narrative clause is a clause that cannot be moved without changing the order in which events must be taken to have occurred. If two narrative clauses are reversed, they represent a different chronology: "I punched this boy/ and he punched me" implies a different sequence of events than "This boy punched me/ and I punched him."

Although "minimal narratives" like these consist of just two narrative clauses, most personal experience narrative is more complex, including more narrative clauses as well as "free" (i.e., movable) clauses that serve other functions. A "fully developed" narrative may include clauses or sets of clauses with one or more of six functions. Each of these six elements of narrative serves a double purpose. Each makes reference to events, characters, feelings, and so on understood to have happened or existed outside of and previous to the conversation in which the story is being told. At the same time, each element also structures the ongoing interaction by guiding the teller and the audience through the narrated events and ensuring that they are comprehensible and worth recounting.

- The *abstract* consists of a clause or two at the beginning of a narrative summarizing the story to come. A person telling a story about a time when he almost died might begin, "I talked a man out of – Old Doc Simon I talked him out of pulling the trigger," then elaborate with a narrative. (Examples are Labov's.) The abstract announces that the narrator has a story to tell and makes a claim to the right to tell it, a claim supported by the suggestion that it will be a good story, worth the audience's time and the speaking rights the audience will temporarily relinquish.
- *Orientation* in a narrative introduces characters, temporal and physical setting, and situation: "It was on a Sunday, and we didn't have nothin'

to do after I – after we came from church"; "I had a dog – he was a wonderful retriever, but as I say he could do everything but talk." Orientation often occurs near the beginning, but may be interjected at other points, when needed. The characteristic orientation tense in English is the past progressive: "I was sittin' on the corner an' shit, smokin' my cigarette, you know"; "We was doing the 50-yard dash."

- *Complicating action* clauses are narrative clauses that recapitulate a sequence of events leading up to their climax, the point of maximum suspense. These clauses refer to events in the world of the story and, in the world of the telling, they create tension that keeps auditors listening.
- The *result* or *resolution* releases the tension and tells what finally happened.
- Often just before the result or resolution, but also throughout the narrative, are elements that serve as *evaluation*, stating or underscoring what is interesting or unusual about the story, why the audience should keep listening and allow the teller to keep talking. Evaluation may occur in free clauses that comment on the story from outside: "And it was the strangest feeling"; "But it was really quite terrific," or in clauses that attribute evaluative commentary to characters in the story: "I just closed my eyes/ I said, 'O my God, here it is!'" Or evaluation can be embedded in the narrative, in the form of extra detail about characters ("I was shakin' like a leaf"); suspension of the action via paraphrase or repetition; "intensifiers" such as gesture or quantifiers ("I knocked him *all* out in the street"); elements that compare what did happen with what did not, could have or might happen; "correlatives" that tell what was occurring simultaneously; and "explicatives" that are appended to narrative or evaluative clauses.
- At the end of the story, the teller may announce via a *coda* that the story is over ("And that was that"), sometimes providing a short summary of the story or connecting the world of the story with the present ("That was one of the most important"; "He's a detective in Union City/ And I see him every now and again").

Below is a transcript of a personal-experience narrative told by a 22-year-old American laborer to a friend who had asked him to be part of a tape-recorded conversation. In this story, the narrator tells about a deer-hunting trip during which he and a friend caught sight of some deer but were struck by their beauty and did not shoot at them. The fact that the usual cultural script for a hunting trip, among men like these, involves "bagging" deer, not simply admiring them, is what makes this memory of the narrator's useful as a potential narrative: It is "storyworthy" (Young, 1987) because it is unusual and surprising. But the surprising quality of the outcome hinges on potential hearers expecting these hunters to be competent and interested in shooting. So the narrator must present himself and his friend as normal, accomplished woodsmen. This requirement gives rise to the overall structure of the story, which is, on the face of it, about a weekend of camping activities (and the expected inactivities), not just the sighting of some deer.

As you read through this analysis of the story, bear in mind that this kind of work is inevitably interpretive. No discourse analyst can make definitive claims about the function of one or another element in story (or any other text), because the speaker's words, as captured in this transcribed text, constitute only one of many elements of the situation in which these words were uttered, understood, and reacted to. As we have seen in chapter 2, understanding what a text might have meant in its original context requires understanding the physical world, the social world, and the linguistic world in which it came to be. As we will see in subsequent chapters, we also need to know much more than the text itself shows us about who was involved in the situation, about their purposes, about their expectations, and about physical and technological aspects of the context such as the medium of discourse. (Transcription note: Dots are used to represent brief pauses, with the number of dots corresponding to the length of the pause.)

orientation: temporal setting, context of events. Word choice also serves an **evaluation** function.

*by late Friday afternoon . . . we were . . . **pretty well** settled in*

evaluation (external)

uh . . . **like I said had a good looking camp . . .**

[Note how this narrator uses intakes of breath, cough, pause to separate the story into its temporal episodes.]

[breath]

orientation: temporal. But note also how the entire temporal structure of the story (the buildup to Sunday morning) also serves an **evaluation** function.

the Saturday that followed the Saturday of that weekend

These clauses cannot be interpreted as narrative clauses, because their order does not model "storyworld" temporal order. ("Lounging around camp" does not necessarily happen before "doing a little bit of hunting.") They are *orientational* (representing the context for the main narrative events), but they simultaneously function as **evaluation**, building suspense.

we just did a lot of shooting and actually just lounging around camp a lot [laughs] ***did a little bit of hunting really just . . . took it good and easy that day***

[another episode break]

[cough]

orientation

but *it was Sunday morning when we got up*

evaluation (external)

that . . . was the high point of the whole camp

narrative clause *orientation/**evaluation*** (The use of this detail helps characterize the protagonists as accomplished hunters.)

we . . . uh . . . got up that morning and . . . ***wearing our camouflage . . .***

evaluation (external and internal): note how the repetition of the idea and the grammatical parallelism of "preferred to see them before they saw us" also function as internal, grammatical kinds of evaluation.

ut to . . . **basically didn't want to be seen by anybody else and preferred to see them before w— them before they saw us**

orientation
narrative clause in simple present ("historical present") tense: note how "happen to" **evaluates** the action by representing the main event of the story as almost accidental.

we were fixing coffee over the campfire
and I **happen to** look up out across this field *at the edge of the woods about three hundred yards out*

orientation: new characters introduced

this . . . six buck deer

evaluation
narrative clause with *orientational* detail (temporal) which serves as **evaluation** as well.

beautiful . . . just majestic as hell
they stood out there *for about a half hour*

orientation/**evaluation**

noses in the wind trying to catch our scent

[another break, from the Sunday episode to the wrap-up of the story]

[breath]

evaluation: note the use of "never" and "really" and compare with what the effect would be if this clause had been "They didn't."

never really did

orientation: re-orients hearers to the temporal setting of the final section of the story; also announces that this is the final part.

*we **finally** decided to show them what we were*

narrative clauses; laughter and choices of phrasing serve as **evaluation**.

and so we **both** stood up
and **[small laugh]** . . . all you saw was six white tails headed the opposite direction

evaluation

but it was truly a fantastic sight

narrative, *orientation*

we closed up camp *that day*

evaluation

and came back **to civilization**

CODA: formulates the point of the story, its consequences, a "moral"

never really been able to forget that day or that campout as a result of it
[long pause]
it's th-
that's the sort of thing i guess that makes life worth living

Discussion

3.9 Using the Labov and Waletzky model that has just been described, try to identify the parts of the personal experience narratives in this conversation. Linda is a 35-year-old African-American woman talking to a friend, Renie, in Linda's kitchen. This part of the conversation arose while Linda was cleaning her kitchen cabinets and noticed how dead-looking they were in color. This led Linda and Renie into a discussion of dead bodies, cemeteries, ghosts, and haunted houses. Note that there may be more than one narrative in this conversation! Transcription conventions used here are these:

- Overlappping talk is signaled with square brackets: ['cause]
  [Um-hm]
- Italics indicate stronger-than-usual stress, accompanied by raised volume: One time *for real*, Renie . . .
- Non-verbal elements of the conversation and notes about voice quality are indicated in double brackets: ((both laugh)).

1	LINDA:	Matter of fact we used to thought our house was haunted too. So it all was there together ['cause] we always
2	RENIE:	[Um-hm]
3	LINDA:	thought the house [was haunted]
4	RENIE:	[Maybe that, maybe,] maybe that's why it was easier for you to walk through the cemetery because, you [had]
5	LINDA:	Yeah, ['cause I thought]
6	RENIE:	that feeling that your house was haunted.
7	LINDA:	We always thought it was haunted. We used to like ah . . .
8	RENIE:	['Cause I]
9	LINDA:	[one time] *for real* when we was living on Grant Street – this is the *truth honest to goodness* – we was all looking out the dining room window, and there was this red truck on the next street over, you know how you how you can see out my backyard now?
10	RENIE:	Um-hm.
11	LINDA:	Me and my cousin Idabell, Stoney and Robert Earl, we was all looking out the window, all of a sudden this truck just *started up by itself.* Honest to *good*ness Renie *it started up by it* [*self!*]
12	RENIE:	[Somebody] was in there.
13	LINDA:	*Nobody* was in that truck!
14	RENIE:	Maybe they were leaning over in it or . . . ((Both laugh.))
15	LINDA:	That tru- It was, had been sitting there and we was looking out the window, we was playing around, the truck just started up by

itself. We ain't seen no head no *noth*ing! We was in the window
((mimics the children's screams)),
((Both laugh.))
screaming and yelling and holding on to each other, Idabell
screaming bloody mur-, "Did you see it? Did you see it?"
((mimicking Idabell's high voice))
Well, we told Mama and them, and they be saying "Aw, you
looked too quick."

16	RENIE:	[Um-hm]
17	LINDA:	["You don't] know what you talking [about."]
18	RENIE:	[Um-hm]

19 LINDA: But I tell you, that house on Grant Street, it was right by the
graveyard, and Daddy used to always tell us that uh the reason
why we thought we saw stuff all the time because it was real,
that somebody had buried something, some gold or something
in the house,

20 RENIE: Um-hm.

21 LINDA: and that the *dead* people would keep would come back to
guard it. 'Cause he said like down South when uh . . . ((both
laughing)) when a rich white man *had* something, a lot of
*mon*ey,

22 RENIE: Um-hm.

| 23 | LINDA: | He would tell us that uh . . . they would kill a [black man] and |
| 24 | RENIE: | [Um-hm.] |

25 LINDA: bury with they money and gold and stuff, and the black man
was so tough his spirit would guard this stuff.
((both are laughing))
He used to tell us [*this*, he used to tell us that all] the time.

26 RENIE: [Wow, I wonder if that's true.]

27 RENIE: I wonder if that just a myth,

28 LINDA: I wonder, because [he be telling us]

29 RENIE: [a downsouth myth.]

30 LINDA: Girl, he be, one time he had us out there *dig*ging, sh-, thought
we heard something that night. We was all scared that night,
out there digging.
Daddy say, *"It's gold in there!"*
Mama say, *Get your ass in this house! Don't listen to your crazy
daddy!*
((both laugh))

3.10 Here is an email message sent by an American man in his thirties to a
Japanese friend, also in his thirties, whom he had not seen for several years.
"Peter" works at a university in Missouri; "Jason" is his son and "Janet" his
wife. Peter seems to have drawn on two discourse schemata in writing this
message: a schema for the structure of email messages, and a schema for a
fairly formal, traditional "friendly letter." Try to describe these schemata and
how they are combined in the message.

Date: Tue, 19 May 1998 13:31:55 -0500 (CST)
From: Peter –
To: Hiko –
Subject: Hi Long Lost Friends

Dear Hiko and All

Of course there are 100 reasons for taking so long to reply to your last Email so pick a number from 1–100.

Good, that's my excuse. I hope things are still as positive as was in your letter. We have just completed the semester. Whew!!! Jason did quite well in his first year of college. I think his GPA is 3.5? As you have heard he will not be pursuing a career in veterinary medicine, although journalism is not what he is after either. I think that in November he will apply to the School of Business. Currently he is working weekends for the veterinary hospital and full time for a construction company. You know the feeling of driving something really big, well this is on a smaller scale, but he is driving a backhoe and bulldozer. It worries us that he really likes the construction job so much. I hope that he doesn't get into the frame of mind that the money in construction is great and there is no need for further college. We have to just keep our mouths closed on this issue. He is still dating Becky his High School sweetheart, they are best friends and if they are thinking of marriage Janet and I haven't heard of it.

Janet is still employed at mental health, but is looking for a job that would make her masters degree pay off. She is really enjoying not being in school. We are having a great time together with this beautiful springtime. We have been working on the yard almost daily. It is the 4th year for our perennial garden. The garden looks like something out of a magazine. We have about 300 bearded iris of all colors and sizes in full bloom. We have daylilies, hostas, coral bell, ivy and just about anything else you can think of in our yard. The newest additions this year is an herb and spice garden. We sit out on our deck in the evening and when a gentle breeze blows over the herbs, we enjoy the aroma of the fresh spices.

As a graduation present, Janet's parents have given a trip. This year we are taking a vacation to New York. We have never been there so this will be a very exciting trip. We will be doing all the things that people do in New York, Statue of Liberty, Empire State Building, Broadway play, Wall Street, we will be "Joe Tourist" for a week. We just can't wait!

I am currently doing a new project. We are copying our language lab language tapes to our server and will have all the tapes on the web this summer. When I have it completed I will send you the web address so you can see for yourself.

Do you have any vacation plans? Is Missouri in your future? I hope that the children have enjoyed their first year in the states.

Let me know what is new,

pete

3.11 In work that builds on van Dijk's research about news article schemata, Allan Bell (1991) shows that a typical wire service news story represents events in the "action" section of a story not in chronological order but in a complex sequence of jumps backward and forward in time, dictated by the news value of the events and of the story as a whole. Bell suggests that this may have implications for how well readers are able to understand news stories. Select a news story from a print or online source and try to adapt Labov's model of narrative to describe its structure. Discuss how the sequence of events in the story is represented.

3.12   Here are parts of the text of two cartoons that play on how children tell
        stories (or, perhaps, how adult cartoonists imagine children's stories). What
        are the differences, in each case, between these stories and the "fully formed
        narratives" Labov's model characterizes?

   a.   (From "Foxtrot," by Bill Amend) A young boy, Jason, writes a story
        about his older sister, Paige.

        "Press M for Murder" by Jason Fox.

        Paige Fox enters her bedroom as she does every day after school.
        Suddenly, a 16-ton weight falls from the ceiling and squishes her dead!!!
        The End

   b.   (From a cartoon in the *New Yorker* magazine entitled "The Litany of
        Fun," by R. Chast) A young boy tells about a school trip.

        . . . and then we got on the bus and then we all had treats and then we sang
        songs and then we played games and then Billy and Kenny got into a fight
        over a Ninja and then we got off the bus and then we had a snack and then
        we stood in line and then we got tickets and then we went into the zoo and
        then we saw the Wild Africa exhibit and then we got back in line and then
        we saw the Hall of Bats exhibit and then we were talking and laughing and
        then we got back in line and then Mrs. Hudson got mad at us . . . and then
        we bought monkey stickers or erasers that had bat heads or T-shirts that
        said "I've been to Herkimer Zoo" or key chains with little whales hanging
        from them and then we walked back to Parking Lot B and then we got on
        the bus and then Mr. Jones drove us home and here I am.

3.13   Here is a short transcript of an Indian student at an industrial training center
        role-playing what he would say if he needed to request his British super-
        visor's permission to take a day off from work (National Centre for Industrial
        Language Training (NCILT), 1978, quoted in Kirkpatrick, 1991: 183):

        Two months ago, somebody accident on the road
        but I am a witness
        but I received a letter yesterday
        because my address change
        but I am going to court in the morning
        but I day off tomorrow
        but I am sorry I can't working tomorrow
        I want to leave for tomorrow.

This would probably be heard by a British supervisor as an awkward way to
make the request, in part because the parts of the request – the request itself
and the reasons for the request – are not in the order a British English
speaker would expect. Role-play or observe several requests like this, and see
if you can generalize about how they are structured in your linguistic and
cultural environment. What generally comes first? Is there a required or

preferred order for the elements that follow? How is this different, if it is, from what the Indian in the example was doing?

The Emergent Organization of Conversation

Look again at Linda's haunted house story in discussion question 3.9 above. Although Linda does most of the talking, Renie talks, too, sometimes at the same time Linda is talking. And yet we probably would not want to call what Renie is doing "interrupting," since there is no evidence that Renie is making grabs for the conversational floor. Rather, Renie makes verbal supportive gestures as Linda talks, saying "Um-hm," asking questions that show she is listening and engaged (e.g., "Wow, I wonder if that's true"). She obviously knows how and when it will seem appropriate to do this. Although Renie is probably not aware of knowing the "rules" for when she can start talking and when she can try to shift the topic slightly with a question, she has obviously learned what to expect in the process of hearing and participating in many other conversations. Casual interaction like this is highly structured.

In older etiquette books or books specifically about the art of conversation, there are rules for how to manage polite conversation. How-to books about job interviewing and other tasks that require special self-presentation skills often include sections or chapters about whom to talk to, what to say and what not to say, what sort of "conversational style" (Tannen, 1984) to adopt. American children may learn explicit rules for how one is supposed to behave in conversation, such as these:

Don't talk with your mouth full.
Don't interrupt.
Don't hog the conversation.
Sex/medical problems/bathroom humor/etc. is not dinner table conversation.

We have many other ways to talk about conversation as well. In English, for example, there are formulaic expressions such as "not being able to get a word in edgewise" or "putting your foot in your mouth," stock ways of discussing people's conversational behavior, such as "So and so talks too much/is too shy/laughs at his own jokes/talks about herself a lot," and terms for kinds of conversations, such as "small talk," "polite conversation," "visiting," or "chatting."

Sociologists and linguists are interested in conversation not only because it is one of the main things we do with language, but because it is a good place to look at how people evoke and create structure in the process of interacting. In spontaneous, casual, everyday conversation, there are no pre-set rules about who talks when, about what, or for how long (no rules such as "oldest first," for example, or "each speaker talks for three minutes"), but conversations are nonetheless not chaotic. Everyone is not always talking at once, and people generally (though of course there are exceptions) do not say things that strike others as bizarre non sequiturs.

Because of the ways we are used to seeing conversations represented in writing, it is tempting to think of a conversation as consisting of a bit of talk by one speaker, then a bit of talk by another, then by another, and so on. These units are often called "turns." In written representations of conversation such as playscripts and interview transcripts, turns are easy to identify: a turn begins when one speaker starts to speak, and ends when he or she stops speaking. Turns, defined this way, are often relevant to how conversations are structured. For example, getting the conversational floor takes less work when a second speaker waits until the first speaker has indicated that he or she is finished talking, via phrase-final intonation or grammar, eye contact or body movement, or some explicit means for allocating the next turn to someone else (asking a question, for example). Another way to say this is that there is a "preference" (Pomerantz, 1984[1979]) in conversation for well-defined boundaries between turns. If a new speaker wants to interrupt a turn, he or she has to talk louder, say something like "excuse me," or acknowledge in some other way that this action is "dispreferred." Another way in which turns are relevant to how conversations are structured is that certain types of turns may call for particular corresponding types of turns to follow them: questions call for answers, complaints for responses, a greeting for a return greeting. When conversationalists fail to respond with the expected turn type, extra work is necessary to "repair" the problem: if a question turn is not followed by an answer turn, the question may be asked again, for example. Pairs of turn types which go together in this way are referred to as "adjacency pairs" (Sacks, 1995: 554–60).

However, it is only in the most pre-structured kinds of conversations (such as formal debates with rules about how many minutes a turn may take) that it is ever completely clear when a turn boundary has been reached. Speakers may (or may not) start their turns when the previous speaker's turn *could be* ending (at the end of a phrase, for example), but they do not always wait until the previous speaker has *in fact* stopped talking. In other words, in most conversations there are frequent occasions when more than one person is talking at once. Such "overlaps" are not always perceived as interruptions; often they are not perceived at all, because they are expected and not disruptive. For some speakers and in some situations, overlapping speech can be seen as cooperative and can help build rapport between speakers (Tannen, 1983). Often a speaker's turn ends not because the speaker has a previously made plan to stop, but because someone else starts. If the timing of conversation is thrown off because a speaker stops before another is ready to start, giving rise to silence, it can be just as awkward, and require repair moves of the same magnitude, as when another starts before the current speaker is willing to stop. In other words, turns to speak in conversation are jointly produced by the interlocutors in a process of negotiation. Besides mutually determining when turns begin and end, co-conversationalists produce sentences and phrases jointly, too (Ochs, Schieffelin, and Platt, 1979; Goodwin, 1979; Tannen, 1989; Ferrara, 1992), supplying words for one another and picking up and reusing one another's sounds, words, and structures. So thinking of conversations as proceeding one speaker and one turn at a time is useful for some purposes, but it can also obscure important features of talk.

Another sort of unit in face-to-face interaction is a conversational move (Goffman, 1981[1976]: 24). This is a unit that is defined functionally rather than (like the turn) structurally. The parallel here is to "moves" in other kinds of games. A move in chess, for example, is the performance of an action that is relevant to the game (so that shifting the location of a piece that has already been taken out of play is not a move, but shifting a piece that is on the board may be a move, assuming it is a shift of the right kind). In social interaction, a move consists of the amount of talk required to perform one action in the "language game" in which interlocutors are engaged. An apology might be a move, for example; the response to an apology might be another; a question might be a move and an answer another move. A move may take one or more sentences, and it may take one or more turns in conversation. For example, asking a favor of someone might take one conversational turn, and agreeing to do the favor might take one turn, as in (a):

a. speaker A: Could you put this letter in the mailbox for me on your
                 way past?
    speaker B: Sure.

Alternatively, the same moves might be accomplished in two turns each, as in (b):

b. speaker A: Could I ask you a favor?
    speaker B: Sure, what is it?
    speaker A: Could you put this letter in the mailbox for me on your
                 way past?
    speaker B: Sure.

In traditional classroom conversations, a teacher's *initiation* can be followed by a student's *response*, then a *feedback* move by the teacher (Sinclair and Coulthard, 1975), as in this example (Stubbs, 1983: 131–2):

TEACHER: can you tell me why you eat all that food – yes   (initiation)
PUPIL: to keep you strong   (response)
TEACHER: to keep you strong yes – to keep you strong   (feedback)

Sinclair and Coulthard refer to the next-level unit consisting of these three moves together as an "exchange." (We return to Sinclair and Coulthard's work on classroom discourse in chapter 4.) Another functional unit in conversation is the adjacency pair, introduced above: a one-turn move followed by a corresponding responsive move.

Like the other unit-types we have discussed, moves, exchanges, and adjacency pairs can be useful tools for analysis. We might remember to ask, though, whether a move has really been made unless and until it has been responded to in an expected way. If you ask a question and your interlocutor fails to respond to it, have you really successfully asked a question? It can be argued, in other words, that moves are mutually constituted, like turns, and it can sometimes be useful to think of them that way for the purposes of analysis. Dividing conversations into moves or adjacency pairs may sometimes obscure other facets of interactions, too. For example, while it may sometimes be useful to think about classroom talk in terms of teacher-initiated exchanges, it can at other times be useful to think about what the teacher is responding to by initiating an exchange. A question may be the beginning of a unit of conversation, but it may at the same time be a response to what preceded it. Many utterances are responses to non-verbal events or to things that happened earlier in the interaction (Goffman 1981[1976]), and the function an utterance serves can always potentially be altered in retrospect, as a result of the reaction it gets.

Some aspects of the sequential organization of conversation – that is, the way conversation unfolds over time – result from what Goffman called "system constraints." These reflect the physical requirements of any communication system. For example, no communication system would work without mechanisms for establishing whether interlocutors are in contact, for allocating the right to speak, and for providing feedback. Other aspects of the structure of conversation, on the other hand, arise from (and reinforce) expectations about how individuals are expected to treat each other. These "ritual constraints" vary from culture to culture and change over time.

For example, telephone calls invariably begin with a "summons": the caller causes the callee's phone to ring. This non-verbal summons goes with an answer as an adjacency pair that opens the interaction. In American telephone calls (Schegloff, 1968), the Answerer usually fills the answer slot with "Hello?" (sometimes "Yes?") and the summons-answer sequence is followed by an identification move by the Caller, as in this hypothetical example.

```
0                ((rings))
1  Answerer:     Hello?
2  Caller:       Hi, this is Kelly. Is Kristen there?
```

In a study of Korean telephone conversations, Lee (2006) found, by contrast, that callers sometimes produced a "second summons," as in Turn

2 in the following example. (I include only the English translation and have simplified Lee's transcription somewhat.)

0		((2 rings))
1	Answerer:	Hello?
2	Caller:	Hello?
3	Answerer:	Yes?
4	Caller:	Yes ma'am it's ((first name))?
5	Answerer:	Oh yes.
6	Caller:	Yes hi?
7	Answerer:	Yes.

Lee explains this pattern by pointing out that, in Korean, speakers must choose different forms of many words depending on the social status of the person they are talking to in relation to their own. Such "honorific" forms are not required in the first two turns, when Answerer and Caller say "Hello." But the third turn ("Yes?") requires the Answerer to have already figured enough about the Caller's identity to decide whether to use an honorific form of the word or not. Lee suggests that the Caller's "second summons," in the form of the "Hello" in Turn 2, provides the Answerer with a sample of the Caller's speech in order to help the Answerer determine what their social relationship is. The Caller then takes the Answerer's cue in Turn 4 of this example, using the equivalent of "ma'am" in response to the Answerer's choice of an honorific form of "Yes" in the previous turn. "Second summonses" in telephone call openings are thus a conventional way of dealing with a particularly Korean interactional requirement, the requirement for the Caller to provide a speech sample to the Answerer to enable the Answerer to decide what honorific forms to use.

As noted, summons-answer sequences are one example of conversational "turn-taking." Humans use turn-taking to regulate many aspects of social life. There are turn-taking systems, for example, which regulate traffic at intersections (at a four-way intersection in the US, drivers are supposed to take turns in the order in which they arrived at the intersection; in Europe the driver to the right has the right of way). There are turn-taking systems for serving customers in stores (sometimes people take a number, sometimes they wait in line, sometimes the person who gets the salesperson's attention first gets served first) and over the telephone ("Your call will be answered in the order in which it was received" represents one common system). And there are formal, codified (that is, written down or memorized) pre-set turn-taking systems for some kinds of face-to-face talk, such as Robert's Rules of Order for meetings in the English-speaking world, or rules for formal debates.

Sociologists Sacks, Schegloff, and Jefferson (1974) were the first to analyze turn-taking in casual conversation. They pointed out that a speaker's turn can consist of a single word, a phrase, or many sentences. There are, however,

Sacks, Schegloff, and Jefferson (1974) list fourteen "grossly apparent" facts about conversation which must be accounted for in any model of how conversation works. Each of these facts raises one or more questions about conversation which discourse analysts have subsequently tried to answer. A few of these questions are listed here.

FACTS ABOUT CONVERSATION	QUESTIONS FOR DISCOURSE ANALYSIS
1 Speaker-change recurs, or at least occurs.	How do speakers know, and how do they indicate to others, when a new speaker can take the floor? What happens when speaker-change does not occur where people expect it to?
2 Overwhelmingly, one party talks at a time.	What happens when more than one person is talking at once? What can such "overlaps" mean to people and accomplish for them?
3 Occurrences of more than one speaker at a time are common, but brief.	What causes overlaps to be brief, in general? Who stops talking when an overlap occurs?
4 Transitions (from one turn to the next) with no gap and no overlap are common. Together with transitions characterized by slight gap or slight overlap, they make up the vast majority of transitions.	How do speakers manage to cooperate to produce smooth transitions? How do they know when a transition is imminent?
5 Turn order is not fixed, but varies.	How do speakers in a group select who will speak next, in the course of ongoing conversation? (See point 12 below.)
6 Turn size is not fixed, but varies.	How do speakers know when a turn has gone on long enough? What do they do when they want to take an unusually long turn (for example, to tell a story)?
7 Length of conversation is not specified in advance.	How do conversations start and end? What are the "pre-closing" signals, for example, that speakers are ending a conversation?
8 What parties say is not specified in advance.	How do participants in a conversation introduce new topics? How do they move from topic to topic?

Figure 3.2   A model of conversational turn-taking

FACTS ABOUT CONVERSATION	QUESTIONS FOR DISCOURSE ANALYSIS
9 Relative distribution of turns is not specified in advance.	Who speaks most in a given conversation? What can it mean to have one person speak more often than others? When the distribution of turns seems wrong to participants (e.g., when one person takes too many turns or not enough), what do others do?
10 Number of parties can vary.	How is a new participant brought into a conversation? How does someone exit from a conversation? Are there cross-cultural differences in how many speakers are expected in particular kinds of conversations, and what their roles are?
11 Talk can be continuous or discontinuous.	How do speakers manage to differentiate between taking up an old conversation again and starting a new conversation?
12 Turn-allocation techniques are obviously used. A current speaker may select a next speaker (as when he or she addresses a question to another party); or parties may self-select in starting to talk.	What are some other ways in which current speakers allocate turns to next speakers? How does "self-selection" work? For example, what happens if two people both try to self-select at the same time?
13 Various 'turn-constructional units' are employed; e.g., turns can be one word long or they can be the length of a sentence.	What would an incomplete turn be? How do children learn to construct utterances that can function as conversational turns?
14 Repair mechanisms exist for dealing with turn-taking errors and violations; e.g., if two parties find themselves talking at the same time, one of them will stop prematurely, thus repairing the trouble.	What are these repair mechanisms?

Figure 3.2   *(cont'd)*

only certain places where another speaker can take over the floor. These places are at the ends of clauses, the ends of phrases, or at other points at which the person who is currently speaking pauses, slows down, or draws out words. In this bit of conversation (from Sacks, Schegloff, and Jefferson, 1974), for example, B starts when A gets to the end of what could be a complete grammatical unit, "You been down here before?" (In this transcription system, italics represent extra stress and square brackets represent where overlapping speech begins.)

A: Uh *you* been down here before [haven't you?
B: [Yeah.

B's contribution is not treated as an interruption (A does not act annoyed about it, and the conversation does not derail), because it occurs in an acceptable place.

Who gets to speak when? When more than one person starts to talk at once, the first person to start is sometimes the one who gets to continue. Other speakers drop out. This technique for allocating turns in conversation is known as "self-selection." Self-selection can cause discomfort or more serious conversational problems when the people who want to take the next turn have different senses of exactly how long the tiny pause between one turn and the next should be. As Tannen shows (1981, 1984), people who tolerate shorter pauses tend to become uncomfortable with what they perceive as awkward silence before longer-pausers become uncomfortable, so they consistently start talking sooner, and consequently they end up talking more. The longer-pausers feel as if they are being excluded from the conversation, and the shorter-pausers think they are being forced to do all the conversational work.

Another way in which turns can be allocated is that the person who is talking can select who gets to talk next. This can be done, for example, by asking someone a question. Here, at a dinner table, Sarah first selects Ben as the next speaker, then Bill. (Parentheses indicate material that could not be interpreted on the tape; double parentheses enclose non-verbal behavior; angled brackets enclose editorial comments.)

SARAH <selecting Ben by name>:   Ben you want some (   )?
BEN: Well alright I'll have a,
                                 ((pause))
SARAH <selecting Bill by name>: Bill you want some?
BILL: No . . .

Turn allocation can also be accomplished in a number of other ways, as illustrated in these examples (also from Sacks, Schegloff, and Jefferson, 1974) in which speakers are attuned to conventions about adjacency pairs. When the American speakers Sacks, Schegloff, and Jefferson studied made a complaint to someone, for example, that person normally got the next turn. Here, Ken complains about Al's behavior, giving Al the floor for a response. Ken's use of the pronoun *you* ("ya") also indicates that he is allocating the next turn to Al.

KEN <to Al>:   Hey ya took my chair by the way.
AL: *I* didn't take your chair, it's *my* chair.

When a compliment was made, the person complimented could claim the next turn for a response, as in this irony-loaded exchange from Sacks, Schegloff, and Jefferson's data:

A <to B>:   I'm glad I have you for a friend.
B: That's because you don't have any others.

Conventions for how to respond to compliments vary greatly. Some speakers, in some cases, and some groups of speakers, believe that compliments should be rejected, as A's compliment is here. In other cases, speakers generally accept compliments. One interesting cross-cultural study of complimenting behavior is Wolfson (1981).

When someone was challenged, that person got the next turn for a response to the challenge. Here, A and B are working together and disagree about whether B should be allowed to take a break. A challenges B, and B rejects the challenge by telling A to "shut up."

A <to B>:   It's not break time yet.
B: I finished my box, so shut up.

Finally, when a request was made the requestee got the next turn. In this example, Raymond uses a declarative sentence, "I don't want this other piece of toast" to request that he be allowed not to eat it.

RAYMOND: Mommy, I don't want this other piece of toast.
MOMMY: You don't? Well, OK, I guess you don't have to eat it.

Looking closely at the process of "talk-in-interaction" has enabled linguists and sociologists to develop new ideas about how discourse works as well as, more generally, how human social life is organized in the ongoing social practice of interacting. Rather than explaining human interactive behavior as the result of general rules or predetermined social roles and relationships, people who engage in what is known as Conversation Analysis (or CA) examine small bits of transcribed conversation in detail, to see how individuals' contributions to conversations are designed and interpreted as responses to what is happening at the moment.

For example, it is possible to think about one common conversational event, disagreement, from two perspectives. The traditional perspective, with its roots in the tradition of rhetoric as planned, public oratory, sees an argument as the result of a situation in which two parties know in advance that they disagree and set out to come to a decision about who has the better case. Each speaker, according to this model, assesses the available "means of persuasion" and constructs arguments that seem likely to work, in light of what the speaker knows about the adversary's background and beliefs. Each then comes into the conversation with a pre-set plan based on pre-formed analyses of the facts at issue and the conversational situation at hand. From a CA perspective, on the other hand (Jacobs and Jackson, 1982), argument is seen as on-the-spot response to the interactional problem of disagreement. People prefer to agree, and when disagreement arises, it has to be remedied. Argument then becomes relevant, and arguments are ideally designed as specific responses to specific, situated problems. From this perspective, argument is not a *kind of* conversation, but rather a *process* that arises in conversation.

Another example of how CA can supplement other approaches to discourse has to do with how knowledge and authority emerge in interaction, as people negotiate the right to make evaluative claims (or "assessments") about the world and respond to others' claims (Pomerantz, 1984[1979]). Speakers may come into interactions with expectations about who is the more authoritative, and people whose social identities give them greater epistemic (knowledge-shaping) power – teachers, judges, or parents, for example – may in some situations have greater rights than others to make assessments. But epistemic power must be claimed and displayed in interaction, and it can be challenged and negotiated. Heritage and Raymond (2005; Raymond, 2000) show how small details of the language people choose when they make and respond to assessments can act as claims to epistemic authority. For example, when both speakers have immediate, personal access to a state of affairs, the second speaker can "upgrade" the first speaker's assessment. Here, J and L exchange assessments of the weather. (Arrows point to assessments.)

```
1  J:   →   T's tsuh beautiful day out isn't it?
2  L:   →   Yeh it's jus' gorgeous.
```

L signals her right to make a "second assessment" (line 2) by saying "Yeh," then upgrades J's assessment by adding "just" and replacing "beautiful" with "gorgeous." In the following example, Jon and Lyn assert greater rights to assess the movie "Midnight Cowboy" than Eve, who has only heard about it second hand.

```
1  JON:        We saw Midnight Cowboy yesterday or [suh- Friday.
2  EVE:                                           [Oh?
3  LYN:  →   Didju s- you saw that, [it's really good.
4  EVE:                            [No I haven't seen it
5        →   Jo saw it 'n she said she f- depressed her
6  EVE:        ter[ribly
7  JON:  →      [Oh it's [terribly depressing.
8  LYN:  →              [Oh it's depressing.
```

As Raymond (2000) shows, using "oh-prefixes" the way Jon and Lyn do in lines 7 and 8 asserts a stronger right to evaluate.

Discussion

3.14   How would you define "conversation"? Does "conversation" occur any time people are in a group talking? For example, is a group therapy session a "conversation"? Is there a default kind of conversation which could be usefully thought of as "ordinary" or "everyday" conversation, or does every conversation have some particular agenda which helps to shape its structure? How would you describe the key characteristics of some of the specific kinds of conversations listed above ("small talk," "visiting," and so on)? In what ways do these genres of face-to-face talk contrast with one another?

3.15   Record and transcribe a few minutes of multi-party conversation. Note the "overlaps": the times when more than one person is speaking. Which of the overlaps are treated, by the participants, as interruptions (for example by being commented on overtly)? Who decides what constitutes an interruption, and on what basis?

3.16   What do you think is the best way to represent silence in the transcript of a conversation? Is it ever possible to attribute silence to one speaker or another, or are all silences mutual?

3.17   How could you transcribe in such a way as to highlight (or at least represent) the fact that conversational contributions are often jointly produced? What might be gained (and lost) from a transcript that did not attribute particular words to particular speakers?

3.18   Describe the structure of a typical telephone conversation in the linguistic/ cultural setting you are most familiar with. Who talks first? What is the "preferred" format of the succeeding turn? Who suggests the first topic? Who initiates the end of the call? How can these expectations be manipulated (by telemarketers, for example) in order to keep people from hanging up the phone? What cross-cultural differences can cause problems? What new conventions have arisen in connection with the use of mobile phones?

3.19   In addition to conventions about who can speak when, conversationalists rely on conventions (of which they are usually unaware) about how topics are introduced, changed, and dropped. Oddly, one way for a speaker to signal that he or she is going to introduce a new topic is to announce the opposite, by saying something like "Not to change the subject, but . . ." More commonly, however, topics in spontaneous conversation are "chained," one giving rise to the next. This passage, adapted from a newspaper column by humorist Dave Barry, is a parody of the topic-chaining process. What can you learn from it about how conversationalists usually move from one topic to another? What is being overdone here? It may be helpful to trace how links are created from one utterance to the next.

From Dave Barry, "Idiots cause high anxiety on the ground." Barry is caricaturing the sort of inane conversation one is often forced to overhear, he claims, while sitting in an airplane stuck on the runway. (The conversation is in capital letters because, according to Barry, the people who carry on this sort of conversation always talk too loudly.)

FIRST WOMAN: I PREFER A WINDOW SEAT.

SECOND WOMAN: OH, NOT ME. I ALWAYS PREFER AN AISLE SEAT.

FW: THAT'S JUST LIKE MY SON. HE LIVES IN NEW JERSEY, AND HE ALWAYS PREFERS AN AISLE SEAT ALSO.

SW: MY SISTER-IN-LAW WORKS FOR A DENTIST IN NEW JERSEY. HE'S AN EXCELLENT DENTIST, BUT HE CAN'T PRONOUNCE HIS R'S. HE SAYS, "I'M AFWAID YOU NEED A WOOT CANAL."

FW: MY BROTHER-IN-LAW JUST HAD THAT ROOT CANAL. HE WAS BLEEDING ALL OVER HIS NEW CAR, ONE OF THOSE JAPANESE ONES, A WHADDYACALLEM, LEXIT.

SW: I PREFER A BUICK, BUT LET ME TELL YOU, THIS INSURANCE, WHO CAN AFFORD IT?

FW: I HAVE A BROTHER IN THE INSURANCE BUSINESS, WITH ANGINA. HE PREFERS A WINDOW SEAT.

SW: OH, NOT ME. I ALWAYS PREFER AN AISLE. NOW MY DAUGHTER . . .

3.20   Look at this excerpt from a conversation between a doctor and a patient. The patient has cancer of the bladder, and the doctor is describing the surgical procedure he would like the patient's consent to perform. (The equal signs indicate that there is no gap between the end of one turn and the beginning of the next.)

DOCTOR: . . . While we do that we just . . . cut you open here, the soft tissues so that I have access to your bladder. So it's just small, like a zipper.

PATIENT: Yeah, yeah.

DOCTOR: Then we get these catheters in place. Then we close you up.

PATIENT: How long would all this =

DOCTOR: = I would say, I'm going to say maybe probably somewhere between sixty, maybe sixty minutes to one and a half hours.

PATIENT: No, I mean the whole uh process.

The patient starts to ask "How long would all this . . . ," the doctor comes in with an answer. What is the evidence in the conversation that the patient perceives this "latching" as interruption? What might the doctor have done to avoid interrupting? The question which the doctor answers is apparently not the question the patient had in mind. How does the patient "repair" this problem by making the doctor aware of this? Can you relate what happens in this excerpt to issues of power and control in conversation? For example, would you expect doctors or patients to interrupt more often? Is this the way doctors and patients often interact? Is it the way they should interact?

Old and New Information and the Organization of Sentences

Why do sentences take the form they do? The traditional answer is usually something like "because of the rules of grammar," or, to put it more accurately, because of the conventions that have arisen as speakers have done things the way previous speakers have done them. When they are speaking English, for example, people tend to put grammatical subjects before predicates in declarative sentences, and English adjectives generally precede nouns. In Arabic, by contrast, subjects typically follow verbs, and in French, the default place for adjectives is after the nouns they modify. When we compare one language with another, some things about the grammars of languages do seem fairly arbitrary. Questions are formed in some languages by adding special words or particles to the beginnings of sentences, for example, and in other languages questions are formed by manipulating the order of the words inside sentences. Neither of these options is inherently better, more logical, or more effective than the other. There may be universal cognitive reasons, having to do with the ways in which humans are equipped from birth to be language learners and language users, why some ways of arranging phrases into sentences are more likely than others, and some arrangements may be impossible, because humans simply cannot process them. But within these constraints there are numerous options. If we compare isolated characteristics of languages' grammars, as they are codified in textbooks and linguists' grammars, it does look as if it is fairly arbitrary what goes where in a sentence.

Within a language, grammar also allows choices, and, if we think only about the meanings of isolated sentences, these choices can also seem arbitrary. As we have already seen, there are almost always several possible ways to organize a given sentence, all of which, if considered in isolation, mean more or less the same thing. For example, English speakers can choose between active and passive constructions, between "The accounting department made a mistake" and "A mistake was made by the accounting department." We can choose between "I remember that one" and "That's the one I remember." "Account Link by Web is your link to your accounts 24 hours a day" conveys the same information as "Your link to your accounts, 24 hours a day, is Account Link by Web." We can say "If you can click a mouse, you can use our services," or "You can use our services if you can click a mouse."

If the order of words in a sentence were truly arbitrary – if exactly the same meaning could be conveyed in more than one way – then we might expect all but one of the alternatives to drop out of the language, since, from the perspective of discourse processing, there could be no point to having more than one way to do exactly the same thing. Just as there are no truly synonymous words, there are no truly synonymous grammatical transformations: if the grammatical conventions of a language allow alternative ways of formulating a phrase or a sentence, these alternatives must serve different functions. What, then, makes people choose one possibility for the construction of a sentence over others in a given situation? In chapter 2, we explored how choices among ways of phrasing "the same" sentence can reflect ideological agendas, explicit or unconscious. Here we turn to another approach to the relationship between the form of a sentence and its function, one that has to do with the referential aspects of sentences, their "literal" meanings.

Discourse analysts who work in the field of "functional grammar" examine how the structure of the particular sentences people choose to use reflects how people process and package information in the longer stretches of discourse of which sentences are parts. There are several strands of linguistic research that take a functional approach to syntax. The best known is probably the "Systemic-Functional" approach developed by M. A. K. Halliday and his associates (Halliday, 1994; Eggins, 2004; Thompson, 1996). Another important strand of functional grammar is associated with research on "grammaticalization," or how language change is shaped by language function (Givón, 1979; Hopper, 1996; Hopper and Traugott, 2003).

One set of questions about how syntactic structure is correlated with communicative function has to do with what sorts of information fill which grammatical slots in a sentence. What kinds of communicative work do grammatical subjects do, for example, and what difference does it make whether grammatical subjects are at the beginning of the sentence? What kind of information tends to be grammaticalized as an object? It has been observed, for example, that in many languages grammatical subjects tend to be used to express given information, and that new referents are more likely to appear as the subjects of intransitive verbs or as objects.

More generally, it has been observed that speakers tend, as the default choice, to put relatively familiar information at the beginning of a sentence, and relatively new, unfamiliar information closer to the end. Hearers accordingly expect this order. There are several ways of labeling these functional parts of sentences, depending on the particular formulation of the idea: some functional grammarians talk about the differences between "given" and "new" information, others about sentence "themes" and "rhemes," others about "topics" and "comments," and some subdivide these categories further. The fact that sentences in discourse generally move from the familiar to the less familiar, or from the "what" to the "what about it," reflects the fact that people appear to process information by first identifying what is being talked about and then attending to what is being said about it. In informal speech, people sometimes use explicit topic + comment structures, literally announcing first what they are going to be talking about, then saying a sentence about it, as in this example:

My father,   he's fit to be tied.
(topic: easily identified)   (comment: new information about him)

In Linda's haunted house story, discussed earlier, was this example:

. . . that house on Grant Street,   it was right by the graveyard
(topic: already mentioned)   (comment: new information about it)

As we can see from these two examples, information can be "already given" in a number of ways. "My father," in the first example, can be said to be given information because its referent is easy to identify unambiguously: the fact that a person says "my father" rather than, for example, "my step-father" signals that there is only one such person who is relevant here. In the second example, "that house on Grant Street" is given information because it has already been talked about in the conversation. Some functional grammarians (such as Prince, 1981) accordingly use a large variety of labels for the specific ways in which referents can be identified.

As conversationalists attempt to create common ground, they can simplify each other's interpretive task by signaling whether they expect others to be able to identify a particular entity. One way to do this is by putting already given referents at the beginning of a sentence. The structure of the noun phrases speakers choose to identify things also sometimes reflects speakers' expectations about how available the referents are to their interlocutors. For given, easily accessible information, shorter, less complex noun phrases can be chosen: I might use *that house* or *it*, for example, if we have just been talking about the house; *my house* if it can be assumed that there is only one. New information, to which hearers presumably do not have activated mental access, requires longer noun phrases: *the president's summer home, one of the houses across the street from mine.* In general, information that is less predictable, more difficult to access, or more discontinuous with the preceding discourse tends to take more words to express (Givón, 1985) and is accompanied by more gestural activity (Levy and McNeill, 1992).

Other strategies speakers may use to warn each other when they introduce new entities into the talk may include using *there is/there are* to push the new entity out of sentence-initial position, as in this example (Cheshire and Williams, 2002: 223). The discussion between Peter and an interviewer, AW, has been about the band that Peter plays in, and the existence of Peter's cousin has not been mentioned before. (Spaced periods represent short pauses.)

AW   and are all the people in this band at school?
Peter er no **there's** my cousin . who's seventeen and he he's not doing it
       though cos he's working

Another strategy for introducing a new entity is to explicitly indicate that the hearer's involvement is needed for figuring out what the speaker is referring to. Cheshire and Williams' British adolescents sometimes use the word *like* for this purpose, as well as sentence-final phrases such as *sort of thing, and stuff*, or *and everything*. Here is an example involving *like*. Interviewer AW has just asked Sam whether he has a job, so the nature of Sam's workplace is brand new to the discourse (Cheshire and Williams, 2002: 224).

AW   where do you work?
Sam   it's just in **like** a fish place

Note that the placement of *like* in the sentence, after the preposition *in* rather than before it, shows that Sam is not comparing his workplace to "a fish place," but identifying it as "a fish place." Verbal hesitations, pauses, and other strategies can also call attention to a new referent that will require the hearer to do extra interpretive work, and sometimes multiple strategies are used together, as in this example (Cheshire and Williams, 2002: 226), where "pop groups" brings in a new referent:

AW   and is there anybody you really admire?
Peter **um well like I think. I mean** I admire some **like** pop groups **and that sort of thing** . . .

Among the eight boys and eight girls Cheshire and Williams studied, the boys "seem[ed] to take more care to mark for the interviewer those items that are unfamiliar" (p. 229). The authors suggest that this may be because the boys were working harder to be informative, seeing the interview as an occasion for exchanging information, while the girls tended to act as if they saw the interview more as an occasion for friendly conversation.

Discussion

3.21 Each person in the class writes a sentence – any sentence. Go around the room reading the sentences aloud in turn, or have them written on the board. Why does the result seem different from connected prose? What is missing? Do you find yourselves trying to find ways to interpret the sentences as if they did have something to do with each other? Why do you suppose this happens?

3.22 In one of these two paragraphs (Vande Kopple, 1986), the expected ordering of information in sentences – familiar information first, new information later – has been systematically violated. Read the two paragraphs and decide which it is. Then use circles and arrows to show how, in the paragraph with the more conventional sentence choices, information presented as new at the end of one sentence turns up again at the beginning of the next, as a familiar topic. How does this structure contribute to the readability of the two paragraphs?

   a.   An excellent example of an epic poem is "The Odyssey." A long narrative or story is usually included in epic poems. Certain conventions almost always mark this story. The epic simile is one of these. The stature of a great hero is enhanced through its use. The ideals of particular societies are personified in such a hero. The trait of bravery, naturally, is among these ideals. But courtesy always accompanies bravery. And many particular ways of acting are included in this courtesy.

b. "The Odyssey" is an excellent example of an epic poem. Epic poems usually include a long narrative or story. This story is almost always marked by certain conventions. One of these is the epic simile. It is normally used to enhance the stature of a great hero. Such a hero personifies the ideals of particular societies. Among these ideals, naturally, is the trait of bravery. But bravery is always accompanied by courtesy. And this courtesy includes many particular ways of acting.

3.23 Record some casual conversation among friends. If they are speaking English, see whether *like* is serving the new-information-labeling function described above for Cheshire and Williams' data. What other functions does the word *like* serve in the conversation? If they are speaking another language, what elements serve equivalent functions?

3.24 Below are six options for a sentence meant to describe a feature of many computer programs. Which version would be best for a new computer user, someone who has never heard of a toolbar? Which would be best for a user who knows what a toolbar is but needs to know where to find it in this particular software application? Why? Think about information flow: what information is presented as new in each sentence? Also note anything else that might be relevant, such as, for example, the contrast between the use of *the* and *your* ("the screen" versus "your screen"), sentence length and complexity, and how the sentences are linked together.

a. There is a row of buttons with icons on them on the toolbar at the top of your screen. This toolbar provides shortcuts for frequently performed operations.

b. The toolbar, at the top of your screen, is a row of buttons. The icons on these buttons represent operations you may perform frequently. You can use the buttons as shortcuts in performing these operations.

c. At the top of the screen there is a row of buttons with icons on them. This row is called the toolbar. By clicking on the buttons, you can perform the operations represented by the icons via a shortcut.

d. By clicking on the buttons on the toolbar (at the top of the screen), you can take shortcuts for operations you perform frequently. The buttons are identified with icons that represent these functions.

e. The toolbar provides shortcuts for operations you perform frequently. It is at the top of the screen. To use it, click on the button whose icon represents the function in question.

f. Your toolbar is at the top of your screen. It gives you shortcuts for operations you perform frequently. The icons on the buttons represent these operations. Use it by clicking on the buttons.

Cohesion

What distinguishes a written text or a conversation from a random list of sentences? As you probably noticed in discussing question 3.21, people will try to interpret any set of sentences they hear or read together as a coherent text, and they can do surprisingly well at this, even if they know that the sentences in fact have no relation at all to one another. This highlights the fact that we rarely, if ever, decide whether a set of utterances or sentences constitutes a text purely on the basis of its structure. We also look outside the text and find situational cues that help us interpret what we are hearing or reading. What happens as people do question 3.21 is that the situation – the fact that the sentences are written or read in sequence – cues people to expect the sentences to function together as a coherent text. That is what accounts for the bizarre, often humorous effect of such a set of unrelated sentences read one after another, and it accounts for people's tendency to attribute meaning to the accidental bits of coherence that arise in such a "text."

But speakers and writers often also provide internal cues as to how the parts of a text are linked together. We have just discussed one kind of cue: putting the familiar first, the less familiar later on within sentences. Another category of cues are those that show how sentences are related to other sentences. These cues create *cohesion* in a text.

The best-known treatment of cohesion is that of Halliday and Hasan (1976). Halliday describes five general grammatical and lexical strategies that speakers use (and hearers expect) for showing how the meanings of parts of different sentences are related to each other. By linking some element in one sentence with some element in another, these cohesive devices create *ties* between sentences. The first of these cohesive devices is *reference*. Referential ties are created when an item in one sentence refers to an item in another sentence, so that in order to interpret part of one sentence readers or hearers have to refer to part of some other sentence. Pronouns are perhaps the main resource people have for referring. A pronoun can point backwards (backward-pointing is called "anaphora"), to an earlier sentence that included the noun it refers to, as well as forwards (this is called "cataphora") in a text. Pronouns can also point to something outside the text ("exophora"). The following example, like the others in this discussion of cohesion, is from the teacher of a writing class, speaking to her students. (The class was recorded and transcribed by Suzanne Cherry.) Here the teacher is encouraging the students to think about similarities and differences among technical and non-technical audiences.

The *executive group*, in many ways, is really similar to the *lay audience*. Right? How, how may **they** be a little bit different?

They, here, points back (anaphorically) to "the executive group" and "the lay audience." Because the meaning of *they* can only be interpreted with reference to the earlier sentence, it creates a cohesive tie between the first sentence and the second.

A second kind of cohesive tie can be created by the use of words or phrases that *substitute* in the same grammatical slot for material elsewhere in the text.

> Do you think, think *we've held most of the high school students* to this point? Hope **so**.

So substitutes here for a clause, *we've held most of the high school students*. It ties the two sentences together by making the interpretation of the second one depend on the first one. Other words and phrases that can create cohesive ties through substitution include *one*, as in *another one* or *the second one*, which substitutes for a noun phrase, and *do*, which substitutes for verb phrases in expressions like *so do they*.

Closely related to substitution is *ellipsis*, which creates cohesive ties via omission, as interpreters have to go elsewhere in the text, or in the context of the discourse, to fill in the blanks. In the classroom transcript, ellipsis ties a student's response to the teacher's question.

> Teacher: Is anyone here a physics major?
> Student: I am ~~a physics major~~.

What is elided here is "a physics major" in the student's response. Saying "I am" rather than "I am a physics major" creates a blank space, so to speak, which can only be filled with reference to the teacher's question.

Fourth, *conjunction* is the use of any one of a variety of strategies to show how sentences are related in meaning to other sentences. One of the signals is the use of conjunctions, words such as *however, because, so, nevertheless,* and *and*. Here, as she explains an assignment, the teacher conjoins utterances with *but* and with *and*:

> Sometimes I'll give you an audience analysis sheet that I want you to fill out and tack onto the assignment. **But** for this particular one, I want you just to use, use all four of those as a general guide to get you started. **And** to answer the kind of questions you need to for this assignment.

Conjunctions explicitly tie the meanings of utterances together, making the meaning of one coordinate with or subordinate to the meaning of the other.

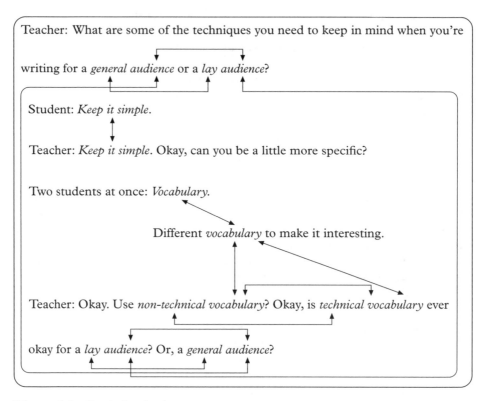

Figure 3.3   Lexical cohesion

Finally, *lexical cohesion* means using the same words repeatedly, or using words that point to one another in various ways, such as by having similar or antonymous (opposite) meanings or by being meronyms (one referring to a whole and one to a part of it: *tree – limb*) or hyponyms (one word refers to a class and the other to an item in the class: *meat – beef*). In the passage from the writing class in figure 3.3, the students and the teacher create a web of cohesive ties by repeating themselves and each other. Cohesive ties are formed here via repetitions of *audience, keep it simple, vocabulary*, as well as by the use of the antonyms *non-technical* and *technical* and the synonyms (in this context) *lay* and *general*. This excerpt highlights the ways in which conversations as well as monologues can be more or less cohesive. It also suggests that making cohesive ties between one's own contributions to talk and one's interlocutors' contributions can have interactional as well as semantic effects. The inter-speaker deployment of cohesive ties is one of the ways in which meanings are jointly constructed in talk. It can thus be an indicator of cooperativeness, as in the above example, where the lexical cohesion contributes to the sense of engagement between teacher and students and cooperation among the students.

Discussion

3.25   Here, again, is one of the extracts from the writing teacher. We identified examples of conjunction in this passage above. What other cohesive strategies are in use here? Which ones create ties to parts of the discourse that presumably came before or after this part? Look for examples of reference, substitution, ellipsis, and lexical cohesion.

> Sometimes I'll give you an audience analysis sheet that I want you to fill out and tack onto the assignment. But for this particular one, I want you just to use, use all four of those as a general guide to get you started. And to answer the kind of questions you need to for this assignment.

3.26   Identify and label the cohesive ties in this selection from a Canadian government tourist brochure about Lake Superior Provincial Park. All such documents must be bilingual in Canada, so the passage appears in English and in French. (Since the French version appears below the English in the brochure, I have put the English version first.) If you can read French, compare and contrast the cohesive strategies employed in the French version with those used in the English version. Could either the English version or the French version be improved via different choices for cohesion?

a.   English version:

> Lake Superior Provincial Park, one of the largest parks in Ontario, is 1,556 square kilometres of northern terrain offering wonderful opportunities for outdoor enjoyment and magnificent scenery. The open waters of Longfellow's "Shining Big-Sea-Water" and its haunting shoreline, a myriad of small jewel-like lakes and rushing rivers, cobble beaches, rugged rocky outcrops of the Canadian Shield, and limitless forests inhabited by a variety of species of wildlife are all part of the wealth to be found in this Natural Environment Park.
>
> With its southern boundary about 130 kilometres north of Sault Ste. Marie, Lake Superior Provincial Park stretches northward almost to Wawa, and east to the Agawa River. Highway 17 cuts through the park, running close to the craggy shore of Lake Superior at the southern end and then heading inland, where it touches a number of small lakes and rivers.
>
> With campgrounds close to the highway, and access to eight different canoe routes and eleven hiking trails, Lake Superior Provincial Park is an ideal destination for a vacation in the wilds. It also offers awe-inspiring stopover spots for motorists travelling between the Sault Se. Marie and the region north of Superior.
>
> At the eastern boundary of the park, the Algoma Central Railway provides access to the park for canoeists.

b.   French version:

> Le parc provincial du lac Supérieur, un des parcs les plus vastes du Nord de l'Ontario, occupe une étendue de 1 556 km carrés. Les visiteurs pourront

s'adonner à de nombreuses activités de plein air dans un cadre absolument grandiose. Ce parc naturel regorge de fabuleuses richesses, ainsi les eaux libres du «Shining Big-Sea-Waters» de Longfellow et les hallucinants contours de son littoral, une multitude de petits lacs scintillants et de rivières bouillonnantes, les plages de galets, les affleurements rocheux du Bouclier canadien, et des forêts immenses qui abritent une variété d'espèces animales et végétales.

La lisière sud du parc se trouve à 130 km au nord de Sault Ste. Marie, tandis que sa bordure nord touche presque la localité de Wawa. La rivière Agawa constitue la frontière orientale du parc. Le parc est parcouru en son milieu par la route 17 qui, à l'extrémité sud, longe de littoral escarpé du lac Superior avant de pénétrer dans l'arière-pays où elle rencontre plusiers lacs et rivières.

Le parc provincial du lac Supérieur est un endroit privilégié pour un agréable séjour dans la nature à l'état sauvage. Il offre aux visiteurs plusiers terrains de camping situés non loin de la route, un total de huit itinéraires de canotage et de onze sentiers de randonnée. C'est avec plaisir que les automobilistes voyageant entre Sault Ste. Marie et la région au nord du lac Supérieur y feront une halte.

À la bordure est du parc, les canoteurs pourront emprunter le chemin de fer de l'Algoma Central pour accéder au parc.

3.27 Lexical cohesion can have a variety of special effects, particularly when employed in unusual ways. We touched briefly above on how lexical cohesion can index cooperativeness and hence be used to build rapport in conversations, but other things can happen, too. Identify all the instances of repetition and partial repetition of words, within and across speakers, in these examples. Then discuss their effects.

a. Part of a conversation between two university students (Hopper, 1990):

RICK:	Have you had dinner yet?
	(0.4 second pause)
CAROLE:	No I haven't. [Have you.]
RICK:	[I- I'm] so hungry, (laughing)
CAROLE:	Are you starving?
RICK:	Yes.
	(0.3)
CAROLE:	Have you ate today?
	(0.4)
	Eaten.
RICK:	(laughs)
CAROLE:	(laughing) I said *eated* (laughs) =
RICK:	= No I- I- I already eated.
	(laughs)
CAROLE:	You already eated?
RICK:	Yes.
CAROLE:	What did you eat at (laughs)

RICK: But I'm going to go- I'm gonna go, ra- now, (laughs)

CAROLE: You gonna go ran.

RICK: I'm gonna go ran.

CAROLE: (laughs)

RICK: (laughs)

CAROLE: Fuck you. (laughs) (He's) gonna go ran now, (laughs) [Leave me alone.]

RICK: [And the- and then-] and then I'm gonna- and then I'm gonna go:n to a movie (laughs)

CAROLE: Gonna gone to a movie?

RICK: Gonna gone to a movie.

CAROLE: *Are* you gonna gone to a movie?

RICK: Yeah.
           (0.2)
           You wanna comed?

CAROLE: (unintelligible)

RICK: (laughs)

CAROLE: I wanna came.

RICK: (laughing) Wanna come.

CAROLE: (laughs) You wanna came (laughs)
           (0.4)
           (laughing) Leave me alone.

RICK: (laughs)

b. Excerpts from plays by playwrights associated with the "theater of the absurd" (Schnebly, 1994).

(i)   Edward Albee, *The American Dream* (p. 105)

GRANDMA: My, my, my. Are you the van man?

YOUNG MAN: The what?

GRANDMA: The van man. The van man. Are you the one come to take me away?

(ii) Harold Pinter, *The Birthday Party* (pp. 17–18)

MEG: Do you want some tea?
            Say please.

STANLEY: Please.

MEG: Say sorry first.

STANLEY: Sorry first.

MEG: No. Just sorry.

STANLEY: Just sorry!

(iii)   Harold Pinter, *The Birthday Party* (p. 9)

> MEG: I've got your cornflakes ready.
>   Here's your cornflakes. Are they nice?
> PETEY: Very nice.
> MEG: I thought they'd be nice.

c. From a conversation between a psychotherapist ("Marian") and her client (Ferrara, 1994):

> SHARON: ((angry tone)) He thinks he's doing me a favor, I'm afraid, by letting me get on my feet financially, and as long as I'm doing ten dollars a month better than I was doing before, they don't have to consider anything else.
> MARIAN: (4) So this father is not a real good father
> SHARON: (1) Well, he's helpin' his kids out.
> MARIAN: (2) You don't want to be one of his kids.
> SHARON: (1.9) I don't want to be one of his kids. I would never have told him some of those things if he hadn't asked me. . . .

Structures and Rules

This chapter has been about some of the ways in which discourse appears to be structured: some of the units into which talk and writing seem to fall, and some of the recurrent ways in which these units seem to be organized into sequences. Many theories for thinking about how repeatable units and sequences come to be make use of terms such as "rules," "conventions," or "constraints." According to such theories, when people act the same way other people do, be it in language or in other arenas of life, it is because they are acting according to convention; a paragraph or story seems coherent and cohesive because its author knows and has has obeyed the constraints (conscious or not) that delimit what paragraph- or story-builders can do; discourse, in short, is "rule-governed."

Many of us are taught to think of discourse as the result of rules from a fairly early age. There are rules at home for what can be talked about at dinner and which words are taboo; there are spelling rules at school, rules about topic sentences, rules about comma splices and split infinitives; conventional ways of writing book reports and college application essays (and even conventional ways of displaying your unconventional creative spark); rules, sometimes masked by potentially misleading encouragement to "do it however you like," for how to write critical essays and lab reports later on. It seems easy and automatic to many discourse analysts to think about the structural facts about texts as being the result of rules. But what are rules?

Where do they come from and what is their role in discourse-building? There are several possible answers.

One way of imagining the relationship between rules and discourse is to see rules as descriptions, or, more commonly, models (since cognitive processes cannot be directly observed) of actual cognitive processes. Rules in this sense are "generative": discourse is generated when speakers and interpreters apply pre-existing procedures, speakers to create utterances and interpreters to arrive at interpretations of their meanings. In this view, rules are "a priori" (Hopper, 1988), existing before and apart from utterances.

In another view, rules are not descriptions of how discourse is (or could be) produced, but rather statistical generalizations about already-uttered discourse, generalizations that are made after the fact. It is possible, in other words, to look at corpora of transcripts or texts and make statements about how they are structured "as a rule" – how they are "usually" structured, in other words – without claiming that these "rules" are actually generative. Reference books about the grammars of languages are compendia of rules of this sort, rules formulated by scholars on the basis of examinations of actual discourse. Statistical rules can only be formulated from a distance, by looking back at what people do. In this view, discourse is not created or interpreted via the application of a priori rules. Instead, structure and meaning are "emergent" (Hopper, 1988), created in the process of interaction as people devise strategies for responding to the immediate situation and solving the immediate communicative problems. This is the view held by many Conversation Analysts and functional grammarians (see, for example, Ochs, Schegloff, and Thompson, 1996).

In the sense of "rule" which is most common in educational settings, rules are prescriptive. They describe a target: fluency in a foreign language, for example, or correct speech or writing. Rules of this sort are like rules of etiquette. Prescriptive rules might enter into discourse-building in a variety of ways, and many teachers and texts do not take an explicit position on how they do. While we sometimes speak, as laypeople, as if standard-sounding speech or native-sounding writing were the result of "following the rules," and textbook exercises sometimes encourage students to apply rules one after another, we do not necessarily mean by this that fluent speakers or good writers actually generate discourse via a mental process involving these rules. Consciously trying to follow prescriptive rules can be paralyzing, like trying to think about how to dance or drive while doing so. In fact, prescriptive rules often turn out to be more useful in retrospective tasks such as editing written text or "monitoring" one's output in a foreign language (Krashen, 1983) than in spontaneous production and interpretation.

When we talk about the units of discourse and how they combine, as we have in this chapter, which view are we taking? It is possible that some readers, perhaps particularly those for whom English is not an early-learned language or who feel they need to be able to write or speak better, will interpret some of the generalizations we have made as prescriptive rules. Any statement about what people *do* is liable to be read as a statement about what people *should do*, whether the author intends it to be read that way or not. And it is possible that some of the generalizations we have made might be useful in that way, at least to the extent that they describe real texts and conversations. But our goal has certainly not been prescriptive in any explicit way: this is not a textbook about how to speak or write.

The generalizations made in this chapter are, on the other hand, explicitly meant to be interpreted as statistical rules, statements about what generally or commonly or usually happens. They are explicitly meant to encourage readers to formulate ways to see if the same things happen, with the same degree of frequency or for the same reasons, in other contexts. They are meant, in other words, to encourage more of the sort of retrospective analysis of discourse of which they are the result. This is explicitly a book about discourse analysis, after all.

To what extent can our statements about discourse structure be thought of as generative rules? To make the claim that intonation units correspond to cognitive processes which are actually in play as people talk, for example, or that Topic – Restriction – Illustration rules are actually applied in the process of composing paragraphs rather than just being a useful way to think about their structure, it would be necessary to adduce actual research about speakers' mental processes. Some discourse analysts (such as Chafe, in his discussions of intonation units) make such claims, and some (such as Becker, in his discussion of paragraphs) do not. Some generalizations about discourse structure might correspond to generative rules. The ability to make generalizations is a basic human trait (this, it might be noted, is why discourse analysts are able to do the work we do), and it might make sense to suppose that some generalizations people make about discourse, as they interact, become part of the process by which discourse is produced and interpreted. Others of the generalizations discourse analysts make, on the other hand, are likely to be simply statistical rules, with no necessary bearing on mental process.

Discussion

3.28   What, if any, is the relevance of discourse analysis for the teaching of writing? Do you think writers can learn to write better by analyzing their own writing, or that of other writers? You may want to ask yourself, for example, whether statistical rules are more likely to be used generatively in edited writing than in spontaneous speech.

3.29   Which kind or kinds of rules – generative, statistical, or prescriptive – would have to enter into the engineering of computer software that can produce and/or understand discourse?

Further Reading

Crookes (1990) discusses several ways of dividing spoken discourse into units. Chafe (1994) takes a cognitive approach to intonation units; Sherzer (1982) and Hymes (1977) talk about poetic lines in Native American discourse. Christensen (1965), Becker (1965), and Christensen et al. (1966) talk about the structure of written paragraphs; van Dijk (1986) and Bell (1991) discuss the structure of news articles. Key sources about the structure of oral narrative are Labov and Waletzky (1967, 1997) and Labov (1972b, 1981). An overview of work influenced by Labov's "Oral Versions" paper is Bamberg (1997). On formal models of discourse, see Hobbs (1983) and Webber (2001). Taboada and Mann (2006) provide an overview of Rhetorical Structure Theory. Goffman (1981[1976]) is a key source on the units of conversation, and Sacks (1995) and Sacks, Schegloff, and Jefferson (1974) contain important early discussions of the emergent organization of conversation. More recent work in Conversation Analysis (CA) is represented in Goodwin (1981), Atkinson and Heritage (1984), Ochs, Schegloff, and Thompson (1996), and Ten Have (1999). Wooffitt (2005) compares CA with other approaches to discourse analysis. A somewhat different approach to the analysis of conversation is associated with Interactional Sociolinguistics (Gumperz, 1982b; Tannen, 1984). Overviews of Hallidayan Systemic-Functional Grammar include Halliday (1994), Eggins (2004), and Thompson (1996). Vande Kopple (1986) is a good overview of the topic of information flow in discourse; other sources are Prince (1981), Chafe (1986, 1994), Givón (1990), and Lambrecht (1994). Examples of functional approaches to how grammatical roles such as subject and object are assigned are Li (1976) and Du Bois (1987). The most important source on cohesion is Halliday and Hasan (1976). Hoey (1991) focuses on lexical cohesion. On "a priori" and "emergent" concepts of rules and grammar, see Hopper (1988).

chapter 4

Participants in Discourse: Relationships, Roles, Identities

Choices about what to say or write, facts about how conversations emerge or texts get written, and conventions as to how discourse is to be interpreted all are influenced by who is involved in producing and receiving it. How a text or conversation is shaped and what it is taken to mean has to do in part with who the audience is understood to be, who the text's producer or producers are, whether the person (or people) who write, sign, or speak the text are responsible for the text's meaning or just relaying it, what the relationships among text- or talk-producers and other participants are and what the participants would like them to be, who else is listening, watching, or reading or might be, and how discourse producers and audiences are related to these overhearers or eavesdroppers. In this chapter we explore a few of the ways in which participants shape, and are shaped by, what goes on in discourse. We look at how the identities of participants in a communicative event, and the relationships among the participants, influence the talk and texts to which the event gives rise, and we examine how talk and text define and "position" the actors involved in it.

One traditional way of thinking about the participants in discourse is to imagine the "author" of a text (or the current "speaker" in a conversation) as the primary source of its structure and meaning, the one who decides what to say, how to say it, and what others should take it to mean. Other participants are then thought of as passive decoders of the message. In this view, if the decoding participants do not accurately reconstruct the speaker's intended meaning, then they have misunderstood, whether because the speaker/author failed to make his or her intentions clear or because the hearers/readers have not used the correct interpretive strategies. In some cultural traditions, in some situations, speakers or writers do play this special role. When speakers or writers are thought to be primarily responsible for determining the "true" meaning of their words, people behave accordingly, looking for the real meaning of a text in its author's intentions – as they do, for example, when making legal arguments based on the original intent of the framers of laws.

But other participants are also always involved in shaping discourse, through their reactions to it, through the ways in which it is designed with them in mind, and through the ways in which their roles make authors' roles possible. As we look in this chapter at the ways in which discourse is shaped by participants (and by the various ways in which people categorize one another as participants in interaction), we will also consider the ways in which discourse shapes participants. We will be reminded that in many ways people's positions in the world are their positions in discourse, since the power to shape the world is, to a large degree, the power to shape how people talk about the world (see chapter 2). People without a voice are often people without a shaping role in the world. For example, being an expert often means being empowered to speak with authority, and having the chance to do so. In many ways – and perhaps increasingly, as we interact more and more with people with whom we are not in physical proximity – the reference groups which guide our behavior are "discourse communities" consisting of the people with whom we talk or whose expectations about what discourse is like are similar to ours.

Power and Community

Two important aspects of social relatedness that are expressed and created in discourse are power and solidarity. Power has to do with the respects in which relationships are asymmetrical, with some participants more able than others to shape what occurs or how it is interpreted. Solidarity has to do with the relatively symmetrical aspects of human relationships. Power and solidarity are both always at play in any relationship (Tannen, 1994: 19–52). Solidarity can be thought of as the counterpart of power in human relations: only in the context of mutual orientation to shared knowledge, membership in common predefined social groupings, or joint activity, do negotiations about control arise. Human life is social – it takes place in the contexts of groups of various sizes. Thus humans need ways to claim membership in groups and to show that they are thereby in some senses in symmetrical relationships with fellow group members. But not all members of human social groups play the same roles. Social groups are often divided into subgroups (such as "social classes," "castes," or "cliques") with differing status and differing access to economic, cultural, or political power.

In some situations, power can be seen as something one subgroup or one person "has" and others do not: power comes with social status. For example, a person who is elected President fifth the US thereby acquires the power to declare war; the chairperson of a committee that follows traditional rules of order has the power to adjourn the committee's meetings; some religious traditions have laws about who makes which decisions in a marriage. Power in this sense is institutionally defined.

But power is also negotiable. People compete for the ability to make things happen, even in situations in which institutionally allotted power might make such competition unequal. In US politics, the legislature can and does try to limit the President's power to declare war. Other committee members can suggest that the chair adjourn a meeting, or they can cause a de facto adjournment by simply getting up and leaving. Women's power in marriages in which men are officially in charge is often considerable. If we think of power as the electric current that makes human interaction possible at all, then it is possible to see power as constantly circulating in any situation. If there were no power, there would be no interaction, just as the lights would go out if the electric current were cut. In this sense, power is not necessarily dominance, but rather more like agency: an individual's ebbing and flowing ability to shape the activity at hand.

Institutionally conferred power and situationally negotiated power are often both in play. For example, Scott F. Kiesling (1997) studied interactions among members of a college fraternity chapter (a social club for university men). In the excerpts below, some of the men are discussing which fellow member should be chosen for the position of "Chapter Correspondent." In the first excerpt, Darter, a younger member who is relatively low in the fraternity's hierarchy of institutionally defined roles, argues for his choice, Richie. Since Darter knew Richie before the others did, as a fellow student in high school, he can claim expertise that the others lack. This gives him potential power to influence the decision. Note how he balances this situational power, based on expertise, with his lack of institutional power.

DARTER: Um *Ri:tchie* may come off like he's really like a dumb ass
          and everything but uh
          he's like one of the smartest people
          I know y'know
          I went to high school with him
          and he was like ranked *fifth* in our class
          and he can write like really well
KIM: He's *A:*sian man, what do you expect?

SPEED: (sarcastically) Is he really?
DARTER: I mean he *types* like unbelievably . . . quick.
          um I just think this would be a good position for him
          to hold because he's a really good writer,
          I mean I've read a lot of papers of his.

Darter begins by anticipating objections to his claim ("Richie may come off like he's really like a dumb ass and everything, but uh . . ."), displaying his awareness that others might object, not only to his suggesting Richie for the open position but to his making a suggestion at all. Several "hedges" – *like, y'know, I mean, I just think, uh* – could be read as signals of unsureness, as could the fact that he speaks quickly (as if he did not think he could hold the floor for long) and in a relatively uninflected, monotonous voice.

But if Darter were really unsure of his support of Richie, he might not have raised the subject to begin with. It may be that rather than *being* unsure, Darter is showing that he is aware that he needs to *act as if* he is unsure. His hedging can be seen as at one time displaying his lack of institutional power, as a junior member of the group, and making a play for situational power, as he manages through a display of apparent powerlessness to get the others to listen to him. The same effect is created via Darter's uses of the intensifiers *really* and *unbelievably*, via his use of the conditional ("this *would be* a good position for him"), and via his repetition of the supporting evidence for his argument, "he can write like really well" / "he's a really good writer." All of these choices display Darter's awareness that people might not automatically take his opinion seriously, but at the same time, all are calculated to make them more likely to do so.

Mack, the focus of the next excerpt, is an older and more institutionally powerful fraternity member. His choice for chapter correspondent is Kurt. Note how Mack's claims to power are expressed. (Mick, chairing the meeting, allocates turns to speak. Pencil, the chapter's graduate-student advisor, reminds people of the proper procedures.)

MICK: Mack. (Calling on him)
MACK: *Okay* . . .
          This is *it* . . .
          Somebody said something about =
PENCIL: = Again, we need to reorganize (?).
MACK: yeah somebody's-
          we need to look at what we have left here
          and there are certain positions
          that everybody fits into perfectly.
          Ernie does *not* fit into this: (0.1)
          I'm not sure where Ernie fits in just yet.
?:   Historian.

MACK: *but* I: a:m afraid that we are going to *waste* uh
           one of the few brains *left.* in someplace that that
           uh Historian has potentially been a
           non-existent position, uh I think for a couple
           semesters yahoo took some pictures,
PENCIL: We're talking about Chapter Correspondent now
MACK: what's that? I know
PENCIL: and he can hold *both* positions.
MACK: I understand that. (0.3)
           But he won't.
           (0.5)
           [I see- I see *Kurt-* I see Kurt- I see *Kurt-*]
PENCIL: [Then talk about Chapter Correspondent.]
           point of order.
?:   we have four left.
PENCIL: point of order.
MACK: I see Kurt as Chapter Correspondent.
           not Richie damn it.

Hedging and other ways of expressing hesitancy or unsureness are not much in evidence in this excerpt. Mack claims the right to influence the decision in this particular situation by virtue of his institutionally-defined power to influence decisions in general. To do this, he reminds people of his right to speak with authority by speaking with authority, making direct claims such as "This is *it*" and "but he won't," talking about what the group "needs to" do rather than making suggestions about what they *could* or *should* do, and speaking for the group by using *we*. He reminds the others of his seniority by evoking institutional memory ("Historian has potentially been a non-existent position"). He makes repeated attempts to get the conversational floor for his suggestion: "I see- I see *Kurt-* I see Kurt- I see *Kurt-*." When he does succeed in recapturing the right to speak, he phrases his objection to Richie as directly as possible: "not Richie damn it."

As they claim or request the right to power, the fraternity men also display and create community. Engaging in joint discourse activities such as the meeting and the decision-making that goes on in its course are among the things that the collection of men do because they are members of the fraternity community. The activity performed by the group reinforces the group: having the meeting and making the decisions displays to the men that they are, at least for these purposes, members of a common community. Showing that they share norms for how to talk like community members also helps the men constitute themselves as a group. They perform their commonality through such things as uses of *we* in reference to people in the room or in the chapter, uses of people's first names or nicknames, references to common knowledge, and uses of in-group jargon.

Communities seen through the lens of discourse have been called "speech communities," "discourse communities," or "communities of practice." Each of these terms highlights different aspects of how social groups can be constituted. In settings in which everyone in a physical community, such as a village, talks to everyone else and uses the same variety of the same language to do so, a "speech community" might be the same as a spatially-defined community, which might also correspond to a community defined by a language variety. A group of people who regularly talk to one another about a particular topic or in a particular situation (researchers in an academic discipline, for example, or the staff of a company) might constitute a "discourse community." The idea that a person is permanently a member of one all-important group, spatially or otherwise defined, whose rules and standards do or should shape every behavior, has often been a powerful one. There have often been reasons for which some people have wanted others to think first and foremost in terms of the nation, "the Community," the company, or some other group. But settings in which people interact exclusively with others who are exactly like them do not really exist, since there is always variation among speakers in how they talk and what they do with talk, there are always activities going on in which some people and not others are involved, and each individual's specific social ties to the other individuals are differently patterned (Milroy, 1987). Different groups of speakers are relevant to an individual at different times and in different ways.

Indexicality

For this reason, people need ways to show which set of social alignments is relevant at the moment, and they need ways to create new sets of alignments. These strategies are sometimes referred to under the cover term "indexicality," and particular strategies are sometimes called "indexes," or "indices," though I will refer to them as "indexical forms" or "indexicals" in what follows. (When it comes to their literal meaning, the terms are synonymous.) An indexical form is a linguistic form or action which, in addition to or instead of contributing to the denotational or "literal" meaning, points to and sometimes helps establish "social" meaning. Indexical forms can point to pre-existing social meaning, but the use of an indexical can also create social meaning. (For example, choosing to use the more elevated-sounding Greek plural "indices" rather than the English-style plural "indexes" may be a way of claiming a certain kind of well-educated, perhaps somewhat pretentious, social identity, not just a way of showing that you already have this identity.)

Almost any aspect of human interaction can function indexically. Engaging in joint discourse activity (whether by working collaboratively on a work or research project or engaging in casual chat, and whether or not these activities are conducted face to face, by people who know each other, or in a single language variety) can index – that is, again, create and/or affirm – shared membership in a "community of practice" (Wenger, 1998). Using the resources of language the same way and evaluating others' speech the same way may sometimes be relevant in the creation and maintenance of communities, as when fellow New Yorkers recognize each other, speakers of Gaelic band together to preserve their heritage, or members of different high-school cliques use slightly different accents (Eckert, 2000). Common ways of doing things with language, such as telling stories (Johnstone, 1990), having arguments (Schiffrin, 1984), or following the necessary sequence of events in an airplane cockpit (Nevile, 2006) can index common affiliation. Small choices among words and phrasings can also index that a person is orienting to one group or another. In languages that have "formal" and "informal" second-person pronouns, choices among them can, for example, index greater or lesser social equality (Brown and Gilman, 1960). Ways of speaking that presuppose shared knowledge characterize tightly-knit social groupings. A discourse community can have particular genres of its own (see chapter 5), such as the "treatments" of species of flora that are written and used by systematic botanists (Swales, 1998), or it can have characteristic jargon or characteristic patterns of interaction. All of these modes of indexicality, as well as others, can function as both signals of group solidarity and claims to group membership.

Discussion

4.1   Here is an excerpt from a transcript of a girls' softball team preparing for a game. Roy is the coach. Pete is the assistant coach. Jodi, Mina, and Jessica are team members. John is the father of a girl on the team. How does Roy express and claim his institutional power, as coach, to be in charge of the situation? How does he in fact assert control when things threaten to get chaotic (as when the girls show that they are not paying attention)? How does he try to create solidarity ("team spirit") at the same time as he asserts his power? Look at such things as pronoun choices, imperatives, "comprehension checks" such as *Okay?* and *Understand?* What is the function of the short sentences? How does repetition work?

ROY: "When am I going in the game? When am I gonna play?" and all that. (imitating the girls' questions)
JODI: Hey, is this thing recording us? (in reference to the tape recorder)
ROY: I, I'll put you in the ball game. Okay? Understand? Anybody not paying attention? Don't think you're gonna play that much, 'cause you're not. We got a ball game. All right? Watch what's going on. Everybody'll get in. Treat everybody equal. Mina, you're leading off, playing left field. That means you bat first.
MINA: I bat first?

ROY: Right. Holly, first base. Sarah, short stop. Jessica, second base. Karol, catching. Shonda, third base. Jodi, you['re] playing rover. I'll tell you where to go when you go out there. Holly, you['re] batting after Jodi. You stay in the dugout to begin with. Okay? Christa Long, center field. You bat after . . . Fern. Carla King, you stay in to start with. Okay? You bat after Christa. You know Christa. Gillian, playing right field. Kelly, you['re] pitching. Then I got Judy Wiener and Jaqui. Scratch the last two 'cause they ain't gonna be here. You gotta tell these score keepers, I guess.

JOHN: Huh?

ROY: Everybody got it? Let's play ball like I know we can play ball. Okay. Remember . . . all the practices we went through. Okay. This is it. This is the big game, man. Season opener. All right. Gotta do it. Can we do it?

JESSICA: Yeah.

JODI: You mean I have to stay in . . .

ROY: Jodi!

PETE: What did he just say?

JODI: Okay.

ROY: Okay. Everybody understand what's going on?

4.2   Powerlessness and inarticulateness are often associated. What features of discourse are seen as indexing inarticulateness in the settings you are familiar with? (For example, people who "mumble" or "don't speak in complete sentences" are sometimes thought to be inarticulate.) Are there situations when inarticulateness can in fact be a way of indexing power? What are some other uses of inarticulateness?

4.3   Anne Graffham Walker (1982) points out that witnesses in court are required to follow rules for telling their stories which are different than the unspoken rules that govern stories in everyday conversation, and that these special rules may not be explained to them. For one thing, in many settings people have the right to talk about what they thought was going on or what appeared to be the case, but in courtroom testimony doing this can result in objections to "hearsay" evidence. The difference between conversational and courtroom norms for narrative can confuse witnesses and make them appear inarticulate or untruthful. Here is an example (Walker, 1982: 15):

PROSECUTOR: And what happened then?

WITNESS: Apparently they were, from what I could understand, they were offering her, uh, gratuity-

DEFENSE: Objection to what=

COURT: =Sustained.

WITNESS: They were offering her-

DEFENSE: [Objection

PROSECUTOR: [Just what you, just what you observed.

WITNESS: Okay. Well, all right, uh – nothing.

Discuss the connections between this sort of inarticulateness – not knowing the relevant interactional rules – and powerlessness. In whose interest is it to have witnesses appear confused and inarticulate? Compare this excerpt with how such conversations are represented in film and on television.

4.4   Here is a memo which was sent by the new principal of a high school to the teachers, a few weeks after his arrival at the school (Varenne, 1978: 638–9). The memo infuriated the teachers. Part of the problem, claims Varenne, lies in how the principal's choices of words and structures indexes, or points to and constructs, his role and his relationship with the faculty members. In what ways are the principal and the faculty members referred to? For example, to whom does each *us* refer, in the first paragraph? What words and phrases can be taken to refer to the audience of the memo, the teachers at this school? What else about how the principal chooses to represent himself and the situation might be responsible for the teachers' objection to the memo? How do power and community (or the lack of it) come into play here? Remember to focus on the details – choices of words and structures – in addition to making general statements about "content."

> Memo
> June 25, 1971
> To: FAC
> From: Foster
>
> There is something intriguing about a teacher surplus which now exists in our country today. It permits us to be very selective in education. It enables us to assign teachers better. It even lets us replace some teachers we should not have hired in the first place. Possibly, at long last, it can stimulate us to be serious about individualizing education.
>   I have listed below some of my thoughts which will obviously convey my ideas and philosophy of education
> 1. Accountability. Teachers must become more and more accountable for student failures. Just as the patient expects the doctor to administer medication, teachers must continue to search for methods and approaches to meet the needs of students.
> 2. "E" and "F" grades. I must emphasize, even though the record shows the student has failed, it is a definite reflection on the teacher and his approach to helping the student learn.
> 3. Teachers must show an awareness of understanding of pupils' human as well as intellectual needs. The student must have a sense of personal worth, a feeling he belongs, and some sense of power to make a difference in shaping his own destiny. This would again infer that the failure of a student is because of the failure of a teacher.

4.5   To what discourse communities do you orient yourself at different times? What characterizes their discursive practices, in other words, the repeated ways they use language? How do shared practices of discourse serve to perpetuate the community? How do newcomers learn how to use discourse to claim affiliation with the group? Is there competition for control of the group's discursive practices such that people try to be better at them than others or perform them more than others?

Stance and Style

Thinking about power and community gives us a macroscopic view of how discourse participants both shape and are shaped by what goes on in discourse. As we move toward a more fine-grained description of some of the ways this process works, the concepts of stance and style are useful. *Stance* (as it is usually called, though *stancetaking* might be a better term) has to do with the methods, linguistic and other, by which interactants create and signal relationships with the propositions they give voice to and the people they interact with. Early work (Biber and Finegan, 1989) focused on "evidentiality" and "affect," examining textual features that can signal the source of speakers' knowledge and their degree of certainty (evidentiality), as well as their attitudes about the propositions they utter (affect). More recently, Hunston and Thompson (2000) have explored the linguistics of "evaluation," or "the expression of the speaker or writer's attitude or stance towards, viewpoint on, or feelings about the entities or propositions that he or she is talking about. That attitude may be related to certainty or obligation or desirability or any of a number of other sets of values" (p. 5). According to Hunston and Thompson, evaluation has three functions (pp. 6–13): expressing the opinion of the speaker/writer vis-à-vis the propositions being expressed, manipulating the hearer/reader's attitude vis-à-vis these propositions (in part by constructing and maintaining relationships between speaker/ writer and hearer/reader), and organizing the discourse, for example, by marking boundaries or highlighting significant parts. Because evaluating a proposition often involves comparing it against a norm, linguistic features associated with evaluation may include such things as comparative adjectives, negation, and adverbs of degree. The language of evaluation may also involve markers of subjectivity, or the perspective of the speaker, such as modals including *might* or *could*, sentence adverbs such as *apparently* or *in my opinion*, and conjunctions and structures that report and attribute speech, as well as markers of value, such as lexical items that are evaluative and indications of whether goals are achieved (pp. 21–2).

Since taking a particular attitude toward propositions – such as uncertainty – may index a particular social relationship or attribute – such as powerlessness – stancetaking inevitably has to do with both epistemic (knowledge-related) and interactional aspects of perspective-taking in discourse, and the same features that index knowledge states and interactional roles can also index social identities. Ochs (1992) models how particular linguistic forms can index evidential stances such as certainty, interpersonal stances such as friendliness or intensity, or social identities such as gender. For example, the use of tag questions – appended questions like "isn't it?" in "It's a nice day, isn't it?" or "do they?" in "They don't really mean that, do they?" – can index uncertainty. This arises from their literal meaning, which is to question an assertion that has just been made by the same speaker. But the fact that tag questions and uncertainty are indexically connected means that using tag questions can also index a non-threatening or even relatively powerless interactional identity. A person might use tag questions not just if she were unsure about the particular assertion she just made, but to avoid challenging an interlocutor's authority in general. So, a witness in court might use more tag questions than the attorney questioning her (O'Barr and Atkins, 1980; Conley and O'Barr, 1998) or a student might use more tag questions than the teacher. Because Americans, like many other cultural groups, often assign people to one of two gender categories, male and female, and since relative powerlessness in interaction is, in mainstream US culture, traditionally expected of people categorized as female, tag questions can also index female gender (Lakoff, 2004[1975]).

Repeated sets of stancetaking moves can become relatively stabilized repertoires, or *styles*, associated with situations or social identities. Styles are (at least to some extent) repeatable. That is to say that sets of stancetaking moves serving a common function are not always assembled from scratch in each new situation. As they produce or interpret talk, people can often draw on already-made generalizations about the stance features that can be used to instantiate a particular style. Styles are often identifiable, by analysts and/ or by participants; some have names. Styles associated with a particular set of contextual factors that confront a speaker with a particular set of rhetorical requirements are sometimes called "registers" (Biber and Finegan, 1994; Finegan and Biber, 2001; see chapter 5). As we will see later on in this chapter, sets of stancetaking choices associated with participant roles or subject positions are sometimes referred to under the rubric of "footing" (Goffman, 1981[1979]) or "framing" (Tannen, 1979, 1993a). A set of stancetaking choices associated with a socio-demographic identity category is sometimes referred to as a "dialect" or a "variety" and may have a popular designation like "Received Pronunciation" (Agha, 2003) or "Pittsburghese" (Johnstone and Baumgardt, 2004; Johnstone, Andrus, and Danielson, 2006).

Styles thus emerge when particular patterns of language use become ideologically linked with locally relevant social meanings (Irvine, 2001). This happens because of the potential indexicality of all language use: forms that regularly occur in a certain context can come to call up and construct that context. Eckert's (1989, 2000) work in a Detroit high school links stancetaking to social identity via styles. Eckert shows that adopting certain variants of vowels is one way adolescents take a stance vis-à-vis local life, just as is cruising in cars (or not), dressing in a particular way, or choosing among school activities. Such activities on all levels can become styles linked with social identities. In the high school Eckert studied, two of these social identities were "jock" and "burnout." In a study of recent immigrants in Australia, Kiesling (2005) shows that a particular set of pronunciation features in the migrants' English work together to project an epistemic and interactional stance Kiesling calls "authoritative connection." This stance, Kiesling claims, is particularly likely to be relevant for members of subordinate groups. Because they work together as a stancetaking strategy, the features get used repeatedly together, and a style (locally labeled with the derogatory term "wogspeak") emerges, ideologically linked with a repeatable social identity, that of the recent immigrant.

Discussion

4.6   In early research about language and gender, it was claimed that the discourse features listed below were characteristic of "women's language." Later research has called various aspects of this claim into question. Discuss this issue in terms of stancetaking and style. Could any feature come to index femaleness if it gets conventionally associated with this category, or are there reasons connected with the kinds of stancetaking traditionally expected of middle-class American women why these particular features should be connected with female identity? Who gets left out of the picture if people are divided into "men" and "women" for the purposes of research?

   a.   speaking "properly"; using language thought of as more correct, more prestigious;
   b.   using fillers and hesitation markers such as *ah, well, umm*;
   c.   using "hedges," that is, expressions that reduce the level of certainty that is claimed: *sort of, I think, I guess*;
   d.   using a wider range of intonation;
   e.   doing supportive "backchanneling" when others are talking by saying things like *right* or *um-hm*;
   f.   talking less than men in mixed-sex conversations.

Social Roles and Participant Structure

People constantly create and renegotiate their relationships with each other in the process of interacting, via discourse moves that make claims to equality, inequality, solidarity, or detachment. But there are situations in which social roles are relatively fixed in advance, and in which people are expected to use and interpret discourse in relatively pre-set ways. Sometimes, discourse roles are even codified in books or explained overtly. For example, foreign-language textbooks may include explanations of the linguistic and other behaviors expected for the roles in which students may be using the language, contrasting how students respond to teachers in different countries, or discussing what is expected of hosts and guests. A common, usually pre-set pair of discourse roles consists of those of server and client. People who train for serving jobs at fast-food restaurants are sometimes told exactly what to say to clients in what order, and what style to adopt if talk outside the "script" is required. Another such relationship is that of teacher and student; another is that of parent and child. People who find themselves in social roles that involve more or less predefined ways of interacting are not thereby forced to act in those ways, of course: every restaurant server has stories, for example, about waiters and waitresses speaking rudely to rude customers, students can speak in unexpected ways to teachers and vice versa, and so on. Breaking the conventions for a discourse role can be an effective move, because it can serve to remind people in the situation what the usual expectations are.

In some situations, it may be unclear to one or more of the participants what role is being assumed by others, or what roles they should themselves adopt, and a person can be acting in more than one role, each associated with a different "voice" or a different "frame" (see chapter 5) for understanding what is going on. This can itself be predictable: people can go into a situation expecting that they will have to negotiate about social and linguistic roles. Alternatively, it can cause difficulties. For example, Bamberg and Budwig (1992) describe the ethical dilemma that can result when people in a hospital who are at the same time staff physicians and medical researchers interact with people who are both patients and potential research subjects. Patients may imagine that the doctors are always acting in the roles of carer and curer, even when the doctors may be acting in the researcher role of detached observer. In such a situation, Bamberg and Budwig wonder whether patients can provide truly informed consent to participate in medical research projects.

One of the many ways in which social identities and discourse roles can be indexed is via forms of address. In some situations address is expected to be reciprocal: everyone calls everyone else by first name, for example, or by a title and last name combination, or by some other formula. In non-reciprocal situations, one person is expected to employ one form of address and the other person another. In English, the choices include first name; nickname or short form of first name; last name only; title (*Dr.*, *Ms.*, *Reverend*) plus last name; title only (*Your Honor*, *Officer*); *Dad*, *Mama*, *Sis*, and other terms for family members or quasi-family members; *sir* or *ma'am*; numerous forms like *luv*, *honey*, *bro*, *sweetie*, *old man*, *mate*, and so on. It is also possible to use no term of address at all. When people's roles vis-à-vis one another change, this can be indexed by shifts in how they address one another. In many discourse traditions, including Javanese and Japanese, choices among address forms are only one aspect of a much larger set of honorific choices speakers make, choices that can require different pronouns, different verbs, different ways of referring to objects, and different pronunciations, depending on the roles of speaker and addressee.

Every time a form of address is used, it helps create, change, or reaffirm a social relationship, in addition to indexing a set of conventional expectations. Calling a professor by his or her first name can, depending on the situation, be either completely expected (even perhaps required) or startlingly unexpected, as can using the title-plus-last-name formula. But whether or not it is the expected choice, a choice of address form is always in some ways a strategic move as well as a response to a situation. How a student addresses a professor can be more or less conventional, but it is always a potential signal of how the student imagines his or her relationship with the professor. Likewise, saying "We're all on a first-name basis around here" is never simply a statement of fact, but an attempt to shape the beliefs and behaviors of others. Choices among forms of address are complex and often difficult. This is especially the case for speakers with less institutionally allotted power, as any student knows.

Discourse roles are indexed via choices on every level, from which word to use to what sort of thing to say. Compare (a), an utterance by a teacher, with (b), a hypothetical utterance in casual conversation (example (a) is from Coulthard, 1985: 123):

a.   (in school) Well, today I thought we'd do three quizzes.
b.   (in casual conversation) Well, today I thought we'd talk about my holiday in France.

The first seems fairly usual, the second might strike some people as somewhat odd, possibly rude. The difference has to do with the fact that, in classrooms, teachers very often have the right to frame interactions, to decide, that is, what will be talked about in what way, and for what purpose. Look at the sequence below, from a British classroom, taken from work by Sinclair and Brazil (1982), reproduced in Coulthard (1985: 125):

Teacher: What does the food give you?
Student: Strength.
Teacher: Not only strength, we have another word for it.
Student: Energy.
Teacher: Good girl, energy, yes.

As we saw in our earlier discussion of the structure of such conversations, this is a fairly typical pattern for teacher–student interactions, consisting of an initiation, "What does the food give you?" a reply, "Strength," some evaluative feedback by the teacher, "Not only strength, we have another word for it," a second reply, "Energy," and more evaluative feedback, "Good girl, energy, yes." Other moves teachers can make are *nominations* (calling on students to speak) and *directives* (telling students to do things, such as "Open your books"); students can *bid* for the floor, by raising their hands or calling out.

Teachers only exist because there are students, and vice versa. People create roles for one another and reinforce the difference between roles as they speak in ways their roles require. Sometimes, this process can push people further and further apart, making their roles and their behaviors increasingly dissimilar. Gregory Bateson (1979: 119) calls this process "complementary schismogenesis." It occurs, for example, when a leader, simply by taking charge, thereby creates a group of people who are dependent on her. Their dependency forces the leader to take control even more firmly, which makes the others even more dependent, until ultimately there is a radical division of labor which did not exist at the beginning of the interaction. The same is true of other discourse roles. Via the ways they talk and the ways they categorize their audiences, speakers assign roles to, or "position" (Davies and Harré, 1990), other participants; via their interpretations and reactions, audiences construct speakers.

One useful way of thinking about how people orient to their own and others' roles is in terms of "footing" (Goffman, 1981[1979]). For Erving Goffman, "a change in footing implies a change in the alignment we take up to ourselves and the others present as expressed in the way we manage the production or reception of an utterance" (p. 128). A footing may be associated with a conventional, named role such as "teacher" or "journalist," or it may signal an alignment of some other sort, such as an alignment to gender. (Goffman uses the example of former US President Richard Nixon commenting repeatedly during press conferences on the clothing of a distinguished journalist, thus insultingly signaling his alignment to her gender rather than her profession.) Telling a story about one's past means shifting from a footing in which one is speaking for one's current self to a footing in which one is speaking in the voice of a past self, and quoting others also involves changes of footing. Footings, and shifts in footing, can be indexed in many ways, as we have seen.

Conventional ways of talking about discourse roles sometimes collapse several footings and make them difficult to disentangle. For example, Goffman points out that a person who utters a sentence may have one or more roles with respect to the utterance. He or she may or may not have the role of *principal* vis-à-vis the utterance, that is, the person or group who has decided what to say and is responsible for its having been said. In addition, the speaker may or may not be the *author* – the person who planned the actual words – or the *animator* – the person who wrote down or spoke the words. We often think of these three footings as coinciding, so that our default expectation may be that the same person is principal, author, and animator. But while these roles often do coincide, this is not the necessary state of affairs. When a speech writer prepares a speech for a politician, for example, the politician is the principal and the speech writer the author. If the speech is then read aloud by a spokesperson, the spokesperson is animator but neither author nor principal. Because, in the Western tradition, we imagine that the people who write novels are typically principal, author, and animator, it is easy for us to miss seeing how all novelists appropriate and rework ideas and words that are already circulating (Bakhtin, 1981[1953]; Pease, 1990).

Speakers can shift footings in the course of interactions. Sometimes this is indexed overtly. Imagine, for example, a meeting between a writer and her editor, who have been friends for years. The editor, after interacting with the writer on the footing of her friend for a time, might say something like "Now, putting on my editor's hat . . ." as a way of indexing a realignment of footing. Shifts in linguistic style can index shifts in footing, as can shifts in physical stance, dress, and so on. Subtle shifts in footing can cause trouble in interaction. For example, Berk-Seligson (2000) shows how a bilingual police officer who was meant to be acting as the interpreter between a Spanish monolingual suspect and an English monolingual police officer repeatedly shifted back and forth between the footing of interpreter and that of interrogator. For example, when the English-speaking officer, who was officially the interrogator, asked the suspect to "tell *me*" something, the "interpreter" often translated with "tell *us*." In the process, he was later found to have coerced the suspect into talking, violating the suspect's right under US law to remain silent under questioning. As a result, the case was dismissed, even though the suspect had confessed to murder.

Discussion

4.7   Describe the patterns of address between teachers and students at your institution. Are the terms relatively negotiable or relatively fixed? How do people learn the system? Do people ever use terms of address to challenge the status quo? Does everyone share the same beliefs about how the system works?

4.8   An endearing term of address, or one that indexes closeness, can sometimes sound threatening, as, for example, when a woman is addressed by a stranger as "baby" or a man challenges another with "I don't know whether I'd do that, bud." Why can terms of endearment function as threats in this way?

4.9   What are some ways in which terms of address that signal family relationships (for example, *brother* or *bro*, *sister*, or *uncle*) can be used metaphorically, in English and in other traditions? What sort of footing can be indexed by the use of a kinship term to address a non-relative?

4.10   Contrast possible and expected discourse moves in a "non-traditional" classroom with those briefly described in this section. How can students and teachers express resistance to the discursive expectations that go with their roles? Can teachers and students change the linguistic ways in which roles are created and expressed? Would this create a more egalitarian classroom? Or does it work the other way around, such that the classroom has to be more egalitarian before the discursive practices can change?

4.11   Here are the opening paragraphs of pamphlets distributed to students and employees of two US universities. The pamphlets are supposed to inform students and employees about sexual harassment: what it is, what to do about it, and what the university's policy about it is. Compare and contrast how the two pamphlets construct roles for the university as an entity vis-à-vis its students and employees. Look first at how nominals (nouns, noun phrases, pronouns) are deployed to refer to the university, to sexual harassment, and to students and faculty. Then look at the verbs and verb phrases that describe what these "characters" do. Then look at the structure of the clauses. Are the characters presented as agents or patients, for example?

Pamphlet A (from a large, public university):

THE UNIVERSITY OF X PROHIBITS SEXUAL HARASSMENT

SEXUAL HARASSMENT violates professional ethics and federal and state law. It subverts the mission of the university and threatens the careers of students, faculty and staff. **SEXUAL HARASSMENT** violates Title VII of the 1964 Civil Rights Act, Title IX of the Education Amendments of 1972, and university policy.

Pamphlet B (from a small, private university):

Y University is dedicated to the free exchange of ideas and the intellectual development of all members of the community. For this exchange and development to take place, the university environment must promote the confidence that will enable us to work, to study, to innovate and to perform without fear of harassment.

Y seeks to maintain a learning and work environment free of sexual harassment. University policies specifically prohibit sexual harassment. Any faculty member, staff member or student found to have violated the university's policy against sexual harassment will be subject to immediate and appropriate disciplinary action, including possible suspension, termination or expulsion.

Audience, Politeness, and Accommodation

One of the oldest observations about discourse to be made in the Western tradition of rhetoric is that effective orators keep their audiences in mind (Ede and Lunsford, 1984; Porter, 1992). Rhetorical and literary theory has suggested various ways of conceptualizing audience and the role of the audience in discourse. An audience may be imagined as a collection of actual people or as an image in the mind of the speaker or writer. An audience may be thought to consist of passive listeners whose emotions and beliefs have to be analyzed so that they will identify with what the speaker or writer says; alternatively, audience members may be thought of as active co-participants in the making of meaning. Anthropologists have shown that audience is not imagined in the same way everywhere and accordingly plays different roles in discourse in different traditions (Duranti and Brenneis, 1986). For example, some Native Americans are said to be relatively silent with strangers and relatively voluble among intimates (Basso, 1970; Scollon and Scollon, 1981: 14–16) whereas European Americans are often the reverse, feeling that silence is an appropriate sign of intimacy but awkward among new acquaintances. Scollon and Scollon claim that Athabaskans are silent with strangers because of the fear that, if people do not already know what each other's beliefs are, they risk imposing differing points of view on one another. In other words, by Athabaskans, speakers and hearers are thought to be highly autonomous, and new "intersubjective" (jointly constructed, negotiated) meanings are thought to be threatening. In other discursive traditions, on the other hand, jointly constructed, highly interactive discourse is highly valued, or thought to be the only source of meaning; audiences are explicitly recognized as "co-authors."

One influential line of research about how discourse is shaped by audience has to do with linguistic "politeness." Politeness, in this technical sense of the term, refers to the ways in which speakers adapt (or fail to adapt) to the fact that their interlocutors, actual or imagined, have social needs like their own. Politeness is one of the main reasons for which people are often indirect, not saying precisely what they mean but implying it. Politeness, in this sense, is much more pervasive and more necessary than the formal etiquette involved in making introductions correctly or using the correct eating utensils.

The idea of linguistic politeness was first proposed by syntacticians (that is, people who study how grammar works) who had been attempting to model the abilities involved in producing and computing the meaning of isolated sentences and began to wonder how best to model the additional knowledge that enables people to use and interpret language appropriately in actual social interaction. One of these theorists was Robin Lakoff (1973, 1974b). Lakoff pointed out that humans seem to operate under a set of very basic constraints in their behavior toward one another. Some of these have to do with the expectation that interlocutors will act cooperatively in meaning-making, making their intentions as clear as possible. (Of course, this expectation is not always met. We will return to the idea of the "cooperative principle" in chapter 7.) In addition, Lakoff claimed, societies need rules that insure that social interaction will proceed smoothly, without undue friction. These are Lakoff's three "rules of politeness" (with alternative labels in parentheses):

1 Formality (Distance): Do not impose on others; be sufficiently aloof.
2 Hesitancy (Deference): Allow the addressee options about whether or not to respond and about how to respond.
3 Equality (Camaraderie): Act as if you and the addressee are equal; make the addressee feel good.

In every interaction, Lakoff claimed, these three requirements must be balanced, since they cannot all be maximized at once. More formality, or distance, may result in less equality, or camaraderie; more equality may result in less hesitancy, and so on. Speech and behavior may be perceived as inappropriate, odd, or rude, when, by the standards of speaker, addressee, or both, the balance is off. A dentist who asks the patient a question when the patient's mouth is stuffed with cotton risks violating the rule of hesitancy (the addressee does not have the option whether or not to respond if responding is not physically possible) in the attempt not to seem overly distant. Saying "May I ask you to open the door?" rather than "Open the door" may in one context seem appropriately formal and deferential, in another context insufficiently egalitarian and hence threatening. Strangers sitting together on buses and planes have to balance their own and their neighbors' need to be friendly with their need not to be imposed on. Making the wrong choices can result in misunderstanding. For example, giving one's interlocutor options, in acknowledgment of his or her need for deference, can appear to be a sign of apathy or disinterest, as in this interchange, in which A and B pass back and forth the option of making a decision:

A: Do you want to go to Jim's party?
B: I don't know, do you want to go?
A: I'm asking you. Make up your mind!

Interactions such as this, which can leave one person thinking the other one does not care, and the other person feeling frustrated at the rebuff of an attempt to be accommodating, can undermine relationships (Tannen, 1986b).

One way to describe how Lakoff's rules of politeness work is in terms of "positive face" and "negative face" (Brown and Levinson, 1987). Brown and Levinson, who proposed this influential idea, claim to base their notion of "face" on that of Erving Goffman (1955). The meaning of "face" in this sense is not unlike the common usage of the term in expressions such as "saving face." As Brown and Levinson describe it (p. 13), "[the] notion of 'face'... consists of two specific kinds of desires ('face-wants') attributed by interactants to one another: the desire to be unimpeded in one's actions (negative face), and the desire (in some respects) to be approved of (positive face)." Brown and Levinson suggest that, while there are cross-cultural differences in what constitutes being unimpeded or being approved of and in how these face-wants are dealt with in conversation, the fact that discourse is shaped by considerations of face is universal. Whenever a "Face-Threatening Act," or FTA, must be performed – a speech action which poses a threat to the addressee's positive or negative face – speakers must employ strategies that mitigate or "redress" the threat.

For example, if asking for the loan of something, a person might redress the threats to his or her own and the requestee's face in various ways. He or she might choose a marker of egalitarian "positive politeness" in order to mitigate the threat to his or her own positive face caused by the fact that asking for something puts a person in a one-down position. For example, the requestor might claim common ground: before asking for the loan of a neighbor's garden shears, one could elicit an expression of common experience by asking, "Do you see how this hedge has gotten out of control?" Alternatively, the requestor could choose the positive politeness strategy of offering to reciprocate: a person asking for a loan of money might say, "I'll pay you back, I promise!" Other positive politeness strategies include using markers of in-group identity; expressing approval of or sympathy with one's addressee; noticing and attending to the hearer's wants, interests, and needs; making offers and promises; and giving reasons.

But asking someone for something is also a threat to the requestee's negative face, or desire not to be dictated to, controlled, or hampered. So the requestor could also use markers of deferential "negative politeness" such as not presuming or assuming to know things about the interlocutor ("You wouldn't have a pencil, would you?") or displaying the desire not to impinge ("I don't want to bother you, but do you have a bicycle pump I could use?"). Other negative politeness strategies include being indirect, apologizing, minimizing the imposition, being overtly deferential (by using a formal address form, for example), and phrasing things as questions rather than as statements. Brown and Levinson show how grammatical features in a variety of languages are geared to making utterances polite.

Subsequent research on linguistic politeness has called Brown and Levinson's model into question in several ways. Research about social interaction in Asian societies (Matsumoto, 1988; Ide, 1989; Mao, 1994) has suggested that Brown and Levinson's concept of "negative face," or the desire to be unimpeded, was better adapted to Euro-American social reality than to social reality in general. While negative face may be relevant in individualistic societies, in which people are thought to be relatively auto-nomous, it may be irrelevant in more collective societies where concern for the interests of the group, rather than one's own interests, drives social interaction. Scholars like Eelen (2001) and Watts (2003: 103–16) argue that Brown and Levinson's way of using the notion of "face" is, more generally, based on the culturally particular idea that speakers have pre-existing selves that they bring into interaction. This is not, they argue, what Goffman originally meant by the term.

In addition to adapting their discourse to expectations about human needs and politic behavior in interaction, people adapt their behavior to the actual linguistic behavior of the people they are talking to, or to their image of the people for whom they are designing discourse. Work on "accommodation theory" (Giles and Powesland, 1975; Street and Hopper, 1982; Thakerar, Giles, and Cheshire, 1982) has shown that styles of speaking often "con-verge" toward (that is, become more similar to) the styles of interlocutors with whom speakers identify and "diverge" from those of interlocutors with whom they do not identify.

An elaboration of this idea is Bell's (1984, 2001) "audience design" theory. Bell suggests that discourse is designed with both actual addressees and potential "referees" in mind. In relatively unselfconscious speech, speakers adapt primarily to their immediate addressees, but strategic "initiative style shifting," which is meant in part to define or redefine the situation, may involve shifting away from the style of the immediate audience and toward a style associated with a non-present reference group. For example, advertisers and newscasters, whose audiences are often not physically present at all, design their discourse quite carefully for the set of consumers they hope to attract, even when not all of the people who actually watch the news or see the advertisements are members of this group. Bell suggests that shifts in style that co-occur with shifts in topic or setting can be understood as the result of calculations (often unconscious but sometimes quite carefully planned) about what sort of speech the audience or reference group expects in that context.

For instance, Al-Khatib (2001) shows that Jordanian TV presenters use linguistic features associated with standard Arabic to different degrees depending on what they imagine the expectations of their audiences to be. One set of features Al-Khatib studied was what Arabic linguists call "vocalization," or how often certain vowel phonemes are pronounced, as opposed to being silent. In Modern Standard and Classical Arabic, these vowels tend to be pronounced, while in colloquial Arabic they tend not to be. He found that when the topic was sports the percentage of standard-sounding vocalized vowels was the lowest, and when the topic was religion the percentage was the highest. Al-Khatib suggests that this is because TV presenters know that audiences expect more standard- or classical-sounding speech in religious contexts and design their own speech accordingly.

In research on accommodation and audience design, "speaking style" is usually defined largely in terms of accent and the use or non-use of relatively prestigious versus relatively stigmatized grammatical alternatives. But accommodation is clearly also at work in more global ways, as people make stylistic and rhetorical decisions on all levels.

Discussion

4.12   With reference to Lakoff's rules of politeness, describe what goes wrong in each of these interchanges. Which rule is being overused, underused, or misinterpreted? From whose perspective? How could communication be made to work better in situations such as these?

a.   At an office:

BOSS, TO SECRETARY: Would you have time to address these envelopes for me?
SECRETARY: After I get through this pile of other stuff.
BOSS: I need them right away.

The secretary is left angry, wondering why, if the "request" was really an order, the boss did not phrase it as an order. The boss wonders why the secretary has acted in such an uncooperative way.

b. At home, between friends

A, coming in: I'm exhausted! I just walked all the way from campus.
B: Why didn't you call? I could have given you a ride.
A: I was afraid you'd be busy.

B is left feeling that A does not trust her, and irritated at A's complaining about being tired when she could have phoned for a ride. A does not understand why B is annoyed, since A had made a point of not imposing on B by not calling.

4.13   In what ways is linguistic politeness built into "user-friendly" software and software documentation? How, for example, can software users be given options about how to respond to messages on their screens? How do software and documentation designers attempt to accommodate the varying face-wants of various potential users, some of whom may want to be left to make their own choices and others of whom may want to be interacted with? Find and describe examples of software and documentation that is particularly effective or ineffective in this regard.

4.14   One series of how-to manuals consists of books whose titles suggest that they are addressed to "dummies" (*Dog Training for Dummies*, *Bartending for Dummies*, *Guitar for Dummies*, and so on). A competing series of books are the *Idiot's Guides* to various things. People who buy or use these books are, in a sense, acknowledging that they are "dummies" or "idiots." In some contexts, calling a person stupid is insulting. But these books are very popular. Could this be explained in terms of politeness theory?

4.15   It is often noted that people interacting electronically are sometimes less polite (in the everyday sense of the word) than they would be if they were talking face to face. "Flaming," for example, one of the first discursive practices explicitly identified with email and real-time electronic chat, consists of making direct, unredressed threats to negative face. On the other hand, new ways of redressing potential threats to positive and negative face have arisen in electronic discourse. For example, "emoticons" and other conventions of punctuation can be used to mitigate face-threats. Describe how this can work. What are some other ways of dealing with potential threats to face in text-based electronic discourse? How do new standards form and how are they disseminated? How do people teach one another the rules, which are for the most part not written down?

4.16   How might the idea of linguistic accommodation account for the fact that people who come from areas with non-standard regional accents, and who have tried hard to "lose" their regional accents, sometimes report finding themselves slipping into their native ways of talking when they go home to visit? If you are such a person, do you ever find your speech *diverging* from that of the people you grew up with when you talk with them? What might account for that?

4.17   When people are interacting in real time and in shared space (physical or electronic), one of the linguistic mechanisms they use to influence each other's
discourse is "repair" (Jefferson, 1974; Norrick, 1991). Repair refers to all the
ways people make corrections to their own or others' talk: by repeating
someone's utterance in a different way, by saying "We don't use that word
here," by saying "What?" or "Pardon me?" and so on. In discourse designed
for non-present "referees," on the other hand, on-the-spot repair by audience
members is less likely and, when it occurs, less immediate. If I object to
something I read in a newspaper or see on a website, for example, my
objections will not result in repair unless I compose and send a response.
How do the producers of newspapers, film, and other discourse designed for
non-present referees try to compensate for the lack of immediate repair and
other kinds of feedback?

4.18   One often-noted difference between print and electronic information media
is that the latter can be "interactive" in different ways. Another way to say
this is that the audience potentially plays different, perhaps enhanced roles
in the shaping of electronic discourse. What are some of these roles? What
are some of the effects of this? Is there more convergence in discourse style,
for example, in electronic discourse than in other modes? Design a study that
would test the hypotheses you generate.

Social Identity and Identification

A universal and probably necessary aspect of how humans deal with other
humans is by categorizing them. We decide how to interact with others
partly on the basis of such categorizations: people may deal with "women"
differently than with "men," with "foreigners" differently than with "fellow
Germans," or with "African-Americans" differently than with "whites."
People often act as if identities were natural and predictable: as if gender
("man" vs. "woman") were a result of biological sex ("male" vs. "female"), as
if nationality were a result of place of birth, as if ethnicity could be predicted
on the basis of skin color or genealogy. In fact, however, no categorization
schemes are really "natural" (see chapter 2). People range on a spectrum of
cultural gender; some choose gender identifications that do not correspond
with their biological sex, and some are physically altered to make the two fit;
and sexual orientations do not map neatly onto biological sexes. A "German"
is not anyone born in Germany, since people with two generations of roots
in Germany can still be perceived, and perceive themselves, as "foreigners,"
particularly if they are "Turks," according to the cultural categorization
system in effect for many people there. Ethnic categorizations and racial
ones do not line up, either. The categorization schemes census-takers and
other demographers use, based on the working assumption that people have

easily describable, stable, predictable social identities, have no logical place for people of mixed backgrounds and mixed identities, or for the ways in which identity can change over the lifespan or from situation to situation.

Thus, it is important for discourse analysts not to let predefined categories such as nationality, sex, and so on dictate how they divide up people or texts, or what questions they ask. For example, a researcher who asks "How do men do x" or "How do Hispanic Americans behave in situation y" may unintentionally render invisible the ways in which being a man may mean different things in different situations or obscure the diversity among Hispanic Americans. It is important to try to let analytical categories emerge in the analysis. It is important, in other words, to leave oneself open to the possibility that the social "facts" that seem obvious and defining to one person or group or in one situation may be irrelevant for another. Social class may be crucial in one situation and beside the point in another; being "ethnic" or "white" or "urban" or "rural" may have very different implications in different situations. Some discourse analysts, in particular those who call what they do ethnomethodology or Conversation Analysis, start from the assumption that categorizations arise exclusively in interaction, and that neither participants in interactions nor people who study interactions need any prior knowledge of what social categorizations are conventionally taken to imply about people (Antaki and Widdicombe, 1998).

However, people do orient to the ways they categorize themselves and are categorized by others, and to the ways others categorize themselves and are categorized, and people create, claim, and express these orientations in their discourse. Discourse analysts have found the idea of performance useful in understanding how social categories are connected to discourse. Everyday interaction requires "performances" (Goffman, 1959) of selves strategically geared to the interactional demands at hand. The term "identity" has been used to describe these performances (Gumperz, 1982a; Bucholtz and Hall, 2005). Identity, in this sense, refers to the outcome of processes by which people index their similarity to and difference from others, sometimes self-consciously and strategically and sometimes as a matter of habit. (The processes themselves might be called "identification.") Thinking of gender, for example, as the performance of certain discursive acts (Butler, 1990), sometimes quite consciously strategic, has the advantage of not implying that everyone who is biologically female is thereby destined to think and act in a certain way, or that early socialization into gender roles necessarily determines how people will behave from then on. The social identities that have received the most attention across the social sciences and humanities are ones associated with race, gender, ethnicity, and nationality. But social identities also arise from other sources (Bucholtz and Hall, 2005). Identities can be associated with discourse participant roles like author or overhearer, temporary situational roles like teacher or chapter correspondent, or categorization schemes that arise in particular local contexts, like social cliques in some schools.

As we saw above, social identities can be indexed by styles of discourse. For example, when a person wants to identify with a certain category of women, she (or he) can adopt ways of talking that are conventionally associated with this group, so as to suggest to others what attributions to make of her (or him), and others may use a person's speech style as a way of categorizing him or her in gender terms. The same goes for styles conventionally associated with ethnicity, region, religion, political stance, and so on. People can adopt sets of features associated with groups with which others would be likely to associate them (as when a man "talks like a man" or an African-American youth sounds African-American), and, since these are ways of talking they may have known for a long time and may have learned early in life, they may be able to do this easily and fluently. But people can also adopt features associated with identities with which others might not normally associate them, as when a male talks like a woman, an Anglo-American uses Spanish-sounding words, or a white London youth sounds for a moment like an Afro-Caribbean or a Punjabi. This has been referred to as "language crossing" (Rampton, 1995a, 1995b, 1999).

Discursive performances of identity can serve various purposes and have various effects. At their most consciously strategic, such performances can be carefully planned and deployed. Some women in the Southern US, for example, use what they refer to as "turning on the Southern charm" as a sexually charged way of manipulating men (Johnstone, 1999). Hall (1995) describes how telephone sex workers make strategic use of gender-marked ways of talking in their jobs. Linguistic performances of regional identity, such as the adoption or showing off of local-sounding ways of talking, can express resistance to perceived cultural homogenization, as people become more and more mobile and interconnected. Discursive performances of "local color" can also help further the goals of the tourist industry, or they can be an individual's livelihood (as, for example, in the case of "professional Texans" or "professional Irishmen" whose best-selling books and television appearances are performances of "Texanness" or "Irishness"). A study by Elinor Ochs Keenan (1974) provides one example of the complexity of the relationships among social identity and speech style. In traditional Malagasy society (the Malagasy are indigenous people of Madagascar), proper, polite behavior is highly indirect. It is thought to be extremely important never to risk offending anyone, so face-threatening acts such as ordering, criticizing, and requesting are very difficult to perform and are supposed to be couched in elaborate politeness. But highly face-threatening acts are often necessary: things have to be bargained for in the market, loans have to be requested, children have to be scolded, complaints have to be made to un-neighborly neighbors. Such acts are typically performed by women, who use direct modes of speech to perform them, thereby violating the norms for Malagasy speech. Women, that is, are expected to violate expectations; the norm for a woman is that she be a "norm-breaker."

Another example of the complex set of ways in which social identity and discourse can be related has to do with what some Americans refer to as "sounding country": sounding as if one is from a small town or a farm or ranch. This can involve features of pronunciation and syntax, or more global choices about how to talk and what to say. Certain discourse practices may be identified with country life, for example: gossip, perhaps, the telling of traditional tales, or talk about the weather. People may talk as if they knew one another and shared one world rather than using a more public, distanced, elaborated way of talking. The connection between rural life and rural-sounding speech was once fairly simple, at least in many cases: people sounded rural because they were from the country. With little mobility or access to ways of using language from elsewhere, country people before the days of easy transportation and broadcasting had no other choice. They might never have heard anyone who sounded any different.

However, in the wake of the shift from a predominantly rural to a predominantly urban population, speech forms identified with rurality can now function as resources for expressing one's identification with values perceived as best nurtured in rural life: community and family orientation, religiousness, political conservatism, pride in "tradition," resistance to the urban and suburban mainstream (Fox, 1997). The symbolic use of country-sounding speech and discourse patterns is characteristic of the Country-Western music industry in the US (Johnstone, 1998). Singers and songwriters may or may not be rural in origin; many live in Nashville, Dallas, and other large cities when they are not on the road, and they are part of a large, public-relations oriented industry. When they "sound country," they evoke (often quite intentionally) an image of a kind of rural life in which neither they nor most of their audience actually participate. Rural-sounding discourse is a way of showing, among other things, that a person is like "plain folks" with traditional values, so it has obvious uses, too, for conservative politicians trying to establish, evoke, or maintain a constituency. Sounding urban, whether or not a person is actually from a large city, likewise has its uses.

To think of identity as performance is to adopt a humanistic, rhetorical perspective on a set of issues on which linguists have often taken a social-scientific, deterministic perspective. The advantage of this is that it highlights the ways in which people decide who to be and how to act, and the extent to which they are responsible for the consequences of such decisions. It highlights the ways in which gender and other aspects of identity are discursive practices (Eckert and McConnell-Ginet, 1992) which may be salient in different ways in different situations, rather than demographic facts about people which cause them to act in certain ways. But we need to keep in mind that people's choices are not unlimited. Just as it is unfair to suggest to students of writing or oratory that anything is possible if one works hard enough at argumentation and eloquence, it is unrealistic to suggest that any identity is available to anyone who chooses to adopt it.

Sociolinguists have shown, for example, that habits of pronunciation acquired early in life (sometimes referred to as "accents") are quite resistant to change. So while it is possible for some people to submerge the linguistic evidence of their regional origin, it is not easy and in many cases not possible at all. In other words, discourse is not *either* completely a matter of strategy and choice *or* completely a function of the "social construction" of individuals and the world. It has to be seen from both perspectives.

Discussion

4.19   One aspect of "language socialization" (Ochs and Schieffelin, 1984, 1986) has to do with the ways people learn how they are expected to categorize themselves socially and how people in those social identity categories are expected to talk. How does this happen? For example, how do boys learn to think of themselves as boys and talk like boys, in your environment? In what ways is language socialization a part of the process of learning to function as a university student?

4.20   Studies suggest that white American teenagers who adopt features of speech that are associated in some people's minds with the vernacular speech of African-Americans (Cutler, 1999) may not necessarily be motivated by the wish to identify with African-Americans. How would you design a study to find out what it means to people to use features of speech that they think of as "belonging" to other groups?

4.21   What features of discourse – pronunciations, grammatical choices, topics, ways of talking, genres – are identified with an urban identity in your environment? With a working-class identity? With a rural identity? With a local identity? Who uses these features as a matter of unselfconscious habit? How can these features be used strategically?

4.22   One linguistic feature which people from Pittsburgh, Pennsylvania think of as characteristic of "Pittsburghese" is the use of the second-person plural pronoun *yunz* (also spelled *yins* or *yinz*). Like other Americans, Pittsburghers think of the greeting "Top o' the mornin' to you!" as stereotypically Irish. For Saint Patrick's Day (widely celebrated in the US even by people who are not of Irish descent), the public relations department of the Pittsburgh public transportation authority had a city bus painted green, with a shamrock and the phrase "Top o' the mornin' to yunz!" on the sides. Can you provide other examples of public, strategic uses of linguistic forms associated with local or national identities? What are they intended to accomplish, and how do they work?

4.23   What are some other examples, in addition to the ones mentioned in this section, of ways in which people perform gender or ethnicity for strategic purposes?

4.24 Do speakers ever make "performance errors" in performances of identity?

4.25 Are performances of identity ever evaluated in the way artistic performances are? You might think, for example, about a beauty pageant or a gay-pride parade. What about performances of identity that are specifically linguistic, such as those of people who express a regional or ethnic identity by adopting certain features of pronunciation, vocabulary, grammar, and style?

Personal Identity: Discourse and the Self

Current ways of understanding social identity and its relationship to discourse are rooted in the idea that the selves we present to others are changeable, strategic, and jointly constructed. We use the resources of language to perform a variety of social identities, geared to the situations we find ourselves in and the ways we are socially positioned by others. But we can also use language to construct and project a coherent, more durable personal identity. This involves showing that we are, in a very basic sense, autonomous agents and that we have temporally continuous life histories, biographies without gaps. Children differentiate themselves from others when they notice that they can make things happen and that different things happen to them than to others; when there are holes in their life histories, people can lose their sanity, and psychotherapy often involves constructing a new, complete life narrative (Schafer, 1981).

We can project this more durable sort of identity – the experience of being the same person from day to day and from situation to situation – through the ways our behavior, linguistic and otherwise, remains the same from situation to situation, despite the inevitable need to adapt. This can involve adopting a consistent personal style, or, conversely, it can involve calling attention to the fact that one is always flexible, across modes of behavior and situations (Johnstone, 1996). It can also involve having a coherent life story to tell, or, more precisely, shaping a coherent life story in the telling of it. As Elinor Ochs and Lisa Capps put it, "Personal narrative is a way of using language or another symbolic system to imbue life events with a temporal and logical order, to demystify them and establish coherence across past, present, and as yet unrealized experience" (2001: 2). Charlotte Linde (1993) shows how this can work, in a study of oral narratives by American professionals. Linde argues that personal narrative is perceived as coherent if it establishes causality and continuity, or successfully explains accident and discontinuity, in the teller's life. She claims that "narrative is among the most important social resources for creating and maintaining personal identity" (p. 98), because life narratives both represent and help to construct three characteristics of personal identity (pp. 98–126). First, through the sequencing of events in narrative and the causal connections among events that narrators establish, stories represent the experience of continuity of the self over time, shaping our experience of inhabiting a lasting personal identity. Second, through markers of person like the pronouns "I", "you," "she," and so on, and because narrative arises in social interaction, life stories represent the relationship of the self to others. This shapes our experience of our perspective on the world as being different from others' perspectives and captures the ways in which personal identities are shaped both by identification with others and in contrast to others. Third, through the retrospective process of creating narratives, and in highlighting what was important in their stories, narrators represent the experience of one's own life as a meaningful whole.

Discussion

4.26   In middle-class European-American society, romantic courtship often involves the sharing of life stories. What situations in your social setting call for people to exchange stories of their lives? Can the requirement of storytelling in these situations be linked to the need to display personal identity? In other words, could you argue, based on your experience, that life stories get told at times when personal identity is at a premium?

4.27   When is it particularly important, in your social setting, to project one or another of a set of temporary social identities, and when is it particularly important to project a coherent personal identity? In what situations is others' behavior evaluated in terms of social identity, and in what situations is it evaluated in terms of personal identity?

4.28   Here is a narrative about choosing a career, from the study by Charlotte Linde discussed above (1993: 196–7):

> Well, uh, it doesn't seem as though there was ever a time, well there was, I was a math major when I was a freshman in college, but in my sophomore year I discovered that I wasn't going to be a great mathematician and uh I seemed to be very good in reading and analyzing books and writing so I became an English major and from then on since I knew that I would go as far in whatever I chose as I could possibly go, getting a Ph.D. became a necessity. And once I had a Ph.D., getting a job as an English teacher seemed the logical choice and that's how I arrived at my profession.

As Linde points out (p. 197), "This example shows a citation of character and ability as the natural determinant of career choice . . ." What linguistic details contribute to creating the sense that the speaker's career was the natural, almost automatic outcome of inherent psychological characteristics? Look, for example, at the use of evidential verbs (that is, verbs that represent ways of acquiring knowledge or degrees of certainty) like *discover*, *seem*, and *know*. List some other ways of saying "I became an English major" (for example, "I chose to major in English") and some other ways of saying "I arrived at my profession," and discuss the potential significance of the choices this speaker made. When does the speaker use the verb *choose*? Is the use of this verb consistent with the cultural plot about career choice (in which "getting a Ph.D. became a necessity") that structures this narrative?

4.29   Ask two or three people to tell you how they arrived at the field of study they're now in or how they came to their current careers. With the narrators' permission, record and transcribe the responses. Do they fit the plot of the story in the previous discussion question? If not, what kinds of cultural "common sense" are reflected in how your respondents talk about their personal identities? What details of language reflect this?

The Linguistic Individual in Discourse

Because features of discourse can be *correlated* in so many ways with "social facts" about speakers, audiences, and other participants, it is sometimes tempting to talk as if such facts *determined* what discourse is like. It is tempting, in other words, to suppose that people talk, sign, write, and interpret in the ways they do because they are authors or audiences; because they are identified as male or female; because of features of ethnicity, region, class; because of the need for linguistic politeness and audience accommodation. To do this, however, is to confuse correlation (the observation that two things tend to occur together) with causation. It is important to remember that no matter how much we know about the social context of discourse, we cannot predict what a particular person will say in a given instance, or how it will be interpreted by another person. However constrained individuals may be by the interactional and social roles they are called on to adopt and the stances and styles available to index these roles, by their relationships with one another and the adaptation and accommodation these relationships call for, and by all the other facets of context we have examined and will be examining – in other words, however people's linguistic resources and choices are limited by the ways in which their behavior forms part of the whole ecology of human social life – the fact that participants in discourse are individual human beings means that discourse is fundamentally creative, even if the linguistic decisions made by one individual are often the same as those made by others.

One reason for this is that no two people speak the same language. As children learn to use talk to deal with the world, they make generalizations based on what they hear and see (and, later, read) around them. It may be the case, as is claimed in generative linguistics, that the human mind is pre-programmed to make certain kinds of generalizations and not others. But the exact generalizations people make depend on their particular sets of "lingual memories" (Becker, 1995). Two people whose linguistic experiences are relatively similar, perhaps because they live in the same place, interact with the same people, and have access to the same linguistic input from the media, may end up making a similar set of generalizations. We refer to this by saying that they "speak the same language." But this is misleading, since it suggests that the two share one single set of rules, when they do not. Standardized, written discourse of the sort people learn to produce and interpret via explicit rules in school is more similar from person to person than other modes of discourse; in fact, we often talk as if a standard language could be contained in a book, such as a grammar or a dictionary. Since scholars have often treated all forms of discourse as if they were like standardized, written discourse, it has been easy to miss seeing that language in this sense is an abstraction, not an object.

A second reason for saying that all discourse is creative is that humans are always in some sense individual agents. There are cultural settings in which showing that one is different from and independent of others is highly valued, and settings in which it is not. But whether or not individualism is valued, individuality is inevitable. Different people experience the world through different eyes, different bodies; they have different life stories; they have different names. Even in the most scripted, controlled discourse situations, such as survey interviewing, different people sound different, not simply for biological reasons but because unless they can be heard as expressing individuated human identities they sound like machines (Johnstone, 1991a; Cheng and Johnstone, 2002). Researchers with a Western, individualistic intellectual bias have a long history of overstating the degree to which individuals' autonomous intentions and choices can account for social practices across cultures, and they have often made the negotiated, collaborative, socially shaped aspects of human identity relatively difficult to see. There is more than a bit of truth to the casual ways in which we attribute features of people's discourse to social identities in one way or another, in saying such things as "That's just how men talk," or "You're just saying that because you're an American," or "That sounds like something a mother would say," but as Anthony Cohen reminds us (1994), we do not like to have our own actions explained in this way, as if we were simply bundles of demographic features or fillers of slots in social systems. Concepts of the self vary widely across cultures, but whether or not we think others have the same sense of self as we do, it is important not to assume that others are so constrained by social forces that they lack the free will to make moral choices.

Summary

This chapter has touched on some of the ways in which discourse is affected by who is involved in it and how participants and their social and discourse roles are imagined and enacted in the situation at hand. Because humans live and interact in social groups, we have ways of claiming and expressing alignment and solidarity with others, such as choices of pronouns and terms of address. We also have ways of creating and displaying social stratification in groups, both through relatively fixed ways of talking associated with relatively fixed social roles (teachers, for example, may perform certain classroom interactional moves in fairly fixed ways) and through continual negotiations for control of the ongoing interaction and its outcome. Hedging (expressing uncertainty or tentativeness) is one way, for example, in which a speaker can show that he or she is in a powerless position, or needs to act that way. One way of thinking about how people orient to their own and others' roles in the social world and in the interaction at hand is in terms of "footing." For example, in a particular interaction a person might be participating sometimes on a professional footing (as a professor or a lawyer), sometimes on a personal footing (as a friend or a mother). Changes in footing are signaled linguistically in various ways, although conventional beliefs about expected or natural footings may complicate interactions and their analysis. For example, in the Western literate tradition it is conventional to imagine that the person who writes a book is also the creator of the ideas in it, so that we try to draw firm boundaries between "original" written work, borrowed ideas (which must be identified and sourced), and plagiarism. This makes it difficult to see that ideas and ways of expressing them are always, necessarily, partly borrowed and appropriated, so that all writing is "multi-voiced."

One of the most fundamental ways in which discourse is designed with interlocutors in mind has to do with linguistic "politeness." Politeness, in this sense, goes well beyond overt social etiquette. It has to do with the ways in which people display (or show that they are ignoring) the fact that the people with whom they interact are human beings with needs like their own. The need for ways to perform "face-threatening acts" which violate these expectations accounts in large part for the fact that there are always multiple ways to say things, varying in directness, formality, and hesitancy. As people interact, they also display their alignments to one another through the ways in which they accommodate, or fail to accommodate, to one another's speech styles. "Audience design" of this sort is sometimes fairly automatic, but when discourse is designed for external referees – the readership of a blog or the viewership of a television advertisement, for example – attempts to accommodate to their expectations may be quite self-consciously strategic.

Part of the process by which interactants figure out what their interlocutors expect, whether consciously or not, is by categorizing them. People decide how to deal with others, in part, on the basis of categorizations by gender, ethnicity, class, where they are from, whether they are "friends" or "enemies," and in innumerable other ways. The labels which we repeatedly use for social identities like these can come to seem like natural predictors of people's behavior. For example, it is easy to imagine that acting "white" or "Hispanic" is an automatic consequence of being born to certain parents or looking a certain way. Social identities are sometimes operationalized this way, as, for example, on census forms. As people interact with one another, however, the degree to which they orient to one identity or another can shift, and, to some extent, people can adopt ways of talking associated with groups they would not usually be thought of as belonging to. For example, someone who is not from a small town might use rural-sounding ways of talking as a way of displaying alignment with the values associated with rural life.

In certain situations it can also be important to project personal identity. Like the temporary social identities we adopt or are positioned in, our sense of a perduring personal identity is both represented and reinforced in discourse, by means of choices about linguistic consistency from situation to situation and through the process of narrating our lives.

It can be argued that people are always "performing" one or more identities. This is not to say, however, that all choices about how to sound and who to be are available to anyone. It is important to remember that factors such as gender, income, education, race, and the like may have a bearing on the range of linguistic resources that is available to a person. Although no speakers are monostylistic – as sociolinguists have shown, everyone's speech varies – some may be more resourceful than others, because more resources are available. It is also important to remember that no matter how detailed our description of the social context of discourse, we can never predict what a particular person will say in a particular instance, or how it will be interpreted. This is because linguistic behavior is ultimately the result of choices by particular people, no two of whom share precisely the same set of linguistic memories.

Further Reading

Power and solidarity were first proposed as key variables in linguistic interaction in the 1960s (Brown and Gilman, 1960). Contemporary critical approaches to discourse and power are represented by Fairclough (1989), Lakoff (1990), and Wodak (1996). The idea of "speech community" was proposed by Dell Hymes (1984[1967]). There have been numerous discussions of "speech community" or "discourse community," as neither term has proven easy to define. Overviews include Dorian (1982), Killingsworth (1996), Swales (1998: 196–208), and Rampton (1998). The idea of "communities of practice" is identified with de Certeau (1984) and Wenger (1998). The idea of indexicality originates with the Pragmatist philosopher Charles Sanders Pierce. It was brought into discourse studies largely through the work of Michael Silverstein (1995[1976], 2003, 2004). For an overview of linguistic features that can serve stancetaking functions in English, see Hunston and Thompson (2000). A thought-provoking collection of articles on various uses of the concept of style is Eckert and Rickford (2001). Discussions of how stance features can come together into styles are Ochs (1992) and Kiesling (2005).

Irvine (1985) provides an overview of research about social status and style. Research on how forms of address index social and discursive roles includes studies by Brown and Ford (1964), Ervin-Tripp (1972), Friedrich (1972), Parkinson (1985), Braun (1988), Duranti (1992), and Davies (1997). On discourse in classrooms, see Heath (1978), Michaels (1981), and Sinclair and Brazil (1982). The major source on footing is Goffman (1981[1979]). Key sources on linguistic politeness are Lakoff (1973, 1974b), Brown and Levinson (1987), and Watts (2003). On speech accommodation theory, see Giles and Powesland (1975), Street and Hopper (1982), and Thakerar, Giles, and Cheshire (1982). Bell (1984) is an introduction to audience and referee design theory; Bell (2001) updates the theory.

The idea that identities are strategic, changeable "performances of self" can be traced to the work of Erving Goffman beginning in the 1950s (Goffman, 1959). Much current research on language and social identity is influenced by John Gumperz (1982a, 1982b) and his students, who often describe what they do as "interactional sociolinguistics." Bucholtz and Hall (2005) take a particularly expansive view of the identity terrain; Brubaker and Cooper (2000) suggest "identification" and "self-understanding" as useful terms for disentangling some of the disparate phenomena that are often subsumed under the term. Hewitt (1986) and Rampton (1995a, 1995b, 1999) describe some of the ways people can use ways of speaking associated with social groups they are not usually identified with; the term "language crossing" is Rampton's. Research on language and gender is often said to have begun with the work of Robin Lakoff (2004[1975]). Butler (1990) talks about gender as being constructed via linguistic performances. Collections of papers that take this perspective on gender and discourse include Hall and Bucholtz (1995) and Bergvall, Bing, and Freed (1996). There are numerous textbooks about language and gender and overviews of scholarship in this area. Holmes and Myerhoff's (2003) handbook maps some of this territory. A collection of key studies is Coates (1998). Other collections of articles include Tannen (1993b), Johnson and Meinhof (1997), Livia and Hall (1997), and Bucholtz, Liang, and Sutton (1999). Overviews of research on language, ethnicity, and race include Fishman (1999) and Harris and Rampton (2003). On discourse and personal identity see Johnstone (1996), Linde (1993); on the role of narrative in the construction and circulation of social and personal identity see Ochs and Capps (2001). On "the linguistic individual," see Johnstone (1996, 2000).

chapter 5

Prior Texts, Prior Discourses

One reason the writing which you are now reading looks and sounds the way it does has to do with my previous experiences with textbooks, and your experience with prior discourse like this (prior textbooks and the situations in which they are relevant) is one of the resources you are using in interpreting it. Our experience with future texts like this will in turn be colored by our experience with this one. In this way, prior discourse and categories of prior discourse are evoked and created as we interact. In other words, one of the ways in which discourse is shaped has to do with what people expect to say or hear, write or see in a given context and how they expect it to sound or look. Speakers evoke things previous speakers have said and rely on hearers' previously created expectations about how to interpret utterances. We select certain aspects of discourse – sounds, words and phrases, structural formulas, styles, communicative situations and activities, text-types, and narrative plots – as repeatable wholes, and we reuse text-building strategies and styles of sounding that others have used, building new meanings and new ways of meaning on the scaffolding of familiar ones.

When ready-made phrases are often reused, we sometimes call them "clichés." We sometimes call reusable patterns of structure "boilerplate." Often reused patterns of speech or writing associated with recurrent communicative roles or situations get names like "baby-talk," "legalese," or "administrator-speak." But despite sometimes derogatory labels for especially salient kinds of repetition, we could not communicate without adapting old ways of speaking to new contexts. A person whose discourse was completely creative – completely unlike anything previously tried – would, after all, be impossible to understand. Even the verbal artists we think of as speaking in the newest, least conventional ways (James Joyce, for example) are mostly repeating. They use words, grammar, figures of speech, and genres that have been used before, and they participate in repeated activities like book publishing, poetry reading, competing for literary awards. Verbal artists of the avant garde may expect their readers to work harder than other writers do, but they expect their readers to draw on familiar interpretive strategies.

Familiar types of story plots have names: comedy, tragedy; love stories, Bildungsromane, and so on. We learn, and teach others, to produce new texts with old structures and sounds: haiku, business letters, conference paper abstracts, technical reports and such. Newer text-types like email messages and web pages draw on older text-types like memos and print advertisements. New text-types inevitably become increasingly conventional, as writers and readers develop expectations about their structure and sound, and as texts that violate those expectations become more and more unusual-looking and difficult to process. New situations call for new combinations of old communicative strategies; new stories borrow and adapt familiar plots; new sentences borrow and adapt familiar structures; and conversationalists repeat and adapt their interlocutors' words and sounds. Repetition and variation – prior texts shaped to new contexts, old expectations drawn on in new situations – are at the heart of how discourse works.

We begin this chapter by looking at some of the ways in which language theorists have talked about the relationship of discourse to prior discourse. We then explore four overlapping ways of thinking about prior text. We think first about text-building strategies which involve people's use and interpretation of on-the-spot repetitions of words, sounds, formulaic phrases, and syntactic building blocks. We then look at two closely related concepts that have been used to categorize more global strategies for adopting and adapting prior discourse and discursive practices: register (sets of expectations, based on what people have heard and read before, about conventional stylistic choices associated with recurrent roles and situations) and genre (sets of expectations about text-types and knowledge-producing activities that are used for particular purposes in particular discourse communities). We then briefly explore plot (sets of expectations, mirroring and shaping basic beliefs about the world, about what makes a coherent story, which ways of talking about characters and actions make sense). Finally, we think more generally about repetition in discourse. We explore the possibility of creativity and truth-telling in the light of the many ways in which prior ways of talking and thinking shape even the texts we think of as the truest and most creative, and we speculate about the role of memory in discourse production and processing.

Intertextuality and Interdiscursivity

Discourse analysts' interest in the ways in which texts and prior texts are connected is often traced to the influence of the Russian linguist Mikhail Bakhtin. Bakhtin wrote (apparently under several names) over a period spanning from the 1920s to the 1940s, but because there was little communication between Soviet scholars and outsiders, his work did not become known in the West until the 1960s, and English translations became available only in the 1980s (Bakhtin, 1981[1953], 1986). In his work about the history of the novel, Bakhtin talked about the "dialogic" qualities of texts, the ways, that is, in which multiple voices (multiple ways of talking, multiple points of view, and multiple things to say) are transformed and reused each time something new is written.

The French scholar Julia Kristeva (1986) introduced Bakhtin's work to Western audiences. Kristeva coined the term "intertextuality" for the ways in which texts and ways of talking refer to and build on other texts and discourses. For Kristeva, "horizontal" intertextuality has to do with how texts build on texts with which they are related sequentially (or syntagmatically, to use the traditional term in linguistics), in other words, the texts (or utterances) which they follow and precede. So, for example, speakers pick up on other speakers' sounds and words and phrases and reuse them; new personal-experience stories in a conversational story-round may pick up on character types or plots from previous ones; or someone spoken to in a particular professional register may respond in the same style. "Vertical" intertextuality refers to how texts build on texts that are paradigmatically related to them in various ways, members, that is, of the same or similar categories. So, for example, an email message may borrow from and transform the conventions of letter writing, or a postmodern parody of a fairy tale may borrow from the plot and character conventions and the language of traditional fairy tales, mixing them with conventions and language from contemporary texts of other kinds, such as TV sitcoms, comic books, and so on.

Texts can bear intertextual traces of other texts in many ways, ranging from the most direct repetition to the most indirect allusion. Norman Fairclough (1992: 118–23) describes some of the possibilities. A text can quote another text, or represent it through paraphrase. A text can be worded in such a way as to presuppose a prior text. For example, definite articles (in English, *the*) often introduce condensed forms of propositions handed down from previous discourse. *The threat to our national security* presuppposes some previous talk or writing in which it was established that there was or is such a threat. Some bits of prior text circulate widely in condensed forms like this, and people may use them without asking themselves whether the propositions they presuppose are actually true. Expressions like these function, in Michel Pêcheux's (1982) terms, as "preconstructeds": formulas that circulate from text to text in ready-made form. Texts can evoke prior texts through negation: saying what something is not presupposes one or more prior texts that have made the opposite claim. Fairclough uses the example of a tabloid newspaper headline: "I Didn't Murder Squealer! Robbey Trial Man Hits Out" (p. 121). By claiming not to have committed the murder, the suspect evokes previous discourse suggesting that he did. Texts can also evoke prior texts through a variety of strategies for distinguishing among different stances that a text-producer can take with regard to the claims the text makes (see chapter 4). Through various "metadiscursive" strategies – ways of making discourse be about discourse – speakers can situate themselves outside their words, pointing to the words' origins in others' talk or writing. For example, we can speak of a "so-called" entity, highlighting the fact that others have used the term, or hedge the description of a quality with "sort of," and defining a term ("by which I mean") highlights the way the speaker has brought it into the discourse from somewhere else. Irony also points to prior discourse; making it obvious that one is using words one doesn't mean gestures to others' sincere uses of the words.

In a study of intertextuality in transcripts of the South African Truth and Reconciliation Commission's amnesty hearings, Susan Lawrence (2006) explores how the texts that set up procedures for the hearings shaped how applicants for amnesty presented their testimony. In order to qualify for amnesty, perpetrators of crimes committed during the apartheid era were required to show that their crimes had been politically motivated. To do this, they and their attorneys turned to the criteria for political motivation described in the legislation that established the Truth and Reconciliation Commission. One criterion had to do with "the object or objective of the act, omission or offence, and in particular whether the act, omission or offence was primarily directed at a political opponent" (Promotion of National Unity and Reconciliation Act No 34, Section 20 (3)(d)). Lawrence shows how one applicant for amnesty described the man whose murder he was responsible for. While the victim was identified most frequently by his name in the applicant's testimony, he was also identified as "an ANC [a political party] member," "a self-proclaimed ANC member," "a self-proclaimed communist," "the ANC dog," "my political opponent," "the enemy," and "your son." With the exception of "your son," all the ways the victim is identified other than by his name can be seen as being intertextually related to the "political opponent" criterion in one way or another. In particular, says Lawrence:

> The Act, in section 20 (2), focuses the definition of a . . . political opponent on any "members or supporters" of "a publicly known political organisation or liberation movement engaged in a political struggle against the State." To call the victim "my political opponent," then, is to repeat the language of the Act; to call him "the enemy" is to relate the two terms through hyperbole; the Act does not speak of enemies, but of opponents. To call the victim "an

ANC member" is to offer a specific instance of a "publicly known liberation movement engaged in a political struggle against the State." Thus the relationship here is synecdochal, in which a specific term (species) is substituted for a general one (genus). To quote characters in the account as having talked of "the ANC dog" is to relate the account and the Act through metaphor. When the victim becomes "a self-proclaimed communist" the figurative relationship becomes one of metonymy, in which something associated with the thing, or an attribute of the thing, is substituted for the thing itself (the pre-transition ANC had strong affiliations with the Communist Party). The figurative intertextual relationship, then, between this nomenclature and section 20 (3) of the Act is variously that of repetition, hyperbole, synecdoche, metonymy and metaphor. Repetition forges the closest ties between the two texts, with metonymy and metaphor creating looser ones; each provides one means by which the account orients to "political opponent."

Texts can also be *interdiscursively* related to prior texts. "Interdiscursivity" refers to ways in which "discourses" (see chapter 1) draw on previous discourses. Just as text-producers reuse and refer to bits of the language of previous texts, they reuse and refer to already existing text-types and the text-producing activities (or "discursive practices") in which they are embedded. So, for example, public debates about issues involving science (such as the teaching of the theory of evolution, the marketing of genetically modified food, or the possibility of a cure for homosexuality) borrow both from discursive practices associated with science, such as the use of statistics to persuade and the adoption of a neutral, disinterested stance on the part of the researcher, and from practices associated with other contexts for talk, such as ways of speaking and thinking associated with science fiction, religion, and politics (Fahnestock, 1986; Stewart, 2005; Myers, 2003).

To describe the process by which texts and discursive practices take up bits of prior texts and practices, the notion of "appropriation" – also drawn from Bakhtin's work – has proven useful. As people learn how to do things in a language, whether as children, as foreign-language learners, or in the context of the daily language-learning in which we are all engaged, they must start by borrowing. Learners begin by mimicking words, structures, purposes, and ways of talking that belong to other people. As they use and reuse these borrowed building blocks, successful learners appropriate them, or make them their own. What starts out as imitation becomes self-expression, as borrowed discourse strategies and pieces of language are fitted into a person's own set of ways of meaning. For example, in their study of a book written by a third-grader (that is, an eight- or nine-year-old), Lensmire and Beals (1994) show how the girl drew on words, themes, purposes, and styles from two sources: a book written by an adult which she had read, and her local peer group. As Lensmire and Beals put it (p. 411): "We are born and develop, learn to speak, read, and write, awash in the words of others. . . . Our words are always someone else's words first; and these words sound with the intonations and evaluations of others who have used them before, and from whom we learned them."

Appropriation can be self-consciously strategic, as, for example, when a saleswoman chooses to use a Southern US accent to charm a potential customer (Johnstone, 1999) or a screenwriter chooses a Southern accent to symbolize the low IQ of a movie character (Lippi-Green, 1997). Appropriation can be strategic in less self-conscious ways, too, and sometimes its effects are created only after the fact, via others' reaction to it. For example, in a study of how code-switching (alternating between languages or varieties) can function as a way of negotiating community membership and ethnic identity among young men in Los Angeles, Adrienne Lo (1999) examined this exchange between Chazz, a Chinese American born in the US, and Ken, a Korean American who moved to the US when he was 16. (Rob, who is not centrally involved in the conversation at this point, is African-American.) All three men are in their early twenties. In this segment, Chazz appropriates a derogatory Korean phrase (represented in bold italic type) referring to Vietnamese people, in order, Lo suggests, to align himself with Ken, the Korean American. Ken responds to the offensive language and the way it miscategorizes him by switching into Japanese (in small capital letters). English translations for the code-switched parts are in single quotes. As the excerpt starts, Ken asks Chazz about the national origin of a girl Chazz says he likes. Lo videotaped the conversation and transcribed it in a format that allows her to see the small details of the interaction. Numbers in parentheses are seconds and fractions of seconds, laughter is transcribed with *huh*, *hah*, *hih*, *h*'s, and *o*'s, colons indicate drawn-out sounds, and non-verbal behavior is described in italics, in double parentheses. Parts connected by equal signs are "latched" (i.e., follow on each other without a break), and parts aligned with brackets are overlaps.

KEN: What is she [the girl Chazz likes] Vietnamese?
          (.6) ((*Chazz's head recoils, he frowns, eyes flash, then smiles*))
CHAZZ: ***Ttangkhong anya!*** ((*smile voice*))
          'She's not a peanut!'
KEN: hh(h)<u>O</u>(h)o(h)::::: ((*Ken recoils back sharply, smiling*))
          (.4)
KEN: What is she then.
CHAZZ: ***Hankwuk yeca***=
          'Korean woman'
KEN: =Korean?
CHAZZ: Yeah ((*Chazz nods*))
KEN: Really.
          ((*Ken looks to the left, grimaces, looks down and reaches for his sandwich*))
          (2.0) ((*Chazz bites lip, looks left*))

KEN: O(h)o(h)o(h) you don't like ***ttangkhong*** then
        ((looking down at table))
CHAZZ: ***Tta(h)gn [khong ssiphal!***
        'Peanut fuck!'
KEN: [huh huh huh ha(h)h hih
        ((Chazz, smiling, looks to camera))
        ((Ken points to the left))
KEN: hih hah hah [hih hh
                    [*(((Chazz silent laughter))*
        (2.0)
KEN: Ok. *((looking down))*
CHAZZ: [hih hih hih hih hih
ROB: [(So everythi-) *((Rob looks at the camera))*
        Damn. Everything's o:n this tape huh?
        hhhuh hh
CHAZZ: Yeah (.) ***Ttangkhong ttangkhongul acwu silhe!***
        'Peanuts, I really don't like peanuts!' *((incorrect use of object marker))*
        (.2)
KEN: O̲:h
        (.8)
KEN: hh hu̲h hhh
        (1.0)
KEN: Do:SHITE hh *((smiling))*
        'Why' *((in Japanese))*

As Lo shows in her longer treatment of the conversation of which this excerpt is part, Chazz's behavior indicates that he thinks his use of the derogatory Korean term *ttangkhong*, literally 'peanut', to refer to Vietnamese people, will align him with Ken, who is Korean and thus, Chazz thinks, will share this attitude about Vietnamese and appreciate Chazz's use of Korean slang. Telling Ken that the girl he likes is Korean, not Vietnamese, is also intended to be an affiliative move. But Ken's behavior shows that Chazz's appropriation of Korean words and Korean ideas has failed in this situation: Ken recoils, says "Really," looks down, and grimaces, and there is a long (2-second) pause. The awkwardness continues, as there is embarrassed laughter, silence, sudden self-consciousness about the camera, and more attempts by Chazz to get a reaction to his appropriation of Korean, including another use of vulgar Korean slang. Eventually, Ken says "why" – in Japanese. Lo suggests that this shift into Japanese is a shift away from Koreanness as Chazz is defining it, as is Ken's refusal to shift into Korean himself. Ken is not, in fact, a member of the generation of Korean Americans who would be likely to use the term 'peanut' in this way, and he appears not to like Chazz's claiming membership in this group for himself or for Ken. (Whether or not Ken also objects to Chazz's way of talking about women, as it is represented here, is not clear from this excerpt.)

Discussion

5.1 In the following passage, A. L. Becker (1994) uses the metaphor of plagiarism to describe intertextuality:

> I repeat others, reshaping their words to new contexts, but only a tiny handful of those others whom I repeat do I acknowledge mainly in order to appropriate their prestige. What I get and repeat from NPR [National Public Radio], "Nova" [a television program], the *New York Times*, the books I read, and the people I talk with is mostly unacknowledged. I am hardly conscious that I am repeating, don't even like to have it pointed out. But very little of what I say or write is original. . . . And I repeat my own prior words, not just those of others. I reshape what I hear and read, make it my own, and use it over and over again, reshaping as I go. . . . None of us can plumb the depths of our plagiarism.

Discuss the difference between plagiarism and intertextuality. What counts as plagiarism in your institution? How does the idea of intertextuality bear on debates about "intellectual property" and copyright?

5.2 According to discourse analysts who draw on Bakhtin's notion of "appropriation," the first step in any kind of language learning is imitating, borrowing. From this start, learners have to move toward making foreign words, structures, styles, and situations their own. If you are or are preparing to be a language teacher, discuss how teachers of foreign languages can facilitate this process. Which foreign-language teaching methods provide the best fit with this way of thinking about language learning? If you have studied a foreign language, describe what it feels like to make a foreign word or structure your own for the first time.

5.3 Here is part of a correspondence between the American architect Frank Lloyd Wright and Pittsburgh businessman Edgar J. Kaufmann, for whom Wright designed a well-known house called Fallingwater. (Letter excerpts from Gangwere, 1999.)

> Dear Mr. Kaufmann:
>
> I don't know what kind of architect you are familiar with but it apparently isn't the kind I think I am. You seem not to know how to treat a decent one. I have put so much more into this house than you or any other client has a right to expect that if I haven't your confidence – to hell with the whole thing.
>
> Frank Lloyd Wright

> Dear Mr. Wright:
>
> I don't know what kind of clients you are familiar with but apparently they are not the kind I think I am. You seem not to know how to treat a decent man. I have put so much confidence and enthusiasm behind this whole project in my limited way, to help the fulfillment of your effort that if I do not have your confidence in the matter – to hell with the whole thing.
>
> Edgar J. Kaufmann

P.S. Now don't you think we should stop writing letters and that you owe it to the situation to come to Pittsburgh and clear it up by getting the facts? . . .

Kaufmann's letter draws directly on the structure and wording of Wright's letter. Yet in saying to Wright almost exactly what Wright said to him, Kaufmann also adds extra meaning. (He refers to this, indirectly, in his post-script.) For one thing, Kaufmann's letter comments on Wright's in an indirect way. For another, perhaps related, thing, Kaufmann's response could be taken as insulting, or it could be taken as funny. Discuss how the exchange works. Are there situations in which people more routinely respond to others in exactly the same way others speak to them? What are the effects of intertextuality in those situations?

5.4   The magazine article in which the Wright–Kaufmann correspondence appeared was visually designed to look somewhat like a Frank Lloyd Wright artifact, with liberal use, for example, of Wright's signature horizontal lines in Wright's signature shade of red. This could be seen as an example of intertextuality, in the sense that the text of the article and its visual design point to each other and both refer to the same previous "texts" in the form of Frank Lloyd Wright sketches and artifacts. Discuss other ways in which the verbal and visual elements of multi-modal discourse (magazine articles, web pages, CD-ROM, and so on) can make reference to each other, or to common prior texts, verbal or visual.

Repetition in Conversation

According to one bit of folklore shared by some American children, conversational repetition is remarkable and even somewhat spooky. In one version of the game, when two children happen to say the same thing at the same time, the first to call out "Jinx!" can claim a Coke from the other. The irony, of course, is that the game is based not only on simultaneous repetition of some prior text, but also on another completely unremarkable kind of repetition: In order to win, you have to say "Jinx, you owe me a Coke!" No other wording will work. Repetition in conversation is not, in fact, rare at all. People constantly repeat themselves and repeat others. There are traditional names for many forms of repetition: *alliteration* for the use of a series of words beginning with the same sound, *parallelism* for repeated grammatical structure, *chiasmus* for repetition in which the order of elements is switched, and so on. Writers and orators can make conscious use of figures of speech such as these, repeating themselves, one might say, very much on purpose and for rhetorical ends. Casual conversationalists repeat, too, less consciously, and perhaps less systematically than do speakers or writers with more self-consciously rhetorical or poetic aims, but remarkably frequently, as Deborah Tannen (1987a, 1987b) and others have shown.

In some situations, repetition of others' words and ways of talking is explicitly encouraged. Psychotherapists' responses to their clients, for example, often include repetitive "mirroring" and "echoing" (Ferrara, 1994). Exact repetition of another's words may even be required, as, for example, in radio talk between pilots and air traffic controllers (Cushing, 1994). Language learners, children or adults, repeat things they hear, and people speaking to language learners (or to people they imagine to be language learners) repeat and expand what the learners say. In short, writers and speakers repeat their own and one anothers' sounds, words, structures, phrases, and meanings, in every context.

Discussion

5.5   Here are five short excerpts from actual or literary conversation. Identify the repetitions in each excerpt. Look for instances of across-speaker and within-speaker repetition, on the levels of sound, words, phrases, and structures. What functions does repetition appear to serve in these examples? Note: It may be helpful to read the transcripts aloud, with each "part" taken by a different speaker.

a.   A conversation (originally in Tojolab'al) between two Tojolab'al (Mexico) women, who are discussing an incident earlier in the day during which a crazy man ran through the village (Brody, 1994).

JUANA SÁNTIS: It's very difficult.
JUANA LOPEZ: It's very difficult.
SÁNTIS: That's how it is when someone gets . . . Who knows how he goes crazy? Or because, or because surely, because he wasn't crazy like a rabid person like they say, because he didn't bite.
LOPEZ: Who knows, mhm.
SÁNTIS: Because the rabid crazy person, like they say, bites.
LOPEZ: He bites.
SÁNTIS: He bites.
LOPEZ: That is what they say about one long ago now from X.

b.   From Tom Stoppard, *Rosencrantz and Guildenstern are Dead* (a play based on Shakespeare's *Hamlet*; the "old man" referred to here is Polonius, the father of Ophelia).

PLAYER: The old man thinks he's in love with his daughter.
ROS: (*appalled*). Good God! We're out of our depth here.
PLAYER: No, no, no – *he* hasn't got a daughter – the old man thinks he's in love with *his* daughter.
ROS: The old man is?
PLAYER: Hamlet, in love with the old man's daughter, the old man thinks.
ROS: Ha! It's beginning to make sense!

c. From Norrick (1994). A conversation about gossip, among friends. Italic
    type is for marked stress, equals signs are for latched speech. The colon
    shows that a syllable was drawn out.

NAN: He'll tell Mary and Mary will tell Mike.
LEE: (laughing) Mary will tell Mike. No, Sue will tell Mike and Mike
       will tell Mary=
SUE: =I'm *not* that kind of *per*son.
NAN: Mary will tell me.
LEE: Ohhh, "I'm not that kind of *per::son.*"

d. From Tannen (1987b). A conversation about dating after a divorce. This
    transcription system represents the way speech is uttered in "intona-
    tion units" (see chapter 3). Accent marks over vowels mark unusually
    stressed syllables; capital letters represent even stronger stress and volume.
    Ellipses represent pause; overlapping speech is represented via vertical
    lines.

D: Then you get bored.
     [[part of conversation left out here]]
P: We:ll, I think I got bored.
D: [laughs]
P: Well I – I mean basically what I feel is
     what I really líke . . . is péople.
     And getting to know them réally wéll.
     And you just CAN'T get to know
     . . . TEN people REALLY WELL.
     You can't dó it.
D: Yeah, right.
     Y' have to there's no
     Yeah there│'s no time.
P: │There's not time.
D: Yeah . . . 'strue.

e. From Neil Simon, *The Good Doctor.*

GENERAL: (*Stands and screams out*) *Out! Out, you idiot! Fool!
              Imbecile! Get out of my sight! I never want to see you
              again. If you ever cross my line of vision I'll have you
              exiled forever . . . WHAT'S YOUR NAME?*
CHERDYAKOV: Ch – Cherdyakov!
              (*It comes out as a sneeze – in the GENERAL's face*)
GENERAL: (*Wiping himself*) You germ spreader! You maggot! You
              insect! You are lower than an insect. You are the second
              cousin to a cockroach! The son-in-law of a bed bug! You
              are the nephew of *a ringworm*! You are nothing, nothing,
              do you hear me? . . . *NOTHING*!

Among the functions of repetition you may have noted in these excerpts are these: Repetition can serve as a form of "backchannelling" in conversation, indicating that interlocutors are listening, understanding, or agreeing. It can signal problems in the conversation and help to repair them. Repeating an utterance can recast it in a humorous or ironic light. Repetition can signal cohesive relationships among utterances or sentences. It can aid in the production of talk, providing speakers who are planning as they go with a reusable template and thus minimizing hesitations and fillers while allowing people to keep the conversational floor as they think of what to say next. Repetition can create rapport, the feeling of harmony among interlocutors which, it can be argued, is one of the primary functions of conversation. On the other hand, repetition can be used to mock another speaker or to show that one is listening only superficially or does not care what the other says (Schnebly, 1994). Paraphrase is apparently a symptom of heightened emotion in excerpt (e), and makes the General's excoriation of Cherdyakov harsher by making it longer. One might say that repetition simply calls attention to the need for implicature – the need to figure out what the extra meaning is – and that its potential functions are thus almost limitless (Merritt, 1994; Johnstone, 1994).

Repetition can serve specialized functions that vary from culture to culture. For example, Joseph Grimes (1972) describes how repetitive "overlays" structure narrative in a number of non-European languages. This story, told by a speaker of New Guinea Pidgin, describes the people's first encounter with Europeans. The story begins with these four clauses:

1   *bipó ol tumbúna i stap nau*
    Once upon a time the forebears lived.

2   *Masta súts i kam núpela*
    Mr. Schutz arrived for the first time,

3   *na ol i – kirap*
    and they became curious,

4   *na ol i ting – támbaran.*
    and they thought him to be an ancestral spirit.

Then the reference jumps back in time to the beginning, as another "plane" is laid over the first. The same ideas are covered again, but in greater detail. Here are the lines on the new overlay that correspond to lines (1) and (2) of the story:

5   *yes – bipó ol tumbúna bilong me, ól mán bilong nóbonob; táim – ól i lúkim núpela – wáitskin. ól kámap long plés bilong ól.*
    Yes: formerly when my forebears, the men of Nobonob, saw the new white man, they came up to their village.

6   *na long díspela taim – am másta súts. i kam núpela.*
    And around this time came Mr. Schutz for the first time.

7   *i kám misin bilong ól.*
    He came on a mission to them.

Although proverbs, ritual greetings, insults, and other formulas play somewhat different roles from society to society (Coulmas, 1981), the use of
formulaic, prepatterned bits of speech is universal.

Discussion

5.6   Over the course of a day, notice and note down as many greeting episodes
      as you can. How much variation is there among them? What verbal formulas
      are used, and how are the formulas varied? In what sorts of situations do you
      find the most formulaic greetings used, and what sorts of situations seem to
      encourage creativity in greeting talk? If you just listen for greeting words such
      as "hi" or phrases such as "How are you?" you may miss less formulaic kinds
      of greetings. So listen to what happens at the beginnings of conversations, no
      matter what it is.

5.7   How do people in your sociocultural context talk about repetition? When is
      repetition valued and when is it disfavored? What are some of the formulaic,
      often-repeated ways people voice their attitudes about repetition?

Register: Repeated Styles for Repeated Situations

One approach to the study of intertextuality and its effects is the analysis of
"register." A register is usually defined as a set of lexical (vocabulary) and
grammatical features that accompany and help to identify discourse that
occurs in a particular recurrent situation. As Ferguson describes it (1994:
20), "A communication situation that occurs regularly in a society (in terms
of participants, setting, communicative functions, and so forth) will tend
over time to develop identifying markers of language structure and language
use, different from the language of other communication situations." Register
variation contrasts with (but also partly overlaps with) the kinds of variation
that are associated with the social characteristics and identities that people
may orient to and index across situations: variation correlated with gender,
ethnicity, social class, and so on. (Sets of typical linguistic choices that are
correlated with such "social facts" about speakers are often called "dialects"
or "varieties," or, in lay usage, "accents.") Instruction in public speaking or
in writing has often been organized around styles associated with academic
tasks or rhetorical purposes or aims (Kinneavy, 1980). The creativity in
giving a eulogy or writing an essay is in adapting the appropriate style to the
particular current situation.

It is difficult to separate register from style (chapter 4), particularly since the term "style" has been used in many different ways (Eckert and Rickford, 2001). For some sociolinguists, including Labov (1972a), style refers to a speaker's level of self-consciousness, so that, for example, a person's style in talk among peers would be expected to be different from that person's style when reading aloud in front of a stranger. Some students of register might say that style is one aspect of register, since style often refers mainly to choices of vocabulary and grammar, while knowing how to function in a register also includes knowing the ways of interacting and general strategies for interpretation that are characteristic of a situation. Others use the term "style" instead of the term "register" (Crystal and Davy, 1969).

One example of a register is legal language, sometimes referred to as "legalese," which can be described as a set of words, structural choices, and interactional patterns that tend to occur in discourse in legal situations (Mellinkoff, 1963; Bowers, 1989; Bhatia, 1993; Conley and O'Barr, 1998). Traditional legal English can be characterized lexically and syntactically. In the traditional legal lexicon, the preference is sometimes for longer expressions over some shorter ones. (This may have its roots in the traditions of oral law, according to which it was thought that an expression would be easier to understand if each part of its meaning was expressed in a separate word.) So, for example, *at this present moment in time* is used for *now, during such time as* for *while, in that place* for *there*, and *in the event that* for *if*. Legal "binomial" expressions involve the use of two terms linked with *and* for a single meaning. (This may be a result of the need, after the Norman conquest of England, to show how French and English legal terms were related.) Familiar legal binomials include *ways and means, null and void, without let or hindrance, annul and set aside*, and *last will and testament*. Legal vocabulary is also sometimes characterized by the use of words that are archaic in everyday usage, such as *aforesaid, forthwith, heretofore*, and *whereby*.

Legal syntax sometimes seems needlessly complex, and this has given rise to "plain language" efforts in the legal profession and in government. Such efforts have had mixed success. This may be because part of the reason for the complexity is the underlying linguistic ideology (see chapter 2) of the legal profession, which holds that if one is careful enough it is possible to remove all ambiguity from a document, or to make it ambiguous in exactly and only the ways the writer wants it to be ambiguous. A particularly egregious-looking example is the following (Crystal, 1987: 386). (Try putting this into "plain English" and see whether you have to make choices about meaning which the authors may have intended to avoid.)

MONEYS to be invested under this Settlement may be invested or otherwise applied in the security of or in the purchase or acquisition of real or personal property (including the purchase or acquisition of chattels and the effecting or maintaining of policies of insurance or assurance) rights or interests of whatsoever kind and wheresoever situate including any stocks funds shares securities or other investments of whatsoever nature and wheresoever whether producing income or not and whether involving liability or not or on personal loan with or without interest and with or without security to any person (other than the Settlor or any Spouse of the Settlor) anywhere in the world including loans to any member of the Specified Class and the Trustees may grant indulgence to or release any debtor (other than as aforesaid) with or without consideration and may enter into profit sharing agreements and give and take options with or without consideration and accept substitution of any security . . .

Some features of a register may serve to make communication faster and easier. Professional jargon, for example, may provide shortcuts to meanings that are needed often in the situation, as, for example, the courtroom exchange "Objection" / "Sustained" does. But as outsiders to the situation know, features of a register can serve to index the use of the register even to a person who does not understand them. Legal language sounds like legal language, in fact, precisely because of some of the features that make it difficult for laypeople to understand. Speaking or writing in a legal-sounding way can help identify a person as an insider to the situation and help create rapport with other insiders, it can help define the situation as a legal one, and it can serve as a move to exclude from participation people who do not control the register, or to put them in the weaker position. Using the linguistic features of a register can be a way of bringing the situation associated with the register into interactional play. For example, a register shift can function as a cue that the initial, friendly-chat phrase of a student–teacher meeting is over and the "official business" of the meeting is beginning. For another example, register shifts often cue beginnings, endings, and internal parts in religious rituals: the beginning of the service, the end of the sermon, and so on.

In order to describe a register, it is necessary to describe the *situation* in which the register occurs and the *linguistic features* of the register. Both of these jobs are complex. Describing a recurrent situation is difficult because it is difficult to know what to describe, and the list of potentially relevant facts about situations can be long. Figure 5.1 presents one such list.

The biggest obstacle to describing recurrent situations is the fact that exactly the same situations never actually recur. (The feeling that a situation is an exact recurrence of an earlier one is what we call "déjà vu," and it is, fortunately, not common.) How much does a situation have to change before it becomes, for the purposes of describing a register, a different situation? For example, is a course with ten students in it the same situation as a course with twenty? Is a Jewish wedding the same situation as a Christian wedding? Using Douglas Biber's list of relevant features (figure 5.1) to help answer these questions would be useful: in each case, the two

I	Communicative characteristics of participants	(a)	Addresser(s): Is there one or more? Is the addresser an institution (such as a university, a government, a corporate body)?
		(b)	Addressee(s): Is the discourse addressed to self or other(s)? Is there one or more than one addressee, or is the number not relevant for defining the situation?
		(c)	Is there an audience in addition to the specified addressee(s)?
II	Relations between addresser and addressee	(a)	Relative status and power: Do addresser(s) or addressee(s) have higher status? More power?
		(b)	Extent of shared knowledge: Do addresser(s) and/or addressee(s) have more specialist knowledge about the topic? More personal, experiential knowledge?
		(c)	Interactiveness: How much do addresser(s) and addressee(s) interact?
		(d)	Personal relationship(s): Do the participants like, respect, fear each other? Are they kin, friends, enemies, colleagues, etc.?
III	Setting	(a)	Characteristics of the place of communication: Is it public or private? In what domain is it: business or workplace, education, governmental or legal, religious, etc.? What, if any, is the role of other media besides, or in addition to, face-to-face interaction? For example, is the communication filmed?
		(b)	Extent to which place is shared: Are participants in the same place? Is the place familiar?
		(c)	Extent to which time is shared: Are participants interacting synchronously, or are they at a temporal remove?
IV	Channel	(a)	Mode: Is the primary channel of communication written, spoken, signed, mixed?
		(b)	Permanence: Is the communication recorded or transient?
		(c)	Medium: If the communication is recorded, is it taped, transcribed, printed, recorded electronically, etc.? If it is transient, is it face-to-face or over the phone, radio, etc.?
		(d)	Is the communication embedded in a larger text from a different register?
V	Relation of participants to the text	(a)	What are the production circumstances for the addresser(s)? Is the text revised or edited? Scripted or planned online?
		(b)	What are comprehension circumstances for the addressee(s)? Does comprehension have to occur online, in real time? If not, what are the time constraints?
		(c)	How do addresser(s) and addressee(s) evaluate the text? Do they evaluate what is said or written in the situation in terms of its importance, value, beauty, popularity, etc., or some combination?
		(d)	What is the addresser(s)' attitudinal stance toward the text? Are they emotionally involved in the communication? Do they feel reverent, excited, bored, etc.?
		(e)	How do the addressee(s) stand with regard to the text? Are they deciding whether or not to believe it? Whether or not to doubt it?
VI	Purposes, intents, and goals	(a)	Factuality: Is the communication in this situation supposed (by the participants) to be based on fact, or is it supposed to be imaginative, speculative, or some mixture?
		(b)	Purposes: Is the purpose of the situation, and the communication in it, to buy or sell things? To persuade? To transfer information? To entertain? To express feelings? Some combination?
VII	Topic	(a)	What is the level of discussion: general, specialized, popular?
		(b)	What is/are the specific topic(s): finance, science, religion, politics, etc.?

Figure 5.1 Situational parameters of variation
Source: Adapted from Biber (1994: 40–1)

candidates would turn out to have more situational features in common than not. But how similar do two occasions have to be in order to count as the same situation, given the fact that every occasion on which people use language is different from every other occasion?

Some situations – ones that are highly institutionalized, and in which standards for behavior are highly codified – are relatively resistant to change. The law is one such situation, and legal register is relatively durable and slow to change. Other registers are more fluid, emerging as needed out of situations that may be repeated just often enough for people to start thinking of them as a category of their own, then fading as the situation stops arising. In the long run, cultural categories of situations and the registers that go with them are always in the process of evolution. Correspondence between distant friends, to give just one example, has evolved from letter-writing to telephoning and electronic communication, and the ways in which distant friends communicate have changed in some respects but stayed the same in other respects.

Describing the linguistic features of a register involves noting what words and structures (if any) occur *only* in the situation in question, as well as noting words and structures that occur frequently in the situation, and ones that tend to occur together (or "co-occur") there. This can be done by starting with a list of linguistic features to check for, or it can be done by looking carefully and repeatedly at examples of a register until recurrent features become salient. The disadvantage of starting with a list means that you are relatively unlikely to notice anything that *is not* on the list, but starting without a list means possibly not noticing some of the things that *would have* been part of a good coding scheme.

Discussion

5.8   Here is part of a will (with the testator's name removed and some other details altered). Some of the features of the language of such documents are these (Finegan, 1982):

- absence of second person pronouns (*you*, etc.);
- absence of imperatives, interrogatives; reliance on declarative sentences;
- frequent use of conditional syntax;
- long sentences.

Which of these features characterize this will? What other features differentiate this register from styles of formal writing associated with other situations? What features reflect particular aspects of the situation in which wills are produced and the situation in which they are put to use? In what ways, if any, could the style of this will be simplified without changing its meaning and force?

Last Will and Testament
of

_____

THE STATE OF TEXAS:
COUNTY OF HARRISON:

I, _____, residing and being domiciled in Harrison County, Texas, now revoke all previous wills and codicils made by me and make, publish and declare this to be my last Will.

I.
Appointment of Executors

1.1 I appoint my husband, _____, hereinafter referred to as "my husband," as Independent Executor of my estate. If my husband should fail or cease to serve as Executor, for any reason, then I appoint my daughter, _____, as Independent Executor of my estate. If my daughter should fail or cease to serve as Executor, for any reason, then I appoint FIRST NATIONAL BANK of Bluebonnet, Texas as Independent Executor of my estate. My Independent Executor, whether original, substitute or successor, individual or corporate, is herein called "my Executor."

1.2 Compensation of Executors. My individual Executor may receive compensation for their services in handling my estate. Any corporate Executor shall receive such compensation for its services as Executor as is then currently being charged for like services by banks in Harrison County, Texas.

1.3 No Executor shall be required to furnish bond or any other security.

1.4 Administrative Powers. From the date of granting of letters until my estate has been entirely distributed, my Executor shall have all rights and powers and be subject to all duties and responsibilities imposed on a Trustee under the provisions of the Texas Trust Act, Art. 7425b., V.A.C.S., as it now exists and as later amended, in addition to all other powers given to independent executors by the laws of Texas and by this instrument. In addition to, not in limitation of the above, I give to my Executor all the powers enumerated in Annex "A" which is attached to and made a part of this Will by reference. I further specifically authorize my Executor to sell all or any part of my estate upon such terms and conditions as my Executor may deem proper, and to partition all or any property of my estate among the beneficiaries in such manner as shall be deemed fair and equitable by my Executor.

5.9 Describe a situational register with which you are familiar. This will require, first, describing the situation (you may want to use the list of parameters in figure 5.1), and, secondly, describing the features of lexicon and grammar that occur in and help to define this situation.

5.10 Here are some excerpts from a parody of the register characteristic of some technical documentation. What features of technical-documentation register are adapted, exaggerated, and played on in this parody? Be specific, here as in every exercise: describe the linguistic features of the text in detail.

CAT v.6.1b: Completely Autonomous Tester, Manufactured by MOMCAT. User Installation and Maintenance Documentation:

Features:
User Friendly
Low Power CPU
Self-Portable Operation
Dual Video and Audio Input
Audio Output
Auto Search Capability for Input Data
Auto Search for Output Bin
Auto Learn Program in ROM
Instant Transition (Energy Saving Standby Mode When Not In Use)
Wide Operating Temperature Range
Mouse Driven
Self Cleaning

Transportation:
A suitable transportation case should be used for transportation to the operating site. Failure to properly ship a CAT unit may result in loss or damage to the unit and serious injury to the user.

Installation Procedures:
Upon receiving the CAT unit, the user should examine the unit to verify that all I/O channels are free of debris and operational. The user should look for minor bugs in or on the system. Bugs are indicative of the MOMCAT production environment. The user may manually remove any bugs. Bring the CAT to operation in an environment temperature of 20degC (+/– 3deg tolerance). Use a quiet room with the primary user(s) present. Open the transportation case and let the CAT unit autoexit. Initialize the self learn-ing program by displaying the output bin. The next step consists in dis-playing the input bins. These should contain H_2O (liquid state, room temperature, 99% purity) and dry energy pellets. Immediately afterwards, you must display the output bin.

If the user already has a CAT unit successfully installed, it may be possible to download the BASIC routines to the new CAT. For the first day or two, the CAT will stay in the self learning mode. When this learn buffer overflows, the CAT will autoswitch to sleep mode. This is normal. The MMU system will store the new information to permanent memory. After 72 hours, the CAT will be interacting with the operating environment. The unit may often be placed in direct sunlight. If all basic environment requirements are satisfied, the CAT system will produce a slight hum. This is normal.

A new CAT should not exit the primary site facility. Full portability comes after extensive burn in. Some users never let the CAT unit autoexit the site. The advantages are longer unit life and fewer bugs. Contact with pirate CAT units may lead to unplanned BATCH iteration. If allowed to exit, some CAT units may try to port across a street. Fatal errors may happen. These errors are never recoverable. Such situations are not covered by warranties.

Applications:
MOUSE is a killer app. This is pre-installed. Many owners use their system for game playing. Some of the better CAT games are:
CACHE
The CAT will CACHE a data code. Similar to the K9 unit game, but the object code must be smaller.
STRING
The CAT attempts to parse a data string.

Caution:
CAT systems are normally user friendly. However, in certain documented situations, a CAT may pose a danger to the user. Repeated jamming or obstruction of air ports may lead to a CAT deploying its auto defense mechanisms. Do not strike a CAT. Twin D-shaped five-pin connectors have an average seek rate of 3 milliseconds. Children should not poke anything into a CAT's I/O ports. CAT may BYTE.

5.11   With what registers do you associate noun strings like these? Are there functional reasons in the situations in question for compressing information in this way? In other words, does this aspect of the register serve a communicative purpose, or does it simply serve to differentiate insiders from outsiders in the situations in question?

- The FEMA-sponsored host area crisis shelter production planning work book
- Enterprise Computing In Higher Education conference series overview
- mission critical Macintosh systems integration challenges
- the November and December timeframes
- the virtually integrated technology architecture lifecycle
- desktop integration, database access, and front-ending
- client/server application development tools
- liquid oxygen liquid hydrogen rocket powered single stage to orbit reversible boost system

Genre: Recurrent Forms, Recurrent Actions

The French word "genre" means "kind." In English, the word has a long tradition of use in literary studies, where it has been used to refer to conventional types of literary texts categorized by how they represent the world: the epic (primarily descriptive), the dramatic (primarily mimetic, or imitative), and the lyric (mixed, but also self-expressive). As long as literary scholars in the West focused on the Western literary tradition, and as long as the set of acceptable literary forms codified in Classical times remained relatively stable, this classification system continued to work, acting as a sort of contract between authors and their readers about what to expect and how to interpret it.

This notion of genre works much less well for other traditions of discourse, however. Linguists and anthropologists working with Native American discourse, for example, have had to remind themselves that genre distinctions are culturally relative. After years of assuming that Native American texts collected in the early part of the twentieth century were prose narratives, people like Dell Hymes (1981b) and William Bright (1981) began to notice that the prose-like way in which the tales and myths had been transcribed obscured their many poetic qualities: rhythm, divisions into lines and stanzas, and so on. Bright suggested that perhaps in some settings all discourse is "poetic," or perhaps none is. While there are formal features (repetition, parallelism, special vocabulary, special ways of framing and keying) that seem to recur across cultures in talk that is "performed" (Bauman, 1977; Bauman and Briggs, 1990) – discourse, that is, meant to focus attention on its linguistic form and/or to be aesthetically appealing – formal features are not enough to determine what sort of discourse will count as what genre in its particular context.

Discourse analysts interested in how writing and other communicative skills are acquired and deployed in professional discourse communities have used the idea of genre in discussing the categories of texts which a person has to learn to recognize, reproduce, and manipulate in order to become a competent member of a particular community. For example, learning to function as a college undergraduate involves learning the conventions of various academic genres such as the research paper, and graduate students in the US have to be able to control and manipulate genres such as the conference paper abstract, the academic curriculum vitae, and so on (Berkenkotter, Huckin, and Ackerman, 1988). Learning a trade or a profession requires coming to control not just a body of facts but a set of text-building skills, embedded in recurrent types of interactions. The relatively fixed text-types that are associated with particular recurrent purposes for writing of speech in a community are referred to as genres. In some uses of the term, the skills, understandings, or activities through which these text-types are produced are called "genre knowledge" (Berkenkotter and Huckin, 1995).

Analyses of the forms of texts can be and have been used to categorize texts (for example, in the archiving of collections of folklore) and to teach people to produce them (for example, in writing classes). A genre is usually defined, by people who are interested in categorizing discourse types, as a conventionalized verbal form associated with a conventionalized purpose or occasion. The large databases of texts and transcribed conversations with which corpus linguists work are sometimes divided into genre categories as a first step for analysts: formal letters, academic prose, casual conversations, legal texts, and so on.

Recurrent text-types mark recurrent social occasions, but they also categorize occasions. Thank-you notes, for example, are conventionally required in certain situations in which gratitude has to be expressed, but the use of a thank-you note can retrospectively redefine a situation as one in which gratitude was relevant, or highlight that aspect of a situation which could also be categorized in some other way. So if a student writes a thank-you note to a teacher who has written her a letter of recommendation, she retrospectively defines the writing of the recommendation as a special favor rather than as a routine part of the teacher's job. As people draw on genre knowledge they perpetuate it, producing new texts that others will put into the genre group. But they also transform it, since each use of a prior model is by necessity a creative use.

In other research, analyses of how genres function in social life are being used to understand and critique how "typification" (Miller, 1984) works in the representation and maintenance of ideology (linguistic and otherwise), in language socialization, in the process of language change, and in communication in institutions. In some situations, ideological and communicative pressures push discourse forms ("genres") and discursive practices ("genre knowledge") in the direction of fixity. In these situations (which may, for example, arise when organizations need to legitimize themselves by acting like similar organizations, or when political pressures lead states to feel they need standardized systems of education and standard procedures for evaluating their success), genres may become relatively standardized and inflexible. Relatively "stable" genres have clearly delineated boundaries and a characteristic, consistent constellation of participants; they are often written rather than oral, and they tend to have names. Fairly stable literary genres include the haiku and the sonnet, each of which has an almost inflexible format and, in the case of haiku, a fairly inflexible topic (enigmas suggested by observations of nature). One fairly stable genre in academic discourse is the scientific research paper (Bazerman, 1988; Swales, 1990; Berkenkotter and Huckin, 1995; Tracy, 1988). A person coming to know and to be able to function in the "lifeworld" of academia – such as a graduate student – could learn a lot about this genre by analyzing sample texts, or by relying on others' analyses of them, and in fact the teaching of academic research genres is a large part of many programs in English for Special Purposes.

But such a person would have to acquire other aspects of genre knowledge in the process of interacting with other academic researchers as they use and evaluate research papers, in the process of learning what counts as new and interesting in research, and in the process of coming to know when creativity is seen, by those in power, as appropriate, and when formulaicity

The terms "register" and "genre" describe similar generalizations about discourse, and not all discourse analysts use these terms in the same ways. Since many people study either genre or register, not both, they have not always had to keep them completely clearly separated. Here is a comparison of what is generally meant by each.

REGISTER	GENRE
Definition: a variety of language (or "style") associated with a recurrent communicative situation or set of communicative roles.	Definition: a recurrent verbal form (or "text-type") associated with a recurrent purpose or activity; "genre knowledge" is the procedural competence required to produce a form and use it.
Examples: testamentary language, scientific discourse, teacher-talk, medical discourse.	Examples: wills, research reports, essay questions, medical consultations.
To describe a register, you need to describe:	To describe a genre, you need to describe:
1 the situation which calls for the register; 2 the linguistic features that constitute the register.	1 the form of texts of the genre; 2 the contexts in which the genre is relevant, in which participants may use the genre to organize, explain what they are doing and why; 3 the activities by which people create and share the knowledge required to produce texts in the genre; 4 how the genre works in interaction: how people draw on the generic conventions in creating new text, how they use genre to categorize situations, how the genre serves to maintain the status quo and/or make change possible.

Figure 5.2   Comparing register and genre

is considered appropriate. Because researchers balance conventionality and creativity, and because the situations in which they present their work vary from time to time and evolve over time, the prototypical academic research paper is quite different now than it was 200 or even 50 years ago. Other form–situation pairings are much less stable. Situation-specific ways of speaking or writing may emerge experimentally in a new organization, for example, as people figure out on the spot what will work and what will not, and there may be debate, overt or covert, about which discursive procedures should be named, fixed, identified as "the way we do things here." As you know if you have ever run an organization, the familiar, relatively fixed genres associated with organizations (bylaws, written agendas, minutes of meetings) can function as procedural scaffolds for action, but they can also lead to inflexibility. Relatively flexible practices of discourse can, on the other hand, take longer and sometimes seem chaotic.

Discussion

5.12   Here are several notes from a young boy, the first written when he was 6 and in his first year of school, the last when he was 12. The person to whom these notes were sent is the boy's aunt, who had sent him a gift on each occasion. For comparison, the boy's notes are followed by two notes written by adults. There is, of course, a name in English for the genre these notes represent: the "thank-you note." Describe the prototypical form of such notes. Are Peter's thank-you notes at each age relatively close to the prototype or relatively creative? How does "genre knowledge" enter into the process by which such notes get written? How does this genre reflect the culture's ways of categorizing people and situations – such that Peter gets socialized into a set of ideas about the world as he learns to write, in this genre and others?

a.   Peter, age 6. Written on a special card meant for children's thank-you notes, featuring a Superman-like "birthday man" holding a gift, and the words THANK-YOU.

> DEAR, [printed on card]
> Aunt ane [= Anne]
> Thank You
> for the stamps
> I will use
> them for
> my cousins.
>   party.
> FROM, [printed on card] Petey

b.   Peter, age 7. Written on a regular post-card.

> Dear, aunt Anne
>   thank you
> for the Make a
> comic book kit. I
> made a comic
> bbok with it.
>
> your neghuge [= nephew],
>
> Peter

c. Peter, age 9. Written on a post-card, on the lines meant for the address (so that he ran out of space).

> Dear Aunt Anne,
>   Thank you for
> the money. I bought a G.I.
> Joe with it.

d. Peter, age 11. Written on the inside of a note-card.

> Petey H.
> 9-20-99
>
> Dear A.H.,
>   Thank you for the money. I got a Memory card. (which is a Memory bank that is able to pluge into my Playstation. Which is a computer used to play games on the T.V.
>
> Love,
> Petey H____

e. Peter, age 12. Written on the inside of a note-card.

> Dear Anne,
>   Thank you for the money. I'm going to use it for a game called Age of the Empires II It's about the Dark ages, all over the world, like Arabia, France, Central America, Mongolia, Scotland, etc. It's really awsome. Contact me soon.
>
> Petey

f. From an adult.

> Dear Anne,
>   Happy New Year!
>   We are enjoying the new napkins with elephants – very dramatic. They go well with
>   book looks good – the boys went back to school yesterday so I should get some time to delve into fiction –
>
> Thanks! Love, Carole

g. From an adult (the first paragraph of a longer note).

> Dear Anne –
>   How often can one expect a canteloupe teapot to arrive, unannounced, during Indian Summer? The pot is an exquisite example of what you remembered I like – dishes with the look of fruits, veggies, + other natural objects. The whole family has been admiring it. Thanks for thinking of me. It's an early and completely special birthday gift.

5.13 How does knowledge about generic situations and generic form and content enter into how we create and interpret parody?

5.14 In a study of 200 "death announcements" in Jordanian newspapers, Mohammed N. Al-Ali (2005) has found these obituaries to have nine structural parts:

1 opening (consisting of two verses from the Qur'an);
2 heading (usually includes the word *naʕiy* 'obituary');
3 announcement of the death;
4 identification of the deceased;
5 specification of surviving relatives;
6 specification of date, age, place, and cause of death;
7 description of funeral and burial arrangements;
8 description of arrangements for receiving condolences (or congratulations, in the case of a "martyr"'s death);
9 closing, usually a particular verse from the Qur'an.

Assemble a corpus of 10 or 20 obituaries from your local newspaper or an online source, and perform an analysis similar to Al-Ali's. How do your obituaries differ from the Jordanian ones and in what respects are they the same?

5.15 How do people acquire "genre knowledge" in new situations, or situations whose details are new each time? For example, how do students figure out, over the course of a semester, what the instructor's expectations for written assignments are? How do newcomers to blogging or instant messaging learn how to do it, what to say, how to interact? Describe a communicative situation or constellation of discourse participants and purposes that was new to you and discuss the process by which you learned how to participate in it. What sorts of things do people say and do in a new situation to try to fix genres and genre activities? What factors contribute to genre flexibility?

Frames, Plots, and Coherence

As we have seen, discourse and humans' lifeworlds constrain each other: discourse is about the world as we experience it, and discourse helps to create our experiential world (chapter 2). This can be seen not only on the level of choices of words and structures that make some worlds easier to imagine than others, but also on the level of the "frames" and "plots" that structure our sense of what is going on now or what happened in the past.

The idea of frames was proposed by cognitive psychologists interested in modeling what is involved in knowing a concept (Bartlett, 1932; Barsalou, 1992). A frame, in this view, is a complex cognitive structure that links together the attributes of a concept in a web of relationships. Activating one node in this web might activate others, so that DRIVER might evoke the frame for CAR, or vice versa. This idea was taken up in linguistics in the theory of frame semantics (Fillmore, 1982; Fillmore and Atkins, 1992). According to frame semantics, every word and grammatical structure is associated with a frame which "relates the elements and entities associated with a particular culturally embedded scene from human experience" (Evans and Green, 2006: 222), and words and structures can only be interpreted in the context of the frame they evoke. Differences among words that refer to the same thing, like *coast* and *shore*, may have to do with the fact that they are associated with different semantic frames: at least for some speakers of English, *coast* is connected to the LAND DWELLING frame while *shore* is connected to the SEAFARING frame (p. 229).

Sociologist Erving Goffman (Goffman 1986[1974]) used the concept of frames, or "frameworks," to describe the "schemata of interpretation" we use as we decide, from moment to moment in daily life, what is going on. For example, picking up a small statue and moving it would be a different event if the relevant frame had to do with playing chess (making a move with a game piece) than if it had to do with curating a museum exhibition (rearranging works of art). Goffman focused attention on moments when frames are "keyed" so that the relevant interpretive schema changes. For example, everyday fighting is keyed in a staged, scripted fight, and theatergoers in the know about the culturally relevant key and frame do not leap from their seats to try to separate actors who are "fighting" in this keyed sense.

The need for framing shapes discourse in both small- and large-scale ways. In a study of how people retold an experimental film they had seen (Chafe, 1980b), Du Bois (1980) explored the uses of definite (*the*, *my*) versus indefinite (*a*, *some*) determiners with nouns. Du Bois observed that once a particular frame had been evoked in a retelling, objects associated with the frame were often treated as if they were already familiar and so marked with definite forms. For example, once a teller had said that there was a boy riding a bicycle in the film, then elements of the BICYCLE and HUMAN frames were treated as known: "*the* handlebars," "*the* fender," "*his* leg." Studying the same film, Tannen (1980) found that American retellers often started with an observation about the film ("The movie opened up on this . . . nice scene"), whereas Greek retellers more often began describing the film's content ("eh . . . (There) was a– . . . a worker"). This suggests that the Americans framed the experimental task as a film critique, whereas the Greeks framed it as description.

Like frames, plots are semantic scaffolds for creating worlds in discourse. They are prior texts for histories, lives, and personal identities (see chapter 4), and other narratives. In the Western tradition, Aristotle was among the first to describe conventional ways in which experience is assimilated to talk. Aristotle's treatise on *Poetics* (1958) includes a detailed characterization of the conventions by which the tragic drama of classical Greece was structured. (The *Poetics* is prescriptive in tone, as if it were a list of rules for potential playwrights, but it is based on the kind of empirical descriptive analysis that was characteristic of Aristotle's approach to philosophy.) Aristotle shows that a common semantic structure underlies the plots of various tragic dramas, a common way of making the play, and, through the play, reality, seem coherent. Here are some excerpts from Aristotle's characterization of tragic plots:

- "Whole" means having a beginning, a middle, and an end. . . . To construct a good plot, one must neither begin nor end haphazardly but make a proper use of these three parts. (p. 16)
- Beauty is a matter of size and order . . . so plots must have a length which can be easily remembered. (p. 16)
- Since [the plot] is the imitation of an action, this must be one action and the whole of it; the various incidents must be so constructed that, if any part is displaced or deleted, the whole plot is disturbed and dislocated. (p. 17)
- The object of the imitation is not only a complete action but such things as stir up pity and fear, and this is best achieved when events are unexpectedly interconnected. (p. 20)
- A good [tragedic] plot must consist of a single and not, as some people say, of a double story; the change of fortune should not be from misfortune to prosperity but, on the contrary, from prosperity to misfortune. This change should not be caused by outright wickedness but by a serious flaw in a character . . . (p. 24)

Though certainly not identical in all ways, a contemporary TV drama produced in the US probably has elements of plot described by Aristotle, or it may acknowledge them via parody. In fact, a software package called StoryCraft uses traditional plots to help people create short stories, novels, and screenplays. According to the web page describing one version of the software, "StoryCraftPro writer's software identifies 18 basic patterns of stories that all the great myths and literary classics fall under, and gives you an instant outline of your story, based upon your choice of one of those patterns, called Story Types" (http://www.writerspage.com/pro.htm). To people repeatedly exposed to narrative "Story Types," such as the ones StoryCraft employs, it may eventually come to seem necessary that stories involve reversals of fortune (something bad or disruptive happens but things work out in the end, or something good happens but its outcome is bad), that there is suspense leading to a resolution, or that starting in the middle of the action and flashing back and forward is marked compared to starting at the beginning and moving to the end. As a result, we may not notice that life often fails to fit such plots neatly. We use plots to fit experience (which is necessarily chaotic) into coherent ways of understanding the world, so how the plots work comes to seem natural, as if it were how the world works. In writing classes as in less formal situations, we tell others to "begin at the beginning" of a story, as if human experience actually came pre-packaged in distinguishable units with beginnings and endings. When people raise topics that do not fit the plot of the ongoing activity, we ask "What does that have to do with it?" knowing, usually without thinking about it, the plot being referred to as "it."

There are conventional ways of showing where one is in a plot. As Longacre (1976: 217–28) points out, climactic moments (Longacre calls them "peaks") in Shakespeare's plays are often moments when all the characters are on stage at once. Linguistic ways of highlighting peaks can include tense shifts, a shift from reported to constructed ("direct") dialogue, a shift to shorter units of talk, or a change in point of view. In the kinds of "fully-developed" personal experience narratives described by William Labov, rising tension in a story's plot is often accompanied by multiple evaluative devices (see chapter 3).

Expected plots vary widely from society to society. As A. L. Becker (1979) shows, for example, the plot of a Javanese shadow theater play, or *wayang*, is built around coincidence rather than around chronologically and causally developing tension and its resolution, as in Western plots. In a *wayang* plot there are numerous time lines, running simultaneously in the play but at different speeds. Each set of actions takes place in a different world, at a different historical period, with different characters speaking different languages. In one, demons in the cosmic void speak in archaic Javanese; in another, gods and goddesses speak Sanskrit; another story involves traditional Javanese heroes; in another, contemporary Javanese characters comment on the other stories in jokey colloquial language. The stories come together spatially, when the characters from different worlds find themselves in the same place at the same moment in the play. These symbolic intersections of the various worlds that are relevant to Javanese life are the key to the play's meaning.

The organizing principles provided by plot are far broader than just constraints on a single genre (such as tragedy or *wayang*), however. Because they are constraints on the way the world is made to seem meaningful and coherent, they are reflected in linguistic preferences, in music and visual art, and in other symbol systems. For example, as Judith Becker (1979) shows, the Javanese calendar system and Javanese music also operate on the basis of cycles and coincidence. Likewise, it can be argued that Western calendars and music reflect the same basic linear, causal coherence principles as Western story plots do.

Discussion

5.16   What are some of the ways in which English and other Indo-European languages might be said to fit with the kind of plot Aristotle described? Think, for example, about the complexity of Indo-European systems of tense compared with those of other language groups, or about the ways in which chronology and causality can be referenced with the same expressions (such as *then, it follows, since*). Thinking back to the Sapir-Whorf hypothesis discussed in chapter 2, discuss whether you think preferences for one plot type or another arise from the linguistic resources available to a group of people, or whether the linguistic resources are a result of the plots they are used for.

5.17 How does the Judeo-Christian origin story presented in the biblical book of Genesis mirror the preference for stories that involve causally-related, chronological series of events leading to a climactic point? Are there also indications in the Old Testament of coherence systems based more on cycles? (Think, for example, about cycles of feast and famine.) Do cyclical ways of thinking and telling sometimes compete with climactic ones in the contemporary world? (Think, for example, about the cyclical "plot" that makes an ecological perspective on the world make sense versus the linear, progressive "plot" of capitalism.)

5.18 Do the life stories with which you are familiar (biographies, oral histories, everyday anecdotes about the past) have recurrent plots? Do the stories people tell about their own and others' lives have high points, for example? Are there reversals of fortune? What is the plot of a "good" life, as reflected, for example, in funeral eulogies or obituaries? Are there conventional plots for "unconventional" lives? Are there standard ways of accounting for why some things happen and others do not? What is the expected role of fate in a human life, for example, for you and people like you?

5.19 Figure 5.3 (see p. 192) characterizes the plots of 58 spontaneous narratives of personal experience collected in Fort Wayne, Indiana (Johnstone, 1990). All the plots involve some sort of conflict or disturbance and its resolution, but the conflict or disturbance can get started in various ways (the protagonist can go looking for trouble, or the trouble can be presented as something that just happened), and the outcome can be successful or unsuccessful. Which of these plot types, if any, would you associate with stories men tell versus stories women tell? With stories children tell versus stories adults tell? With other social and cultural differences in role or identity?

Summary

The form and function of any text is partly the result of what other texts are like and what their functions are. One commonly used term for the relationships between texts and prior texts is "intertextuality." Intertextuality refers to the ways in which all discourse draws on familiar formats and texts, previously used styles and ways of acting, and familiar plots. This chapter introduced several ways of analyzing intertexuality. We began by focusing on the smallest bits of repetition in discourse, the ways in which speakers and writers borrow, adapt, and reuse sounds, words, phrases, and structures,

	Danger is courted	Danger is encountered
Danger is averted	• Social danger (embarrassment) courted; averted through luck: The protagonist pays respects to the wrong corpse at a funeral home, having neglected to ask directions, but fortunately nobody notices the faux pas. • Social danger (failure) courted; averted through skill: The protagonist enters dairy judging competitions at progressively higher levels, and keeps winning them. • Physical danger is courted; averted through verbal skill: The protagonist almost gets into a fight, but says just the right clever thing to defuse the situation.	• Physical danger encountered; averted through luck: The protagonist's car skids off the road in the snow, but fortunately protagonist and passenger are not hurt and damage to the car is minor. • Social danger (failure) encountered; averted through skill: The protagonist's car keeps failing to start, but the protagonist figures out what the problem is and solves it. • Epistemological danger (the supernatural) encountered; averted by being explained: The protagonists think they hear spirit voices, but there turns out to be an explanation for the noise.
Danger is not averted	• Social danger (embarrassment) courted and not averted; a lesson is learned: Two young people run through the neighborhood naked, on a dare, and collide with a teenager by accident; they are embarrassed and chastened. • Physical danger courted and not averted: The protagonist, who has misbehaved, tries to hide from the maid, who is in pursuit, but is caught. The protagonist learns a lesson about character.	Stories in this category are rare in this particular corpus. People seem to be willing to tell stories about failures for which they set themselves up, but not about failures that seemed fated. • Social danger (failure) encountered and not averted; a lesson is learned: The protagonist talks about setting up an insurance adjustment company after seeing several truck accidents, but never does, because it just wasn't in the cards.

Figure 5.3 Plot types in Fort Wayne stories

from their own previous talk and writing and from others'. We then turned to the analysis of register, repeated styles of lexicon and grammar associated with recurrent situations such as the courtroom, the classroom, or the computer lab. Genre analysis, which we touched on next, has to do with the study of how recurrent purposes for discourse result in recurrent speech acts and actions and recurrent verbal forms. Scientific journal articles, for example, are embedded in a body of expertise about writing format and style, about the right way of balancing familiar facts with new, interesting claims, about the editorial and publication process, about how to interpret the order of multiple authors' names, and so on. On an even less conscious level, groups of people who live in similar worlds of experience and talk may interpret the world in terms of similar frames and plots, similar ways of adapting the inchoate flow of experience to shared images of what makes the world coherent. Experiences which cannot be adapted to familiar frameworks may seem deeply disruptive.

All creativity has to be embedded in the familiar. Even the most boundary-bending performances – Dada nonsense-syllable poetry, a musical composition consisting of silence, a monochrome black painting, a science-fiction alien world – work only insofar as they arise out of and comment on more familiar forms of talk, music, art, or life, and, like writers and conversationalists, composers and visual artists sometimes borrow quite consciously from prior works. (In music, this is sometimes referred to as "sampling.") Complete repetition is impossible: even a rote recitation of a familiar prayer or greeting formula takes place in a new context each time. Complete creativity is also impossible, because there would be no way to interpret it, thus no way to recognize it as creative.

The idea of intertextuality raises some new and confusing difficulties for people and societies accustomed to thinking of a text or an utterance as a novel creation by the person who writes or utters it. One set of difficulties has to do with the notion of intellectual property, which is the basis for copyright law and systems for the payment of royalties to authors and composers. If all texts are necessarily reworkings of prior texts, what does it mean to talk about an idea or a book or a song as belonging to one particular person? What is an author, and what rights, if any, do authors have? A related difficulty has to do with speakers and writers' responsibilities for what they say or write. If all discourse is multi-voiced, the result of an endless and probably untraceable series of appropriations, borrowings, repetitions, variations on themes, then who is responsible for the truth of what gets said or written, or for the accuracy of an interpretation? Can we even talk about "truth" and "accuracy"? Provisional answers to questions like these are being worked out in the daily lives of people and cultures, as we work out systems for balancing sharing and creating, freedom to borrow and responsibility to cite on the internet, for example.

For people who are interested in what it means to know how to use language, the idea of intertextuality raises new questions about the knowledge that underlies this ability. Traditional ways of thinking about linguistic competence, as a set of rules speakers use to generate utterances or sentences or connect forms with meanings, are built on the idea that talk is mostly creative. If, however, discourse is mostly repetition, then we need to think more carefully about the role of memory in language-knowledge. When you learn a new language, perhaps what you have to acquire are new "lingual memories" (Becker, 1995) rather than new rules; perhaps a grammar is a set of strategies for manipulating prior texts rather than a set of rules for creating brand new ones.

Further Reading

A good overview of intertextuality and interdiscursivity is Fairclough (1992), chapter 4. Bakhtin (1981[1953], 1986) and Kristeva (1986) are key sources for anyone wanting to delve further into the theory and its implications. On repetition in conversation, see Tannen (1987b) and Johnstone (1987, 1994). Coulmas (1981) is a collection of articles about formulaicity and "prepatterned speech." Early studies of situational variation are Malinowski (1923) and Firth (1935). One of the most influential students of register in North America, in particular "simplified registers" such as baby talk and foreigner talk, was Charles Ferguson (1971, 1982, 1983, 1985, 1994). A good overview of British approaches to register (in the context of Systemic Functional Grammar) is Eggins and Martin (1997); key works in this framework are Crystal and Davy (1969), Gregory and Carrol (1978), Ure (1982), and Ghadessy (1997). A variety of ways of approaching register are represented in Biber and Finegan (1994), which includes several studies that employ Biber's (1988) quantitative factor-analysis approach. Important sources on genre theory are Todorov (1976) and Bakhtin (1986); good examples of research on genre can be found in Bazerman (1988), Swales (1990), Bhatia (1993), Kress (1993), and Berkenkotter and Huckin (1995). On frame analysis in sociological theory, see Goffman (1986[1974]). Tannen (1979) discusses the use of cognitive frame theory in discourse analysis. A collection of studies that use this kind of frame analysis is Tannen (1993a). Linde (1993) and Polanyi (1985) talk about the plots of stories told by middle-class, white Americans; the essays in Becker and Yengoyan (1979), about coherence systems in Southeast Asia, provide an instructive contrast. The idea of plot was also crucial in structuralist folklore (Propp, 1968) and literary theory (Culler, 1975).

chapter 6

Discourse
and Medium

Discourse is shaped by its medium. The structure as well as the potential functions of a stretch of discourse may differ depending on whether it is spoken, written, or signed, whether it combines other modalities (such as pictures or music) with language, and whether it arises in face-to-face interaction or in an interaction by telephone, television, radio, or computer. Starting or ending a conversation over the telephone is different from starting or ending a conversation with someone who can be seen. The social relationships created over email or in "virtual" environments online may be different from those created in face-to-face talk or written letters. A real-time electronic conversation requires different strategies for getting the floor and different conventions for what can be said and how it can be said than does a radio call-in discussion or a dinner-table conversation. The grammatical choices that are preferred in carefully pre-planned speeches or reports are not always the same as the choices people make when they are planning at the same time as they are talking or writing. Websites that combine visual information with words require different design decisions than does print.

Such differences are sometimes tied to factors which we have touched on earlier. People who communicate online, for example, may belong to different discourse communities to begin with than people who do not, and they may bring into the new communication medium prior texts, aspects of their senses of the world, social roles, and conventions for discourse structure and audience design that come from previous interactions elsewhere, in other media. People with the skill, inclination, and technological resources to blog or instant-message may be on average younger, wealthier, and better educated than the population as a whole, for example, and these facts about them might have some bearing on the conventions they develop for electronic talk.

But people also develop new ways of using language in the process of communicating in new media, and these new discourse practices are sometimes tied to constraints and possibilities afforded by the media themselves. For example, the development of the punctuation-mark faces called "emoticons" that are used to express an email writer's attitude about what she or he is writing is partly attributable to the fact that it is relatively difficult to express attitudes of this sort in email in other ways. In many email platforms, font choices cannot be used to point to "metamessages" that would be conveyed in face-to-face interaction via tone of voice or facial or manual gesture. (Capitalization of anything but word-initial letters is, of course, conventionally used in email discourse to represent raised voice volume in speech, and it conveys metamessages of anger or urgency.)

Other aspects of new discursive practices we associate with new media are due not to possibilities and limitations imposed by technology itself, but by new ideas about language (or "language ideologies"; see chapter 2) that come to be associated with new ways of communicating. These ideas vary from group to group, person to person. For example, for some people and in some situations, writing may seem to be a particularly authoritative medium, because things that are written down do not change. Thus one believes what one reads. For others, orally-transmitted knowledge may seem more believable, because what people say to particular people, in particular situations, may be thought to have a kind of immediate, situational relevance that more distanced written texts lack.

We begin our examination of discourse and medium by sketching the history of scholarship about orality and literacy and discussing, in general terms, the role of mediation in discourse and some of the dimensions along which discourse in different media may be different. We then examine some of the ways in which discourse can vary structurally depending on its medium. We look at structural differences that can be correlated with greater or less opportunity for advance planning, with the primary sense channel involved in the interaction (hearing versus vision), with the degree of textual fixity and coherence enabled by the medium, and with the immediacy or distance, in time or space, of the interaction. We then turn to the topic of how interpersonal relations are reflected and created in discourse in various media. We touch on differences having to do with whether interlocutors are relatively involved with or detached from one another and how this affects their behavior toward one another, and we look at how collaboration works, or fails to work, across discourse media and at what it might mean to talk about "community" in contexts in which interlocutors may never meet face to face. Finally, we examine ideologies connected with, and uses of, media in a variety of settings. We look, for example, at how attributes such as power and gender are constructed in different media (if they are relevant at all), at the variations in the politics of authorship, text, and readership which different media make possible or likely. Finally, we touch on multimodal discourse.

Early Work on "Orality and Literacy"

Students of language have often claimed that the object of their inquiry was spoken language, not writing. Speaking, after all, precedes writing in the history of the human species and in the lives of most human individuals; writing is thought to represent speech (even if people sometimes try to pronounce things the way they are written), not the other way around. But the kind of detached, retrospective thought about language that makes grammatical and rhetorical analysis feasible is really only possible in the context of writing. It is only possible to think about relatively fixed connections between forms and meaning – linguistic signs, grammar rules, repeatable discourse structures and discursive practices like frames, plots, and genres – if words are relatively fixed in form and meaning the way they are in written texts such as dictionaries, and if structures are relatively fixed the way they are in grammar books and books about discourse (such as this one!). Linguistics has always been permeated with metaphors from writing (Harris, 1981). For example, the tree diagrams used to represent syntactic structures are said to branch to the "left" or "right." But speech unfolds in time, not in space: oral discourse proceeds from earlier to later, not from left to right or from right to left. Sign-language discourse is both spatial and temporal, but unless it is recorded it is as ephemeral as speech. It is writing systems (and not even all writing systems), rather than speech and in a different way than for signing, in which "left" and "right" and other spatial images are relevant.

It can, in fact, be argued that the entire endeavor of discourse analysis depends on thinking of oral discourse as if it were written. As was discussed earlier (chapter 1), we cannot analyze talk in real time. This is not just because we cannot process information fast enough, but because it is impossible to categorize the forms or functions of elements of discourse before experiencing the whole of the discourse in question. To analyze what we have heard or read, we have to look back at it. In order to perform this retrospection we create written versions, called transcripts, to look at. Although conscientious discourse analysts keep listening to their audiorecordings or viewing their video throughout the process of analysis, the details of the analysis are usually worked out through reading and rereading the transcript.

Starting in the 1960s, work by sociologists and sociolinguists that was explicitly about spoken discourse started to reveal some interesting and unexpected differences between the relatively standardized, written-like language most grammars described (even grammars that purportedly described spoken language) and the things that happened in speech. Concurrently, scholars in fields ranging from communications to classics began to discover spoken language, too. Once oral discourse began to receive real attention, it began to become clear that it is very different from written discourse. Speakers apparently organize their thoughts differently than writers do, use different grammatical strategies, and say different things. According to some scholars, people in "oral cultures" experience the world in completely different ways.

One important influence came from comparative literature and the study of "oral literature." (Since the word "literature" comes from the Latin *litterae*, or 'letters', "oral literature" is really an oxymoron.) Surrounded by writing as we are, we can find it difficult to think of words as transient airwave shapes (or, in the case of sign language, transient visual impressions) rather than as permanent, unchanging marks. We may find it difficult to imagine a body of knowledge that is verbally transmitted, never written down, never archived, never put into an encyclopedia or onto the internet, never recoverable in exactly the same form. This is why the "Homeric question," the question of who wrote the pre-classical Greek epics the *Iliad* and the *Odyssey*, had seemed intractable. The *Iliad* and the *Odyssey* have been seen since antiquity, in the Anglo-European literary tradition, as among the best, purest, truest, most inspired secular poems ever composed, so people were curious about their authorship. During the nineteenth century, philologists began to pay attention to the fact that the *Iliad* and the *Odyssey* were different from other literary works and other Greek texts, and that the two texts were different from each other in some ways. The question arose whether they were really both written by the same person, or indeed written at all. It was even suggested that Homer, who according to tradition was blind, may not have been literate.

Milman Parry (who lived from 1902 to 1935; his work was collected and published, in 1971, by his son) was the first to discover the real key to Homer. Everything that is distinctive about the epics, Parry claimed, was due to the fact that they were composed orally. Epic poets (or "rhapsodes," from Greek *rhaptein* 'to stitch' and *ōide* 'song') stitched together long poems out of a stock of pre-established, traditional phrases, or "formulas." Standard formulas fit standard themes, such as the challenge to a duel or the gathering of an army or naval fleet. Key characters were referred to with formulas that varied depending on where in the metrical line the character was mentioned, as were standard physical referents, such as "rosy-fingered dawn" or "the wine-dark sea." Among other things, the idea that the epics were reconstructed, at each telling, out of pre-existing formulas helps explain the fact that there is a mixture of different dialects of Greek, from various eras, in the versions of the epics that were eventually written down.

The epics told by the twentieth-century bards in Macedonia whom Parry studied turned out to be similarly stitched together out of prefabricated parts. Since then, other such oral traditions of epic poetry have been described and found to be built, similarly, in formulaic ways.

But why would the Greeks or the Macedonians have wanted to listen to poems made up of strings of pre-formulated clichés? Erik Havelock (1982[1963]) suggested a larger explanation. Literature does not have the same function in an oral tradition, said Havelock, as in a literate one. Epics like the *Iliad* and the *Odyssey* were ways of remembering the past. Such epics functioned as history as well as entertainment. The production, processing, and distribution of knowledge in a world in which things are not written relies on verbal formulas linked to formulaic characters (heroes and villains) and formulaic situations, so that knowledge can be reconstructed and redistributed again and again, as the key texts are spoken and listened to. In contexts in which knowledge cannot be stored (in libraries, archives, notebooks, or databases), it has to be repeated, or else it is lost.

One of the best known general treatments of "orality and literacy" is that of Walter J. Ong (1982). According to Ong, orally transmitted knowledge is different from knowledge in literate lifeworlds in several ways. First, discourse in an oral context is different in *structure*. If writing is not available, what you know is what you can recall. Thus knowledge has to be represented differently, in such a way as to make it memorable. In structural terms, this means that you need repetition, balance, and rhythm. If you think of the longest text you learned orally, not by seeing it written down – an often-recited prayer, for example, a nursery rhyme, or the words to a patriotic pledge or a song – you probably find yourself moving along in it via patterns of sound and rhythm. Discourse in an oral lifeworld is primarily additive rather than subordinative. Syntax is simpler, and there is less embedding and more cohesion via repetition and parallelism. It is also copious. Since there is no opportunity for checking back, redundancy is especially necessary, for listeners as well as for speakers.

Secondly, according to Ong, discourse in oral contexts is different in *theme*. Discourse tends to be about heroic characters in agonistic (that is, diametrically opposed) relationships: the king and the peasant, the good sister and the evil sister. Knowledge is close to the human world, and explanations for what happens are not highly abstract. Third, discourse in an oral lifeworld has different *functions*. In a world without writing, words tend to seem like events, not objects, because they leave no lasting trace. Speech is action, not simply a sign of supposedly pre-existing thought. Thus words can be powerful and magical. Discourse is aggregative: once an idea and a memorable utterance are connected, they are unlikely to be disconnected, so traditional texts are added to, rather than re-worked, as new truths are constructed or discovered. Analysis, a process that involves looking back and picking apart, is less likely in the absence of fixed forms of discourse such as writing. Oral discourse is also conservative, because knowledge that depends on

Structural features: What do texts sound like?
- Repetition, balance, rhythm
- Simple, additive syntax
- Greater redundancy

Thematic features: What are texts about?
- Larger-than-life heroes and villains in diametric opposition
- Close to human lifeworld; concrete

Functional features: What do texts do?
- Words are actions and can be powerful.
- Discourse aggregates knowledge rather than analyzing it.
- Discourse conserves knowledge rather than creating it.
- History is flexible, serves current needs.

Figure 6.1 Features of orally-transmitted knowledge
Source: Adapted from Ong (1982)

human memory is valuable and felt to be worth preserving. The nature of history is different, since, if a people's whole history is stored in memory, history can be modified to suit current exigencies. People remember the historical stories they need in order to explain their present circumstances, to resolve disputes, to decide on the succession of leaders, and so on. The stories that are not useful do not continue to be transmitted and remembered.

In an article entitled "The consequences of literacy," Goody and Watt (1968) suggested that Greek culture changed dramatically with the advent of relatively widespread literacy among Greek men. It was at this stage, they said, that the Greeks developed a sense of history as opposed to myth, a sense of the past as objectively real, as well as a system of logic, a systematic way of deciding once and for all (it was thought) about the truth or falsity of a proposition. Goody and Watt suggested that universal literacy, which it is often thought is a step on the way to democracy and equality in a society, may in fact lead to social stratification, as distinctions come to be made based on what and how much people read. For example, there can be a gap between the oral culture of home and the literate culture of school, and culture transmitted in writing can be avoided in a way that orally-transmitted culture cannot: a person does not have to read. When a people's records are in writing, eventually no one person can have read them all, so knowledge is not widely shared the way it is in an oral setting.

Scholars such as Ong and Goody and Watt have been criticized for making overly broad and sweeping distinctions between oral ways of thinking and literate ones, distinctions which can too easily be used to make other people seem exotic and irrational. For example, explaining the reading and writing difficulties of certain schoolchildren as resulting from the "oral culture" of their home communities can make it more difficult to notice other factors, such as poverty, bad educational policy, or poorly trained teachers, that may actually have a lot more to do with the problem. In general, dividing human societies into "literate" ones and "oral" ones vastly oversimplifies the range of ways in which humans make use of writing and other communication technologies. There are many kinds and many uses of literacy, as we will see. However, the idea that medium affects, and is affected by, what people do with discourse continues to be a powerful and useful one.

Discussion

6.1   One area in which the knowledge which many of us have is primarily oral is family history. In what ways, if any, does the discourse of your family's history conform to Ong's characterizations of orally transmitted knowledge? For example, is it selective? What functions does it serve? Are the characters divided into heroes and villains? At a family gathering, record some family history talk to see if it shares the structural, thematic, and functional characteristics Ong described (see figure 6.1). In some families, one person or another takes on the role of genealogist, collecting information about names, marriages, children, and their dates, and assembling them into a family tree. Compare and contrast the way a family is represented in a family tree with the way a family is represented in oral family-history talk.

6.2   In what other realms have you acquired knowledge mainly in oral ways? You might think, for example, about things you learned before you could read. Some possibilities: Children's games, elements of religious practice such as prayers and hymns, nursery rhymes, skip rope rhymes, children's songs. Referring to the text of this section and figure 6.1, discuss whether and how this knowledge seems "oral," structurally, thematically, and functionally.

6.3   Proverbs are one familiar example of knowledge organized for an oral world. Collect ten proverbs, from your memory or by asking other people. What generalizations can you make on the basis of this data about structural features characteristic of proverbs? What functions do proverbs serve, in your experience? Do proverbs serve as tools for recalling, organizing, and disseminating knowledge in your environment? In what contexts? Does the body of cultural knowledge encoded in the proverbs you are familiar with constitute a coherent, consistent system of beliefs or recommendations for behavior?

Literacy and Literacies

When generalizations about orality and literacy that had been developed in the context of Western culture began to be tested in other settings, it became clear that literacy does not always involve the same activities and that its consequences are not always the same. What writing and reading are used for and how they affect people's lives and ways of thinking depends on how writing and reading are conceived of in local terms. One of the early studies calling into question the idea that literacy necessarily gives rise to dramatic cognitive and cultural change was that of Scribner and Cole (1981), who studied the acquisition and uses of literacy in three languages among the Vai people of Liberia. Scribner and Cole found that many of the cultural and psychological effects that had been attributed to literacy in the abstract were actually the results of the particular educational practices associated with particular uses of literacy. Taking an ethnographic approach to the study of literacy, which involves looking carefully at particular technologies for writing and their uses in particular societies and for particular purposes, analysts such as Street (1984, 1993), Heath (1983), and Finnegan (1988) showed that rather than talking about "literacy" it is more accurate to talk about "literacies," and that the effects of technology on human behavior are mediated by ideology – beliefs about what literacy means, how it can supplement or supplant oral discourse, what its uses ought to be. As one such analyst puts it (Kittay, 1988: 226): "The change of medium does not inevitably mean that one understands utterances differently. For example, the degree to which literacy replaces orality depends upon circumstances more of cultural than technological evolution." People and groups of people are not either literate or non-literate: there are many possible ways in which written discourse can be incorporated into human life and in which writing can affect discourse. This realization has given rise to many detailed studies of uses and effects of literacy in a variety of settings.

One of these studies (Kittay, 1988) traces various developments which, in the course of the Middle Ages in Europe, were linked to writing's becoming decoupled from spoken utterances and reading decoupled from listening. In the early Middle Ages, writing was "oral." The person who uttered words was not usually the person who wrote them down, and *scribere* referred only to writing down, inscribing words from dictation. Partly because there were no spaces between words in the orthography of the time, written documents needed to be read aloud in order to be interpreted. Furthermore, in the monasteries, writing and reading were religious practices which, for doctrinal as well as practical reasons, required reading aloud, so that writing was a "reenactment of the utterance as spoken" (p. 216).

In the later Middle Ages, however, several developments served to separate some kinds of writing from speaking. One was the development of the practice of glossing the Christian Scriptures, that is, the writing of marginal or interlinear comments about how they should be interpreted. While the Scriptures themselves were still meant to be interpreted as the transcribed speech of particular historical figures, these supplementary explications were "not attached to a time and place outside the book but [were] now in a context understood as a page of writing" (p. 218). They were to be understood, that is, not as things which *someone* once *said*, but as things which *a book says*. In connection with this, the Bible was divided into chapters, verses, and lines, which could be referred to via numbers. Another development was the cleric, someone trained and protected by the church who would travel around writing things, often for secular purposes. Writing began to be seen as "a portable skill, on demand and applied to a diverse set of tasks" (p. 221).

Kittay shows that in the course of the Middle Ages, writing moved from being part of an activity that involved spoken words from the beginning (dictation) to the end (reading aloud) to being an activity in its own right, an activity that did not have to involve speaking, or the idea of a speaking originator, at all. Thinking of writing as detached from the circumstances of speech means that it is possible to analyze written words in retrospect. This eventually made possible the practice of scholastic argumentation, academic discussion about the true meanings of texts based on the kind of close analysis which is only possible when discourse exists in a permanent visual form. This, then, is an *oral* practice based on *writing*, something which would have been impossible at the beginning of the Middle Ages, when written practices were based on speaking.

In this way, through a series of particular historical developments, Europeans and their descendants eventually came to see writing as more authoritative than speaking. The idea that the way to discover the truth was through analyses of fixed texts – be they traditional writings or records of experiments or observations – came to shape not just the interpretation of sacred texts but Western scholarship in general. This idea, we might note, is the basis for a pedagogical system in which textbooks (like this one) are the organizing principle for courses, the basis for oral discussion, and the source of the information students are most likely to have to produce for examinations. Similarly, written wills and contracts, written instructions, written histories and literature came to be seen as more binding, more believable, and more valuable than their oral counterparts. Because writing is seen as more authoritative than speech, people sometimes suppose (despite the fact that the English writing system is notoriously un-phonetic) that the correct way to pronounce a word must be the way it is written (as when the *t* in *often* or the second *e* in *vegetable* is sounded). The tendency toward such "spelling pronunciations" can even affect the process of language change. For example, Chambers (1993: 140–2) describes some Canadian youngsters who, after they moved to Oxfordshire, England, tended to stop pronouncing words like *butter* in the North American way, replacing the North American flap sound [D] between the vowels (so that *butter* sounds like *budder*) with the more British-sounding [t]. (A "flap" is produced when the tongue hits the top of the mouth once, very briefly.) However, the youngsters did not lose the North American habit of pronouncing /r/ after vowels (in words like *north*, *nor*, or *water*) rather than dropping it. They thus moved toward British pronunciation in the first respect but not in the second.

Chambers suggests that this has to do with the fact that the shift from [D] to [t] is in the direction of pronouncing words as they are spelled, whereas the shift from pronouncing /r/ to not pronouncing it would be in the opposite direction, making pronunciation less like spelling.

A contrasting situation to the European one, a situation in which writing is not seen as more authoritative than speaking, is that of the Nukulaelae Islanders described by Besnier (1995: 77–9). A common practice among these Polynesians is for people who write letters to friends and relatives abroad to give travelers oral messages for the letter recipients that repeat what the letters say. Nukulaelae people explain this practice by saying that the message-bearers are meant to "help" the letter recipients to understand the letters, in light of the fact that some people have poor handwriting, that the Tuvaluan language in which they write does not have a consistent orthographic system, and that people do not have much practice in reading letters. Besnier points out, however, that many people have no trouble reading in other contexts, which calls these explanations into question. He suggests that the practice of supplementing written messages with oral ones has more to do with Nukulaelae attitudes about writing and speaking (pp. 78–9):

> Underlying local ideologies is the view that certain forms of oral communication are more reliable than writing. At best, letters are seen to complement oral messages: unlike letters, which can be and often are misplaced among the innumerable plastic bags, buckets, boxes, and woven coconut-frond baskets that many Nukulaelae Islanders travel with, oral messages will not slip between the woven fronds of baskets, fall into the ocean during reef-crossings in rough weather, and get soiled to the point of illegibility in contact with cooked swamp taro. Thus, rather than leading an autonomous existence from oral communication in the local communicative ideology, letters are closely associated with orality.

Because writing is seen in Western societies as an index of prestige and authoritativeness, debates about which varieties of language should be written and how nonstandard varieties should be represented on the page (if at all) can be highly contentious. In popular usage, a way of talking that does not have a writing system is sometimes thought of (inaccurately, from the point of view of sociolinguistics) as not really a language, but a "dialect" or "slang." Brown (1993) talks, for example, about the conflicts surrounding decisions, both personal and institutional, about the writing of the French spoken in Louisiana in the southern US. Various dialects and uses of French came to Louisiana, during the eighteenth century, with colonists from France, French Canadian migrants, and slaves from Haiti (p. 70), and Louisiana French now consists of several overlapping ways of talking which are all thought of locally as nonstandard. It has only recently begun to be written, and the need for multiple complex choices about how to write it makes

Louisiana French, in the words of one anthologist (Ancelet, 1980: 10), *la langue problématique*, the problematic language. This has to do with the fact that, as Barry (1989: 5–8) puts it:

> It is not simply a question of how and what to write, but in what language . . . Standard French, Cajun French, Creole. The choice of a word is a commitment, a risk, a conflict. What word to choose: "je vais," "j'vas," "mo va"? How do you write a language which is only oral? What risk does one run when confronted by the empty page? . . . The dilemma of language is present for the writer in each line, each word.

As writers make choices like the ones Barry describes, they are not just transcribing what local speech sounds like at the moment. They are also fixing it in form, turning instances of talk into a standardized, codified, named language. Because of the perceived authoritativeness of writing, choices about what Louisiana French should look like in print will ultimately come to serve as descriptions of what "real" Louisiana French is like, and as prescriptions for how to speak and write it. (See also Johnson, 2005, on the debate surrounding a 1996 effort to standardize the spelling of German.)

Once a variety of language has a standardized orthography, representing it in nonstandard ways can have social consequences. Jaffe and Walton (2000) report on a study that uncovered some of these consequences. Jaffe and Walton showed people texts written with varying degrees of approximation to the actual sound of casual speech, rather than to standard spelling conventions, and they asked their research subjects to describe the people they imagined speaking each passage. The first sentence of one of the manipulated texts was this (adapted from p. 586):

History Lessons (Standard orthography)
When I was a kid, I thought history was one of the dumbest subjects that could ever be taught.

History Lessons (Lightly modified)
When I wuz a kid, I thought hist'ry wuz one o' the dummest subjects that could ever be taught.

History Lessons (Heavily modified)
Wen Aye wuz uh kid, Aye thawt histree wuz wun uh thih dummess subjeks tha' koud ever bee tawt.

Jaffe and Walton's research subjects did not hesitate to connect nonstandard orthography in the representation of speech directly with the social identity of the imagined speaker. Specifically, the researchers "found that people uncritically and spontaneously read nonstandard orthographies as indices of low socioeconomic status" (p. 561), and when they asked people to read the text out loud, they found that many read the texts with nonstandard orthography as if they represented a nonstandard dialect of English rather than simply representing anyone's casual speech, as they do.

Electronic media have given rise to some new ways of imagining reading and writing. For example, since anyone who has access to the internet can "publish" there, ownership of discourse and information on the internet is often perceived as publicly shared in a way print text is not. It is sometimes claimed that new communications technology is making traditional ways of thinking about authors, readers, information, and texts obsolete. According to Landow (1992), hypertext reconfigures the "politics" of text in several ways. The relative ease and acceptability of creating new sites for, downloading, printing, or copying from online texts, together with the possibility of creating links between documents of different origins, calls into question traditional law and belief about who owns a text and the information in it, such as regulations concerning copyright. The ease of access to the internet (though this is often overestimated; many people still have no access at all), along with the increasing online availability of books and other texts, calls into question traditional restrictions on who is allowed to know what, restrictions once reinforced via such things as closed library stacks and the cost of books and newspaper subscriptions. In most of the world, anyone who has a computer, internet access, and the relevant skills can create websites on which they can post whatever they like and participate in collaborative knowledge-building activities like blogs, wikis, and discussion boards. This challenges traditional mechanisms through which publishers and designated experts such as academics control what counts as an authoritative, canonical text, and how such texts should be read.

Discussion

6.4   In English and in other languages there are formulaic expressions that give voice to the belief that writing lends authority or closure. For example, to indicate that plans are still flexible, we might say "It's not written in stone." What are other such expressions?

6.5   Are there occasions in your experience when reading is a social rather than a solitary activity – when multiple people have to be involved in the interpretation of a written text, for example? Are there occasions when writing has to be supplemented by speech before it is seen as really authoritative?

6.6   One currently popular use of alphabetic literacy in the US is represented on "vanity" automobile license plates such as UCHOWUR ("You see how you are") and in this inscription in a high-school yearbook:

UR 2 good
+2 be
4gotten

Find some more examples of this phenomenon and describe how it works. How do oral and literate skills have to be drawn on in the creation and interpretation of texts like these? What attitudes about literacy underlie this phenomenon?

6.7   Are you familiar with settings in which literacy serves functions different from those it serves in mainstream settings? You might think, for example, about non-sanctioned uses of writing such as passing notes or sending surreptitious text-messages in school or in meetings, "tagging" (the writing of stylized signatures or monograms on public surfaces), graffiti, or writing computer code for the purpose of hacking into corporate or governmental computer systems. Describe the functions of literacy in these settings and the beliefs about reading and writing that make them possible. People are not taught in school to do things like these with writing. How are literacies like these acquired?

6.8   How do reading and writing work in religious settings with which you are familiar? Think, for example, about choral readings of prayers; reading from the Christian Bible, the Torah, or the Qur'an; the functions of Missals, prayer books, and so on; the role of memorization; whether and how sermons are expected to be based on written texts. Is the ability to read music an aspect of literacy in some religious settings? How are the uses of literacy in religious settings you are familiar with different from the uses of literacy in secular settings?

6.9   A magazine supplement about how to encourage young children to become readers says, "Here in the Information Age, the ability to read proficiently is crucial to success" (Starting Points-Pittsburgh, 1999). What do you think "proficiency" in reading should entail in "the Information Age"? How does this compare with what proficiency in reading might have entailed a century ago? What does the fact that the definition of proficiency in reading has changed over time suggest about the practice of labeling people as either "literate" or "illiterate"?

6.10   How does the "politics of representation" enter into debates about how to write languages or varieties you are familiar with? For example, how should the speech of people who use African-American-sounding English be written? Should creole languages be written in the standard orthography of the language from which most of their vocabulary comes, which is often the language of former colonizers? What are the reasons for, and the effects of, representing southern German dialects in nonstandard orthography? Would it ever be a good idea to write Arabic the way it sounds (which is very different from place to place) rather than writing it in the conventional standardized way, which does not reflect local differences? What debates arise surrounding how and when Japanese or Chinese should be written in Roman alphabetic characters? In whose interest is it to standardize the mark-up systems (such as HTML) which are used to format hypertext documents? Do you know how such decisions are currently made?

Communication and Technology

All discourse is mediated. Face-to-face oral–aural communication involves the use of the articulatory organs and muscles to produce sound, which must then be converted into neural impulses via the ear. Face-to-face communication also often involves modes like gesture, gaze, and the positioning of the body in space, and print discourse, images, musical sounds and other modes may serve as resources in face-to-face talk too. When people have difficulty speaking or hearing, they sometimes replace one bodily medium with another, using hand and facial gesture instead of the voice, as in the languages of the deaf, or looking at lips rather than listening to sound. Alternatively or in addition, some mechanical and even some information-processing functions of the body can sometimes be augmented or replaced with technologies such as artificial larynxes, electronic voices, hearing aids, alphabet boards, or ear implants. Bioengineering and computer technology are rapidly blurring the line between the communication media provided by the "natural" world and the human body, and the "artificial" media. Furthermore, material objects of all sorts serve as carriers of meaning, not just the ones we think of as communications media, like radio or telephones. For example, Ron Scollon (2001) shows how objects such as crayons, papers, books, pots and pans, and food, sometimes together with bits of language, all served as "mediational means" as one child was socialized by her caregivers into activities involving giving and taking. We should be alert to the fact that there is no communication without technology or its equivalent, and we should be aware that the idea that face-to-face oral–aural communication is the most "natural" or the "best" source of data about how humans use language is based on the mistaken assumption that a clear line can be drawn between communication settings in which human-to-human contact is mediated and settings in which it is not.

No matter what the medium of communication is, it affects the discourse that it enables or accompanies. Giving instructions requires different kinds of talk when the process can be mediated by a map or diagram than when it cannot. It is possible to do different things with sign than with oral language, because gestures are sometimes more iconic than words are (that is, they more often look like what they represent), and because gestures can be combined in ways words cannot. Because face-to-face oral–aural discourse is usually supplemented with visual cues, people have to interact somewhat differently over the telephone, when the lights are out, or when vision is otherwise impaired. Some of the ways in which visual cues can be replaced with linguistic ones can be carried over into talk that is mediated not by the telephone but by computer, but since email and synchronous computer-mediated chat are written, not spoken, some different things have to be done. A multimedia presentation such as a set of PowerPoint slides or or a video game can include images, sound, and writing and may sometimes draw on other modalities as well, such as smell or touch. It can be asynchronous, like letters or email, or synchronous, like face-to-face talk or some online chat. Each set of technological constraints brings with it a different set of possibilities, preferences, and restrictions. For example, word-processing facilitates some ways of composing and not others, as did the use of styluses on clay, chisels on stone, pigment on parchment, or fountain-pen writing on paper before it.

As we have seen, the uses and effects of all media, not just writing, are in part the results of systems of belief, or ideology. A medium of communication is not simply an object or a technology, but rather a set of interlocked technological, social, and linguistic practices. For example, the fact that the internet is more "interactive" than a library may be partly the result of the ways in which internet technologies facilitate interactivity, but it is also partly a result of beliefs about how the internet should be used, about how it fits into the repertoire of things we do with discourse, about who the "typical" or most likely users are, and so on. It is easy to lose sight of how ideology enters into the process by which new media are incorporated into human life in the excitement about the potential of "global" technologies such as television and computers: the fact that a technology is available everywhere does not mean it will everywhere play the same roles. It is important to keep this in mind in our discussions of newer technologies, since much of the research about their uses and effects has, to date, been carried out in fairly homogeneous Westernized settings.

In general, what are the dimensions along which medium might influence discourse? For one thing, medium and discourse form may be related. Discourse in one medium may be more complex syntactically, have more words, be less cohesive or cohesive in a different way, have a different kind of macrostructure, or perhaps less structure, and so on. Secondly, medium and discourse processing may be related. It may, for example, be easier to recall or interpret information in one format than in another. Thirdly, discourse medium and interpersonal relations might be related. For example, one medium might be better for sharing feelings than another, one medium might enable collaborative work more effectively than another, conversation might be more oriented towards interpersonal rapport in one medium and more oriented toward information exchange in another. Different media might encourage people to regulate their behavior and imagine their rights and responsibilities in different ways. Fourth, medium might be implicated in knowledge-making and knowledge use. For example, one medium might encourage the idea that one interactant is the author and others the readers, whereas another medium might encourage the idea that text and knowledge are jointly constructed; one medium might facilitate the making of abstractions or critical judgments more than another; a more ephemeral medium might make self-reflection less likely whereas a more permanent medium might encourage it. In the sections that follow, we explore several of these dimensions.

Discussion

6.11   Develop some hypotheses about ways in which the use of various electronic
       media – email and email based bulletin boards or distribution lists, synchronous
       ("real-time") systems such as Internet Relay Chat (IRC), instant messaging,
       the World Wide Web and hypertext in general – shapes discourse. Might the
       structure of discourse in each of these media be different from face-to-face
       or print discourse? How, for one thing, might the shape, size, and configura-
       tion of a computer screen affect computer-mediated written communication?
       Describe some newer electronic genres of discourse. Are these new genres asso-
       ciated with new purposes for discourse? New relationships among participants?
       Discuss how discourse analyses could be used to test your hypotheses.

6.12   Information on web pages is often presented in smaller chunks than it would
       be in print. Paragraphs are often shorter, and material that might be on one
       page in a print document is sometimes divided into multiple linked sub-
       documents. To what extent is this a result of facts about internet techno-
       logies (computers, computer monitors, hypertext and browser software, etc.),
       and to what extent is it the result of facts or beliefs about readers of web
       pages? Does the Web "construct" a different sort of reader than paper-based
       media do?

Planning and Discourse Structure

One thing that might make discourse in one medium differ from discourse
in another is the amount of planning that is possible. Modes of discourse
that take place in real time, such as face-to-face speaking or signing, involve
relatively little planning. More planning is possible, and sometimes expected,
in situations in which discourse can be drafted, edited, or rehearsed before
it enters into interaction. The writing of a book is clearly such a situation.
But not all carefully planned discourse is written (some formal speeches are
planned in advance, for example), and not all unplanned discourse is oral
(some kinds of computer-mediated talk involve discourse that is written,
read, and responded to almost simultaneously). Ochs (1979b) suggests that
relatively planned discourse may differ from relatively unplanned discourse
in a number of ways.

   For one thing, in relatively unplanned discourse, speakers tend to rely on
the immediate context, rather than on syntax, to express ideas. For example,
referents may not be mentioned when it can be assumed that interlocutors
already know or can easily figure out what the subject of a sentence or the
topic of a conversation is. When a referent is expressed, it may be part
of what Ochs calls a "referent + proposition" construction. In this extract
from a conversation between two college students, the speaker expresses a

proposition that might be expressed in writing as "We have eight books to read in our Twentieth-Century Art course":

Ohhh, I g'ta tell ya *one* course,
the mo- the modern art the twentieth century art,
there's about eight books.

Note how she begins by talking about the social activity in which she and her interlocutor are engaged ("I g'ta tell ya"), then identifying the topic ("one course"), specifying it with a string of appositive noun phrases ("the modern art," "the twentieth century art"), and finally beginning a new clause to make a comment about the now-specified referent ("there's about eight books"). This kind of topic + comment organization is typical of relatively unplanned discourse, as is the strategy of modifying nouns by adding nouns after them rather than with adjectival elements that come before them. Both of these features could be said to reflect the real-time processing of discourse in speech. Whole propositions tend to be semantically linked via parataxis in unplanned discourse, too, that is, by being next to each other rather than by being explicitly connected with words such as *thus* or *because* or *after*.

For another thing, in producing relatively unplanned discourse speakers tend to rely on syntactic strategies and structures they learned relatively early in life, while relatively planned discourse may be characterized by structures learned later on. For example, relative clauses are more typical of planned discourse than of unplanned. This sometimes has to do with the greater verbal specification of detail that is possible (and, when visual cues are absent as in writing, often necessary) in planned discourse: a person who refers to a character in a spoken story as "this woman" might refer to her in a written version as "a woman *whose back was turned*." Planned discourse makes greater use of the passive voice than does unplanned discourse, and unplanned discourse makes greater use of the present tense. In spontaneous speech someone might tell a story involving *this guy* who was standing on *this subway platform*, whereas if the person were to write the story she might talk about *the man* and *the platform*. Demonstrative pronouns such as *this* point outside of discourse to the world; articles such as *the* point back inside the discourse, often, to whether or not the referent has been mentioned in the preceding talk.

Repetition within utterances is also more common in relatively unplanned discourse than in relatively planned discourse. Often this has to do with the need for an online way of repairing potential or actual misunderstandings or incomplete understandings. If a speaker has not used exactly the right word, she might, for example, repeat it and then suggest a better one:

This *fella* I have uh "*fella*." This *man*, he had uh f- who I have for linguistics is really too much.

Because of the need for repairs such as this, unplanned discourse may be less compact than more planned discourse. By the same token, in relatively unplanned discourse, the same referent or the same proposition, if expressed again, tends to be expressed in the same way, and the same speech act tends to be performed in the same way if performed again. People repeat, in other words, not only within their own utterances but across utterances, and across speakers. This may involve the repeated use of phrases, as in this example, where B repeats "right" and "something right" from utterance to utterance:

   A: (You sounded so // far)
→B: *Right*
   A: Yeah
→B: See I- I'm doin' *something right* t'day finally.
   A: Mm
→B: I finally said *something right*.

Repetition may also be on the level of phonology, as speakers pick up and repeat the sounds others use.

In other work about discourse planning and its consequences, Tannen (1982a), Chafe (1982) and others have suggested similar ways of characterizing the differences. Figure 6.2, which is based on lists by Tannen (1982a), summarizes these findings. A larger-scale approach to studying the differences in structure among different genres of spoken and written discourse is that of Biber (1988). Biber identified 67 features, taken from lists of features like those in figure 6.2, that had been said to differentiate between spoken (or spoken-like) and written (or written-like) modes of discourse. He then noted each occurrence of each of these features in 241 samples of speech and writing representing 23 types: newspaper reports, fiction, letters, transcripts of face-to-face conversation, broadcast debates and interviews, spontaneous and planned speech, and so on. Statistical analysis of the data showed which sets of texts were similar and showed that the 67 features clustered into six sets, representing six dimensions along which the texts varied. Dimension 1, involved vs. informational production, has to do with whether the focus is on information or on interpersonal rapport. The presence or absence of personal pronouns would, for example, be one way to locate a given text along this dimension. Dimension 2 has to do with whether the text has primarily narrative or non-narrative concerns. Tense choices, including the use of the simple past tense, would be one thing that would locate a text at the narrative end of the scale. Along dimension 3, texts vary according to whether reference is relatively explicit or relatively situation dependent. Nominalizations and certain kinds of relative clauses are correlated with explicitness, for example. Dimension 4 ranges texts according to whether they are characterized by the overt expression of persuasion or not (conditional structures and certain modal verbs such as *must* and *will* tend to be found in texts that are overtly persuasive), and dimension 5 has to do with whether information is relatively abstract or non-abstract. (Agentless passives tend to characterize texts that are close to the abstract end of the

Relatively unplanned discourse	Relatively planned discourse
dependence on morphological and syntactic features learned early in life	use of complex morphological and syntactic structures learned later in life
reliance on immediate context to express relationships between ideas	relationships between ideas made explicit in words, with formal cohesive devices, topic sentences
preference for deictic modifiers (*this man*)	preference for articles (*a man, the man*)
preponderance of repair mechanisms	scarcity of repair mechanisms
repetition of sounds, words, syntactic structures	less repetition and parallelism
avoidance of relative clauses	use of relative clauses
more use of present tense, especially in narrative	more use of other tenses
less use of passive	more use of passive
fewer nominalizations, participles	more nominalizations, participles
more appositives for modification	more attributive adjectives
more coordination	more subordination
less compact, more words	more compact, dense, "integrated" (Chafe)

Figure 6.2 Some features of planned and unplanned discourse
Source: Based on Ochs (1979b), Tannen (1982a), Chafe (1982)

scale, for example.) Dimension 6 has to do with whether information is elaborated "online" or not. Online elaboration may, for example, be correlated with the use of certain kinds of subordinate clauses strung out after the main clause rather than embedded in it.

Biber's analysis makes it possible to think about variation among texts in various media as a set of differences, each correlated with different facts about what the media make easy or difficult, likely or unlikely. For example, in a comparison of Biber's findings about oral and print genres with some examples of computer-mediated discourse, Collot and Belmore (1996) found that the electronic bulletin-board messages they studied had some characteristics of written print genres and some characteristics of oral genres. On the basis of a count of the grammatical features Biber found to be associated with each dimension, they found that the messages were fairly involved, fairly overt in the expression of persuasion, fairly abstract, elaborated online, and more non-narrative than narrative. In other words, the b-board messages

Biber (1988) developed these six dimensions by looking at which subsets of particular features (passives, personal pronouns, verbs in the simple past tense, and so on) tended to be found together in his corpus of texts. He then explored where various text-types (newspaper reports, conversations, broadcast interviews, and so on) tended to fall along each dimension. For example, newspaper reports are relatively informational (dimension 1) and relatively narrative (dimension 2) while a conversation among friends might be relatively involved (dimension 1) and relatively narrative (dimension 2). Thus, newspaper reports and conversations would differ more on dimension 1 than on dimension 2.

1   involved production ------------------------------------- informational production
2   primarily narrative ------------------------------------- primarily non-narrative
3   relatively situation-dependent reference ------------ relatively explicit reference
4   little overt expression of persuasion ------------ overt expression of persuasion
5   relatively non-abstract information ------------- relatively abstract information
6   information is elaborated "online" -------- information is elaborated "offline"

Figure 6.3   Dimensions of textual variation
Source: Biber (1988)

were the most like Biber's public interviews and personal and professional letters.

Discussion

6.13   Here are written and spoken versions of the same information. The data was collected by a student of Deborah Tannen's (Tannen, 1982a), who asked a friend to talk about her daughter and, two or three weeks later, to write down what she had said. What differences are there between the two versions, and to what can they be attributed? (You may find it useful to refer to the list of features in figure 6.2.)

a.   Spoken version of a story (contributions from the audience are in parentheses; ellipses represent pauses, with more dots indicating longer pauses, and colons represent drawn-out sounds):

> . . . A:nd u:m . . . Dale is going to go to A- . . . junior high school. She's going into the ninth grade. . . . But they put the ninth graders . . . in with the. . . . all right. The way they've got it, they're in a period of transition at their school system now, OK? (Yeah.). . . . And . . . the ninth grade . . . is with, because the high school's overcrowded I guess they're building a new high school? So they're . . . they're putting the . . . eighth . . . and the ninth . . . in . . . the junior high. (Hmmm.) U:m . . . Dale . . . is going into the ninth grade, . . . and. . . . she is supposed to be going into high school normally, . . . But she, because of this situation, will be in . . . junior high. . . . This is a school, . . . that is . . . seventh . . . uh eighth and ninth graders only, . . . two thousand . . . Out in a sticky place like Willingboro New Jersey. (Laughs.) Two thousand. It's only eighth and ninth graders.

b. Written version of the same description, by the same person:

> Dale, in the ninth grade, will go to junior high school, which for this academic year consists of only the 8th and 9th graders, for a total of 2,000 students.

6.14 Here is an excerpt from a transcript of a writing teacher talking to her class, reading them an anecdote in the process. The excerpt thus includes talk that is partially planned (the text from which she reads – although this text represents a range of styles), partially relatively unplanned (her own comments – although you may note variation between more writerly and more spontaneous-sounding talk here, too). Pick out the more planned-sounding features and the more unplanned-sounding features. Is this mixed spoken-written style characteristic of instructional discourse?

1   Okay. Now a kind of a shift between style and audience. Like I said when we started this unit on style [puts a transparency on the overhead projector], style, like everything else in writing, depends on audience. However, there are some principles of good style that you can learn that will pretty well stand you in good stead, no matter what the audience. But, of course, other things in style depend on whom you're writing for. Now this is real, a real example, it's not made up. [reads]
8   A plumber wrote to the National Bureau of Standards to ask if
9   hydrochloric acid was effective for cleaning out clogged drains.
10   Someone at the bureau replied, in typical bureaucratic language,
11   "The efficacy of hydrochloric acid is indisputable, but the corrosive
12   residue is incompatible with metallic permanence."
13   Sounds like that typical beauty is in the eye of the beholder thing. [reads]
14   The plumber wrote back, thanking the bureau for agreeing with
15   him. Another member of the bureau tried to straighten the plumber
16   out with the following message: "We cannot assume responsibility
17   for the production of a toxic and noxious residue with hydrochloric
18   acid and suggest that you use an alternative procedure."
19   Okay. Did you follow that?
20   The plumber thanked the bureau a second time, saying that the
21   bureau should suggest the use of hydrochloric acid to other people.
22   Uh-oh. Definitely a communication breakdown.
23   Finally, the problem was passed to a department head who wrote
24   the plumber, "Don't use hydrochloric acid. It eats the hell out of
25   the pipes."

6.15 When do people make strategic use of discourse that sounds unplanned when it is in fact highly planned? Is it ever possible to make unplanned discourse sound as if it was planned?

6.16 Develop hypotheses about the differences that might exist between the following genres of discourse along each of Biber's six dimensions (see figure 6.3):

a. a press conference by a government leader vs. a radio call-in talk show;
b. a scientific research report vs. a literary-critical essay;
c. a corporate intranet email message vs. a memo on paper;

    d. an online catalog for clothing or electronic gear vs. a paper one;

    e. a friendly conversation with a professor vs. a conversation intended for advising.

How, in each case, might differing expectations about each feature and the grammatical choices by which it is expressed create misunderstanding? (For example, why might some email, in professional settings, seem inappropriately casual to some readers? Why might politicians sometimes come across as uncaring? Why might a literary critic find it frustrating to read a scientist's research report, and vice versa?) For a larger project, you could use Biber's (1988) lists of features along each dimension to test one of your hypotheses.

6.17   In a magazine cartoon, an auditor for the Internal Revenue Service (the US federal government taxing agency) is depicted as saying the following over the telephone:

> Your tax return, Mr. Ferguson, for 1985 shows that you want four hundred twenty-one dollars and sixty-six cents of the amount you overpaid applied to your 1986 estimated tax. However, we applied only one hundred sixty-six dollars and twenty cents to that tax, because we adjusted your account. The correction will be explained in a separate notice. Since we have not applied the full amount, you may want to: (1) correct your copy of the tax return, (2) amend your declaration of estimated tax, and (3) increase your estimated-tax payments. Otherwise, you may be charged a penalty for underpayment. No further action is required of you, Mr. Ferguson. Thank you for your coöperation.

In addition to parodying of the sort of bureaucratic register (see chapter 4) Americans associate with messages from the government, part of the joke is that only a government bureaucrat would talk on the telephone in exactly the same way he would write. What is it about the language of the passage that would make it ill suited for oral conversation over the telephone? What characteristics would make it difficult to process in real time, for example? What would be likely to happen, in an actual telephone conversation, that would cut this passage short?

Fixity, Fluidity, and Coherence

Print discourse is relatively fixed in form. A book, for example, contains the same words in the same order when you pick it up as it did when you last put it down. Once a book is in print, it is usually impossible to change the order of the words, the chapters, or the sections without reprinting the book. (An exception might be a book that was bound with a ring binder and had removable pages, like some cookbooks.) The difficulty is partly a result of physical characteristics of the medium (you could tear out the pages of a book and rearrange them, but, with most books, you could not then reattach the pages to the binding), and partly the result of cultural conventions about books and reading (books are not meant to make sense if you reorder the pages, and, since it is supposed to be possible to read a book more than once, or for multiple people to read it, you are not supposed to tear the pages out of books). If the book contains a story, the parts of the story are the same, and they appear in the same order, from reading to reading. (This is true whether or not the story is presented chronologically.)

Hypertext discourse is less fixed in some ways. Hypertext links make it possible for readers to choose how to proceed from section to section of a document, and to do so differently from one time to the next. This means that a hypertext document does not have a single structure, but many possible structures, and it may not have to be conceptually unified in the same way a book or an article is. As a result, it can be claimed (Bolter, 1991; Landow, 1992; Murray, 1997), hypertext documents are not coherent in the way print documents are. It is the reader who creates the coherence, not the writer. Since readers make transitions from part to part in various ways, conjunctions, for example, may be less useful than they are in more "writer-based" prose, since conjunctions create cohesion from the writer's perspective. Electronic conversations can also be said to be less coherent in some ways than face-to-face conversations are. Because many software platforms for online chat transmit messages in only one direction at a time, people cannot provide simultaneous feedback, and because messages are posted in the order in which the system receives them, the system of conversational turn-taking (chapter 3) may be disrupted. For example, a response may not follow a question, but be "interrupted," on the screen, with turns that are parts of different adjacency pairs, sometimes with different addressees. While speech cannot overlap in the way it can face to face, different conversational exchanges often overlap, as unrelated messages by speakers in various conversational subgroups appear "interleaved" on the screen. An example from a study by Susan Herring (1999: 5) shows how difficult it can be to figure out what is going on in this medium, at least for an analyst reading it after the fact rather than experiencing it in real time:

1. <ashna> hi jatt
2. *** Signoff: puja
3. <Dave-G> kally I was only joking around
4. <Jatt> ashna: hello?
5. <kally> dave-g it was funny
6. <ashna> how are u jatt
7. <LUCKMAN> ssa all
8. <Dave-G> kally you da woman!
9. <Jatt> ashna: do we know eachother?. I'm ok how are you
10. ***LUCKMAN has left channel #PUNJAB
11. *** LUCKMAN has joined channel #punjab
12. <kally> dave-g good stuff:)
13. <Jatt> kally: so hows school life, life in geneal, love life, family life?

14. <ashna> jatt no we don't know each other, i fine
15. <Jatt> ashna: where r ya from?

Two conversations are going on here, one between ashna and Jatt and the other between Dave-G and kally. At the end of the excerpt, Jatt starts an exchange with kally. David Crystal, discussing this excerpt, points out that the way the conversations appear interlocked on the screen "destroy[s] any conventional understanding of adjacency pairing" (2001: 158), or the way in which one conversational turn creates a space for a relevant next turn. Notice, though, how the chat participants use people's names to designate whose turn it is to speak in the conversation they are participating in ("how are u jatt"; "kally you da woman"). This might not be necessary if they could use eye contact or other visual or spatial cues to keep the conversations separate.

As Susan Herring points out (1999), the violation of expectations about turn-taking can lead to incoherence, and participants in text-based online chat like this may accordingly have lowered expectations about how relevant conversational turns should be. Herring suggests that this may be part of the reason why some software robot programs that talk can make people think they are human even when the robots' contributions might seem bizarre in human–human conversation. Herring shows that people who talk online respond to medium-induced incoherence in two ways: by devising strategies for mitigating it, such as ways of signaling whose turn it is to speak or whether or not one is ready to relinquish the floor, and by putting it to use in playful, creative ways.

Humans interacting with computers also sometimes encounter incoherence, and one way they respond to it may be to fall back on expectations and strategies they learned in human–human interaction. For example, Robin Wooffitt and colleagues (Wooffitt et al., 1997) discuss this interaction between a user and a simulated computer system acting as a travel agent (adapted from Wooffitt et al., 1997: 144–5; numbers in parentheses represent pauses long enough to time, and parenthetical periods represent shorter pauses):

1 User: I'm enquiring about em the flights coming from
                      Crete .h there's one due in: (.) to Gatwick (0.2)
                      approximately ten o'clock this morning .h. but I've
                      heard (.) there's some problems (.) do you know if
                      there's any flight delays
              (4.0)
2 System: Please wait.
              (27.0)
3 System: *Please (0.3) repeat (.) the (.) point (.) of departure*
              (1.2)
4 User: *.hh Well >th–< the- it's flying from Crete*
              (4.3)

5   User: ***To Gatwick***
            (1.2)
6   User: ***Arriving at Gatwick***
            (4.3)
7   System: I'm (.) sorry (0.7) British (.) Airways (0.5) do not
                          have (.) any (.) flights (0.5) from (.) Crete (0.3)
                          arriving (.) this (.) morning

In line 3, the simulated computer System requests the User to repeat the
point of departure of the flight about which the User is inquiring. The
User's response ("it's flying from Crete") is followed by a silence of more
than 4 seconds, upon which the User, unprompted, states the flight's point
of arrival (Gatwick). After another silence, the User restates the point of
arrival, again unprompted. Wooffitt et al. suggest that the User interprets
the long silence as an indication that there is something wrong with his or
her response which is causing the System to fail to understand. Resorting to
expectations about interaction among humans, the User tries to repair this
problem by providing extra information. Ian Hutchby, who discusses this
example (2001: 165) refers to this fallback strategy as "the persistence of
conversation" in human–computer interaction.

People using a new medium often begin by falling back on familiar discourse structures and practices, but, over time, they develop new ones, adapted
to what kinds of discourse practices the medium can facilitate and to local
ideas about its usage. For example, Ilkka Arminen and Minna Leinonen
(2006) show how the openings of mobile phone calls in Finland have diverged
from the structure of landline call openings in ways that can be linked to
mobile phone technology and to the ways mobile phones often get used, in
Finland, to coordinate ongoing activity. Here is the opening of a typical
landline call, from Arminen and Leinonen's data (2006: 342). (The transcription is in Conversation Analysis style, with many kinds of detail that
are not directly relevant to the discussion here. *.hh* represents a burst of
laughter, and brackets indicate both overlapping talk and, in the case of the
Finnish *no*, a word with no direct equivalent in English. I have italicized the
English translations to make them stand out better from the Finnish originals.)

1   R: (0.5) Mäki:>sellä<   ((the ending is said quickly))
        (0.5) at Mäki:>nen<   *((at + familyname))*

2   C: n:o: M:irja tässä hei.   .hh [hh .hh
        [ ] Mi:rja here hi:.   *.hh [hh .hh*

3   R: [no $he:ih$=
                                 [[] $hi::h$=

4   C: =#e# no ku- #ö# kuule tuota: mmh ö m- meinasin
        =#e# [] li- #uh# listen e:rm mmh uh m- I meant

5   kyssyy paria asiaa ku taas >neuvoa tartte:
     to ask couple of things as again >I nee:d advice

Like other typical landline calls, this one starts with the Recipient identifying herself, using the family name ("at Mäkinen"). The Caller then identifies herself ("Mirja here") and greets the Recipient ("hi"). The Recipient
returns the greeting, then the Caller broaches a topic ("Listen . . . I meant
to ask a couple of things").

Mobile calls, by contrast, often start with an exchange of "recipient designed" greetings. Because the digital technology underlying mobile telephones makes it possible for call recipients to see the names of their callers
before answering the call, they can omit the initial identification moves
heard in landline calls and start with a greeting selected on the basis of who
the caller is. (In some parts of the world, "caller identification" systems
make this possible on landline phones, too, and one might expect a similar
change in conversation-opening practices.) A mobile phone opening from
Arminen and Leinonen's data is this (2006: 346):

1   R: no moi,
        [] hi

2   (0.3)

3   C: no mo:i,
        [] hi:,

4   (.)

5   C: ooks sää lähössä,
        are you leavin,

6   (.)

7   R: e,
        no,

Arminen and Leinonen claim that the slight pause in line 4 of this example
is typical of mobile calls. They suggest that it occurs because there are two
conflicting sets of expectations in play at this point in the call: (1) the
expectation that, because the Caller has just spoken, it is the Recipient's
turn to speak, and (2) the expectation that the Caller initiates the first topic
of the call.

Discussion

6.18   Design a small pilot study that would compare cohesion in hypertext with
        cohesion in print, and carry it out. See chapter 3 to remind yourself of the
        linguistic features that can be used to create cohesion in written text. Is
        hypertext less cohesive than print, or is it cohesive in different ways? You

might also think about the ways in which visual cohesion, across linked web documents, might sometimes supplement or replace elements of verbal cohesion such as conjunction or ellipsis.

6.19   What would designers of online chat software need to know about face-to-face conversation in order to design a system that is minimally frustrating or confusing?

6.20   When people first started using the telephone, they had to find ways to compensate for the lack of visual cues from their interlocutors. What strategies have telephone users developed for replacing or doing without some of the visual information that is unavailable in telephone conversation? In your setting, are mobile phones associated with novel interactional strategies and conventions such as the new conversation-opening structure described above in the Finnish case?

Medium and Interpersonal Relations

Biber's factor analysis, discussed above, identified some ways in which texts can differ which have to do not with planning, but with the kinds of interpersonal relations the texts reflect and help create. As Chafe puts it (1980a), face-to-face oral discourse is often more "involved" than more planned genres are. Involvement is signaled by a number of features that characterize more oral or oral-like texts. Figure 6.4 is Tannen's (1982a: 8) list of features that create involvement in discourse, based on work by Chafe. Although they are often typical of face-to-face conversations, these features are not limited to such situations, of course. People interacting in other media sometimes attempt to create the feel of face-to-face talk. For example, to display aspects of interpersonal involvement that might be displayed visually

- Devices by which the speaker monitors the communication channel (such as rising intonation, pauses, requests for back-channel responses)
- Concreteness and imageability through specific details
- A more personal quality; use of first-person pronouns
- Emphasis on people and their relationships
- Emphasis on actions and agents rather than states and objects
- Direct quotation
- Reports of the speaker's mental processes
- Fuzziness (ambiguity, loose cohesion)
- Emphatic particles (e.g., *really*, *just*)

Figure 6.4   Features that can create interpersonal involvement in discourse
Source: Tannen (1982a), based on Chafe (1982)

in face-to-face interaction, such as emotional affect or irony, people using other media sometimes employ creative transformations of the writing system. Katoka (1997) shows, for example, how young Japanese women use "invented punctuation marks, pictorial signs, and intentionally transformed letters" to express emotion in letters to their friends (p. 109). Email "emoticons" can serve a similar function, and they can also be used to suggest that the writer is joking or being sarcastic. Maynor (1994) describes a number of other ways in which orthography is manipulated in email to "make writing more like speech" (p. 49).

Many studies have illustrated other ways in which computer-mediated discourse of certain kinds simulates the relative interpersonal involvement of face-to-face talk. Gains (1999) shows, for example, that in some settings (academia, but not business), email messages take the form of "pseudo-conversation," with subject headers like "COFFEEEEEEEEEEEEE!" informal closings such as "Stay well," and informal grammatical choices. In addition, some messages seem to presuppose ongoing conversations in being responses to implicit conversational moves by others: "yup it got through fine and dandy"; "Thanks love, yes I feel in torture." That some email writers imagine what they are doing as highly interactive is also shown by their uses of self-corrections and rhetorical questions. Werry (1996) shows how online synchronous chat can also mimic the style of face-to-face interaction. As with email, writers use orthographic manipulations to represent intonation and supply other paralinguistic cues. They use each other's nicknames often, to show whom they are addressing, and, in various ways, they work to create a shared immediate context for the interaction. (One online metaphor for the shared physical context of face-to-face talk is the chat "room.")

On the other hand, it is also claimed that computer-mediated communication can be more "depersonalized" than face-to-face interaction. People whose immediate stimulus is written words and who are face to face with a computer screen rather than a human being sometimes seem to orient more to the medium than to the audience. There is evidence, for example, that people are more willing to divulge sensitive information such as debt, psychosis, and alcohol use in a computerized psychiatric interview than in an interview with a human, even though they know that a human will eventually see the information (Greist and Klein, 1980). In a comparison of group problem solving face-to-face and via computer, Kiesler and her colleagues (Kiesler, Siegel, and McGuire, 1984) found that the computer-mediated groups had more difficulty with the task and that the members of those groups treated each other more rudely. The computer groups took longer than the face-to-face groups to reach consensus, and they talked less, argued more vehemently, and were more likely to swear, insult other group members, make hostile comments, and engage in name-calling. Subsequent studies have continued to find these effects, though the nature of the task in which people are jointly engaged plays a role in the extent to which depersonalization makes a difference.

It is sometimes claimed that the electronic media liberate interlocutors from some of the stereotyping and discrimination that can occur in face-to-face talk. People interacting online, at least in certain contexts, cannot see each other and may not have to provide their real names or any information about such things as race, age, sex, or appearance. Thus they might be less likely to interact through a screen of predetermined assumptions about their interlocutors' social status, authoritativeness, sexual availability, and so on. By reducing the number of cues about social identity and status, computer-mediated communication is said to have the potential to democratize inter-action (Spears and Lea, 1994; Turkle, 1995).

As we have seen throughout this book, however, discourse is never a transparent medium for the exchange of information. The ways in which language shapes the world are particularly obvious, in fact, when the world interactants share consists entirely of language, as it does in some electronic settings. Social identity and social status are not facts about people which either "come through" in communication or do not; they are interactive processes that are created in discourse. Like other "social facts" about people, gender, for example, is at least as much a result of linguistic performances by individuals and talk about individuals by others as it is a result of how people look or what their voices sound like. Research by discourse analysts has shown that gender-marked ways of talking and talk that reflects stereo-types about gender are as prevalent in cyberspace as elsewhere, as people express gendered identities and orient to gender in the ways they interact with others. In studies of the discourse of electronic discussion groups, Herring (1993; Herring, Johnson, and DiBenedetto, 1995) has shown that messages by female participants tend to be more aligned and supportive, men's more oppositional, and that men sometimes object to women's styles of participation. Rodino (1997) summarizes many other studies that explore how conventional ways of indexing gender are drawn on and manipulated in online interaction, as interactants create identities that draw on gender stereotypes in complex ways.

Discussion

6.21 Is the conversational quality of some computer-mediated communication a result of the fact that people often report feeling a sense of intimacy with people they meet online, or is it the other way around: could the feeling of intimacy be an artifact of the conventionally conversational style of the medium?

6.22 Using the lists in figures 6.2 and 6.4, describe what gives the following email exchange a spoken-like quality. What features of the messages are *unlike* face-to-face speech? (X is the instructor of a course in which undergraduates are learning to use document-design software. Y, a graduate student, is her assistant. Metamucil, a laxative dietary supplement, is often referred to in jokes about aging in the US.)

Date: Mon, 22 Feb 1999 09:09:14 -0500 (EST)
From: <X@university.edu>
To: <Y@university.edu>
Subject: Re: Friday PageMaker Quiz

Y,
How was the party? I've got to mail that woman.

I don't need the quiz grades until March 4th. And as for meeting, this week it's going to be crazy. I have the [conference] thing in the works and oh so much more):, but I do want to talk about your concerns tieh PageMaker and the class. Could I call you tonight or tomorrow evening. I don't want you to run your phone bill up and I already pay for service to [the city]. So, send me your number and a good time to call.

Thanks,

X

Date: Mon, 22 Feb 1999 09:21:54 -0500
From: <Y@university.edu>
To: <X@university.edu>
Subject: Re: Two questions

X,
The "party" was eh . . . put together on short notice, I'll just say that. It was good to see Sue again and some of her furniture looks good in my apartment. As for calling, I'll be home tomorrow past 8:30 pm . . . I watch "SportsNight" from 9:30pm-10. So, anytime pre- or post that would be fine. And I don't know that I have concerns anymore. I realize that these people are undergrads, so they may not take learning the program as seriously as the people in my program do. Does this mean I'm growing old???? Oh god, next thing you know I'll be complaining because those damn child-proof caps keep me from opening my daily dose of metamucil.

Y
Oh, yeah, the CD thing I'm trying to do for you has failed twice. Sigh. I'll give it one more shot before giving up.

6.23   One way in which people who are engaged in online interaction in English can claim gendered identities is via the screen names they choose (in situations in which people use screen names), which can be conventionally female or male or refer to male or female characters other interactants know. What other lexical or grammatical choices or interactional strategies can serve this purpose?

Analyzing Multimodal Discourse

Most of the approaches to discourse discussed in this book arose in a cultural and technological context in which valued forms of communication took place in one mode or another. Serious written documents (unlike unserious genres such as comic books) had few or no illustrations, serious paintings (unlike illustrations or advertisements) had few or no words, serious music (unlike rock, jazz, or hip-hop) was to be listened to, sometimes with eyes closed, and musicians were dressed and arrayed in such a way as to divert attention from the visual elements of the experience (Kress and Van Leeuwen, 2001: 1). As a result, communicative labor was specialized: writers worked with words, artists and designers worked with images, musicians worked with sound.

New technologies and new ways of imagining communication have blurred these boundaries. The same people now often work in multiple modes. Many writers are expected to know something about visual design and vice versa; multimedia art involves visual, verbal, and sonic elements; contemporary art music now more often involves visual display, as more vernacular genres of music always have. The increasing presence of multimodal communication in public life has called discourse analysts' attention to the ways in which discourse can be (and in many cases has always been) multimodal.

One heuristic for the study of multimodal discourse has been proposed by Gunther Kress and Theo Van Leeuwen (2001). They suggest that descriptions of discourse, whether mono- or multimodal, should consider four interrelated sources of resources and constraints: discourse, design, production, and distribution. Figure 6.5 describes each of these.

Kress and Van Leeuwen point out that meaning can be added at any stratum. Designers (in this broader-than-usual sense) work with available ideas about the world, but by putting them in the context of a particular imagined constellation of participants they reinforce some aspects, downplay others, add nuance. Producers (again, in Kress and Van Leeuwen's technical sense of the word) work with designs, sometimes fairly mechanically but often not. Choices about how to write a novel or a script (even if the plot is pre-selected), how to shoot a film, or how to perform a role obviously have very large implications for how the "product" is responded to. Meaning is also conferred in the distribution parts of the process. Where a book is shelved in a bookshop or what other books it is linked to by an online bookseller; whether a particular copy is hardback or paperback, a first edition or not; how a film is marketed, how much a ticket costs and how difficult it is to get one; whether or not a download is available and legal; all these aspects of distribution affect how people interpret the artifact and in turn shape how future artifacts are designed.

In some modes of discourse, the four strata may appear to be merged. For example, in a face-to-face conversation, speakers and listeners may all be involved in discourse (having ideas), design (deciding what to say), production (deciding how to say it), and circulation (speaking or signing the words and interpreting them) – although, as we have seen, the existence of circulating prior texts and ideas and the interactive qualities of how form and meaning are produced mean that no particular speaker or hearer is ever the sole creator of discourse. Kress and Van Leeuwen claim, however, that

Stratum of discourse	Definition	Example
Discourse	"Socially constructed knowledges of (some aspect of) reality" (Kress and Van Leeuwen, 2001: 4). Discourses provide ideological scaffolds for discourse. (This is similar to the Foucauldian notion of discourses; see chapter 2.)	The "ethnic conflict" discourse of war explains wars in terms of ethnicity, leaving out the influences of things like colonialism, economics, or ideological conflict.
Design	Uses of meaning-making resources like discourses, in all modes. Designs bring discourses into actual communication situations, changing shared knowledge into interaction (which reinforces the shared knowledge).	A thriller set in the context of an "ethnic conflict" brings the "ethnic conflict" discourse of war into use in an interaction between the person or people who plan the thriller and a reader or moviegoer.
Production	"The actual material production of the semiotic artefact" (p. 6) in one or more media. This requires technical skills such as using oil paint, playing the clarinet and reading music, or writing in English.	The producers of the ethnic-conflict thriller, in this sense, are the people who turn the idea into an actual screenplay or novel: writers using language, book designers using layout and typography, directors and camera operators using light, actors using their bodies and voices, and so on.
Distribution	The recording, reproduction, and broadcasting of the product. This can involve a different set of actors, engaged in a different set of activities.	Compositors, printers, book reviewers, and booksellers are all involved in the distribution of the thriller novel; recording engineers, studio public relations staffs, and movie theater operators are involved in the distribution of the film.

Figure 6.5 Strata of discourse
Source: Based on Kress and Van Leeuwen (2001)

"we live in a world where discourse, design and production no longer form a unity."

6.24 Use Kress and Van Leeuwen's "strata" as a heuristic to describe the actors and activities that might be involved in producing:

a. a poster advertising an activity sponsored by a university social group,
b. a political blog,
c. a personal page on a social networking website,
d. a TV advertisement,
e. a book of poetry with illustrations,
f. an interactive video game.

Summary

We began this chapter by reviewing some of the work on "oral literature" that first drew attention to the ways in which discourse and, some claimed, culture could differ depending on whether people used writing or not. Scholars such as Ong and Goody suggested that knowledge disseminated orally is different both in form (more copious, more repetitive, more formulaic, more rhythmical, and so on) and in function (more normative, more conservative) from knowledge that is written down. Research about orality and literacy in a wider variety of settings showed that literacy can take various forms and serve various functions, related to varying underlying beliefs about what it means to read and write and what sorts of activities reading and writing are accordingly embedded in. For example, written information is not invariably seen as more authoritative than spoken information, and the fact that writing is considered more authoritative in the Western tradition (where, for example, a written contract is binding in ways an oral agreement is not) is the result of a series of particular historical developments.

Turning to the topic of communication and technology more generally, we examined ways in which varying degrees of planning might affect the structure of discourse in various media. For example, more complex syntax might be not only possible but necessary in written discourse, when the absence of the sense channels available in face-to-face interaction means that more details have to be specified in words. We then discussed ways in which different media call for different ways of creating coherence and explored the implications of the varying amounts of fluidity and interactivity afforded by different media. Using examples from human–computer interaction and mobile telephone use, we looked at how people interacting via a new medium may at first draw on strategies that are familiar from older media. Then we touched on several issues involving the relationship between discourse medium and interpersonal relations. We examined the often-noted semi-conversational style of some computer-mediated communication, as well as the ways in which computer mediation sometimes appears to reduce people's sense that they are interacting with other people and, accordingly, to reduce the need for linguistic politeness (chapter 4). We also touched on the ways in which social identities and identifications such as gender, which might in some ways be less obvious in communication via computer than in face-to-face interaction, nonetheless appear to figure strongly in people's choices of how to interact and how to treat others. Finally, we touched on the topic of multimodal discourse, discussing one set of conceptual tools that can be used to describe how discourse that involves multiple modalities and media is produced and interpreted.

Further Reading

On the "Homeric question," see Parry (1971) and on the growth of literacy in ancient Greece, see Havelock (1982[1963]). The idea that the medium affects the message was proposed in the 1960s by Marshall McLuhan (1962); the idea that oral and literate cultures are different in fundamental ways is associated with Ong (1982) and Goody and Watt (Goody, 1977; Goody and Watt, 1968), among others. On ideologies and uses of literacy, key sources are Scribner and Cole (1981), Street (1984), and Heath (1983). An overview is Collins (1995); two interesting collections of articles are Keller-Cohen (1994) and Street (1993). A fairly recent discussion of the politics of orthography is a theme issue of the *Journal of Sociolinguistics* edited by Jaffe (2000). On the politics of hypertext, see Landow (1992). Sources that deal with technology and communication in general include Cicourel (1985) and Tuman (1992). Scollon (2001) and Scollon and Scollon (2004), working in the framework of activity theory, describe how discourse and social action are shaped by the available "mediational means," technological and non-technological. Norris (2004) proposes methods for transcribing and analyzing "multimodal interaction" involving gesture, proxemics, and other modalities along with language.

An overview of research by linguists on spoken (and spoken-like) and written (and written-like) discourse is Chafe and Tannen (1987). Important studies of planned and unplanned discourse and on oral and literate features in general are Ochs (1979b), Tannen (1982a), Chafe (1982, 1994), and Biber (1988). Collections of studies include two edited by Tannen (1982b, 1984). Herring (1996) includes several studies of structural characteristics of computer-mediated discourse. Claims about the effects of hypertext's fluidity have been made by Bolter (1991), Landow (1992), and Murray (1997), among others; on coherence and incoherence in online conversation, see Herring (1999). Galegher, Kraut, and Egido (1990) is a collection of studies by social psychologists about how computers enhance or interfere with cooperative work. Rodino (1997) provides a good overview of research on language, gender, and computer-mediated communication.

The discussion of multimodal discourse in this chapter is based on the work of Kress and Van Leeuwen (2001). A somewhat different approach, though also rooted in systemic-functional linguistics, is represented in O'Halloran (2004), who draws on the work of O'Toole (1995). Another edited volume, representing a wider variety of approaches, is Levine and Scollon (2004).

chapter 7

Intention and Interpretation

All discourse is both adaptive and strategic. Everything people say arises out of the existing situation; options for text-building are always hugely limited by the predictable ways in which new discourse echoes past discourse and responds to ongoing discourse and by the ways speakers' choices and their right to make choices are shaped and limited by their social positioning. On the other hand, however, everything people say is also in some sense a result of choices, conscious or unconscious, about how to shape the context that shapes talk. All discourse is both a reaction to the world and an intervention in it.

The idea of purpose can sometimes appear irrelevant. The process of discourse-building sometimes seems fairly automatic, and its results more or less determined in advance. Someone says "How are you?" and you say "Fine," not really intending to accomplish anything in particular but simply because "fine" is the obvious thing to say, and silence might seem rude. People rarely delve into one another's intentions in saying "Fine" in answer to "How are you?"; to do so might in fact seem odd or hostile. Sometimes people sound exactly the way sociolinguists might expect them to sound on the basis of demographic facts about them such as region of origin, gender, and age, and on the basis of facts about the situation such as who the audience is and how self-conscious the speakers are. Sometimes speakers and writers make exactly the adaptations to new media we would expect them to make; language learners sometimes appear to rely on text-building and persuasive strategies from their first languages in precisely the way we would expect. The outcome of an interaction may have very little to do with the interlocutors' purposes, in any case. It is all too common for a comment proffered as a suggestion to be taken as a promise, for an interaction intended, by all parties, to be persuasive to turn out to make everyone angry, or for an assertion of institutional power by a woman to be taken as an expression of unseemly masculine toughness. Because discourse is (and has to be) predictable in many ways, and because, as social scientists, many analysts of discourse are accustomed to noticing regularity rather than idiosyncracy, discourse analysts have tended to focus on the ways in which the shape of discourse is determined by social and situational factors.

Culture-specific language ideology may make purpose more or less relevant to how people produce and interpret discourse in particular situations and settings. In Western societies, very broadly speaking, the process of languaging is often understood as explicitly goal directed, and it often strikes us as appropriate to query a speaker's intentions and to use motive to account for text. The question "What are you trying to accomplish by saying this?" is frequent and useful in a US fiction-writing workshop, for example. Political speeches, advertising campaigns, and many other genres of discourse are judged by what they were intended to do and whether they succeeded in fulfilling their producers' purposes. As I wrote this textbook, I thought constantly about what I wanted it to look like, sound like, be structured, and be used for, and how I hoped it would influence people. Whether they are aware of it or not, what speakers, hearers, and audiences are trying to accomplish often has something to do with what their language is like.

The approaches to discourse which we have been examining in the previous chapters have highlighted the ways in which what a person can do with language in a given situation is limited and channeled by factors over which individual speakers and interpreters have little control. But a complete attempt to understand how discourse works has to consider the purposive aspects of discourse-shaping and discourse-interpreting, too. In this chapter, we touch on a few of the ways there are for thinking about goals, purposes, and intentions and their relationships to texts, and we consider when and where models like these are useful.

Speech Acts and Conversational Implicature

When you say something you are doing something: talking is action on several levels. On one level, speakers perform what are called *locutionary acts*. Let us use as an example a person signing in a language such as ASL,

American Sign Language. When people who do not understand ASL watch a person sign, they are attuned to what the signer is doing physically, to the movements and expressions of hands and face. The layer of action which non-signers could describe corresponds to layer of action that involves the production of sound in spoken languages or the production of marks on a page or screen in writing. At the next level of locutionary interpretation, someone with a dictionary and a grammar of the language in question could parse such a strip of gesture and expression or sequence of sounds or marks into a structured sequence of segments associated with conventional meanings. For example, the sentence "Drop over for dinner sometime" is a sentence of five words with an understood second-person pronoun *you* as its subject. Because it is imperative, there is no overt sentence subject. The sentence is about the future in some sense even though the verb is not marked for tense; it includes a temporal adverbial (*sometime*) that points to the future. It refers to an action (*drop over*) and to a meal (*dinner*). *Drop over* is a phrasal verb, so *over* is a particle rather than a preposition in this context and does not need an object as it would in a prepositional phrase like *over the hill*. And so on. Dictionaries and grammars describe language on this level. They describe the possible locutionary acts in a language: the inventory of possible sounds and/or gestures, how these elements can be combined into words and how words can combine into larger units, and how each word could be glossed, or "literally" translated.

Being able to interpret the locutionary force of an utterance is not, however, all it takes to understand the utterance. It is possible to know exactly what someone said and still not understand it. Students of foreign languages who have to use their new language for the first time in real-life discourse often quickly discover this. Consider the example above. When an American says, "Drop over for dinner sometime," is she making a suggestion or giving an order? Is "Drop over for dinner sometime" a request for immediate action (should you get out your calendar and set a date?) or is it just a way to end a conversation, or an indication that the speaker would like your relationship with her to continue? If she never mentions the idea again, should you be offended? Will she be offended if you do not show up at her house some evening, or will she seem puzzled or annoyed if you do?

Really knowing how to act in English or ASL thus means being able to interpret a speaker's or a signer's action on another level besides that of locution. It means being able to make useful guesses about which *illocutionary* action a speaker may be performing by making an utterance. In other words, it means being able to make useful guesses about what the utterance is meant to accomplish. It means being able to tell, if someone says "Drop over for dinner sometime" in the course of a conversation or correspondence, that the person is probably not promising to issue an invitation to a meal (although she might), but rather suggesting that she would like to be a friend. It means knowing that if a person says "It's cold in here" it might mean that someone should close the window, or that if you are asked "Could you turn the TV down?" it may not be a question about your ability, so that answering "I could if I wanted to" might not be very friendly. It means knowing that to say "I do" as a bride or groom in a wedding is a different kind of action than to say "I do" in answer to the question "Does anybody have a piece of gum?"

Discussion

7.1   Here are some short interchanges taken from newspaper cartoons. In each case, the cartoonist has played with the fact that a single locutionary act can perform multiple illocutionary actions. Use the idea of locutionary vs. illocutionary acts to explain what makes each one humorous.

    a.   A young student is taking a written test. Question on the test: "Can you name the first ten Presidents?" Student writes "No," thinking to himself, "There's *one* correct answer!"

    b.   A man is dozing on the sofa. From the other room: "Bob. The garbage." The caption: "Take as directed."

    c.   MOTHER: (to teenaged daughter, displaying jacket the mother has picked up off the floor) Whose jacket is this?

        DAUGHTER: Your mind must be starting to go, Mom. Don't you remember you bought it for me a month ago?

        MOTHER: When I say, "Whose jacket is this?" I really mean "Come here and hang it up."

        DAUGHTER: How about when you say "Answer the door"? Do you really mean "Pass the potatoes"?

        MOTHER: What do you suppose I mean when I say, "Watch your step, kiddo"?

    d.   Man to another man at bus stop: "Excuse me, do you know what time it is?"

        Other man: "Sure. It's 8:18."

        First man, taking out his pocket watch: "No, I'm sorry . . . you're off by three minutes."

7.2   Sign in the bathroom of a hotel room: "For your convenience, towels are provided at the Health Club and Pool. Please enjoy your stay." What do you suppose the illocutionary force of this message was meant to be? How do you know?

How do we figure out what people are doing – what illocutionary speech acts they are performing – when they talk or write or sign? And why is it necessary to do so? Why don't speakers simply say what they are doing? Why, for example, doesn't the sign in the hotel bathroom say "*We request that you not take the bathroom towels to the health club and pool*"?

Sometimes people do announce their illocutionary intentions, using phrases like "I hereby declare" or "I promise" or "I baptize you so-and-so." Using one of these verbs, in the right context, itself *performs* the action: to say "I promise" is to make a promise, to say "I order you to be there" is to give an order; the action of saying "The meeting is adjourned" adjourns the meeting. Verbs such as these are accordingly called *performative* verbs. Performative verbs are sometimes used in situations in which it is important that a person's intentions in saying what he or she says be absolutely unambiguous. (One such situation is the law.) In other contexts, explicit performatives are less common, and people indicate their illocutionary intentions in more indirect ways. Rather than saying "I promise to call," we say "I'll call"; rather than saying "I hereby request that you take out the garbage," we say, "The garbage . . ."; rather than saying "I order you to be home by 11," we say "We'll expect you home by 11." Being indirect about illocutionary intentions is often more polite than being explicit, because indirectness gives addressees options for how to interpret utterances (see chapter 4). Indirectness is necessarily ambiguous, though, requiring people to guess about what other people's intentions might be. How do people make such guesses? How, for example, do competent users of English know that in the right context "Will you carry my umbrella?" "Could you get the phone?" "I'd really like to take a break now," and "I think we should vacuum the carpet" could all be interpreted as requests for action?

According to the theory of speech acts associated with J. L. Austin (1962) and J. R. Searle (1969), we interpret indirect speech acts with reference to the situations in which utterances are made. We know, for example, that an utterance can only be successful (or "felicitous") as a request when these "felicity conditions" are in effect:

1   An utterance is a potential request only if the speaker wants something to happen in the future. (This means that if we know that a person does not really want us to disappear forever, we do not interpret "Oh, get lost!" as an actual request.)
2   An utterance is a potential request only if the speaker believes that the requestee is able to perform the action. (This means that asking someone with both arms in casts to close the window would seem like a cruel joke rather than a serious request.)
3   An utterance is a potential request only if the speaker is sincere, really intends the request to be interpreted as a request. (This is why it is so difficult to decide whether apparent requests for assistance with suicide should be acceded to.)

If interlocutors share such conventions about how contexts and speech acts are connected, then a speaker can show that a request is being made simply by alluding to one or another of these contextual conditions. That is, a speaker can make a request by alluding to a desire for future action (condition 1): "I wish somebody would go get coffee." Or a speaker can make a request by alluding to condition 2, the hearer's ability to perform the action: "Could you get some coffee?" Or a speaker can make a request by alluding to his or her sincerity (condition 3): "I'd really love some coffee." Because we have conventional ways of being indirect, we are able to be polite, to allow others to save face.

Another way of modeling how indirect speech acts are interpreted is the theory of "conversational implicature" associated with H. P. Grice (1975). Grice suggested that people interpret indirectness by orienting to a set of broad shared conventions about what to expect from others in conversation. The overarching principle is the "cooperative principle," or CP, and four "maxims" describe the particular expectations that shape how efficient, co-operative meaning-making is achieved. Grice's cooperative principle and the four maxims are laid out in figure 7.1. To summarize, Grice claimed that, in the default case, people expect one another to cooperate in conversation rather than contributing random utterances, and to say thing that are true, relevant to the ongoing conversation, clear, and as concise as possible. When

---

The cooperative principle
Make your conversational contribution such as is required, at the stage at which it occurs, by the accepted purpose or direction of the talk exchange in which you are engaged.

The maxim of quantity
1   Make your contribution as informative as is required (for the current purposes of the exchange).
2   Do not make your contribution more informative than is required.

The maxim of quality
1   Do not say what you believe to be false.
2   Do not say that for which you lack adequate evidence.

The maxim of relation
1   Be relevant.

The maxim of manner
1   Avoid obscurity of expression.
2   Avoid ambiguity.
3   Be brief. (Avoid unnecessary prolixity.)
4   Be orderly.

Figure 7.1 Conventions for conversational implicature
Source: adapted from Grice (1975)

speakers do not follow one or more of these rules, then they are inviting hearers to figure out why. The elements of an utterance's meaning that are determined with reference to these principles are called "implicatures."

Even when someone is following the default rules, implicature is required. For example, if A says "I don't have anything to write with," and B responds "I have a pen," A should be able to assume, based on the CP and maxims, that B's contribution is relevant to what A has said. A might conclude, on this basis, that B is offering to lend A the pen.

But the maxims can also be "flouted," or strategically ignored. Here is an example (from Levinson, 1983: 104):

A. Let's get the kids something.
B. Okay, but I veto I-C-E C-R-E-A-M-S.

In spelling out the word "ice creams," B is saying more than is strictly necessary, thus flouting the maxim of quantity. A assumes that B's flouting of the maxim is intentional and meaningful and arrives at the conclusion that B does not want the word "ice creams" used in front of the children.

Speech act theory and the theory of conversational implicature have been criticized on several grounds. For one thing, these theories have been shown to rely on Western ideas about meaning and its relation to "reality." Both these models of interpretation rely on the idea that meaning is located primarily in speakers' intentions, and that hearers arrive at the meaning of an utterance by calculating what these intentions must have been. Anthropologists who study non-Western societies have noted that this idea rests on the assumption that individuals can convey meanings that are independent of how their utterances are interpreted by others, the assumption, in other words, that meaning is located in the speaker's mind rather than being jointly created as people interact. This belief is far from universal; not all societies imagine that the way to determine how to react to an utterance is to figure out what the speaker intended by it, or even that intention is required at all in order for meaning to be created. J. W. Du Bois (1993) explores several instances of divination that illustrate "meaning without intention." In these cases, meaning is created as people come to agree on an interpretation of the essentially random results of the toss of a basket of cowrie shells, the spinning of a string, or the death or survival of a poisoned chicken. Michelle Rosaldo (1982) shows that, for the Ilongots of the Philippines, the fundamental purpose of talk is to establish and negotiate social relations rather than to exchange meanings. Ilongot orators make assertions, for instance, not so much to point to truth but to claim the right to make assertions. Whether or not the speaker is "sincere" – that is, whether or not the assertion corresponds to observable reality – is less relevant than is the fact that the utterance reinforces the speaker's right to speak. Since calculating what counts as a promise requires deciding whether the speaker is sincere or not, the Ilongot do not have a speech-act category parallel to Western promises. In general, what counts as "sincerity" or "truth" is culturally relative and dependent on local ideologies.

A second critique of speech act theory and the theory of conversational implicature has to do with how difficult it is to pin down exactly how they work in actual interaction. Discourse analysts who study records of actual talk rather than hypothetical examples tend to find that any utterance can point to any meaning if the parties involved tacitly agree that it can. Thus what is needed is not a description of a particular set of interpretive rules, like felicity conditions or the CP and the maxims, but a more general theory about how people arrive at understandings about how forms and meanings are connected, in the process of interaction. We need a theory of how utterances, and other modes of communicative behavior, point to the particular contexts in which they can be invested with meaning. We touched on one such theory, the theory of indexicality, in chapter 4. We turn to a related theory in the next section.

Discussion

7.3   The most direct way to make a promise, in English, is to use the words "I promise." Is there a word that corresponds directly to "promise" in other languages you know? If "promising" is a relevant cultural category, what are some more indirect ways to make a promise? For example, if I say "I'll give you a call sometime," would that be interpreted as a promise in your linguistic and cultural context? What other speech acts could be performed with the utterance "I'll give you a call sometime" besides promising? (Could "I'll give you a call sometime" be intended or interpreted as a threat, for example?) How does the potential ambiguity of this utterance give rise to misunderstanding? What are some relatively direct and relatively indirect ways to make a recommendation, in English? To give advice? To turn down a request? To make an order?

7.4   What is the most direct way, marked with a performative verb, of making an apology in English? What are some indirect ways of making an apology? What are some of the felicity conditions for making an apology?

7.5   Refusing a request or an invitation is a difficult interactional task in Japan, where saving face is considered extremely important, so that it is very important not to risk threatening others' face-wants (see chapter 4). Ueda (1974) lists 16 ways of responding to requests which she claims are all widely understood in Japan to be ways of saying "no." All but the first (the use of the word "no") are indirect. Among them are these:

1   actually using the word "no" (*iie*): rare in conversation, occurs mainly in written activities such as filling out forms;
2   using a vaguer form of negation ("I think not");

3 using an expression which could mean either "yes" or "no";
4 saying nothing;
5 asking a counter-question ("Why do you ask?");
6 making a tangential response, changing the subject;
7 leaving the room;
8 equivocating, lying;
9 criticizing the question, for example, claiming that the question is ambiguous, unclear, or not worth answering;
10 claiming to be forced to refuse to answer;
11 using a conditional ("Yes, but only if . . .");
12 saying yes, but expressing doubts about ability to fulfill the request;
13 delaying ("I'll think about it"; "I'll let you know tomorrow.").

Which of these strategies can be observed within your own linguistic/cultural settings? In which kinds of situations is each appropriate? Are other strategies used instead or in addition? Design a study that would (1) use systematic methods of observation to collect data about indirect request-refusals, and (2) develop and test hypotheses about when and why various strategies are used. To collect data, could you use a questionnaire? Could you set up role-playing situations in which people refuse requests? Or should the study be based on observations of naturally occurring interaction? To test hypotheses about function, would you ask people what they use various strategies for, or would you examine how request-responses are reacted to by other people in the conversation? What else could you do?

7.6 Which of Grice's conversational maxims are flouted in each of these examples, and what is the resulting implicature (in other words, how do hearers calculate what the speaker might mean)?

   a. A letter of recommendation for a job candidate: "To whom it may concern: Ms. Smith was employed by our firm for three years. She was always prompt. Sincerely, . . ."
   b. Fair is fair.
   c. CHILD: I'm going to watch TV.
       MOTHER: How is your math homework going?
   d. FATHER: What happened in school today?
       SON: Nothing.
   e. His heart is made of stone.
   f. (From Levinson, 1983: 112) Miss Singer produced a series of sounds corresponding closely to the score of an aria from *Rigoletto*.

7.7 Many Americans think that misunderstandings could be eliminated if people would just "say what they mean." Is it possible for people to say only and exactly what they mean? Why not? Phrase your answer in such a way that someone with no training in discourse analysis could understand it.

7.8 Discuss the issue of "saying what one means" in human–computer interaction. Can computer software that talks (or writes) to people perform indirect speech acts? Does human indirectness create potential problems for software design? Could indirectness be reduced or eliminated in human–computer interaction? Would it be better, for example, to train humans using a computer travel-booking system to say "When does the next flight leave?" rather than the more indirect "Can you tell me when the next flight leaves?", or would it be better to train the computer program to understand indirect requests for information? Why?

Contextualization Cues and Discourse Marking

Speakers may sometimes expect their audiences to employ conventional interpretive strategies such as those we have just discussed to infer how they intend their utterances to be understood. But we have other resources as well for assigning meaning to utterances. Various linguistic and para-linguistic resources indicate more overtly how talk can be interpreted. Whether or not speakers intend these interpretations, hearers can use these resources to arrive at them. The "metacommunicative" (or "metapragmatic") aspect of discourse is sometimes quite explicit: speakers sometimes say things like "What I mean to be saying is x," or "Now, here's the main point," or "I'm not saying this to make you angry." Often, however, the cues as to how words can be taken are embedded in smaller details of how people say what they say.

Elements of discourse which serve metacommunicative functions have been referred to as "contextualization cues" (Gumperz, 1982a: 130–52). For example, pause and final intonation can signal the potential end of a turn at talk (Sacks, Schegloff, and Jefferson, 1974), suggesting to another speaker that it is possible to start a new turn. A change in intonation and stress can change the force of an utterance: "I said sit down" could be a simply an informative answer to "What did you say?" or "I beg pardon?", but "I said, *SIT DOWN*" would be more likely to be taken as an angrily repeated order. The word *well* can show that something unexpected (a surprising response, a shift from one activity to another) is about to happen in a conversation (Schiffrin, 1987: 102–27). A switch from one language to another, in a bilingual's talk, may indicate a shift from background to foreground information or a change of intended addressee (Gumperz, 1982a: 79). Any choice a speaker makes about how to word or perform an utterance can function as a cue about how it might be interpreted, so that contextualization is a facet of every element of discourse. As an illustration of how the contextualization process works, we focus here on a subset of contextualization cues, a set of words and phrases including *and, so, well,* and the like, which can function as "discourse markers" (Schiffrin, 1987).

Discourse markers show what a speaker can be seen as doing on several different planes. Let us use *so* and *because* as examples. In traditional grammatical terms, both *so* and *because* fall into the rather vaguely defined category of "function words." *So* is labeled a "coordinating conjunction" and *because* a "subordinating conjunction." This terminology suggests something about one of the uses of *so* and *because*: to mark semantic relations among clauses. ("Coordination" and "subordination" turn out to be quite difficult to define, however.) Some dictionaries mention that *so* is also "used as an introductory particle" (*Webster's Ninth New Collegiate Dictionary*, 1983). Traditional descriptions of their use do not give the full picture of the deployment of words like *so* and *because* in discourse, however. Schiffrin (1987: 191–227) shows that *so* marks effects and *because* marks causes or reasons on structural and semantic levels as well as on the level of speech act and communicative action. In other words, speakers offer reasons and talk about causes and effects on several planes.

On the plane of reference, *so* or *because* can be used to indicate causality. For example, in an academic discussion group I recorded, someone who was talking about a very repetitive style of conversation among the people she studied said, "You're going crazy *because* you're getting your own talk back" and "Phatic community is [important for this group], *so* you have to have that same damn conversation over and over again." We can call these *causal* uses of *because* and *so*. They can in fact be paraphrased using the verb *cause*, as in "Getting your own talk back *causes* you to go crazy" or "The fact that phatic community is important *causes* people to have the same conversation over and over again."

Alternatively, *so* and *because* can mark logical inferences or warrants of the kind that could be paraphrased in syllogisms. Here, in the same academic discussion, the speaker used *so* to introduce the inference: "When you say the same thing, the referential meaning stays the same. *So* when we say the meaning has changed, we mean something other than the referential meaning has changed." *So* could be paraphrased with *therefore* here. *Because* introduces the warrant (that is, the supporting proposition) in the example below. Here people were discussing a Pinter play in which the expression "very nice" is repeated over and over: "The prior text is the course of the drama, *because* 'very nice' outside of that context just has a neutral, conversational [meaning]." These uses of *because* and *so* can be referred to as *inferential*.

On yet another level, *so* and *because* can give reasons for speakers' actions in the discourse, marking speakers' "motives," as Schiffrin puts it (1987: 202). In this excerpt, a member of the discussion group uses both conjunctions this way in making a point about the danger of imputing intention to speakers (a point that is relevant to our discussion of speech acts and implicature above):

> But intentions are always so dangerous. How can we know what someone's intentions are? And you sometimes end up imputing your intentions to other people. . . . I can maybe say what effects are had upon me, but maybe there

are other effects that I am feeling that I can't articulate. *So* it always seems like there is a little bit of danger in looking at intentions and effects, *because* how can anyone really know?

The best paraphrase for *so* as it was used here is not *therefore*, since what follows *so* is not a logical consequence of what preceded it. "X, *so* y" in this use means "x leads me to say y." "X *because* y," as *because* is used in this example, means "my evidence for x is y." These uses of *so* and *because* can be called *evidential* uses. They mark relationships between assertions and reasons for uttering them.

In addition to these uses of *so* and *because*, all of which mark reasons on one level or another, *so* can also function to mark where a speaker is in his or her turn to talk. *So* sometimes introduces summaries or rephrasings at or toward the ends of speakers' turns, as when, in the same conversation, one speaker summarized: "She was seeing [repetition] as a unitary phenomenon within a single culture and a single language, *so* she was finding the unity," or when she signaled the end of her conversational turns with *so* "*so* that's my little bit" or "I'm confused. *So* are you going to clear this up?" We can call these *boundary-marking* uses of *so*.

Boundary-marking uses of discourse markers are important in relatively monologic narrative as well as in conversations in which there are more participants and the conversational floor is more contested. As we saw earlier on (chapter 3), spoken narrative must be produced in chunks, which narrators need to mark off from one another. There is a variety of ways in which this marking can be done. Some narrative discourse marking strategies are so conventional as to be clichés: "meanwhile, back at the ranch," as a marker of a return to the main sequence of events at the end of a digression, is one such. One conventional way of signaling the beginning of narrative chunks is with *so*. What follows is a conversational narrative about a car wreck which, according to the narrator, was mistakenly attributed to alcohol, when the real cause was the driver's suffering a collapsed lung. The word *so* consistently signals shifts to increasingly crucial and suspenseful episodes in the story. (Not all uses of *so* serve this function, of course. Those that do are highlighted. You might try to identify the functions of the others.)

[Did I ever tell you about when I wrecked my '73 Mercury, er a Comet GT actually? Well I was bowling and uh, there was – it was the day after Valentine's Day, and we had the day off from work.

So I went bowling with a couple guys from work and uh, I had about a beer when I went over there and I had about a beer per game while we were bowling and uh – Well, we bowled about four games, and it was in the middle of the afternoon.

So I was driving home, and it was on Washington, nnuh, it was on Jefferson, and I was going east bound, and I got about a quarter of a mile, and my lung collapsed, and I blacked out and folded the car in a tree. And, I was still unconscious, and when I woke up and I saw all these sirens around me and everything, and I looked over to my left, and you know, about eight inches away was the tree, you know. And I opened my mouth and I pulled out a piece of glass about this big out of my mouth, and I have no windshield at all, and the car was half smashed, and there's just this cop in the passenger's side window reaching in to see if I was okay. And he dragged me out of there, then he stood me up, asked me a couple questions, and looked in the back seat and saw all those beer cans in the back seat you know. And uh, I, standing out there with the guy, and I just woke up from being unconscious, and he goes, "You been drinking?" And I said, "Well, yeah, I had a few beers this afternoon," which was a mistake saying that right there.

So he puts me in this car and drives me downtown. And meanwhile, I was supposed to go to Bloomington at four o'clock, so I was supposed to go home, and John and Jon were gonna pick me up.

So there's – while I was taken downtown, they're standing outside my door, wondering if I'm home, 'cause they're all set and all packed for Bloomington. And they turned around on the porch, and they see this tow truck driving my car all bashed up down the road, and they're wondering where the hell I am. Well, down to the police station, they took me downstairs, and they gave me the Breathalyzer test, and they told me to breathe in this thing. I got a .14. And then they made me walk this straight line while they videotaped me. And I had only been conscious for about fifteen minutes you know, after this wreck.

So they took me downtown, down to the, they booked me and took me down to the basement, opened the cell door, took all my possessions, put them on the table, and opened the cell door, and I was just about to walk in there, and I sat down on the chair, and the nurse – there was this lady – goes, "You sure you don't want to be checked out?" And I go "*Hell yes* I want to be checked out!"

So she goes "Okay," and I get up and the cop, get back in the cop car, go back downtown. He drives me up to Saint Joe hospital, checked me into the emergency room. I ended up laying on the bed, they cut me open, put a chest tube in. And so here I am sitting with this big tube coming out and oxygen going up my nose and a big intravenous thing. And I end up being in the hospital for a whole week you know, and I still got arrested for drunk driving.

The first two *so*'s in the car wreck story introduce story sections that gradually narrow the orientational focus from the day after Valentine's Day, to the afternoon of that day, to the afternoon's activity of drinking beer and bowling, to the subsequent car trip. Later *so*'s introduce new stages in the action. There are two attempts to start a section about being taken downtown to the police station, the first one aborted when the teller digresses to an evaluative side-story about his friends' reaction to seeing his wrecked car towed by. (Note how the digression is marked with the discourse marker *meanwhile*.)

So he puts me in this car,
and drives me downtown,
and *meanwhile* [digression to side story]

So they took me downtown, down to the,
they booked me,
and took me down to the basement . . .

The final *so* begins the denouement of the story – the section Labov (1972b) calls the resolution. The teller is on the verge of being thrown in jail when a nurse finally notices him and asks, "Are you sure you don't want to be checked out?"; he says "Hell yes!" and the nurse's "okay" means that instead of going to jail he is taken to the hospital:

So she goes "Okay,"
and I get up,
and the cop – get back in the cop car,
go back downtown,
he drives me up to Saint Joe hospital . . .

Discourse markers and other metacommunicative strategies are some-times thought of as belonging to shared sets of conventional options among which speakers choose and to which hearers turn as they interpret speakers' utterances. In other words, discourse markers are sometimes seen as having meanings in much the same way as other words and phrases have meanings, although the meaning of a discourse marker may not be referential. The discourse marker *well*, for example, is thought to signal unexpected conver-sational action because, and only if, the speaker and the hearers share the prior knowledge that *well* is one of the strategies that can be used for this purpose. But not all discourse markers are conventional. In fact, discourse marking strategies may be completely unconventional, completely idiosyn-cratic. Non-conventional ways of showing what one is doing as one talks are one aspect of a person's individual voice; they are among the things that enable us to recognize a specific person's style as distinct from those of other people.

Unusual uses of discourse markers can seem meaningful in multiple ways. This can be seen in this excerpt from a conversational narrative, where *and* is used, in the final line, in a somewhat unconventional context. A teacher is talking about a speech given by a student in a public-speaking class.

1   Um and this one guy . . . talked about how he and his family went to Hong Kong for . . . Christmas one year.
2   And there are two parts to Hong Kong and they're separated by a bay I guess= (audience member: =right)
3   So there's a ferry. (1-second pause)
4   Well he and his group, his family and . . . friends . . . they got separated and (1.2-second pause)
5   he hopped on the ferry thinking they were following him.
6   *And* . . . they weren't.

And typically indicates continuity. It typically joins parts of utterances that serve a joint purpose, propositions whose logical status is the same, or speech actions that continue previous actions. In a context such as the one in this example, in which the speaker introduces a contrast between the protagonist's expectation and what actually happened, we might expect *but* rather than *and* ("He hopped on the ferry thinking they were following him, but they weren't"). As Brian Sinclair-James points out in his analysis of this passage (1992), the presence of *and* here serves to set up an expectation on the hearers' part which is not realized. In suspending the expected flow of the narrative in this way, *and* serves as an evaluative device, in Labov's (1972b) sense, highlighting the contrast between what would have been expected and what actually happened, which is what makes the story tellable.

Discussion

7.9   Discuss the other uses of discourse markers – *and*, *so*, and *well* – in the extract above from the Hong Kong ferry story. What functions do these words serve? Are these their typical functions? Why might the speaker have paused after *and* at the end of line 4? Are there other possible explanations for this pause? How could it be determined which possible explanation is correct – or could it be determined at all?

7.10 A rhetorical move that is often effective in argumentative discourse is to state the claim against which one is going to argue, then state a counter-claim to it, which is then argued for. Ellen Barton (1993, 1995) provides these examples to illustrate how "epistemic" discourse markers such as *of course* and *but* are sometimes used in signaling this move:

   a.   *Of course*, even higher education has plenty of room for improvement. As critics have rightly noted, colleges could do a far better job of serving underprivileged and minority students and of managing their financial affairs. *But* the criticism often obscures considerable virtues. (Damon, 1990: A48)
   b.   The affirmative-action cause has failings, *of course* . . . *But* righting ancient wrongs is complex work. (DeMott, 1991: A40)
   c.   *To be sure*, the defects of communist systems do not automatically cancel out those of our own. *But* what, if anything, does Marxism have to offer to understand and repair the defects of contemporary Western societies? (Hollander, 1990: A44)

   Other sets of "double discourse epistemics" Barton found serving this function are these:

      true enough . . . but
      granted . . . but
      now (in the sense of "granted") . . . but

perhaps . . . however
yet . . . rather
fully . . . but
I am sometimes told . . . but

Write claim-counterclaim paragraphs using three of these sets. Do people ever use *true enough* or *granted* to introduce claims which they are *not* going to argue against? Find other examples of this rhetorical move in your reading, and see what other strategies authors use to mark the structure of the argument. Discuss whether, and if so how, research like Barton's could be used in the design of teaching materials for courses on oral or written argument.

7.11   Design a study to explore how *okay* functions in (a) classrooms, (b) survey interviews, (c) service interactions in shops, (d) casual conversation among friends. Carry out a small pilot study and report on the results. If you pursue this topic further, you may want to refer to Merritt (1980) and Condon (1986).

Rhetorical Aims, Strategies, and Styles

When people know in advance that they will have to persuade others to new beliefs or courses of action, discourse may be quite consciously designed for strategic purposes. Carefully crafted rhetoric (in the technical sense, not in the everyday sense in which "mere rhetoric" is sometimes used to refer to persuasive strategies perceived as insincere or unfairly manipulative) can be heard, for example, in political debate, in courts of law, in sermons, letters to the editor, public meetings, even some family disputes. The history of Western rhetoric began partly in the need for techniques for preplanned oratory which argued for one side of a contested issue over the other, and rhetorical theory has often treated all persuasive discourse as if it were entirely the result of conscious, author-controlled strategies for dealing with dispute. Twentieth-century rhetoricians pointed out that dispute is not the only context in which persuasion becomes necessary, and that rhetoric can be usefully taught and practiced as a way of exploring all sides of an issue rather than for arguing for one against another (Young, Becker, and Pike, 1970). They also pointed out that in the sense that all discourse is oriented toward creating "identification" (Burke, [1945]1969) with audiences, all discourse is rhetorical. But when the need for persuasion is felt before the fact, rather than arising in the course of conversation, then it makes sense to think about how people deal with these exigencies as potentially the result (at least in part) of preplanned strategic choice rather than on-the-spot adaptive response.

Although discourse analysts have paid more attention to spontaneous talk than to planned talk, attending to the linguistic details of persuasive discourse has proven to be a useful way of understanding how misunderstandings arise, as well as how they are dealt with. This is because there is enormous variation in what can strike people as persuasive in different contexts. For example, public debate in mainstream contexts in the US is thought to require displays of rationality and logic, and displays of emotion are sometimes thought of as a sign that the speaker lacks self-control or is trying to manipulate the audience unfairly. It is commonly understood that orators do not always live up to these expectations, but they can be criticized for this. In the rhetorical tradition of Burundi, by contrast, "reliance upon appeals to the emotions as the chief technique of rhetoric is taken for granted as right and natural and indeed the whole ground of its utility. There are no reservations about the desirability of flattery, untruths, taking advantage of weakness of character or profiting from others' misfortune" (Albert, 1972: 75).

A persuasive strategy that is effective and acceptable in one forum may fail in another, particularly if pre-acknowledged differences of opinion make people reluctant to do the interpretive work required. In the Western tradition, logic (or at least the appearance of logic) is often thought to be superior to other ways of persuading, and carefully crafted arguments in public forums often draw on the language and structure of formal, syllogistic reasoning. This excerpt from "Letter from a Birmingham Jail" by Martin Luther King, Jr., a religious leader and the most prominent American civil rights activist during the 1960s, exemplifies this persuasive strategy. Constructed on the model of a proof, the passage draws structurally and linguistically on formal logic. King writes here (Washington, 1986: 293–4) in defense of people like himself, who choose civil disobedience over obedience to unjust laws, such as the laws in effect at that time that segregated whites and blacks in public places.

> Now what is the difference between [just and unjust laws]? How does one determine when a law is just or unjust? A just law is a man-made code that squares with the moral law or the law of God. An unjust law is a human law that is not rooted in eternal and natural law. Any law that uplifts human personality is just. Any law that degrades human personality is unjust. All segregation statutes are unjust because segregation distorts the soul and damages the personality.

The central argument here is a logical syllogism with a major premise (a truth that is assumed to be universally acknowledged, here of the form *all p are q*, where *p* stands for laws that degrade human personality and *q* stands for unjust laws), a minor premise (a particular truth: *r* are *p*, where *r* stands for segregation laws) and a conclusion that constructs a new true proposition by combining the major and minor premise via the rules of logic (therefore, *r* are *q*). In other words, the argument is this: Laws that degrade human personality are unjust. Segregation laws degrade human personality. Therefore segregation laws are unjust.

The language of the passage is reminiscent of that of logical disputation, too. King's short sentences begin, in sets of two, by posing a logical question in somewhat the same way as a professor or a textbook might:

1   Now what is the difference between [just and unjust laws]?
2   How does one determine when a law is just or unjust?

The next two sentences sound like definitions one might find in a dictionary. They have the form of a standard definition, "an *x* (the thing to be defined) is a *y* (the category) which *z* (the distinguishing characteristics that set *x* apart from other members of category *y*)." Presenting a claim as if it were a well-established definition lends to it the authority of the canonical, codified claims about how the world is that are found in dictionaries and encyclopedias.

x	y	x
3 A just law	is a man-made code	that squares with the moral law or the law of God.
4 An unjust law	is a human law	that is not rooted in eternal and natural law.

The next three sentences form another parallel set. Each begins with a logical (and grammatical) quantifier, *any* or *all*, and all have the form of logical premises, any *x* is *y*; any *not-x* is *not-y*. The logical connection between the minor premise (7b) and the conclusion (7a) is signaled with the discourse marker *because* used in its inferential sense

5   Any law that uplifts human personality is just.
6   Any law that degrades human personality is unjust.
7a   All segregation statutes are unjust
7b   because segregation distorts the soul and damages the personality.

Perelman and Olbrechts-Tyteca (1969) use the term "quasilogical" for arguments that draw on the structure and wording of argumentation in formal logic or mathematics, but which are not in fact logical in the strict sense. An example of such an argument is this: "Let's invite Kathy to the party. She and Chris would probably get along, since they're both friends of Ann's." The speaker has constructed what looks like an argument based on the logical principle of "transitivity": if A implies B and B implies C, then A implies C. But friendship is not a transitive relationship – the fact that person A likes person B and person B likes person C does not mean that person A will necessarily like person C. So the argument is quasilogical. The language of logic is used quasilogically in the King passage above, in sentences 5 and 6. Because they are parallel in structure, these two sentences sound as if they bear a logical relationship to one another: If any law that uplifts human personality is just, then any law that degrades human personality is unjust. Note, however, that while King's larger argument in the passage about segregation laws is logically valid (anyone who accepts the premises would have to accept the conclusion), this small sub-argument is not. The claim that any x is y does not imply that anything that is not x is not y. (The fact that any cat is a mammal does not imply that anything that is not a cat is not a mammal.)

Another category of persuasive strategies are ones that could be called "presentational" (Johnstone, 1989). In contrast to quasilogical persuasion, with its underlying metaphor of persuasion as a process of rational convincing, presentational persuasion could be said to be based on the assumption that being persuaded is being moved, being swept along by a rhythmic flow of words and sounds the way we are sometimes swept along by poetry. The goal of presentational persuasion is to make the claim for which one is arguing maximally present in the audience's consciousness, by repeating it, paraphrasing it, calling aesthetic attention to it. The language of presentational persuasion is characterized by its rhythmic, paratactic flow. Readers or hearers are swept along by parallel clauses connected in coordinate series. Visual metaphors can also help make a claim seem to be present, as if the claim were actually in the audience's line of vision: audiences can be asked to "look," "see," or "behold." Presentational discourse can also make use of "rhetorical deixis" (Lakoff, 1974a), the use of terms such as *here*, *now*, and *this*, from the realms of space and time, in reference to ideas. In contrast to the denser style of quasilogical discourse, presentational discourse is characterized by features that create interpersonal involvement (see chapter 6).

One example of presentational discourse is from Martin Luther King, Jr.'s well-known "I Have a Dream" speech. King's widow later alluded to the presentational power of the speech when she described its effect by saying that "it seemed as if the Kingdom of God appeared" (Washington, 1986: 217). Here is an excerpt (Washington, 1986: 217–18):

> We have also come to this hallowed spot to remind America of the fierce urgency of now. This is no time to engage in the luxury of cooling off or to take the tranquilizing drug of gradualism. Now is the time to make real the promises of democracy; now is the time to rise from the dark and desolate valley of segregation to the sunlit path of racial justice; now is the time to lift our nation from the quicksands of racial injustice to the solid rock of brotherhood; now is the time to make justice a reality for all God's children. It would be fatal for the nation to overlook the urgency of the moment. This sweltering summer of the Negro's legitimate discontent will not pass until there is an invigorating autumn of freedom and equality.

King makes use here of a number of presentational strategies. There are long patterns of syntactic parallelism, and parallelism within parallel structures, in the clauses beginning with "now is the time":

Now is the time	to make real the promises of democracy;
now is the time	to rise from the dark and desolate valley of segregation to the sunlit path of racial justice;
now is the time	to lift our nation from the quicksands of racial injustice to the solid rock of brotherhood;
now is the time	to make justice a reality for all God's children.

There is repeated poetic alliteration and imagery, as, for example, in the phrase "the dark and desolate valley of segregation," and there are repeated appeals to here and now.

Another strategy for persuasion is the use of stories and other ways of creating analogies between prior situations and the current one. Biblical stories and stories from other religious texts are often used this way, as are parents' stories about "when I was your age." Fleeting analogies in the form of proverbs and maxims can serve as attempts to persuade. Analogical rhetoric persuades by teaching, reminding its audience of time-tested values by having them make lateral leaps between past events and the lessons learned from them, and current issues.

Differing expectations about what a speaker or writer's general strategy for persuasion will be and how persuasive discourse will sound can lead to communicative difficulty. Gumperz (1982a: 187–203) discusses an example involving a political speech given by an African-American radical during the 1960s, during which the audience became increasingly hostile and which eventually resulted in the speaker's arrest for allegedly threatening murder. Gumperz explores what went wrong by analyzing the speech and comparing it with a sermon in an African-American protestant church. He suggests that the problem, in large part, had to do with the speaker's use of the persuasive style of an African-American sermon in speaking to an audience of people who were not familiar with this style and hence misinterpreted the speaker's tone. Part of Gumperz' analysis has to do with what is called "style-shifting" or "code-switching": a speaker's shifting back and forth between two or more varieties of a language or ways of speaking. Most of the political speech was delivered in standard-sounding English, but the speaker used informal, vernacular features when he felt that there were rhetorical reasons for doing so, and the audience, not being familiar with the preaching style of the traditional African-American church, did not understand the rhetorical force of these style-shifts and heard them as insulting.

Gumperz points out that African-American preaching, which has been commented on since the eighteenth century, is noted for vigorous, intensive, expressive audience participation, including shouting and clapping. The themes of sermons are from Southern white fundamentalist Christianity, but the structure of the performance is similar to that of certain West African religious rituals which were transplanted to the Caribbean (and which are also found in Brazil). These rituals typically involved an invocation and call to a deity, followed by the manifestation of the deity in the form of a dance by an initiate. A speaker in a trance would then deliver the deity's message to the audience. Modern African-American religious services also have the basic structure of a dramatic exchange between leader, deity, and audience. By shifting styles, as well as through the use of other contextualization cues (Wharry, 2003), the preacher indicates that he or she is speaking sometimes with his or her own voice, sometimes in the voice of God, sometimes in the congregation's voice. The preacher's delivery may intensify during the course of the service; by the end, he or she may be speaking in an almost trance-like way in the voice of the Lord.

The modern sermon Gumperz analyzes begins with several short, declamatory lines that make a bridge between the preceding music and rhythmic clapping and the sermon. (Single slashes indicate minor, nonfinal phrase boundaries, double slashes major, final boundaries. Dots indicate pauses. Shifts into more vernacular style of more than a word or two are indicated with italic type. Gumperz' system for transcribing prosody also involves other conventions which I have not duplicated here, since I will not discuss the texts in as much detail as Gumperz does.)

1.   God is //
2.   God is // (louder)
3.   God is / . . . standing by //
4.   It's wonderful to know / that God / . . . God is standin by //
5.   Praise the Lord //

Then the preacher shifts to a more expository style, with longer intonation phrases and a more conversational tone:

6.   I hope that you / don't forget the announcement /
7.   We expectən yə to be with us /
8.   Praise the Lord //
9.   We're expectin you to be with us /
10. This week Tuesday through Friday night ah Thursday night and all the district /
11. Tuesday through Thursday night in the revival service and all the district workers are asked to be here on Friday night
12. and ah / . . . *don fəget if yə enywhere in yə car right now* you / . . .
13. you can probably sense the glory of the Lord in this place //
14. *jəs jump in yə car an* run right on down here to the Ephesian church //
15. Immediately after the broadcast we'll be havin a musical service here // Sister Golda Haynes and her daughter saxophone player from ah / all the way from ah / all the way from St. Louis Missouri // they'll be here in a late musical tonight // . . .
16. So you rush right on down and join with us in the church tonight //
17. *An yəll hear sm mo əf this good thing //*

The expository style continues as the preacher introduces the topic of the sermon:

18.   Callin your attention briefly to the sixth chapter of Hebrews //
19.   Begin reading at the seventeenth verse /

As the sermon progresses, the preacher's style gradually becomes more declamatory and less expository. In addition, there are more frequent switches into what Gumperz calls "folk" or "people" style: more vernacular, informal speech, with some different words and pronunciations. These style-switched phrases usually repeat or comment on something the preacher has already said. Lines 12 and 17 above represent such switches. Others, later in the sermon, are these:

28.   You trust / . . . otherwise you wouldn't go driving down the road / with that automobile weighin almost three tons // three tons and you / . . .
29.   *rippin down the road sixty five seventy /* . . . *and eighty mile an hour /* . . . but you have
30.   He [Nixon] got into office / because he said he could stop / . . . the Korean war . . .
31.   But this one / he said / he can stop the Vietnam war // . . . *But look like he bout to get another one start //*

By the end of the sermon, Gumperz says, the preacher's stylistic distinctions collapse, and he is speaking in a mixture of all three styles, declamatory, expository, and folk. Symbolically, the minister and the audience are one.

The speech Gumperz describes was delivered at a political rally by a leader of the Black Panther Party, to an audience of university students that was no more than 10 percent African-American. In it, the speaker tried to draw a parallel between the US occupation of Vietnam and the "occupation" of America's mostly African-American inner cities, and between the fate of the Vietnamese and that of the urban poor. Although the audience consisted of people who were likely to sympathize with the speaker's political position, things started to go wrong almost immediately. The audience began to laugh and made derisive remarks, and the speaker started to attack the Nixon administration's policies in the inner cities. He ended up talking about "killing" people who try to interfere with the work that the Black Panther Party was doing, including providing free breakfasts for children. The audience's shouts of "Peace, peace" expressed their disapproval of what they perceived as threats of violence.

Like the sermon above, the speech starts with an invocation, in short, declamatory parallel phrases:

1.   All power to the people // black power to the black people // brown power to the brown people // red power to the red people // and

yellow power to Ho Chi Minh / and Comrade Kim Il Sung / the courageous leader of the 40 million Korean people //

Then the speaker switches to an expository style, with longer phrases in relatively standard-sounding English and one switch into a folk style in line 9:

2. The Black Panther party / . . . takes the position // . . . that we want all black men / exempt from military service //
3. And that / . . . we believe / that black people should not be forced / . . . to fight in the military / to defend the racist government / . . . that does not support us //
4. We will not fight and kill other people of color / in the world / who like black people / are victims of US imperialism / . . . on an international level / and fascism domestically //
5. So recognizin that / recognizin fascism / recognizing the occupation / of all the pigs / in the black community // . . . then it becomes evident / that there is a war involved / . . . There is a war of genocide / being waged against black people right here in America /
6. So then we would like to ask the American people: "do they want peace in Vietnam?"
   (waits for response and gets none)
7. Well do you?
   (audience: "Yes.")
8. Do you want peace in the black community?
   (audience: "Yes.")
9. *Well you goddamned sure cain't get it / . . . with no guitars / . . . you sure cain't git it / . . . demonstratən //*
10. The only way that you're gonna get peace in Vietnam / is to withdraw the oppressive forces / from the black communities right here in Babylon //

Later in the speech, the speaker asks the audience members to give him information about people they know who are missing in action or prisoners of war in Vietnam, so that the Black Panther Party can negotiate with the North Vietnamese for their release, in return for the release of Black Panther members imprisoned in the US. The audience objects to this idea, whistling and jeering. The speaker responds by switching back into the declamatory sermonic mode. His phrases and the pauses between them shorten, the intonation falls more abruptly, and he moves toward the vernacular end of his phonological and lexical repertoire, as indicated in the italicized sections:

11. We say / down with the American fascist society / Later for Richard Millhouse Nixon / the motherfucker //
    (audience: shouts of derision)

12. Later for all the pigs of the power structure / Later for all the people out here / . . . that don't want to hear me curse / Because that's all that I know how to do / That's all that I'm going to do / I'm not gonna ever stop cursin / not only are we gonna curse / . . . we're gonna put into practice / some of the shit that we talk about //

13. Because Richard Nixon / is an evil *mæːn* //
    (increasing audience protests)

14. This is the motherfucker / . . . that unleashed / . . . the counter-insurgent teams / . . . upon the Black Panther party //
    (more audience shouts)

15. This is the man / . . . that's responsible / . . . for the attacks on the Black Panther party / . . . nationally //

16. This is the man / . . . *that send his vicious / . . . murderous dogs / . . . out into the black community / . . . and invade upon our Black Panther party breakfast programs / . . . destroy food / . . . that we have for hungry kiːdz / and expect us / . . . to accept shit like that idly* //

17. fuck that motherfucking man / We will kill Richard Nixon / . . .
    (increasing audience protests)

18. We will kill any motherfucker / . . . that stands in the way of our freedom //

19. *We ain't here for no god damned peace / because we know / . . . that we we cain't / have no peace / . . .* because this country was built on war //
    (As audience begins to get out of hand:)

20. And if you want peace / you got to fight for it / fight for it / fight for it //

21. So we propose this / propose this //
    (crowd noise: Right on, right on, Peace peace Peace Peace Peace.)

22. Right on / Right on / Peace / peace / peace //

As Gumperz (1982a: 201) explains it, "In trying to regain his audience automatically, i.e., without conscious reflection, the speaker has fallen back on strategies similar to those used by the preacher in our first example. His style here is clearly people style. Thus anyone who knows the rhetorical conventions involved will recognize that the word 'kill' must be interpreted in its metaphoric, black meaning: 'to destroy someone's influence.' In other words, if the speaker is using black code-switching and prosodic strategies, he cannot mean to threaten the life of the president."

Gumperz' explanation of what went wrong in this situation is cast in terms of cultural differences: the speaker's beliefs about how persuasion works and expectations about what oratory is like, drawn from a cultural tradition with which the audience was unfamiliar, differed from the audience's expectations. The audience, mostly white, was unfamiliar with the persuasive style of the speaker, who was African-American. There were, of course, other things at play, too. For one thing, the audience appears to have become engaged in a sort of contest with the speaker for the floor, attempting to drown him out. It is also quite possible that, despite the general sympathy of university crowds of the era with the politics of groups like the Black Panthers, racism may have played a role, in which case it might not have made very much difference which persuasive strategies the speaker tried. As important a role as differences in background knowledge, belief, and experience can play, it would be a mistake to explain any miscommunication purely in terms of cultural differences. Sometimes cultural differences pose little or no obstacle to interaction. The good will of interactants or its absence, their attentiveness or inattentiveness to the process at hand, is often what separates understanding from misunderstanding.

Discussion

7.12   Can you think of other examples of occasions on which someone's use of the wrong style of persuasion for the situation has resulted in misunderstanding?

7.13   Although it did not work well in the case Gumperz described, the African-American homiletic (sermon-giving) style has sometimes been very effective in American political life. Among the American political figures who have made use of this style of persuasion are Rev. Jesse Jackson and Dr. Martin Luther King, Jr. Does Martin Luther King, Jr.'s "I Have a Dream" speech have some of the characteristics Gumperz describes? (You will need to listen to the speech as well as read it.)

7.14   In what situations are stories used persuasively? When is poetic-sounding language persuasive? When does the repetition of a claim make it more persuasive? When are logical (or logical-sounding) arguments persuasive? Think of examples both within your society and from other groups you are familiar with.

7.15   In a study of US committee meetings, Bailey (1983) found that although displays of emotion were officially thought to be inappropriate in the decision-making process, they in fact served several purposes:

- Displays of emotion could signal commitment to a position.
- Displays of emotion could signal what sort of a self a person was adopting.
- Displays of emotion could serve as indicators of what a person was likely to do or what kind of response a person was expecting.
- One kind of display, a display of silliness or irresponsibility, could return people to the rational mode, serving to say "Let's get serious now."

Observe how displays of emotion work in a meeting you attend. How do people display emotion, in language and otherwise? When do such displays shift the key of the interaction toward greater seriousness and when do they seem to be problems that have to be repaired? What else do they do?

7.16   How do the following quasilogical arguments work? What logical principles do they draw on? What logical vocabulary do they draw on? How would you evaluate these arguments? Are they fair, for example?

a.   You have to expect Jason to get into trouble now and then. Boys will be boys.
b.   I once ran a red light on purpose, right in plain sight of a police officer, and didn't get stopped. That just goes to show you that the police never give traffic tickets around here.
c.   He doesn't like anything I cook, so maybe he'll like your cooking.
d.   When I telephoned your customer service number to bring this matter to your attention, I was put on hold for an hour. As a result, I am writing to cancel my account with you.
e.   It is a truth universally acknowledged, that a single man in possession of a good fortune must be in want of a wife. However little known the feelings or views of such a man may be on his first entering a neighbour-hood, this truth is so well fixed in the minds of the surrounding families, that he is considered as the rightful property of some one or other of their daughters. (Jane Austen, *Pride and Prejudice*, ch. 1)

Verbal Art and Performance

Our response to discourse is always partly aesthetic. Humans attend to how discourse sounds or looks as well as to what it refers to and what it is meant to accomplish. Discourse that looks or sounds better may be more persuasive, more memorable, more effective, better at creating conversa-tional rapport (Tannen, 1989). Substance is not independent of style, as anyone knows who has ever designed a speech, a poem, an advertisement, a website, or an article. The diagram in figure 7.2, based on two diagrams in a very influential paper by the Russian linguist Roman Jakobson (1960), captures one useful way of thinking about the relationship between the aesthetic aspects of discourse and its other aspects. Each element in capital letters in figure 7.2 represents one element of the process of communica-tion: there must be an ADDRESSER, an ADDRESSEE, and a MESSAGE with some sort of CONTENT. The participants must be in CONTACT with each other, and they must at least in some sense draw on the same set of CONVENTIONS for producing and interpreting discourse. In a given instance of communica-tion, one or another of these elements may be foregrounded, so that the discourse can be thought of as having one primary *function*. If what is most salient is the exchange of information, the primary purpose of discourse may be *referential*. An instruction manual might be in this category, for example. If what is mainly going on is an attempt to create contact, discourse is *phatic* in function. Examples of primarily phatic discourse might include routine greetings in the hallway each morning, or more literal attempts to

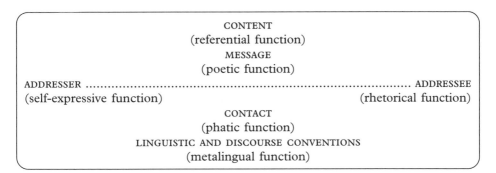

Figure 7.2   Functions of discourse
Source: Adapted from Jakobson (1960: 353, 357)

establish or check contact such as "Hello? Hello? Are you there?" on the phone or "Please respond to let me know you have received this message" on email. Discourse primarily focused on the addresser can be called *self-expressive*; when discourse is focused on the addressee it is *rhetorical*; talk about talk, such as the discourse found in dictionaries, or conversational questions about what words mean or how to interpret what someone says ("Was that supposed to be a question?") is *metalingual*. When the focus of discourse is on the message itself, the actual look, sound, and structure of the discourse, then it is *poetic* in function. ("Poetic," in this sense, means something like "artistic," not necessarily "poetry-like.")

Discourse never has a single function only. While content might, for example, be the focus in technical documentation, such documentation will not work referentially (people will not use it, or will fail to understand it) unless attention is paid to the implied persona of the author and to the look and sound of the documents, unless the documents are available to the right people, unless they are clearly written in ways that do not violate readers' expectations too much, and unless unfamiliar words and phrases are defined. Even technical documentation, in other words, is poetic, self-expressive, rhetorical, phatic, and metalingual, in addition to being referential. On the other end of the spectrum, experimental genres such as the abstract poetry of the Dadaists of the World War I era, written in nonsense syllables so as to be completely free of the need to refer to anything or obey the rules of syntax, were not thereby completely poetic in function. Experiments like Dadaist poetry work, in part, precisely by raising difficult questions about meaning, and they always strike us as self-expressive (Who would do such a thing?), rhetorical (How am I supposed to respond?), phatic (Hello? What's going on here?), and metalingual (This must be a language I don't under-stand), too.

Discourse of which the primary function is poetic is sometimes referred to as "verbal art." (This is a better term than "literature" for our purposes,

- Special codes (archaic or especially "poetic"-sounding language, for example)
- Figurative language
- Syntactic parallelism
- Special paralinguistic features (such as a louder, higher, or lower voice, for example)
- Special formulae ("Once upon a time," for example)
- Appeals to tradition (for example, a Mandinka griot might start a performance with "What I have myself heard / What I have heard from my parents / That is the account which I shall put before you.")
- Disclaimers of performance (claiming to be incompetent, for example: "I'm not very good at telling jokes.")

Figure 7.3 Ways of keying verbal performance
Source: Bauman (1977: 16)

since verbal art is often not written, nor is all verbal art culturally privileged the way literature is.) When people interpret discourse as verbal art – when they focus on the form of the message itself, in addition to other aspects of the discourse – they bring to bear interpretive conventions that are different in some ways from those they rely on in other contexts. Just as they need to contextualize their discourse on the level of speech acts and actions, indicating whether they are promising or predicting, continuing in the same vein or changing course, speakers, writers, and signers need to indicate that their discourse can be or should be interpreted as verbal art. They do this by means of contextualization cues that show that they are "performing." Bauman (1977: 16) lists contextualization cues or "keys" to performance that can be heard in many different traditions of verbal art (figure 7.3). Although the conventions for interpreting and evaluating performed speech differ from situation to situation, it is often considered fair to critique verbal art in special ways. It is fair to evaluate verbal art not just on the basis of whether it is true, understandable, or effective, but also on the basis of the particulars of its form: its words, its structure, its sound, its look, its delivery.

Rhetorical performances such as those we looked at in the previous section can be more or less pre-planned, more or less consciously strategic. Some rhetors read from scripts written for them by professional strategists; others simply start out with a general idea in mind – a biblical passage, for example – and design their talk as they go along. The same is true of verbal art. Speakers can move back and forth between relatively performed and relatively non-performed speech (Hymes, 1981b: 79–259); sometimes a small chunk of speech in an otherwise non-poetic stretch of discourse suddenly strikes people as artistic and gets commented on that way (as when a speaker makes an unintentional rhyme and says "I'm a poet and I don't know it"). Literary texts of the canonical Western sort – written, reviewed by editors, and published in a fixed form – are, by contrast, always perform-ances. This point has been made by Mary Louise Pratt (1977) in her discussion of the literary speech act. Every element of a literary text is assumed to be designed with strategy in mind, so that apparent violations of expectations of any sort – expectations about structure, about genre, about participants, about medium, about intention and its signaling via context-ualization cues – are conventionally treated as purposeful and meaningful. So, for example, a particularly garrulous conversationalist might not be assumed to mean anything in particular by talking more than was needed to get the point across, but the garrulous narrator in Sterne's *Tristram Shandy* is assumed to be overly talkative for a reason (Pratt, 1977: 163–6). Some-one telling a spontaneous anecdote in conversation who says the same thing twice might be assumed just to have had a small memory lapse, but if the same event is represented twice in a novel the repetition is taken to be meaningful. Susan Ehrlich (1997) shows, for example, that the repetition of narrative events in literary texts can signal shifts in point of view.

Discussion

7.17   A book about language, such as this one, is clearly metalingual in function. It is also referential. Is it rhetorical? Self-expressive? Poetic or phatic in any way?

7.18   What are some ways – verbal and non-verbal – in which people establish and/ or check that they are in contact at the beginning of a face-to-face conversa-tion? How is the lack of some of these face-to-face possibilities compensated for in other media, such as the telephone or electronic discourse? Can the authors of books always assume that they are in contact with readers, by virtue of the fact that someone who is reading a book has already picked it up and turned to a place to start reading?

7.19   Is it possible for discourse not to be self-expressive? Is it possible, in other words, to have no sense of the persona of a speaker or writer? Are there kinds of speaking and writing in which this is the aim? Is this a realistic goal?

7.20   Referring to Bauman's list in figure 7.3, describe how performance is "keyed" in the following: a poetry slam; a public reading by a novelist; a children's book; a traditional story-telling situation; a person introducing a limerick or a joke into a conversation.

7.21   On what grounds are readers and literary critics entitled to evaluate literary works, and what kinds of critiques are considered unfair or irrelevant? Get ideas by reading a book review, participating in a reading group, noticing what goes on in a literature course, or listening to a TV show on which books are discussed.

Summary

This chapter has considered ways in which speakers' intentions have been thought to shape discourse. We examined how speakers indicate what they mean by what they say, and how hearers interpret such metacommunicative signals. First we examined the conventions by which utterances are interpreted as actions on various levels: conventions for indicating and interpreting whether an utterance is a promise, or an apology, or an order; conventions for indicating and interpreting how utterances bear on previous and subsequent utterances and for indicating and interpreting speakers' motives for saying what they do: how utterances are taken to function in arguments, how they are taken to fill conversational slots, how they are taken to be logically connected. As speakers and audiences contextualize what they hear, indicating and interpreting how it fits with what is going on in the talk and in the world, they rely on conventions about how locutionary acts are related to illocutionary intentions, and on contextualization cues that serve to signal such relationships. We focused in particular on one set of contextualization cues, known as discourse markers.

We then turned to a more global level, considering the ways in which discourse can be thought of as "performance." We examined how strategic choices about tactics for persuasion might shape rhetorical discourse and how these tactics might vary from situation to situation, resulting in the potential for making the wrong choice. We examined conventions for interpreting verbal art, rooted in the assumption that everything in a literary text is a result of strategy.

Further Reading

The primary sources on speech act theory are Austin (1962), Searle (1969), and Grice (1975). A useful overview is Levinson (1983), chapters 3 and 5. A somewhat different way of thinking about the connections between utterances and the attribution of communicative intentions, focused more on general cognitive strategies and less on particular interpretive conventions, is Sperber and Wilson's (1986) "relevance theory." Blum-Kulka (1989) is an interesting and accessible discussion of the roles of various sorts of conventionality in the interpretation of indirectness. Blum-Kulka, House, and Kasper (1989) and Kasper and Blum-Kulka (1993) are overviews of research on "interlanguage pragmatics," or cross-linguistic and cross-cultural comparisons of how speech acts are performed. Gumperz (1982a) introduces the idea of contextualization and describes some of the metalinguistic cues that can be used in the interpretation of utterances. Silverstein (1979) uses the term "metapragmatics" for the ways in which the contexts in which a text is meant to be understood are indexed in the text. Schiffrin (1987) is the key source on discourse markers. On markers of evidentiality in discourse (such as *because* and *so*), see Chafe and Nichols (1986), Biber and Finegan (1989), and Hunston and Thompson (2000).

Studies of cross-cultural variation in persuasive styles and strategies include those of Albert (1972), Rosaldo (1973), Kochman (1981), Paine (1981), and Johnstone (1989). On performance and its role in verbal art, see Jakobson (1960), Bauman (1977, 1986), and Bauman and Briggs (1990). Clark (1997) is an interesting discussion of how cognitive scientists attempting to model the process of understanding have been hampered by the failure to consider the ways in which meaning resides in audiences' creative interpretations as well as in speakers' intentions and in texts.

chapter 8

Some General Themes

A Heuristic Approach to Discourse Analysis

In the preceding chapters, we have considered six facets of discourse analysis, each corresponding to one particular set of questions that can be usefully asked about a text or a transcript. Asking first about how discourse shapes and is shaped by the world as we experience it, we explored ways of asking systematic critical questions about the relationship between discourse and what seems real, natural, or true about the world. We wondered how languages, and ways of doing things with language, constrain and shape the ways in which we categorize things, describe things, and explain things. We explored how people imagine language works and what they imagine it is for, and saw how those elements of ideology shape what people do with talk, what they do not do, how they interpret discourse.

Secondly, we examined the role of structure in discourse. We explored the role of grammar on all levels – repeated ways of putting elements in order. We saw that the best ways of describing the ordering of words in clauses, and of utterances in texts, are often functional: grammars of sentences and grammars of texts alike both reflect and constrain the ways in which information is processed and social interaction maintained. Structure, in the sense of fixed rules or templates for the arrangement of elements, is always an abstraction: what people do as they produce and interpret discourse may or may not be to attempt to reproduce a template or follow a set of rules. Discourse is fundamentally the result of flexible strategies, not fixed rules: no interaction is exactly like any other, there is always another way of doing things, idiosyncracy and novelty are always possible and usually interpretable. But people also need and use fixity. If we could not talk and think about what we do in terms of repeatable structural patterns, we could not think or talk about what we have in common with other people with whom we communicate. We push toward grammar in this way when we talk about what we do with language, whether in prescriptive guides to usage (which state rules for sentences), in the written bylaws of organizations (where there are rules for the conduct of meetings and so on), or in our strategies, embedded in every utterance, for pointing to and commenting on what we are doing at the moment so as to coordinate our grammars with those of our interlocutors.

Third, we explored the ways in which the participants in discourse – producers, distributors, consumers, present or absent, sanctioned or unsanctioned – influence the choices that are made about text-building and interpretation. Consciously or not, discourse is always designed with an eye to details of social relatedness such as power and solidarity and the need to treat others as human beings. Conversely, we explored how texts construct interactants, how every utterance could be said to contain instructions about who you need to be in order to utter it and who you need to be to understand it. Certain social roles could be said to be constructed almost entirely in discourse. Being a teacher or a student, for example, could be said to consist entirely in doing certain things with language. Other roles have more obvious physical or economic correlates. Being a woman, for example, might sometimes be an entirely discursive activity (someone could be a woman in an internet interaction simply because of choices about how to talk and what to say, and via other people's verbal reactions), but being a woman in some other contexts might require certain physical characteristics and/or entail a particular kind of position in an economic system. We looked at how performances of identity orient interlocutors to the social and personal identities that are relevant at the moment.

The fourth facet of discourse we explored was repetition, on all levels. We examined the continual tension between newness and familiarity, creativity and constraint, "speaking the present" and "speaking the past" (Bloch, 1971). We looked at how speakers build new utterances out of pieces of things other people are saying now and have said in the past, and we looked at how we repeat and vary styles of speaking and writing, situations for speaking and writing, formal discourse structures and ways of learning and using them, stories and even lives. We noted again the fundamental tension in discourse and in human life generally between creativity and constraint, the tension between the inevitable need always to do something new with talk (because each particular situation is new) and the inevitable need always to do something familiar (so people will understand it).

Since we do not share minds or bodies, human interactions are always mediated: there are always layers of talk and ideas between individuals. Discourse is one of these layers, and the ways in which discourse is circulated are others. Accordingly, we turned next to the various connections between the technology of discourse (be it the "natural" technology of lungs, larynx, hands, articulatory muscles and so on, or human-engineered technologies such as writing, recording, and other ways of communicating at distances beyond seeing or shouting range) and the structure and function of discourse. We looked at how writing and ideas about writing can shape what people say and what they do with discourse, and we explored the ways in which differences in medium could give rise to differences in structure and in interactional style, differences in expectations about conversational coherence and narrative plot, differences in what people do together and how well people work together.

Finally, we turned to the connections between discourse and people's purposes, intentions, and goals. We looked at how speakers tell each other what they mean to be doing, through the sentence forms they choose, the words they use, their discourse marking strategies. We looked at the variation in the rhetorical strategies speakers have for evoking or creating shared understandings. We looked at the signals people use to align others to their overall aims in speaking (persuasion, self-expression, artistry, and so on).

Taken together, these six sets of questions about the resources for and constraints on discourse constitute an analytical heuristic. A heuristic is a discovery procedure, a systematic way of exploring a topic to see what is particularly interesting or problematic or puzzling about it or looking at a problem to see how to go about solving it. Heuristic algorithms for problem-solving are crucial in mathematics (Polya, 1973[1957]), since there is no mechanical way to construct a logical proof. In computer science, heuristic procedures are the alternative to solving problems via brute computational time and energy (Michalewicz and Fogel, 2000). Systematic discovery procedures have a long history in descriptive linguistics (Bloomfield, 1942) and continue to be important both in field elicitation and for analysis (Bouquiaux and Thomas, 1992[1976]). A heuristic is not a mechanical procedure, and it is not a way of uncovering truth. As Bloomfield said with regard to the analysis and recording of languages, the analysis of discourse is "an art or a practical skill" (Bloomfield, 1933: 93), not a rigid procedure with a unique outcome. The approach to discourse analysis that has been introduced in this book is a way of asking questions that uncovers more specific, focused questions and possible answers for them.

Several more general themes have come up repeatedly. These have to do with how texts are built and interpreted, with the relationship between discourse and language, and with the best ways of studying text-building and the larger processes in which it is embedded.

Locations of Meaning

Our discussions throughout this book raise an important general issue about discourse. This has to do with where the meaning of a text is located. Let us consider four possibilities:

1 The meaning of a text is what the speaker means.
2 The meaning of a text is what the text itself means.
3 The meaning of a text is its meaning to its audiences.
4 The meaning of a text is in all these places.

One way of talking about what a text means is to talk about what its producer meant by it. In everyday talk about meaning, Americans often appeal to this sense of where meaning is located, in the speaker's intentions, and the approaches to discourse surveyed in chapter 7 focus on the connections between speakers' intentions and strategic choices and the meanings of the things they say. When misunderstandings arise, speakers often say, "That's not what I meant!" or "You didn't understand me," making the implicit claim that what the speaker intends to mean is the true meaning of an utterance. To repair misunderstandings, speakers rephrase what they said. In literary studies, the idea that the meaning of a text is what the author meant is reflected in critical approaches that involve biographical work about authors in attempts to uncover what the author might have meant. When we wonder about speaker-meaning, we ask, in the past tense, "What did you/he/she mean by that?"

Another influential approach to meaning in literary studies, called the "New Criticism," was based on the idea that the meaning of a text is in the text. The New Critics' idea was that the way to understand a text is to avoid the "intentional fallacy" involved in the attempt to determine what the author might have had in mind, focusing instead on extremely detailed, rigorous reading of the text. In discourse studies, Conversation Analysts take a similar methodological approach. This sense of the location of meaning also circulates in everyday life, as when we tell a student who we think has not understood a passage to read it again, or when we look up unfamiliar words in a dictionary. We appeal to text-meaning when we ask a third party, not part of the interaction, to tell us what an utterance or a text means. When we query meaning from this perspective, we ask, in the present tense "What does this mean?"

A third place to look for meaning is in audiences. Meaning in this sense is meaning to someone. In literary studies, "reader response" and "reception" criticism clearly locate meaning in hearers and readers. In everyday interaction, we appeal to this locus of meaning when we say "What I got out of that movie was . . ." or when we say "I'm confused" instead of "You're unclear." Various popular approaches to therapeutic intervention in misunderstanding make use of the technique of eliciting what utterances mean to the people who hear them, asking people to tell each other about how each interprets what the other says. Phrases that remind people to do this include "What I'm hearing you say is . . ." The potential difference between meaning by a speaker and meaning to a hearer is a frequent source of humor, as in a cartoon in which the boyfriend says, over the phone, "The office is crazy today," whereupon the girlfriend thinks "Our movie date is off . . ." He says "I might have to stay a few minutes late" and she thinks "Dinner is canceled," and so on. The extreme version of the audience-oriented view of meaning would be that a text could mean anything at all, depending on who was reading or hearing it – a view which gives rise to skepticism about the possibility of talking about meaning at all.

An influential view of meaning among students of discourse in linguistics, rhetoric, and anthropology locates meaning in the abstract space between hearers, speakers, and texts, saying that meaning is "socially constructed," or "jointly produced." This view of meaning underlies attempts to understand communication that are based on "negotiated meaning" (Flower, 1994) and explorations of "the audience as co-author" (Duranti and Brenneis, 1986), attempts that focus on the evidence, in interactions, that people are adapting to and influencing each other's interpretations. In this view, too, texts have no "true meanings"; meaning is indeterminate, since different social actors, with different minds, come to different conclusions.

People's senses of how language works – their linguistic ideologies – often encourage them to look for meaning in one place rather than another. In the dominant Western tradition, as we have noted, authors and texts are often thought of as the most authoritative sources of meaning, and the idea that meaning is the result of interpretation by audiences has sometimes seemed threatening. In debates about the law that are based on disputes about the meaning of texts such as the US Constitution, each side accuses the other of being untrue to the authors' intentions, of not reading the words of the text carefully enough, or of indulging in excesses of creative interpretation. Religious debates are often debates about the location of meaning: is the true meaning of the foundational scriptures to be found in the scriptures themselves, or is it also important to consider how God, or the writers of the scriptures, would intend people to read them, or how earlier theologians have interpreted them? Some accounts of the differences between men and women, such as that of Tannen (1990), claim that men tend to locate meaning in speakers' intentions whereas women tend to locate meaning in interpretation.

Discourse analysts should consider meaning from all of these perspectives, and the approach to discourse analysis taken in this book tries to encourage that via systematic attention to audiences and speakers as well as to texts. But discourse analysts do not work with interactions. We work – as we must, and as all other students of human interaction must – with *records* of interactions, which we experience as repeatable, re-readable, re-watchable, analyzable texts. This fact sometimes encourages us to privilege texts over speakers or hearers as definitive sources of meaning. We need to be careful to do what we can to minimize the problem.

Discourse as Strategy, Discourse as Adaptation

The development of discourse analysis is historically linked to the study of the strategic aspects of discourse. In the context of the first European democracy, in classical Greece, those people who had the rights of citizens (at that time actually a fairly small subset of the population) needed to be able to make their own cases in courts of law, and the systematic study of speech-making and persuasion arose originally as the underpinning of practical education in oratory. The earliest Western analyses of discourse were those underlying the methods of the Greek sophists, who taught people how to make effective speeches, and the theoretical discussions of rhetoric by Aristotle (in the *Rhetoric*), Plato (in the dialogue "Phaedrus" and elsewhere) and their successors (Kennedy, 1980). The study of the larger-scale choices involved in the design of discourse (choices about topic development, organization, style, and delivery) were the subject matter of education in rhetoric which has been part of the Western educational tradition, in one form or another, for its entire history.

The study of smaller-scale resources for discourse (sentence-level grammar, the meanings of words, the sounds of words and phrases, prosody) has always been connected in the Western educational tradition with the study of literature, so that it, too has always focused attention on highly planned, edited discourse. The fact that popular ideas about discourse tend to stress its purposive, crafted, facet is a result of the fact that the various traditions of rhetoric and poetics have for centuries had an enormous influence on how people were educated in writing, reading, and public speaking. In this view, discourse is the means by which people make things happen: people use discourse to persuade, to cause others to act, to change the world. Because of this, conscious, strategic choice has often been stressed over other aspects of how discourse is shaped and interpreted. In school, for example, students have often been led to suppose that anyone, in any situation, can be eloquent and persuasive if he or she knows how to design discourse effectively. This focus on strategy was also characteristic of twentieth-century Saussurean linguistics, the immediate disciplinary context for linguistic discourse analysis, which developed in large part out of the concerns of philologists who studied literary texts.

This set of ideas about discourse underlies the productive tradition in rhetorical studies, the tradition of analysis in the service of strategic, conscious, designed communicative action. By analyzing the potential audience in advance, by inventorying one's storehouse of logical, emotional, and ethical appeals, through systematic inventional strategies for developing topics and lines of argument, and by marshaling language's resources of sound and structure, a rhetor can choose the best thing to say for the situation. This view of discourse could be said to characterize the more rhetorical approaches in sociolinguistics, too. Although relatively few socio-linguists explicitly describe their goal in rhetorical terms, those that see speakers as agents, texts as the result of choice, and grammar and all the other strategies there are for text-building as resources provide ways to think about how people could change how they talk or decide on better things to say. Interactional sociolinguistics is one example (Gumperz, 1982a, 1982b; Tannen, 1984, 1989; Scollon and Scollon, 1981), with its focus on "discourse strategies" and the ways in which people can be empowered as rhetorical agents by learning to analyze their own and others' interactional styles. Among students of variation and change in language, LePage and Tabouret-Keller (1985) and others who think of the details of utterances as the results of "acts of identity" by individual speakers also take what could be called a rhetorical approach to text-building, as do people who study strategic uses of "language crossing" (Rampton, 1995a, 1999) or "referee design" (Bell, 1984).

A somewhat different view of discourse has its roots in the reflective tradition of literary study and philosophy rather than in the productive tradition of written composition and public speaking. In this view, the controlling metaphor for discourse might be said to be adaptation rather than strategy. From this perspective, discourse is part of the continual, automatic dance of coordination that is human social life. Ways of talking circulate; people are "spoken through" as they produce texts out of prior texts, ready-made sentiments, and pre-molded formulas for voicing them. In this view, texts are best understood as responses to situations, often more automatic, less conscious, and less designed than speakers may imagine, and often allowing far less choice than they may imagine.

In this tradition, discourse analysis is used primarily in the service of description. The primary role of discourse analysis in this tradition is to uncover the ways in which discourse is outside of the control of rhetorical agents, shaped by larger social forces; the ways in which strategy and choice are more illusory than we might like to think. In this view, grammar and the other sources of influence on discourse are more likely to appear as constraints than as resources. In sociolinguistics, this approach to discourse is reflected in areas such as Conversation Analysis (Sacks, 1995; Sacks, Schegloff, and Jefferson, 1974; Goodwin, 1981; Atkinson and Heritage, 1984; Ten Have, 1999), which focuses on the ways in which discourse is organized "sequentially" as a series of responses to immediately prior discourse rather than as the result of strategic choice. In variation study, approaches that could be said to reflect this way of thinking about discourse see the details of people's utterances as situationally cued and automatic, particularly in the unselfconscious "vernacular" mode which is often the focus of attention (Labov, 1972a, 1994); in social psychology, models of unconscious processes by which speakers automatically "accommodate" to one another's styles (Giles and Powesland, 1975; Street and Hopper, 1982; Thakerar, Giles, and Cheshire, 1982) also stress the adaptive facet of discourse. People who work in the theoretical context of Critical Discourse Analysis (Fairclough, 1992; Wodak, 1996) focus on the ways in which people's discursive behavior is less the result of free choice, and more the result of external sociopolitical pressures, than people are led to believe.

It is not always easy to reconcile these perspectives. From the discourse-as-adaptation perspective, people who think of discourse as strategy are deluding themselves. They are under the influence of an outdated ideology that makes it appear that individuals can be autonomous agentive authors of original ideas and words. From the discourse-as-strategy perspective, people who think of discourse as adaptation can seem cynical and passive, unwilling to explore what they could do to help accomplish the practical tasks that need to be done, such as helping students learn to write or speak effectively and otherwise giving voices and choices to people who are silent. I have suggested in this book that we take both perspectives. In other words, I have tried to suggest that while there are ways in which discourse is necessarily adaptive, aspects of text-building in connection with which the idea of strategy is irrelevant, there are also ways in which discourse is necessarily strategic. Throughout the book, I have tried to stress both the ways in which discourse represents adaptation in the context of constraint and the ways in which discourse represents strategy in the context of resources.

Language and Languaging

Doing discourse analysis, and thinking about discourse analysis, leads almost inevitably to questions about the conventional notion of "a language." When we start to look at actual extended instances of talk rather than analyzing hypothetical sentences or isolated phrases elicited from field informants, we begin to notice that neither linguists' "descriptive" grammars nor the pedagogical grammars used in teaching language account for all of what people actually do as they interact through talk, sign, or writing. Sentence structures which, according to such grammars, are incomplete, incorrect, or even impossible are in fact routine in some situations. People use words that are not in the dictionary, and others understand them. Most grammars have nothing to say about the ways in which gesture and gaze and paralinguistic cues such as intonation contribute to meaning-making.

Furthermore, thinking systematically about the processes by which texts are built and interpreted in actual interactions causes us to notice that the relationship between "language" and "discourse" is not convincingly described in the conventional vocabulary of language pedagogy or linguistics, either.

People do not actually appear to do what they do by "using" a body of "language" or "knowledge of language" or "linguistic competence" that they already possess. Language seems, instead, to be created by speakers as they interact, noticing, repeating, and sometimes making reflective generalizations about what other people do, in the process of evoking and creating a world. To think of discourse as "language use" means imagining that "language" could exist prior to being "used," but in fact people learn how to talk by talking, whether as children or as adults, in the continual process of exploring new ways of being and acting.

More and more linguists and other theorists of communication have noticed these things. Becker (1991, 1995) suggests that "language" is not an object, but a process, "languaging." Becker draws on the work of phenomenologist Ortega y Gasset (1957: 242), who points out that "what [linguistics] calls 'language' really has no existence, it is a utopian and artificial image constructed by linguistics itself. In effect, language is never 'a fact,' for the simple reason that it is . . . always making and unmaking itself." Linguists who associate themselves with the "integrationalist" school (Harris, 1980, 1987; Hopper, 1992; Toolan, 1996; Taylor, 1997) also suggest that language should be imagined not as an object (a body of knowledge) but as a process, embedded in and inseparable from the rest of the process of human social life. In this view, language is an activity. For certain purposes, people reflecting back on this activity sometimes try to create static models of the verbal elements of interaction that recur. These are what are called "grammars" or "grammatical rules," and they can be useful, for example, when a person is learning to interact in a new world of discourse (a world with different categories, different sounds, different prior texts, different people, different media, different purposes). Just as it can be useful to have teachers and textbooks to provide shortcuts into new interactional worlds, I have argued that individual speakers may well create their own shortcuts, their own grammars. But understanding language cannot consist entirely of describing sets of conventional ways of languaging, as useful as such sets can be to language learners or to designers of talking software. Understanding languaging means understanding the process of discourse through which people constantly figure out what to say, how to say things, and how to understand what others say, in the process of interacting with others.

We still lack a vocabulary that corresponds to this way of thinking about language. We still use "language" as a noun. To do otherwise in an introductory book such as this one would be distracting. But I have tried, here and there throughout the book, experimenting with some alternatives, some unusual ways of referring to what are commonly referred to as "languages." Sometimes I have used the conventional formulations, speaking of texts as being "in English" or speakers as "speaking Chinese," or talking about what "the Arabic language" provides in the way of constraints on discourse that is "in Arabic." But I have also experimented with other ways of referring to these ideas. Rather than talking about "the English language" I sometimes talk about "the traditions associated with English." Instead of "speaking Chinese" I have tried formulations like "drawing on the resources of Chinese." Instead of "language," I have occasionally talked about "languaging." Discourse analysts ought to take the lead in developing some new conventions for talking about what we study; I hope this tentative effort encourages others to rethink some of our formulations.

Particularity, Theory, and Method

Discourse analysts often work with small sets of data: the discourse surrounding a single incident, five or ten conversations rather than hundreds of experimental trials, three or nine interesting and rich cases rather than a representative sample of a whole population. Sometimes we work with a single text at a time. Our work, if it is done well, is descriptively "thick" in Geertz' (1973) sense. We would often rather describe the small differences between different particular cases than generalize about mostly-shared features in a way that would facilitate comparisons of large sets of cases, and when we do work with large data sets, the way corpus linguists do, we tend to decide what to count not by using predetermined coding schemes but on the basis of preliminary smaller-scale analyses. We are often interested in discovering not just the main reasons for things, but as many reasons as we can. We are interested in the details of the texts we study and in the processes that give rise to these details. Our work is, in other words, often focused on the particular rather than the general, and, as a result, our results are better suited for suggesting how processes of human interaction work than for making generalizations about the results of these processes.

It is tempting, though, for discourse analysts to make such generalizations. Large-scale social theories are tempting, for one thing, because they suggest large-scale solutions to social problems. If we could figure out the reason why men and women miscommunicate, we could show men and women how not to miscommunicate. If we could find the root cause of linguistic discrimination in a pan-human, natural struggle for power, then perhaps we could solve the problem by redirecting power relations. If we could explain the process of learning to write in terms of genre, then all we would have to do in university writing classes is show students how to analyze and duplicate academic prose. But one-dimensional explanations suggested by large theories often turn out not to work, and large generalizations based on small studies (even sometimes ones based on large studies) turn out to be untrustworthy. Generalizations about "what women do," for example, turn out to be accurate only as statements about what the particular women that were studied did. Connections between language and social identity turn out to be extremely complex, so that disparities in how linguistic choices are socially evaluated cannot be explained solely in terms of disparities in "prestige," "power," or "symbolic capital." Learning to write in new ways has to do with learning the structural conventions and lexical formulas of new genres, but it also has to do with developing new social relationships, new senses of self, new ways of seeing the world. Large-scale theories almost inevitably obscure the fact that human actions, discursive and otherwise, are always multiply determined, the result of a large number of intersecting factors, one of which is the particular human being who is acting for a particular set of purposes in a particular situation. If we make premature decisions about what we are seeing based on expectations about what we will see provided by theories we select in advance, we risk failing to pay attention to the multiplicity of resources and constraints that surrounds any human action.

The trouble, of course, is that it is impossible not to have expectations. That is, it is impossible for observations to be "theory-neutral." On the most basic neurological level, we could not perceive anything if we did not have a way of interpreting sensory information, and a way of interpreting is inevitably based on a set of expectations about what is relatively likely and what is not. It may be relatively easy, at least sometimes, to identify and try to set aside large theories, perhaps particularly the ones that have names (the theory that class struggle is at the root of all human behavior, the theory that women's experience is always fundamentally different from men's, the theory that free competition in the economic marketplace eventually leads to social equilibrium). We can also work to become self-conscious about the widespread popular theories that sometimes go unnamed (the theory that people from different countries are fundamentally different, the theory that accent reflects moral character, the theory that change is good or the theory that change is bad). But it is always very difficult to identify the small theories with which we inevitably approach any new phenomenon.

For this reason, it is crucial to think carefully about what our approaches to new phenomena are like. It is crucial to have a disciplined, systematic way of thinking about new things, to minimize the distorting, focus-narrowing effects of theories, large and small. In other words, clearly articulated research methodology is essential, because methodology helps protect us from premature theorizing. Discourse analysis, as I have presented it here, can provide some of the rigor and systematicity that is sometimes missing in interpretive work about discourse in the critical tradition, which is often less particularistic and sometimes jumps sooner to theory.

From Text Outward

When you study a text or a transcript, you are always in some sense trying to understand it. But to understand a text completely would be to arrive at its true meaning, and, since meaning is always particular and situational (in other words, what a text means depends on who is uttering it, why, when, who is listening, and so on), this is impossible. Analyses of discourse are always partial and provisional. Any particular utterance presupposes an entire world, an entire set of psychologies, an entire linguistic history. If discourse analysis is always partial, how much is enough? If we could, in theory and given enough time, spend a lifetime on a phrase and still not have finished describing the world, where do we stop? How far outward from the text do we need to go?

The answer depends, obviously, on our goals in doing the analysis. If the question is "Do English speakers typically encode agents as grammatical subjects?" then all that is needed is to see whether or not, in a corpus of utterances, the semantic agent usually appears as the grammatical subject. But if the question is "Why do English speakers encode agents as subjects?" or "How do conventions about representing agency in texts reflect dominant epistemologies?" or "How does a social institution constitute itself via representations of itself as agent?" then the task has to be larger. Some discourse analysts, often linguists who are primarily interested in linguistic structure and language change, ask questions of the former kind. Many others, linguists but also other people whose research questions are about the connections between language and social life rather than about language per se, ask questions of the latter kind. Such people often find it necessary to work far outward from texts into their cognitive and sociocultural contexts, and they often find that the way to do this is to combine discourse analysis with the methods of ethnography or statistical analysis, with the conceptual frameworks of rhetorical or social theory, with research findings from psychology, history, or language acquisition, and so on.

People who study discourse ask many different kinds of questions, and they need many different theoretical and methodological tools to answer them. What I have described in this book is a methodological tool that has been useful, or is potentially useful, in disciplinary and interdisciplinary inquiry of many sorts. Discourse analysis, as I have described it here, is rigorous to the extent that it is grounded in the closest possible attention to linguistic and contextual detail. Discourse analysis starts in linguistic analysis, and many of the people who developed the ways of working I have described in this book have been linguists. Linguists are skilled and practiced at attending to the details of language form and function, and we have these skills to offer to people from other research traditions who wonder about the role of discourse in human life. Discourse analysis is systematic to the extent that it encourages analysts to develop multiple explanations before they argue for one. Interdisciplinarity is thus not just an attractive feature of discourse analysis but a central fact about it. Discourse analysts have often drawn on disciplines other than linguistics for possible ways of explaining things, and we should continue to search as widely as we can.

Glossary

This glossary includes only technical terms, mainly from linguistics, which are not defined in the discussion in which they first appear. For more complete discussions of many of these concepts, consult an encyclopedia of language or linguistics such as Crystal (1987), Bright (1992), or Asher and Simpson (1994).

agent Each noun phrase (a noun phrase is noun plus its associated determiners and modifiers) in a clause has a role with respect to the meaning of the verb. A noun phrase which represents who or what initiates, controls, or is responsible for the action of the verb is an agent. In simple, active clauses in English, the agent noun phrase is often the grammatical subject: _Juana phoned the doctor_. In passive clauses, the agent noun phrase may be part of a prepositional phrase introduced with _by_ (_Ten protestors were arrested by the State Police_), or the agent of the action may not be expressed at all (_Ten protestors were arrested_). Agency may be expressed in many other ways as well, as, for example, with the noun suffix _-er_ in English, which turns a verb (_to run_, for example into an agentive noun (_a runner_).

aspect The length or type of activity represented by a verb. In English, _I went_ is in the simple past tense. _I was going_ is past tense, continuous (or progressive) aspect. *I have gone* is present tense, perfective aspect. Other languages make other aspectual distinctions.

classifier In many languages, nouns must be accompanied by words or affixes which indicate which of a set of semantic categories they belong to. Such classes may, for example, have to do with the shape of the object represented by the noun. (Nouns representing long things might, in such a system, require a different classifer than nouns representing round things.)

contrastive pragmatics The study of speech acts and conversational implicature across languages. See *pragmatics*.

contrastive rhetoric The study of styles of persuasion and/or the organization of discourse across languages.

embedding Clauses that appear inside other clauses are embedded. For example, in the sentence *He watched me go out*, the clause *I went out* is embedded as the direct object of the verb *watch*.

epistemic See *evidential*.

ethnography A branch of anthropology focused on the description of culture. Ethnographers use various techniques, principal among them participant observation, to arrive at characterizations of human beliefs and practices as they are understood by the people they study.

evidential (**also *epistemic***) Any grammatical or lexical strategy for indicating how the information expressed in an utterance was acquired or how certain it is, as in *Change is <u>clearly</u> inevitable*; *<u>I believe</u> I've met you before*; *War <u>is</u> peace*. In some languages, evidentiality must be explicitly indicated in every sentence that expresses an assertion.

gloss A rough word-by-word translation, often used in displaying the results of a linguistic analysis to people who do not know the language being analyzed.

grammatical person See *person, grammatical*.

grammaticalization The process by which elements once freely added to a phrase or clause to express shades of meaning may eventually become part of the fixed grammar of a language. For example, the English phrase *going to* (sometimes spelled as one word, *gonna*), used for the immediate future (*This is <u>going to</u> pose a problem*), is a grammaticalized use of the verb *go*. In this usage, *go* no longer indicates a direction of motion but now fills a grammatical function instead.

hedging The use of strategies that distance the speaker from the meaning or the implications of an utterance. Evidentials can function as hedges (*You're probably right*), as can, for example, modal verbs (*That might be a good idea*) or tag questions (*This is the place to turn, isn't it?*).

hermeneutics The study of the principles of the interpretation of texts, originally with reference to interpretations of the Bible but now used more widely.

heuristic (**noun**) A systematic approach to problem-solving or discovery, such as a set of questions to ask or procedures to follow.

honorific A form that varies depending on the relative social status of discourse participants.

imperative The sentence type exemplified by *Shut the door*. In English, imperative sentences do not have subjects, but instead begin with the verb.

interlocutor A person engaged in a verbal interaction, particularly as one of the principal, sanctioned participants, not simply as an overhearer.

intertextuality The ways in which texts are related to other texts. (See chapter 5.)

intonation The meaningful use of pitch in speech. An assertion may be distinguished from a request for clarification on the basis of intonation, for example: *It's ten o'clock. It's ten o'clock?*

intransitive See *transitivity*.

lexical Adjectival form of *lexicon* (a set of words) or *lexeme* (one *lexical item* or word). A *lexical* phenomenon is one involving words, as opposed to, for example, grammatical structures.

morpheme The smallest unit of meaning. The word *cat* has one morpheme; the word *cats* has two, *cat* and the plural suffix *-s*.

morphology The study of words and their internal structures.

orthography The use of writing systems, including, for example, alphabets, as media for language.

parse (**verb**) To analyze the structure of a phrase, clause, or sentence.

part of speech One of the set of categories traditionally used to classify words by function. Parts of speech include noun, verb, adjective, adverb, conjunction, etc.

person, grammatical A system that categorizes how speakers indicate the roles of participants in interaction. Person may be indicated via pronouns and verb endings, and in other ways. First-person pronouns in English are *I* and *we*, second-person pronouns are *you*, and, in vernacular varieties, forms like *y'all* or *you'uns*, and third-person pronouns are *he, she, it*, and *they*.

philology The study of ancient texts and the languages in which they were written. Nineteenth-century philology gave rise to modern historical-comparative linguistics and is a precursor of contemporary discourse analysis.

phonetics The study of speech sounds. *Articulatory phonetics* is the study of how the sounds used in languages are produced by the vocal organs and muscles. *Acoustic phonetics* is the study of the physical properties of speech sounds.

phonology How speech sounds are deployed in languages. Not every difference in sound makes a difference in meaning, and phonologists explore how humans and human languages categorize sounds in order to assign them to one *phoneme* or another. For example, the first sound in *pit* is followed with a puff of air (called "aspiration") and the second sound in *spit* is not. Yet speakers of English hear both of these sounds as instances of the phoneme /p/. Speakers of Thai would hear them as two different phonemes, on the other hand.

pragmatics The study of how utterances are deployed and interpreted in interaction. Includes theories about speech acts and conversational implicature that model what is required for the interpretation of a sentence beyond understanding its literal meaning.

presupposition What is assumed in using or interpreting a sentence, as opposed to what is asserted. To give a famous example, someone who says *The king of France is bald* presupposes that there is a king of France.

prosody The use in language of pitch, loudness, tempo, and rhythm.

rhetoric The study or practice of discourse, often focused on argumentation or persuasion in public speech or writing. The discipline of rhetoric originated in the study and practice of oratory in classical Greece, but current rhetorical study encompasses many genres of discourse.

semantics The study of meaning.

sociolinguistics The study of the relationships between language and society. Sociolinguists study such things as the roles played by social pressures and patterns of social interaction in language change; the uses of language in the creation and maintenance of social relations and personal identities; and language planning and language policy.

stylistics The study of literary style, either in general or in the work of particular authors.

syllogism In Aristotelian logic, a set of three propositions consisting of a major premise (*If it's raining, the picnic's canceled*), a minor premise (*It's raining*), and a conclusion (*Therefore the picnic's canceled*).

syntactician Someone who studies syntax. See *syntax*.

syntax The arrangement of elements in a phrase or clause; the ways in which users of a language characteristically use patterns of arrangement of elements to convey meaning. Often used instead of "grammar" to avoid the prescriptive connotations of the latter term.

Tagmemics A system for describing languages developed by American linguist Kenneth Pike, in which each linguistic unit is described simultaneously in terms of its physical form and its functions within the system of a language.

tense The time of the action represented by a verb, with respect to the interaction in which the verb is used. *I walk* is in the present tense, *I walked* is in the past tense.

transitivity A verb used in a transitive sense requires an object (*I walked the dog*); a verb used in an intransitive sense does not (*No thanks, I'll walk*).

utterance A stretch of speech produced by a single speaker. An utterance may or may not consist of a complete grammatical unit.

References

Adams, K. (1999) "Critical linguistics": Alternative approaches to text in the American tradition. In R. Darnell and L. Valentine (eds.), *Theorizing the Americanist Tradition*, Toronto: University of Toronto Press, pp. 351–64.

Adams, K., and Winter, A. (1997) Gang graffiti as a discourse genre. *Journal of Sociolinguistics*, 1, 337–60.

Agha, A. (2003) The social life of a cultural value. *Language and Communication*, 23, 231–73.

Al-Ali, M. N. (2005) Communicating messages of solidarity, promotion and pride in death announcements genre in Jordanian newspapers. *Discourse and Society*, 16(1), 5–31.

Albert, E. M. (1972) Culture patterning of speech behavior in Burundi. In J. J. Gumperz and D. Hymes (eds.), *Directions in Sociolinguistics: The ethnography of communication*, New York: Holt, Rinehart and Winston, pp. 72–105.

al-Husari, S. (1959) *Maa Hiya al-Qawmiyya?* Beirut: Daar al-kilm li-al-Maalaayiin.

Al-Khatib, M. A. (2001) Audience design revisited in a diglossic speech community: A case study of three TV programs addressed to three different audiences. *Multilingua*, 20, 393–414.

Althusser, L. (1971) Ideology and ideological state apparatuses. In *Lenin and Philosophy and Other Essays*, London: Verso, pp. 121–73.

Ancelet, B. (ed.) (1980) *Cris sur le bayou*. Montreal: Editions Intermède.

Antaki, C., and Widdicombe, S. (eds.) (1998) *Identities in Talk*. London: Sage.

Aristotle (1958) The poetics (ed. and tr. G. M. A. Grube). In *On Poetry and Style*. New York: Bobbs-Merrill.

Arminen, I., and Leinonen, M. (2006) Mobile phone call openings: Tailoring answers to personalized summonses. *Discourse Studies*, 8(3), 339–68.

Asher, R. E., and Simpson, J. M. Y. (eds.) (1994) *The Encyclopedia of Language and Linguistics* (10 vols.). Oxford/New York: Pergamon.

Atkinson, J. M., and Heritage, J. (eds.) (1984) *Structures of Social Action*. Cambridge: Cambridge University Press.

Austin, J. L. (1962) *How to Do Things with Words*. Oxford: Clarendon Press.

Bailey, F. G. (1983) *The Tactical Uses of Passion: An essay on power, reason, and reality*. Ithaca, NY: Cornell University Press.

Bakhtin, M. M. (1981[1953]) *The Dialogic Imagination* (ed. M. Holquist, tr. C. Emerson and M. Holquist). Austin: University of Texas Press.

Bakhtin, M. M. (1986) *Speech Genres and Other Late Essays* (ed. C. Emerson and M. Holquist, tr. W. McGee). Austin: University of Texas Press.

Bamberg, M. (ed.) (1997) *Oral Versions of Personal Experience: Three decades of narrative analysis*. Special issue of *Journal of Narrative and Life History*, 7, 1–415.

Bamberg, M., and Budwig, N. (1992) Therapeutic misconceptions: When the voices of caring and research are misconstrued as the voice of curing. *Ethics and Behavior*, 2, 165–84.

Barry, D. (1989) A French literary renaissance in Louisiana: Cultural reflections. *Journal of Popular Culture*, 23, 47–63.

Barsalou, L. (1992) Frames, concepts and conceptual fields. In A. Lehrer and E. Kittay (eds.), *Frames, Fields and Contrasts*, Hillsdale, NJ: Lawrence Erlbaum, pp. 21–74.

Bartlett, F. C. (1932) *Remembering: A study in experimental and social psychology*. Cambridge: Cambridge University Press.

Barton, E. (1993) Evidentials, argumentation, and epistemological stance. *College English*, 55, 745–69.

Barton, E. (1995) Contrastive and non-contrastive connectives: Interpersonal functions in argumentation. *Written Communication*, 12, 219–39.

Basham, C., Fiksdal, S., and Rounds, P. (eds.) (1999) *The Notion of Person*. Special issue of *Language Sciences*, 21(3), 223–369.

Basso, K. (1970) To give up on words: Silence in Western Apache culture. *Southwestern Journal of Anthropology*, 26, 213–30.

Bateson, G. (1979) *Mind and Nature: A necessary unity*. New York: Bantam Books.

Bauman, R. (1977) *Verbal Art as Performance*. Rowley, MA: Newbury House.

Bauman, R. (1983) *Let Your Words Be Few: Symbolism of speaking and silence among seventeenth-century Quakers*. Cambridge: Cambridge University Press.

Bauman, R. (1986) *Story, Performance, and Event: Contextual studies of oral narrative*. Cambridge: Cambridge University Press.

Bauman, R., and Briggs, C. (1990) Poetics and performance as critical perspectives on language and social life. *Annual Review of Anthropology*, 19, 59–88.

Bazerman, C. (1988) *Shaping Written Knowledge: The genre and activity of the experimental article in science*. Madison: University of Wisconsin Press.

Becker, A. L. (1965) A tagmemic approach to paragraph analysis. *College Composition and Communication*, 16, 237–42.

Becker, A. L. (1975) A linguistic image of nature: The Burmese numerative classifier system. *International Journal of the Sociology of Language*, 5, 109–21.

Becker, A. L. (1979) Text-building, epistemology, and aesthetics in Javanese shadow theater. In A. L. Becker and A. Yengoyan (eds.), *The Imagination of Reality: Essays in Southeast Asian coherence systems*, Norwood, NJ: Ablex, pp. 211–44.

Becker, A. L. (1989) On the difficulty of writing: Silence. In B. S. Morris (ed.), *Disciplinary Perspectives on Thinking and Writing*, Ann Arbor: University of Michigan, English Composition Board.

Becker, A. L. (1991) A short essay on languaging. In F. Steier (ed.), *Research and Reflexivity*, Thousand Oaks, CA: Sage, pp. 226–34.

Becker, A. L. (1994) Repetition and otherness: An essay. In B. Johnstone (ed.), *Repetition in Discourse: Interdisciplinary perspectives, vol. II*, Norwood, NJ: Ablex, pp. 162–75.

Becker, A. L. (1995) Ann Arbor: University of Michigan Press.

Becker, A. L. (1995[1986]) The figure a classifier makes: Describing a particular Burmese classifier. *Beyond Translation: Essays toward a modern philology*. Ann Arbor: University of Michigan Press, pp. 211–30.

Becker, A. L., and Yengoyan, A. A. (eds.) (1979) *The Imagination of Reality: Essays in Southeast Asian coherence systems*. Norwood, NJ: Ablex.

Becker, J. (1979) Time and tune in Java. In A. L. Becker and A. Yengoyan (eds.), *The Imagination of Reality: Essays in Southeast Asian coherence systems*, Norwood, NJ: Ablex, pp. 197–210.

Bell, A. (1984) Language style as audience design. *Language in Society*, 13, 145–204.

Bell, A. (1991) *The Language of News Media*. Oxford: Blackwell.

Bell, A. (2001) Back in style: Reworking audience design. In P. Eckert and J. R. Rickford (eds.), *Style and Sociolinguistic Variation*, Cambridge: Cambridge University Press, pp. 139–69.

Bennett-Kastor, T. L. (1994) Repetition in language development: From interaction to cohesion. In B. Johnstone (ed.), *Repetition in Discourse: Interdisciplinary perspectives*, Norwood, NJ: Ablex, pp. 155–71.

Benveniste, É. (1986[1971]) Subjectivity in language (tr. M. E. Meek). In H. Adams and L. Searle (eds.), *Critical Theory since 1965*, Tallahassee: University Presses of Florida, pp. 728–32.

Bergvall, V. L., Bing, J. M., and Freed, A. F. (1996) *Re-thinking Language and Gender Research: Theory and practice*. New York: Longman.

Berkenkotter, C., Huckin, T. N., and Ackerman, J. (1988) Conventions, conversations, and the writer: A case study of a student in a rhetoric Ph.D. program. *Research in the Teaching of English*, 22, 9–44.

Berkenkotter, C., and Huckin, T. N. (1995) *Genre Knowledge in Disciplinary Communication*. Hillsdale, NJ: Lawrence Erlbaum.

Berk-Seligson, S. (2000) The Miranda warnings and linguistic coercion: When the police alternate between interpreter and interrogator. Lecture presented at CIAFIC, Buenos Aires, Argentina, September 18.

Besnier, N. (1995) *Literacy, Emotion, and Authority: Reading and writing on a Polynesian atoll*. Cambridge: Cambridge University Press.

Bhatia, V. K. (1993) *Analysing Genre: Language use in professional settings*. London: Longman.

Biber, D. (1988) *Variation Across Speech and Writing*. Cambridge: Cambridge University Press.

Biber, D. (1994) An analytical framework for register studies. In D. Biber and E. Finegan (eds.), *Sociolinguistic Perspectives on Register*, New York: Oxford University Press, pp. 31–56.

Biber, D., and Finegan, E. (1989) Styles of stance in English: Lexical and grammatical marking of evidentiality and affect. *Text*, 9, 93–124.

Biber, D., and Finegan, E. (eds.) (1994) *Sociolinguistic Perspectives on Register*. New York: Oxford University Press.

Billig, M., and MacMillan, K. (2005) Metaphor, idiom, and ideology: The search for "no smoking guns" across time. *Discourse and Society*, 16, 459–80.

Bloch, M. (1971) Symbols, song, dance and features of articulation. *European Journal of Sociology*, 15, 55–81.

Blommaert, J. (2005) *Discourse*. Cambridge: Cambridge University Press.

Blommaert, J., and Bulcaen, C. (2000) Critical discourse analysis. *Annual Review of Anthropology*, 27, 447–66.

Bloomfield, L. (1933) *Language*. New York: Holt.

Bloomfield, L. (1942) *Outline Guide for the Practical Study of Foreign Languages*. Baltimore, MD: Linguistic Society of America.

Blum-Kulka, S. (1989) Playing it safe: The role of conventionality in indirectness. In S. Blum-Kulka, J. House, and G. Kasper (eds.), *Cross-cultural Pragmatics: Requests and apologies*, Norwood, NJ: Ablex, pp. 37–70.

Blum-Kulka, S., House, J., and Kasper, G. (eds.) (1989) *Cross-cultural Pragmatics: Requests and apologies*. Norwood, NJ: Ablex.

Bolinger, D. (1980) *Language, the Loaded Weapon*. London/New York: Longman.

Bolter, J. D. (1991) *Writing Space: The computer, hypertext, and the history of writing*. Hillsdale, NJ: Lawrence Erlbaum.

Bouquiaux, L., and Thomas, J. M. C. (1992[1976]) *Studying and Describing Unwritten Languages* (tr. J. Roberts). Dallas, TX: Summer Institute of Linguistics.

Bourdieu, P. (1991) *Language and Symbolic Power*. Cambridge: Polity Press.

Bové, P. A. (1990) Discourse. In F. Lentricchia and T. McLaughlin (eds.), *Critical Terms for Literary Study*, Chicago: University of Chicago Press, pp. 50–65.

Bowers, F. (1989) *Linguistic Aspects of Legislative Expression*. Vancouver, Canada: University of British Columbia Press.

Braun, F. (1988) *Terms of Address: Problems of patterns and usage in various languages and cultures*. Berlin: Mouton de Gruyter.

Brewster, P. G. (1940) *Ballads and Songs of Indiana*. Bloomington: Indiana University Press.

Bright, W. (1981) Literature: Written and oral. In D. Tannen (ed.), *Georgetown University Round Table on Languages and Linguistics 1981*, Washington, DC: Georgetown University Press, pp. 271–83.

Bright, W. (ed.) (1992) *International Encyclopedia of Linguistics* (4 vols.). New York: Oxford University Press.

Brody, J. (1994) Multiple repetitions in Tojolab'al conversation. In B. Johnstone (ed.), *Repetition in Discourse: Interdisciplinary perspectives*, vol. II, Norwood, NJ: Ablex, pp. 3–14.

Brown, B. (1993) The social consequences of writing Louisiana French. *Language in Society*, 22, 67–101.

Brown, G., and Yule, G. (1983) *Discourse Analysis*. Cambridge: Cambridge University Press.

Brown, P., and Levinson, S. C. (1987) *Politeness: Some universals in language usage*. Cambridge: Cambridge University Press.

Brown, R., and Ford, M. (1964) Address in American English. In D. Hymes (ed.), *Language in Culture and Society*, New York: Harper and Row, pp. 243–4.

Brown, R., and Gilman, A. (1960) The pronouns of power and solidarity. In T. Sebeok (ed.), *Style in Language*, Cambridge, MA: MIT Press, pp. 253–76.

Brubaker, R., and Cooper, F. (2000) Beyond "identity." *Theory and Society*, 29, 1–47.

Bucholtz, M. (2000) The politics of transcription. *Journal of Pragmatics*, 32, 1439–65.

Bucholtz, M., and Hall, K. (2005) Identity and interaction: A sociocultural linguistic approach. *Discourse Studies*, 7, 585–614.

Bucholtz, M., Liang, A. C., and Sutton, L. (eds.) (1999) *Reinventing Identities: The gendered self in discourse*. Oxford/New York: Oxford University Press.

Burke, K. ([1945]1969) *A Grammar of Motives*. Berkeley: University of California Press.

Burling, R. (1970) *Man's Many Voices: Language in its cultural context*. New York: Holt, Rinehart and Winston.

Butler, J. (1990) *Gender Trouble: Feminism and the subversion of identity*. New York: Routledge.

Cameron, D. (1995) *Verbal Hygiene*. London/New York: Routledge.

Carroll, J. B. (ed.) (1956) *Language, Thought, and Reality: Selected writings of Benjamin Lee Whorf*. Cambridge, MA: The Technology Press of MIT and John Wiley and Sons.

Carroll, J. B., and Casagrande, J. (1958) The function of language classifications in behavior. In E. Maccoby, T. Newcomb, and E. Hartley (eds.), *Readings in Social Psychology*, New York: Henry Holt, pp. 18–31.

Chafe, W. (1980a) The deployment of consciousness in the production of a narrative. In W. Chafe (ed.), *The Pear Stories: Cognitive, cultural, and linguistic aspects of narrative production*, Norwood, NJ: Ablex, pp. 1–50.

Chafe, W. (ed.) (1980b) *The Pear Stories: Cognitive, cultural, and linguistic aspects of narrative production*. Norwood, NJ: Ablex.

Chafe, W. (1982) Integration and involvement in speaking, writing, and oral literature. In D. Tannen (ed.), *Spoken and Written Language: Exploring orality and literacy*, Norwood, NJ: Ablex, pp. 35–54.

Chafe, W. (1986) Cognitive constraints on information flow. In R. Tomlin (ed.), *Coherence and Grounding in Discourse*, Amsterdam: John Benjamins, pp. 21–51.

Chafe, W. (1994) *Discourse, Consciousness, and Time*. Chicago: University of Chicago Press.

Chafe, W., and Nichols, J. (1986) *Evidentiality: The Linguistic Coding of Epistemology*. Norwood, NJ: Ablex.

Chafe, W., and Tannen, D. (1987) The relation between written and spoken language. *Annual Review of Anthropology*, 16, 383–407.

Chambers, J. K. (1993) Sociolinguistic dialectology. In D. Preston (ed.), *American Dialect Research*, Amsterdam/Philadelphia: John Benjamins, pp. 133–64.

Cheng, M. S., and Johnstone, B. (2002). Reasons for reason-giving in a public-opinion survey. *Argumentation*, 16, 401–20.

Cheshire, J., and Williams, A. (2002) Information structure in male and female adolescent talk. *Journal of English Linguistics*, 30, 217–38.

Christensen, F. (1965) A generative rhetoric of the paragraph. *College Composition and Communication*, 16, 144–56.

Christensen, F., Becker, A. L., Rodgers, P. C., Jr., Miles, J., and Karrfalt, D. H. (1966) Symposium on the paragraph. *College Composition and Communication*, 17(2), 60–87.

Cicourel, A. V. (1985) Text and discourse. *Annual Review of Anthropology*, 14, 159–85.

Clark, H. H. (1997) Dogmas of understanding. *Discourse Processes*, 25, 567–98.

Coates, J. (ed.) (1998) *Language and Gender: A reader*. Oxford: Blackwell.

Cohen, A. P. (1994) *Self Consciousness: An alternative anthropology of identity*. London: Routledge.

Collins, J. (1995) Literacy and literacies. *Annual Review of Anthropology*, 24, 75–93.

Collot, M., and Belmore, N. (1996) Electronic language: A new variety of English. In S. C. Herring (ed.), *Computer-mediated Communication: Linguistic, social, and cross-cultural perspectives*, Amsterdam/Philadelphia: John Benjamins, pp. 13–28.

Condon, S. (1986) The discourse functions of OK. *Semiotica*, 60, 73–101.

Conley, J. M., and O'Barr, W. A. (1998) *Just Words: Law, language, and power*. Chicago: University of Chicago Press.

Conrick, M. (1998) Linguistic perspectives on the feminisation of professional titles in Canadian French. *British Journal of Canadian Studies*, 13, 164–80.

Coulmas, F. (ed.) (1981) *Conversational Routine: Explorations in standardized communication situations and prepatterned speech*. The Hague: Mouton.

Coulmas, F. (ed.) (1986) *Direct and Indirect Speech*. Berlin: Mouton de Gruyter.

Coulthard, M. (1985) *An Introduction to Discourse Analysis* (new ed.). London: Longman.

Coupland, N., and Coupland, J. (1997) Discourses of the unsayable: Death implicative talk in geriatric medical consultations. In A. Jaworski (ed.), *Silence: Interdisciplinary perspectives*, Berlin/New York: Mouton de Gruyter, pp. 117–52.

Coupland, N., Coupland, J., and Giles, H. (1991) *Language, Society and the Elderly*. Oxford: Blackwell.

Croft, W., and Cruse, D. A. (2004) *Cognitive Linguistics*. Cambridge: Cambridge University Press.

Crookes, G. V. (1990) The utterance, and other basic units for second language discourse analysis. *Applied Linguistics*, 11, 183–99.

Crookes, G. V., and Rulon, K. (1985) *Incorporation of Corrective Feedback in Native Speaker/Non-native Speaker Conversation*. Technical report, vol. 3. University of Hawaii, Honolulu: Center for Second Language Classroom Research, Social Science Research Institute.

Crystal, D. (1969) *Prosodic Systems and Intonation in English*. Cambridge: Cambridge University Press.

Crystal, D. (1987) *The Cambridge Encyclopedia of Language*. Cambridge: Cambridge University Press.

Crystal, D. (2001) *Language and the Internet*. Cambridge: Cambridge University Press.

Crystal, D., and Davy, D. (1969) *Investigating English Style*. New York: Longman.

Crystal, D., and Quirk, R. (1964) *Systems of Prosodic and Paralinguistic Features in English*. The Hague: Mouton.

Culler, J. (1975) *Structuralist Poetics: Structuralism, linguistics, and the study of literature*. Ithaca, NY: Cornell University Press.

Cushing, S. (1994) *Fatal Words: Communication clashes and aircraft crashes*. Chicago: University of Chicago Press.

Cutler, C. A. (1999) Yorkville crossing: White teens, hip hop, and African American English. *Journal of Sociolinguistics*, 3, 428–42.

Damon, W. (1990) Colleges must help foster a spirit of inquiry in the nation's schools. *Chronicle of Higher Education*, 25 April, p. A48.

Davies, A. (1982) Spaces between silences: Verbal interaction in Quaker meetings. *Nottingham Linguistics Circular*, 11(1), 44–63.

Davies, B. and Harré, R. (1990) Positioning: Conversation and the production of selves. *Journal for the Theory of Social Behaviour*, 20, 43–63.

Davies, C. (1997) Social meaning in southern speech from an interactional socio-linguistic perspective: An integrative discourse analysis of terms of address. In C. Bernstein, T. Nunnally, and R. Sabino (eds.), *Language Variety in the South Revisited*, Tuscaloosa: The University of Alabama Press, pp. 225–41.

de Certeau, M. (1984) *The Practice of Everyday Life*. Berkeley: University of California Press.

DeMott, B. (1991) Legally sanctioned special advantages are a way of life in the United States. *Chronicle of Higher Education*, 27 February, p. A40.

Donald, M. (1993) *Origins of the Modern Mind: Three stages in the evolution of culture and cognition*. Cambridge, MA: Harvard University Press.

Dorian, N. C. (1982) Defining the speech community to include its working margins. In S. Romaine (ed.), *Sociolinguistic Variation in Speech Communities*, London: Arnold, pp. 25–33.

Du Bois, J. W. (1980) Beyond definiteness: The trace of identity in discourse. In W. Chafe (ed.), *The Pear Stories: Cognitive, cultural, and linguistic aspects of narrative production*, Norwood, NJ: Ablex, pp. 203–74.

Du Bois, J. W. (1987) The discourse basis of ergativity. *Language*, 63, 805–55.

Du Bois, J. W. (1993) Meaning without intention: Lessons from divination. In J. H. Hill and J. T. Irvine (eds.), *Responsibility and Evidence in Oral Discourse*, Cambridge: Cambridge University Press, pp. 48–71.

Dunmire, P. L. (2005) Preempting the future: Rhetoric and the ideology of the future in political discourse. *Discourse in Society*, 16, 481–513.

Duranti, A. (1992) Language in context and language as context: The Samoan respect vocabulary. In A. Duranti and C. Goodwin (eds.), *Rethinking Context*, Cambridge: Cambridge University Press, pp. 77–99.

Duranti, A., and Brenneis, D. (1986) *The audience as co-author*. Special issue of *Text*, 6, 3.

Eckert, P. (1989) *Jocks and Burnouts: Social categories and identity in high school*. New York/London: Teachers College Press.

Eckert, P. (2000) *Linguistic Variation as Social Practice*. Oxford: Blackwell.

Eckert, P., and McConnell-Ginet, S. (1992) Think practically and look locally: Language and gender as community-based practice. *Annual Review of Anthropology*, 21, 461–90.

Eckert, P., and Rickford, J. (eds.) (2001) *Style and Sociolinguistic Variation*. Cambridge/New York: Cambridge University Press.

Ede, L., and Lunsford, A. (1984) Audience addressed/audience invoked: The role of audience in composition theory and pedagogy. *College Composition and Communication*, 35, 155–71.

Edwards, J. A., and Lampert, M. D. (1993) *Talking Data: Transcription and coding in discourse research*. Hillsdale, NJ: Lawrence Erlbaum.

Eelen, G. (2001) *A Critique of Politeness Theories*. Manchester, UK: St. Jerome.

Eggins, S. (2004) *An Introduction to Systemic Functional Linguistics* (2nd ed.). London/New York: Continuum.

Eggins, S., and Martin, J. (1997) Genres and registers of discourse. In T. A. van Dijk (ed.), *Discourse Studies: A multidisciplinary introduction. Discourse as structure and process*, London: Sage Publications, pp. 230–56.

Ehrlich, S. (1997) Literary texts and the violation of narrative norms. *Journal of Narrative and Life History*, 7, 321–9.

Ervin-Tripp, S. (1972) On sociolinguistic rules: Alternation and co-occurrence. In J. J. Gumperz and D. Hymes (eds.), *Directions in Sociolinguistics: The ethnography of communication*, New York: Holt, Rinehart, and Winston, pp. 213–50.

Evans, V., and Green, M. (2006) *Cognitive Linguistics: An introduction*. Edinburgh: Edinburgh University Press.

Fahnestock, J. (1986) Accommodating science: The rhetorical life of scientific facts. *Written Communication*, 3, 275–96.

Fairclough, N. (1985) Critical and descriptive goals in discourse analysis. *Journal of Pragmatics*, 9, 739–63.

Fairclough, N. (1989) *Language and Power*. London: Longman.

Fairclough, N. (1992) *Discourse and Social Change*. Cambridge: Polity Press.

Fairclough, N., and Wodak, R. (1997) Critical discourse analysis. In T. A. van Dijk (ed.), *Discourse as Social Interaction*, London: Sage, pp. 258–84.

Ferguson, C. (1971) Absence of copula and the notion of simplicity: A study of normal speech, baby talk, foreigner talk and pidgins. In D. Hymes (ed.), *Pidginization and Creolization of Languages*, London/New York: Cambridge University Press, pp. 141–50.

Ferguson, C. (1977) Baby talk as a simplified register. In C. Snow and C. Ferguson (eds.), *Talking to Children: Language input and acquisition*, Cambridge: Cambridge University Press, pp. 209–35.

Ferguson, C. (1982) Simplified registers and linguistic theory. In L. Obler and L. Menn (eds.), *Exceptional Language and Linguistics*, New York: Academic Press, pp. 49–66.

Ferguson, C. (1983) Sports announcer talk: Syntactic aspects of register variation. *Language in Society*, 12, 153–72.

Ferguson, C. (ed.) (1985) *Special Language Registers*. Special issue of *Discourse Processes*, 8, 4.

Ferguson, C. (1994) Dialect, register, and genre: Working assumptions about conventionalization. In D. Biber and E. Finegan (eds.), *Sociolinguistic Perspectives on Register*, New York: Oxford University Press, pp. 15–30.

Ferrara, K. (1992) The interactive achievement of a sentence: Joint productions in therapeutic discourse. *Discourse Processes*, 15, 207–28.

Ferrara, K. (1994) Repetition as rejoinder in therapeutic discourse: Echoing and mirroring. In B. Johnstone (ed.), *Repetition in Discourse*, vol. II, Norwood, NJ: Ablex, pp. 66–83.

Ferrara, K., and Bell, B. (1995) Sociolinguistic variation and discourse function of constructed dialogue introducers: The case of *be + like*. *American Speech*, 70, 265–90.

Fillmore, C. (1982) Frame semantics. In Linguistic Society of Korea (ed.), *Linguistics in the Morning Calm*, Seoul: Hanshin Publishing, pp. 111–37.

Fillmore, C., and Atkins, B. T. (1992) Toward a frame-based lexicon: The semantics of RISK and its neighbors. In A. Lehrer and E. Kittay (eds.), *Frames, Fields and Contrasts*, Hillsdale, NJ: Lawrence Erlbaum, pp. 75–102.

Finegan, E. (1982) Form and function in testament language. In R. J. DiPietro (ed.), *Linguistics and the Professions*, Norwood, NJ: Ablex, pp. 113–20.

Finegan, E., and Biber, D. (2001) Register variation and social dialect variation: The register axiom. In P. Eckert and J. R. Rickford (eds.), *Style and Sociolinguistic Variation*, Cambridge: Cambridge University Press, pp. 235–67.

Finnegan, R. (1988) *Literacy and Orality: Studies in the technology of communication*. Oxford: Blackwell.

Firbas, J. (1992) *Functional Sentence Perspective in Written and Spoken Communication*. Cambridge: Cambridge University Press.

Firth, J. R. (1935) The technique of semantics. *Transactions of the Philological Society*, 36–72.

Fishman, J. (ed.) (1999) *Handbook of Language and Ethnic Identity*. Oxford: Oxford University Press.

Fishman, P. (1978) Interaction: The work women do. *Social Problems*, 25, 397–406.

Flower, L. (1994) *The Construction of Negotiated Meaning: A social cognitive theory of writing*. Carbondale: Southern Illinois University Press.

Fludernik, M. (1993) *The Fictions of Language and the Languages of Fiction: The linguistic representation of speech and consciousness*. London/New York: Routledge.

Foley, W. A. (1997) *Anthropological Linguistics: An introduction*. Malden, MA: Blackwell.

Foucault, M. (1972) *The Archaeology of Knowledge and the Discourse on Language* (tr. S. S. Smith). New York: Harper.

Foucault, M. (1980) *Power/Knowledge: Selected interviews and other writings, 1972–1977* (ed. C. Gordon). New York: Pantheon.

Fowler, R., Hodge, B., Kress, G., and Trew, T. (eds.) (1979) *Language and Control*. London: Routledge and Kegan Paul.

Fox, A. A. (1997) "Ain't it funny how time slips away?" Talk, trash, and technology in a Texas "redneck" bar. In B. Ching and G. W. Creed (eds.), *Knowing your Place: Rural identity and cultural hierarchy*, New York/London: Routledge, pp. 105–30.

Friedrich, P. (1972) Social context and semantic feature: The Russian pronominal usage. In J. J. Gumperz and D. Hymes (eds.), *Directions in Sociolinguistics: The ethnography of communication*, New York: Holt, Rinehart, and Winston, pp. 301–24.

Friedrich, P. (1986) *The Language Parallax: Linguistic relativism and poetic indeterminacy*. Austin: University of Texas Press.

Gains, J. (1999) Electronic mail – a new style of communication or just a new medium? An investigation into the text features of e-mail. *English for Specific Purposes*, 18, 81–101.

Gal, S., and Irvine, J. (1995) The boundaries of languages and disciplines: How ideologies construct difference. *Social Research*, 62, 967–1001.

Galegher, J., Kraut, R. E., and Egido, C. (eds.) (1990) *Intellectual Teamwork: Social and technological foundations of cooperative work*. Hillsdale, NJ: Lawrence Erlbaum.

Gangwere, R. J. (1999) Merchant prince and master builder. *Carnegie Magazine*, March/April, pp. 12–17.

Gee, J. P. (2005) *An Introduction to Discourse Analysis: Theory and method* (2nd ed.). London: Routledge.

Geertz, C. (1973) *The Interpretation of Cultures*. New York: Basic Books.

Gerard, I. (2006, January 6) Aboriginals must integrate, says Lib MP. *The Australian*. Available: http://www.news.com.au/story/0,10117,17740233-2,00.html. Accessed January 5, 2006.

Ghadessy, M. (ed.) (1997) *Register Analysis: Theory and practice*. London: Continuum.

Gibney, F. (1953) *Five Gentlemen of Japan: The portrait of a nation's character*. Rutland, VT: Tuttle.

Giles, H., and Powesland, P. (1975) *Speech Style and Social Evaluation*. London: Academic Press.

Givón, T. (1979) *On Understanding Grammar*. New York: Academic Press.

Givón, T. (1985) Iconicity, isomorphism, and non-arbitrary coding in syntax. In J. Haiman (ed.), *Iconicity in Syntax*, Amsterdam: John Benjamins, pp. 187–219.

Givón, T. (1990) *Syntax: A functional-typological introduction*. Amsterdam: John Benjamins.

Goffman, E. (1955) On face work: An analysis of ritual elements in social interaction. *Psychiatry*, 18, 213–31.

Goffman, E. (1959) *The Presentation of Self in Everyday Life*. Garden City, NY: Doubleday Anchor Books.

Goffman, E. (1981[1979]) Footing. In *Forms of Talk*, Philadelphia: University of Pennsylvania Press, pp. 124–59.

Goffman, E. (1981[1976]) Replies and responses. In *Forms of Talk*. Philadelphia: University of Pennsylvania Press, pp. 5–77.

Goffman, E. (1986[1974]) *Frame Analysis: An essay on the organization of experience*. Boston: Northwestern University Press.

Goodwin, C. (1979) The interactive construction of a sentence in natural conversation. In G. Psathas (ed.), *Everyday Language: Studies in ethnomethodology*, New York: Irvington Publishers, pp. 97–121.

Goodwin, C. (1981) *Conversational Organization: Interaction between speakers and hearers*. New York: Academic Press.

Goody, J. (1977) *The Domestication of the Savage Mind*. Cambridge: Cambridge University Press.

Goody, J., and Watt, I. (1968) The consequences of literacy. In J. Goody (ed.), *Literacy in Traditional Societies*, Cambridge: Cambridge University Press, pp. 27–84.

Graham, L. R. (2005, September) Studying up collaboratively at the UN permanent forum. *Anthropology News*, 17.

Gregory, M., and Carrol, S. (1978) *Language and Situation: Language varieties and their social contexts*. London: Routledge.

Greist, J. H., and Klein, M. H. (1980) Computer programs for patients, clinicians and researchers in psychiatry. In J. B. Sidowski (ed.), *Technology in Mental Health Care Delivery Systems*, Norwood, NJ: Ablex, pp. 161–82.

Grice, H. P. (1975) Logic and conversation. Syntax and semantics, vol. 3. In P. Cole and J. Morgan (eds.), *Speech Acts*, New York: Academic Press, pp. 41–58.

Grimes, J. E. (1972) Outlines and overlays. *Language*, 48, 513–24.

Grimes, J. E. (1975) *The Thread of Discourse*. The Hague: Mouton.

Groopman, J. (2000) Hurting all over: With so many people in pain, how could fibromyalgia not be a disease? *The New Yorker*, November 13, pp. 78–92.

Guilloton, N., and Cajolet-Laganière, H. (2005) *Le Français au Bureau* (6th ed.). Quebec: Gouvernement du Québec.

Gumperz, J. J. (1982a) *Discourse Strategies*. Cambridge: Cambridge University Press.

Gumperz, J. J. (ed.) (1982b) *Language and Social Identity*. Cambridge: Cambridge University Press.

Gumperz, J. J., and Levinson, S. C. (eds.) (1996) *Rethinking Linguistic Relativity*. Cambridge/New York: Cambridge University Press.

Hall, K. (1995) Lip service on the fantasy lines. In K. Hall and M. Bucholtz (eds.), *Gender Articulated: Language and the socially constructed self*, New York/London: Routledge, pp. 183–216.

Hall, K., and Bucholtz, M. (eds.) (1995) *Gender Articulated: Language and the socially constructed self*. New York: Routledge.

Halliday, M. A. K. (1994) *An Introduction to Functional Grammar* (2nd ed. (rev.)). London: Edward Arnold.

Halliday, M. A. K., and Hasan, R. (1976) *Cohesion in English*. London: Longman.

Hardin, C., and Maffi, L. (eds.) (1996) *Color Categories in Thought and Language*. Cambridge: Cambridge University Press.

Harris, R. (1980) *The Language Makers*. London: Duckworth.

Harris, R. (1981) *The Language Myth*. London: Duckworth.

Harris, R. (1987) *The Language Machine*. London: Duckworth.

Harris, R., and Rampton, B. (eds.) (2003) *The Language, Ethnicity and Race Reader*. London: Routledge.

Harris, Z. (1952) Discourse analysis. *Language*, 28, 1–30.

Hatim, B. (1998) Discourse analysis and translation. In M. Baker and K. Malmkjaer (eds.), *Routledge Encyclopedia of Translation Studies*, London/New York: Routledge, pp. 67–71.

Hatim, B., and Mason, I. (1990) *Discourse and the Translator*. London: Longman.

Havelock, E. A. (1982[1963]) *Preface to Plato*. Cambridge, MA: The Belknap Press of Harvard University Press.

Heath, S. B. (1978) *Teacher Talk: Language in the classroom*. Washington, DC: Center for Applied Linguistics.

Heath, S. B. (1983) *Ways with Words: Language, life, and work in communities and classrooms*. Cambridge: Cambridge University Press.

Henley, N. M., Miller, M., and Beazley, J. A. (1995) Syntax, semantics, and sexual violence: Agency and the passive voice. *Journal of Language and Social Psychology*, 14, 60–84.

Heritage, J., and Raymond, G. (2005) The terms of agreement: Indexing epistemic authority and subordination in talk-in-interaction. *Social Psychology Quarterly*, 68, 15–38.

Herring, S. C. (1993) Gender and democracy in computer-mediated communication. *Electronic Journal of Communication* (Online) 3(2). Available: http://ella.slis.indiana.edu/~herring/ejc.txt.

Herring, S. C. (ed.) (1996) *Computer-mediated Communication: Linguistic, social, and cross-cultural perspectives*. Amsterdam/Philadelphia: John Benjamins.

Herring, S. C. (1999) Interactional coherence in CMC. *Journal of Computer-Mediated Communication* 4(4) (Online). Available: http://jcmc.indiana.edu/vol4/issue4/herring.html.

Herring, S., Johnson, D., and DiBenedetto, T. (1995) "This discussion is going too far!" Male resistance to female participation on the Internet. In M. Bucholtz and K. Hall (eds.), *Gender Articulated: Language and the socially constructed self*, New York: Routledge, pp. 67–96.

Hewitt, R. (1986) *White Talk, Black Talk*. Cambridge: Cambridge University Press.

Hill, J., and Irvine, J. (eds.) (1992) *Responsibility and Evidence in Oral Discourse*. Cambridge: Cambridge University Press.

Hill, J., and Mannheim, B. (1992) Language and world view. *Annual Review of Anthropology*, 21, 381–406.

Hobbs, J. (ed.) (1983) *Formal Models of Discourse*. Special issue of *Text*, 3(3).

Hodge, R., and Kress, G. (1988) *Social Semiotics*. Cambridge: Polity Press.

Hodge, R., and Kress, G. (1993) *Language as Ideology* (2nd ed.). New York: Routledge.

Hoey, M. P. (1991) *Patterns of Lexis in Text*. Oxford: Oxford University Press.

Hoffman, E. (1989) *Lost in Translation: A life in a new language*. New York: Penguin.

Hollander, P. (1990) Communism's collapse won't faze the Marxists in academe. *Chronicle of Higher Education*, May 23, p. A44.

Holmes, J., and Myerhoff, M. (eds.) (2003) *The Handbook of Language and Gender*. Malden, MA: Blackwell.

Hopper, P. J. (1988) Emergent grammar and the a priori grammar postulate. In D. Tannen (ed.), *Linguistics in Context: Connecting observation and understanding*, Norwood, NJ: Ablex, pp. 117–34.

Hopper, P. J. (1992) Times of the sign. *Time and Society*, 1.

Hopper, P. J. (1996) Some recent trends in grammaticalization. *Annual Review of Anthropology*, 25, 217–36.

Hopper, P. J., and Traugott, E. C. (2003) *Grammaticalization* (2nd ed.). Cambridge: Cambridge University Press.

Hopper, R. (1990) Speech errors and the poetics of conversation. Paper presented at the Speech Communication Annual Meeting. Chicago.

Houbedine-Gravaud, A.-M. (1988) *L'une n'est par l'autre (ou genre et sexe en français contemporain)*. Genre et Langage: Actes du colloque tenu à Paris X Nanterre, December 14–16, Paris.

Hunston, S., and Thompson, G. (eds.) (2000) *Evaluation in Text: Authorial stance and the construction of discourse*. New York: Oxford University Press.

Hunt, K. W. (1966) Recent measures in syntactic development. *Elementary English*, 43, 732–9.

Hutchby, I. (2001) *Conversation and Technology: From the telephone to the internet*. Cambridge: Polity Press.

Hymes, D. (1972) Models of the interaction of language and social life. In J. J. Gumperz and D. Hymes (eds.), *Directions in Sociolinguistics: The ethnography of communication*, New York: Holt, Rinehart and Winston, pp. 35–71.

Hymes, D. (1977) Discovering oral performance and measured verse in American Indian narrative. *New Literary History*, 7, 431–57.

Hymes, D. (1981a) Discovering oral performance and measured verse in American Indian narrative. In D. Hymes (ed.), *In Vain I Tried to Tell You: Essays in Native American ethnopoetics*, Philadelphia: University of Pennsylvania Press, pp. 309–41.

Hymes, D. (1981b) *In Vain I Tried to Tell You: Essays in Native American Ethnopoetics*. Philadelphia: University of Pennsylvania Press.

Hymes, D. (1984[1967]) Linguistic problems in defining the concept of "tribe." In J. Baugh and J. Sherzer (eds.), *Language in Use: Readings in sociolinguistics*, Englewood Cliffs, NJ: Prentice-Hall, pp. 7–27.

Ide, S. (1989) Formal forms and discernment: Two neglected aspects of linguistic politeness. *Multilingua*, 8, 223–48.

Irvine, J. T. (1985) Status and style in language. *Annual Review of Anthropology*, 14, 557–81.

Irvine, J. T. (2001) "Style" as distinctiveness: The culture and ideology of linguistic differentiation. In P. Eckert and J. R. Rickford (eds.), *Style and Sociolinguistic Variation*, Cambridge: Cambridge University Press, pp. 21–43.

Jacobs, S., and Jackson, S. (1982) Conversational argument: A discourse analytic approach. In J. R. Cox and C. A. Willard (eds.), *Advances in Argumentation Theory and Research*, Carbondale and Edwardsville, IL: Southern Illinois University Press, pp. 205–37.

Jaffe, A. (ed.) (2000) *Non-standard Orthography and Non-standard Speech*. Theme issue of *Journal of Sociolinguistics*, 4(4), 497–634.

Jaffe, A., and Walton, S. (2000) The voices people read: Orthography and the representation of non-standard speech. *Journal of Sociolinguistics*, 4, 561–87.

Jakobson, R. (1960) Concluding statement: Linguistics and poetics. In T. Sebeok (ed.), *Style in Language*, Cambridge, MA: MIT Press, pp. 350–77.

Jakobson, R. (1968) Poetry of grammar and grammar of poetry. *Lingua*, 21, 597–609.

Jaworski, A. (ed.) (1997) *Silence: Interdisciplinary perspectives*. Berlin/New York: Mouton de Gruyter.

Jaworski, A., and Coupland, N. (eds.) (1999) *The Discourse Reader*. London/New York: Routledge.

Jefferson, G. (1974) Error correction as an interactional resource. *Language in Society*, 3, 181–99.

Johnson, S. (2005) *Spelling Trouble? Language, ideology and the reform of German orthography*. Clevedon, UK: Multilingual Matters.

Johnson, S., and Meinhof, U. (eds.) (1997) *Language and Masculinity*. Oxford: Blackwell.

Johnstone, B. (ed.) (1987) *Perspectives on Repetition*. Special issue of *Text*, 7(3), 205–311.

Johnstone, B. (1989) Linguistic strategies and cultural styles for persuasive discourse. In S. Ting-Toomey and F. Korzenny (eds.), *Language, Communication, and Culture*, Newbury Park, CA: Sage, pp. 139–56.

Johnstone, B. (1990) *Stories, Community, and Place: Narratives from Middle America*. Bloomington: Indiana University Press.

Johnstone, B. (1991a) Individual style in an American public-opinion survey: Personal performance and the ideology of referentiality. *Language in Society*, 20(4), 557–76.

Johnstone, B. (1991b) *Repetition in Arabic Discourse: Paradigms, syntagms, and the ecology of language*. Amsterdam/Philadelphia: John Benjamins.

Johnstone, B. (1994) *Repetition in Discourse: Interdisciplinary perspectives*, vols. I and II. Norwood, NJ: Ablex.

Johnstone, B. (1996) *The Linguistic Individual: Self-expression in language and linguistics*. New York: Oxford University Press.

Johnstone, B. (1998) "Sounding country" in urbanizing Texas: Private speech in public discourse. *Michigan Discussions in Anthropology*, 13, 153–64.

Johnstone, B. (1999) Uses of Southern speech by contemporary Texas women. *Journal of Sociolinguistics*, 3, 505–22. Special issue on "Styling the Other," ed. B. Rampton.

Johnstone, B. (2000) The individual voice in language. *Annual Review of Anthropology*, 29, 405–24.

Johnstone, B., et al. (1994) Repetition in discourse: A dialogue. In B. Johnstone (ed.), *Repetition in Discourse: Interdisciplinary perspectives*, Norwood, NJ: Ablex, pp. 1–20.

Johnstone, B., Andrus, J., and Danielson, A. (2006) Mobility, indexicality, and the enregisterment of "Pittsburghese." *Journal of English Linguistics*, 34, 77–104.

Johnstone, B., and Baumgardt, D. (2004) "Pittsburghese" online: Vernacular norming in conversation. *American Speech*, 79, 115–45.

Joseph, J. E., and Taylor, T. J. (eds.) (1990) *Ideologies of Language*. New York: Routledge.

Kasper, G., and Blum-Kulka, S. (eds.) (1993) *Interlanguage Pragmatics*. New York: Oxford University Press.

Katoka, K. (1997) Affect and letter-writing: Unconventional conventions in casual writing by young Japanese women. *Language in Society*, 26, 103–36.

Keenan, E. Ochs (1974) Norm-makers, norm-breakers: Uses of speech by men and women in a Malagasy community. In R. Bauman and J. Sherzer (eds.), *Explorations in the Ethnography of Speaking*, Cambridge: Cambridge University Press, pp. 125–43.

Keller-Cohen, D. (ed.) (1994) *Literacy: Interdisciplinary conversations*. Cresskill, NJ: Hampton Press.

Kendon, A. (1972) Some relationships between body motion and speech. In A. W. Siegman and B. Pope (eds.), *Studies in Dyadic Communication*, New York: Pergamon, pp. 177–213.

Kennedy, G. (1980) *Classical Rhetoric and its Christian and Secular Tradition from Ancient to Modern Times*. Chapel Hill, NC: University of North Carolina Press.

Kiesler, S., Siegel, J., and McGuire, T. W. (1984) Social psychological aspects of computer-mediated communication. *American Psychologist*, 39, 1123–34.

Kiesling, S. F. (1997) Power and the language of men. In S. Johnson and U. H. Meinhof (eds.), *Language and Masculinity*, Oxford: Blackwell, pp. 65–85.

Kiesling, S. F. (2005) Variation, stance, and style: Word-final -*er*, high rising tone, and ethnicity in Australian English. *English World-Wide*, 26, 1–44.

Killingsworth, M. J. (1996) Discourse community. In T. Enos (ed.), *Encyclopedic of Rhetoric and Composition*, New York: Garland, pp. 194–6.

Kinneavy, J. L. (1980) *A Theory of Discourse: The aims of discourse*. New York: Norton.

Kirkpatrick, A. (1991) Information sequencing in Mandarin letters of request. *Anthropological Linguistics*, 33(2), 183–203.

Kittay, J. (1988) Utterance unmoored: The changing interpretation of the act of writing in the European Middle Ages. *Language in Society*, 17, 209–30.

Kochman, T. (1981) *Black and White Styles in Conflict*. Chicago: University of Chicago Press.

Koller, V. (2005) Critical discourse analysis and social cognition: Evidence from business media discourse. *Discourse and Society*, 16, 199–224.

Kramarae, C., Schulz, M., and O'Barr, W. M. (1984) Introduction: Toward an understanding of language and power. In C. Kramarae, M. Schulz, and W. M. O'Barr (eds.), *Language and Power*, Beverly Hills: Sage, pp. 9–22.

Krashen, S. (1983) *The Natural Approach: Language acquisition in the classroom*. Englewood Cliffs, NJ: Alemany Press/Regents/Prentice-Hall.

Kress, G. (1993) Genre as social process. In B. Cope and M. Kalantzis (eds.), *The Powers of Literacy: A genre approach to teaching writing*, Pittsburgh, PA: The University of Pittsburgh Press, pp. 22–37.

Kress, G., and Van Leeuwen, T. (2001) *Multimodal Discourse: The modes and media of contemporary communication.* London: Arnold.

Krieger, L. M. (1997) AIDS drug cocktails fail 53% in study. *San Francisco Examiner,* September 29 (Online). Available: http://www.sfgate.com/cgi-bin/article.cgi?file=/examiner/archive/1997/09/29/NEWS3491.dtl.

Kristeva, J. (1986) *The Kristeva Reader* (ed. T. Moi). Oxford: Blackwell.

Kulick, D. (2005) The importance of what gets left out. *Discourse Studies,* 7, 615–24.

Labov, W. (1972a) *Sociolinguistic Patterns.* Philadelphia: University of Pennsylvania Press.

Labov, W. (1972b) The transformation of experience in narrative syntax. In *Language in the Inner City,* Philadelphia: University of Pennsylvania Press, pp. 35–396.

Labov, W. (1981) Speech actions and reactions in personal narrative. In D. Tannen (ed.), *Georgetown University Round Table on Language and Linguistics,* Washington, DC: Georgetown University Press, pp. 219–47.

Labov, W. (1994) *Principles of Linguistic Change: Internal factors.* New York: Blackwell.

Labov, W., and Waletzky, J. (1967) Narrative analysis: Oral versions of personal experience. In J. Helm (ed.), *Essays on the Verbal and Visual Arts,* Seattle: University of Washington Press, pp. 12–44.

Labov, W., and Waletzky, J. (1997) Narrative analysis: Oral versions of personal experience. Special issue on Oral Versions of Personal Experience: three decades of narrative analysis, ed. Michael G. W. Bamberg, *Journal of Narrative and Life History,* 7, 3–38.

Lakoff, G. (1987) *Women, Fire, and Dangerous Things: What categories reveal about the mind.* Chicago: University of Chicago Press.

Lakoff, G., and Johnson, M. (1980) *Metaphors We Live By.* Chicago: University of Chicago Press.

Lakoff, R. (1973) The logic of politeness, or minding your p's and q's. In C. Corum, T. C. Smith-Stark, and A. Wiser (eds.), *Proceedings of the Ninth Regional Meeting of the Chicago Linguistic Society,* Chicago: Chicago Linguistic Society, pp. 292–305.

Lakoff, R. (1974a) Remarks on "this" and "that." *Proceedings of the Tenth Annual Meeting of the Chicago Linguistic Society.* Chicago: Department of Linguistics, University of Chicago, pp. 345–56.

Lakoff, R. (1974b) What you can do with words: Politeness, pragmatics and performatives. In *Berkeley Studies in Syntax and Semantics,* vol. 1, University of California, Berkeley: Institute of Human Learning, pp. 1–55.

Lakoff, R. (1990) *Talking Power: The politics of language.* New York: Basic Books.

Lakoff, R. T. (2004[1975]) *Language and Woman's Place: Text and commentaries.* (Mary Bucholtz, ed.). New York: Oxford University Press.

Lambrecht, K. (1994) *Information Structure and Sentence Form: Topic, focus, and the mental representation of discourse referents.* Cambridge: Cambridge University Press.

Landow, G. P. (1992) *Hypertext: The convergence of contemporary critical theory and technology.* Baltimore, MD: Johns Hopkins University Press.

Lawrence, S. (2006) The intertextual forging of epideictic discourse: construals of victims in the South Africa Truth and Reconciliation Commission amnesty hearings. George Mason University, Fairfax, VA.

Lecours, A. R., and Joanette, Y. (1980) Linguistic and other aspects of paroxysmal aphasia. *Brain and Language,* 10, 1–23.

Lee, S.-H. (2006) Second summonings in Korean telephone conversation openings. *Language in Society*, 35, 261–283.

Lenneberg, E. H. (1967) *Biological Foundations of Language*. New York: John Wiley.

Lensmire, T. J., and Beals, D. E. (1994) Appropriating others' words: Traces of literature and peer culture in a third-grader's writing. *Language in Society*, 23, 411–26.

LePage, R. B., and Tabouret-Keller, A. (1985) *Acts of Identity: Creole-based approaches to language and ethnicity*. Cambridge: Cambridge University Press.

Lévi-Bruhl, L. (1926) *How Natives Think*. New York: Knopf.

Levine, P., and Scollon, R. (eds.) (2004) *Discourse and Technology: Multimodal discourse analysis*. Washington, DC: Georgetown University Press.

Levinson, S. C. (1983) *Pragmatics*. Cambridge: Cambridge University Press.

Levy, E. T., and McNeill, D. (1992) Speech, gesture, and discourse. *Discourse Processes*, 15, 277–301.

Li, C. (ed.) (1976) *Subject and Topic*. New York: Academic Press.

Linde, C. (1993) *Life Stories: The creation of coherence*. Oxford: Oxford University Press.

Lippi-Green, R. (1997) *English with an Accent: Language, ideology and discrimination in the United States*. London/New York: Routledge.

Livia, A. (2001) *Pronoun Envy: Literary uses of linguistic gender*. New York: Oxford University Press.

Livia, A., and Hall, K. (eds.) (1997) *Queerly Phrased: Language, gender, and sexuality*. Oxford/New York: Oxford University Press.

Lo, A. (1999) Codeswitching, speech community membership, and the construction of ethnic identity. *Journal of Sociolinguistics*, 3, 461–79.

Lofty, J. S. (1999) "Never use I": So whose voice speaks for me? *Language Sciences*, 21, 251–63.

Longacre, R. E. (1976) *An Anatomy of Speech Notions*. Lisse: Peter de Ridder Press.

Lucy, J. A. (1992) *Grammatical Categories and Cognition: A case study of the linguistic relativity hypothesis*. Cambridge: Cambridge University Press.

Lucy, J. A. (1997) Linguistic relativity. *Annual Review of Anthropology*, 26, 291–312.

Lunsford, A., and Connors, R. (1992) *The Saint Martin's Handbook* (2nd ed.). New York: Saint Martin's.

Malinowski, B. (1923) The problem of meaning in primitive languages. In C. K. Ogden and I. A. Richards (eds.), *The Meaning of Meaning*, New York: Harcourt, Brace, pp. 296–336.

Malmkjaer, K. (2005) *Linguistics and the Language of Translation*. Edinburgh: Edinburgh University Press.

Malmkjaer, K., and Anderson, J. M. (eds.) (1995) *The Linguistics Encyclopedia*. London/New York: Routledge.

Mann, W. C., Mattheissen, C. M. I. M., and Thompson, S. A. (1992) Rhetorical structure theory and text analysis. In W. C. Mann and S. A. Thompson (eds.), *Discourse Description: Diverse linguistic analyses of a fund-raising text*, Philadelphia: Benjamins, pp. 39–78.

Mann, W. C., and Thompson, S. A. (1988) Rhetorical structure theory: Toward a functional theory of text organization. *Text*, 8(3), 243–81.

Mannheim, B. (1986) Popular song and popular grammar, poetry and metalanguage. *Word*, 37, 45–75.

Mansfield, K. (1923) *Bliss, and Other Stories*. New York: A. Knopf.

Mao, L. R. (1994) Beyond politeness theory: "Face" revisited and renewed. *Journal of Pragmatics*, 21, 451–86.

Matsumoto, Y. (1988) Reexamination of the universality of face: Politeness phenomena in Japanese. *Journal of Pragmatics*, 12, 403–26.

Mautner, G. (2007) Mining large corpora for social information: The case of *elderly*. *Language in Society*, 36, 51–72.

Maynor, N. (1994) The language of electronic mail: Written speech? In G. D. Little and M. Montgomery (eds.), *Centennial Usage Studies* (Publication of the American Dialect Society, 78), Tuscaloosa: University of Alabama Press, pp. 48–54.

McLuhan, M. (1962) *The Gutenberg Galaxy: The Making of Typographic Man.* Toronto: University of Toronto Press.

Mellinkoff, D. (1963) *The Language of the Law.* Boston: Little, Brown.

Merritt, M. (1980) On the use of OK in service encounters. In R. Shuy and A. Shunkal (eds.), *Language Use and the Uses of Language*, Washington, DC: Georgetown University Press, pp. 162–72.

Merritt, M. (1994) Repetition in situated discourse: Exploring its forms and functions. In B. Johnstone (ed.), *Repetition in Discourse: Interdisciplinary perspectives*, vol. I, Norwood, NJ: Ablex, pp. 23–36.

Michaels, S. (1981) "Sharing time": Children's narrative styles and differential access to literacy. *Language in Society*, 10, 423–43.

Michalewicz, Z., and Fogel, D. B. (2000) *How to Solve It: Modern heuristics.* Berlin/New York: Springer.

Miller, C. (1984) Genre as social action. *Quarterly Journal of Speech*, 70, 151–67.

Mills, S. (2004) *Discourse: The new critical idiom* (2nd ed.). London: Routledge.

Milroy, J., and Milroy, L. (1985) *Authority in Language: Investigating language prescription and standardization.* London/New York: Routledge and Kegan Paul.

Milroy, L. (1987) *Language and Social Networks* (2nd ed.). Oxford: Blackwell.

Moerman, M. (1988) *Talking Culture: Ethnography and conversation analysis.* Philadelphia: University of Pennsylvania Press.

Murray, J. H. (1997) *Hamlet on the Holodeck: The future of narrative in cyberspace.* New York: The Free Press.

Myers, G. (1996) Strategic vagueness in academic writing. In E. Ventola and A. Mauranen (eds.), *Academic Writing: Intercultural and textual issues*, Amsterdam/Philadelphia: John Benjamins, pp. 3–17.

Myers, G. (2003) Discourse studies of scientific popularization: Questioning the boundaries. *Discourse Studies*, 5, 265–79.

National Centre for Industrial Language Training (NCILT) (1978) *Content, Analysis, and Methodology for the Teaching of Discourse Skills.* London: NCILT.

Nevile, M. (2006) Making sequentiality salient: *And*-prefacing in the talk of airline pilots. *Discourse Studies*, 8, 279–302.

Niedzielski, N., and Preston, D. (1999) *Folk Linguistics.* Berlin: Mouton.

Norrick, N. R. (1991) On the organization of corrective exchanges in conversation. *Journal of Pragmatics*, 16, 59–83.

Norrick, N. R. (1994) Repetition as a conversational joking strategy. In B. Johnstone (ed.), *Repetition in Discourse: Interdisciplinary perspectives*, vol. II, Norwood, NJ: Ablex, pp. 15–28.

Norris, S. (2004) *Analyzing Multimodal Interaction: A methodological framework.* New York/London: Routledge.

O'Barr, W., and Atkins, B. K. (1980) Women's language or powerless language. In S. McConnell-Ginet, R. Borker, and N. Furman (eds.), *Women and Language in Literature and Society*, New York: Praeger, pp. 93–110.

Ochs, E. (1979a) Transcription as theory. In E. Ochs and B. B. Schieffelin (eds.), *Developmental Pragmatics*, New York: Academic Press, pp. 43–72.

Ochs, E. (1979b) Planned and unplanned discourse. In T. Givón (ed.), *Syntax and Semantics*, vol. 12: *Discourse and Syntax*, New York: Academic Press.

Ochs, E. (1992) Indexing gender. In A. Duranti and C. Goodwin (eds.), *Rethinking Context: Language as an interactive phenomenon*, New York: Cambridge University Press, pp. 335–58.

Ochs, E., and Capps, L. (2001) *Living Narrative: Creating lives in everyday storytelling*. Cambridge, MA: Harvard University Press.

Ochs, E., Schegloff, E., and Thompson, S. A. (eds.) (1996) *Interaction and Grammar*. New York: Cambridge University Press.

Ochs, E., and Schieffelin, B. B. (1984) Language and socialization: Three developmental stories and their implications. In R. Shweder and R. A. LeVine (eds.), *Culture Theory: Essays on mind, self, and emotion*, Cambridge: Cambridge University Press, pp. 276–320.

Ochs, E., and Schieffelin, B. B. (eds.) (1986) *Language Socialization Across Cultures*. Cambridge: Cambridge University Press.

Ochs, E., Schieffelin, B. B., and Platt, M. (1979) Propositions across utterances and speakers. In E. Ochs and B. B. Schieffelin (eds.), *Developmental Pragmatics*, New York: Academic Press, pp. 251–68.

O'Connell, D. C., and Kowal, S. (2000) Are transcripts reproducible? *Pragmatics*, 10, 247–69.

O'Halloran, K. L. (ed.) (2004) *Multimodal Discourse Analysis: Systemic-functional perspectives*. London/New York: Continuum.

Ong, W. J. (1982) *Orality and Literacy: The technologizing of the word*. London/New York: Methuen.

Ortega y Gasset, J. (1957) *Man and People*. New York: Norton.

Ortega y Gasset, J. (1959) The difficulty of reading. *Diogenes*, 28, 1–17.

Orwell, G. (1949) *1984*. New York: Penguin.

Orwell, G. (1968) Politics and the English language. In S. Orwell and I. Angus (eds.), *The Collected Essays, Journalism, and Letters of George Orwell*, vol. IV: *In front of your nose, 1945–1950*, New York: Harcourt, Brace and World, pp. 127–40.

O'Toole, M. (1995) A systemic-functional semiotics of art. In P. H. Fries and M. Gregory (eds.), *Discourse in Society: Systemic-functional perspectives* (Meaning and choice in language: Studies for Michael Halliday, 2), Norwood, NJ: Ablex, pp. 159–79.

Paine, R. (1981) *Politically Speaking: Cross-cultural studies of rhetoric*. Philadelphia: Institute for the Study of Human Issues.

Parkinson, D. (1985) *Constructing the Social Context of Communication: Terms of address in Egyptian Arabic*. New York: Mouton de Gruyter.

Parry, M. (1971) *The Making of Homeric Verse: The collected papers of Milman Parry* (ed. A. Parry). Oxford: Clarendon Press.

Pease, D. E. (1990) Author. In F. Lentricchia and T. McLaughlin (eds.), *Critical Terms for Literary Study*, Chicago: University of Chicago Press, pp. 107–17.

Pêcheux, M. (1982) *Language, Semantics and Ideology*. London: Macmillan.

Perelman, C., and Olbrechts-Tyteca, L. (1969) *The New Rhetoric: A treatise on argumentation* (tr. J. Wilkenson and P. Weaver). Notre Dame: The University of Notre Dame Press.

Pike, K. L. (1967) *Language in Relation to a Unified Theory of the Structure of Human Behavior*. The Hague: Mouton.

Pinker, S. (1994) *The Language Instinct*. New York: William Morrow.

Polanyi, L. (1985) *Telling the American Story: A structural and cultural analysis of conversational storytelling*. Norwood, NJ: Ablex.

Polanyi, L. (1988) A formal model of the structure of discourse. *Journal of Pragmatics*, 12, 601–38.

Polya, G. (1973[1957]) *How to Solve It: A new aspect of mathematical method* (2nd ed.). Princeton: Princeton University Press.

Pomerantz, A. (1984[1979]) Agreeing and disagreeing with assessments: Some features of preferred/dispreferred turn shapes. In J. M. Atkinson and J. Heritage (eds.), *Structures of Social Action: Studies in conversation analysis*, Cambridge/Paris: Cambridge University Press and Editions de la Maison des Sciences de l'Homme, pp. 57–101.

Porter, J. E. (1992) *Audience and Rhetoric: An archaeological composition of the discourse community*. Englewood Cliffs, NJ: Prentice-Hall.

Pratt, M. L. (1977) *Toward a Speech Act Theory of Literary Discourse*. Bloomington: Indiana University Press.

Prince, E. F. (1981) Toward a taxonomy of given-new information. In P. Cole (ed.), *Radical Pragmatics*, New York: Academic Press, pp. 223–55.

Prince, E. F. (1992) The ZPG letter: Subjects, definiteness, and information status. In W. C. Mann and S. A. Thompson (eds.), *Discourse Description: Diverse linguistic analyses of a fund-raising text*, Philadelphia: John Benjamins, pp. 295–325.

Propp, V. (1968) *Morphology of the Folktale* (tr. L. Scott). Austin: University of Texas Press.

Rampton, B. (1995a) *Crossing: Language and ethnicity among adolescents*. London: Longman.

Rampton, B. (1995b) Language crossing and the problematisation of ethnicity and socialization. *Pragmatics*, 5, 485–513.

Rampton, B. (1998) Speech community. In J. Verscheuren, J.-O. Ostman, J. Blommaert, and C. Bulcaen (eds.), *Handbook of Pragmatics*, Amsterdam: John Benjamins, n.p.

Rampton, B. (ed.) (1999) *Styling the "Other."* Special issue of the *Journal of Sociolinguistics*, 3, 421–556.

Raymond, G. (2000) The voice of authority: The local accomplishment of authoritative discourse in live news broadcasts. *Discourse Studies*, 2, 354–79.

Reddy, M. (1993) The conduit metaphor. In A. Ortony (ed.), *Metaphor and Thought* (2nd ed.), Cambridge: Cambridge University Press, pp. 164–201.

Reisigl, M., and Wodak, R. (2000) *Discourse and Discrimination: Rhetorics of racism and antisemitism*. London: Routledge.

Renkema, J. (2004) *Discourse Studies: An introductory textbook* (2nd ed.). Philadelphia: John Benjamins.

Reyes, A. (2002) "Are you losing your culture?" Poetics, indexicality, and Asian American identity. *Discourse Studies*, 4, 183–99.

Rodino, M. (1997) Breaking out of binaries: Reconceptualizing gender and its relationship to language in computer-mediated communication. *Journal of Computer-Mediated Communication* (Online) 3(3). Available: http://www.ascusc.org/jcmc/vol3/issue3/rodino.html.

Rosaldo, M. Z. (1973) I have nothing to hide: The language of Ilongot oratory. *Language in Society*, 2, 193–223.

Rosaldo, M. Z. (1982) The way we do things with words: Ilongot speech acts and speech act theory in philosophy. *Language in Society*, 11, 203–37.

Sacks, H. (1995) *Lectures on Conversation* (ed. G. Jefferson, with an introduction by Emanual A. Schegloff). Cambridge, MA: Blackwell.

Sacks, H., Schegloff, E. A., and Jefferson, G. (1974) A simplest systematics for the organization of turntaking for conversation. *Language*, 50, 696–735.

Said, E. (1978) *Orientalism*. New York: Vintage Books.

Sapir, E. (1921) *Language*. New York: Harcourt, Brace, and World.

Sapir, E. (1929) The status of linguistics as a science. *Language*, 5, 205–14.

Sapir, E. (1949) *Selected Writings of Edward Sapir in Language, Culture, and Personality* (ed. D. G. Mandelbaum). Berkeley: University of California Press.

Schafer, R. (1981) Narration in the psychoanalytic dialogue. In W. J. T. Mitchell (ed.), *On Narrative*, Chicago: University of Chicago Press, pp. 25–49.

Schegloff, E. A. (1968) Sequencing in conversational openings. *American Anthropologist*, 70, 1075–95.

Schegloff, E. A., and Sacks, H. (1973) Opening up closings. *Semiotica*, 8, 289–327.

Schieffelin, B. B., Woolard, K. A., and Kroskrity, P. V. (eds.) (1998) *Language Ideologies: Practice and theory*. New York: Oxford University Press.

Schiffrin, D. (1984) Jewish argument as sociability. *Language in Society*, 13, 311–35.

Schiffrin, D. (1987) *Discourse Markers*. Cambridge: Cambridge University Press.

Schiffrin, D. (1994) *Approaches to Discourse*. Malden, MA: Blackwell.

Schiffrin, D. (1996) Narrative as self-portrait: Sociolinguistic constructions of identity. *Language in Society*, 25, 167–203.

Schiffrin, D., Tannen, D., and Hamilton, H. E. (eds.) (2001) *Handbook of Discourse Analysis*. Malden, MA: Blackwell.

Schilling-Estes, N. (1998) Investigating "self-conscious" speech: The performance register in Ocracoke English. *Language in Society*, 27, 53–83.

Schnebly, C. (1994) Repetition and failed conversation in the Theater of the Absurd. In B. Johnstone (ed.), *Repetition in Discourse*, vol. II, Norwood, NJ: Ablex, pp. 98–112.

Schultz, P. (1991) Pumpernickel. In J. Myers and R. Weingarten (eds.), *New American Poets of the '90s*, Lincoln, MA: David R. Godine, p. 342.

Scollon, R. (1976) *Conversations with a One-Year-Old: A case study of the developmental functions of syntax*. Honolulu: University of Hawaii Press.

Scollon, R. (2001) *Mediated Discourse: The nexus of practice*. London/New York: Routledge.

Scollon, R., and Scollon, S. W. (1981) *Narrative, Literacy, and Face in Interethnic Communication*. Norwood, NJ: Ablex.

Scollon, R., and Scollon, S. W. (2004) *Nexus Analysis: Discourse and the emerging internet*. London/New York: Routledge.

Scribner, S., and Cole, M. (1981) *The Psychology of Literacy*. Cambridge, MA: Harvard University Press.

Searle, J. R. (1969) *Speech Acts: An essay in the philosophy of language*. Cambridge: Cambridge University Press.

Sherzer, J. (1975) Semantic systems, discourse structures, and the ecology of language. In R. W. Fasold and R. W. Shuy (eds.), *Studies in Language Variation*, Washington, DC: Georgetown University Press, pp. 283–93.

Sherzer, J. (1982) Poetic structuring of Kuna discourse: The line. *Language in Society*, 11, 371–90.

Sherzer, J. (1983) *Kuna Ways of Speaking: An ethnographic perspective*. Austin: University of Texas Press.

Sherzer, J. (1987) A discourse-centered approach to language and culture. *American Anthropologist*, 89, 295–305.

Sherzer, J., and Urban, G. (eds.) (1986) *Native South American Discourse*. New York: Mouton de Gruyter.

Sherzer, J., and Woodbury, A. C. (eds.) (1987) *Native American Discourse: Poetics and rhetoric*. New York: Cambridge University Press, 3.

Silverstein, M. (1979) Language structure and linguistic ideology. In P. R. Clyne, W. F. Hanks, and C. Hofbauer (eds.), *The Elements: A parasession on linguistic units and levels*, Chicago: Chicago Linguistics Society, pp. 193–247.

Silverstein, M. (1995[1976]) Shifters, linguistic categories, and cultural description. In B. G. Blount (ed.), *Language, Culture, and Society: A book of readings*, Prospect Heights, IL: Waveland Press, pp. 187–221.

Silverstein, M. (2003) Indexical order and the dialectics of sociolinguistic life. *Language and Communication*, 23, 193–229.

Silverstein, M. (2004) "Cultural" concepts and the language-culture nexus. *Current Anthropology*, 45, 621–45.

Silverstein, M., and Urban, G. (eds.) (1996) *Natural Histories of Discourse*. Chicago: University of Chicago Press.

Sinclair, J. M. (1991) *Corpus, Concordance, Collocation*. Oxford: Oxford University Press.

Sinclair, J. M., and Brazil, D. (1982) *Teacher Talk*. Oxford: Oxford University Press.

Sinclair, J. M., and Coulthard, M. (1975) *Towards an Analysis of Discourse*. London: Oxford University Press.

Sinclair-James, B. (1992) "And" as technique: The suspension of contrary action. Unpublished manuscript, Texas A&M University.

Snow, C. E., and Ferguson, C. (eds.) (1977) *Talking to Children: Language input and acquisition*. Cambridge: Cambridge University Press.

Spears, R., and Lea, M. (1994) Panacea or panopticon? The hidden power in computer-mediated communication. *Communication Research*, 21, 427–59.

Sperber, D., and Wilson, D. (1986) *Relevance: Communication and cognition*. Cambridge, MA: Havard University Press.

Starting Points-Pittsburgh (1999) Reading is power: A look at early literacy in our area and what we all can do to help encourage children to read. *Pittsburgh Magazine* (special advertising supplement), September, pp. 57–65.

Stewart, C. O. (2005) A rhetorical approach to news discourse: Media representations of a controversial study on "reparative therapy." *Western Journal of Communication*, 69, 147–66.

Street, B. V. (1984) *Literacy in Theory and Practice*. Cambridge: Cambridge University Press.

Street, B. V. (ed.) (1993) *Cross-cultural Approaches to Literacy*. Cambridge: Cambridge University Press.

Street, R. L., and Hopper, R. (1982) A model of speech style evaluation. In E. B. Ryan and H. Giles (eds.), *Attitudes Towards Language Variation: Social and applied contexts*, London: Edward Arnold, pp. 175–88.

Stross, B. (1974) Speaking of speaking: Tenejapa Tzeltal metalinguistics. In R. Bauman and J. Sherzer (eds.), *Explorations in the Ethnography of Speaking*, Cambridge: Cambridge University Press, pp. 213–39.

Stubbs, M. (1983) *Discourse Analysis: The sociolinguistic analysis of natural language*. Chicago: University of Chicago Press.

Stubbs, M. (1996) *Text and Corpus Analysis*. Cambridge: Cambridge University Press.

Swales, J. M. (1990) *Genre Analysis: English in academic and research settings*. Cambridge: Cambridge University Press.

Swales, J. M. (1998) *Different Floors, Different Voices: A textography of a small university building*. Mahwah, NJ: Lawrence Erlbaum.

Synge, J. M. (1935) *The Complete Plays*. New York: Random House.

Taboada, M., and Mann, W. C. (2006) Rhetorical Structure Theory: Looking back and moving ahead. *Discourse Studies*, 8, 423–59.

Tannen, D. (1979) What's in a frame? Surface evidence for underlying expectations. In R. Freedle (ed.), *New Directions in Discourse Processing*, Norwood, NJ: Ablex, pp. 137–81.

Tannen, D. (1980) A comparative analysis of oral narrative strategies: Athenian Greek and American English. In W. Chafe (ed.), *The Pear Stories: Cognitive, cultural, and linguistic aspects of narrative production*, Norwood, NJ: Ablex, pp. 51–87.

Tannen, D. (1981) New York Jewish conversational style. *International Journal of the Sociology of Language*, 30, 133–49.

Tannen, D. (1982a) Oral and literate strategies in spoken and written narratives. *Language*, 58, 1–21.

Tannen, D. (ed.) (1982b) *Spoken and Written Language: Exploring orality and literacy*. Norwood, NJ: Ablex.

Tannen, D. (1983) When is an overlap not an interruption? In R. DiPietro, W. Frawley, and A. Wedel (eds.), *First Delaware Symposium on Language Studies*, Newark: The University of Delaware Press, pp. 119–29.

Tannen, D. (1984) *Conversational Style: Analyzing talk among friends*. Norwood, NJ: Ablex.

Tannen, D. (1986a) Introducing constructed dialogue in Greek and American conversational narrative. In F. Coulmas (ed.), *Direct and Indirect Speech*, New York: Mouton de Gruyter, pp. 311–32.

Tannen, D. (1986b) *That's Not What I Meant: How conversational style makes or breaks your relations with others*. New York: William Morrow.

Tannen, D. (1987a) Repetition in conversation as spontaneous formulaicity. *Text*, 7, 215–43.

Tannen, D. (1987b) Repetition in conversation: Toward a poetics of talk. *Language*, 63, 574–605.

Tannen, D. (1989) *Talking Voices: Repetition, dialogue, and imagery in conversational discourse*. Cambridge: Cambridge University Press.

Tannen, D. (1990) *You Just Don't Understand: Women and men in conversation*. New York: William Morrow.

Tannen, D. (ed.) (1993a) *Framing in Discourse*. New York: Oxford University Press.

Tannen, D. (ed.) (1993b) *Gender and Conversational Interaction*. Oxford: Oxford University Press.

Tannen, D. (1994) *Gender and Discourse*. New York: Oxford University Press.

Tannen, D. (1999) *The Argument Culture: Stopping America's war of words*. New York: Ballantine.

Tannen, D., and Saville-Troike, M. (eds.) (1985) *Perspectives on Silence*. Norwood, NJ: Ablex.

Tarone, E., Dwyer, S., and Icke, V. (1988) On the use of the passive in two astrophysics journals. In J. Swales (ed.), *Episodes in ESP: A source and reference book for the development of English for Science and Technology*, London: Pergamon, pp. 191–205.

Taylor, T. J. (1997) *Theorizing Language: Analysis, normativity, rhetoric, history*. New York: Pergamon.

Tedlock, D. (1983) *The Spoken Word and the Work of Interpretation*. Philadelphia: University of Pennsylvania Press.

Ten Have, P. (1999) *Doing Conversation Analysis: A practical guide*. London: Sage.

Thakerar, J. N., Giles, H., and Cheshire, J. (1982) Psychological and linguistic parameters of speech accommodation theory. In C. Fraser and K. R. Scherer (eds.), *Advances in the Social Psychology of Language*, Cambridge: Cambridge University Press, pp. 205–55.

Thompson, G. (1996) *Introducing Functional Grammar*. London: Edward Arnold.

Thurlow, C., and Jaworski, A. (2006) The alchemy of the upwardly mobile: Symbolic capital and the stylization of elites in frequent-flyer programmes. *Discourse in Society*, 17, 99–135.

Titscher, S., Meyer, M., Wodak, R., and Vetter, E. (2000) *Methods of Text and Discourse Analysis* (tr. B. Jenner). London: Sage.

Todorov, T. (1976) The origin of genres. *New Literary History*, 8, 159–70.

Toolan, M. (1996) *Total Speech: An integrational linguistic approach to language*. Durham, NC: Duke University Press.

Tracy, K. (1988) A discourse analysis of four discourse studies. *Discourse processes*, 11, 243–59.

Tuman, M. (ed.) (1992) *Literacy Online*. Pittsburgh, PA: University of Pittsburgh Press.

Turkle, S. (1995) *Life on the Screen: Identity in the age of the Internet*. New York: Simon and Schuster.

Ueda, K. (1974) Sixteen ways to avoid saying "no" in Japan. In J. C. Condon and M. Seito (eds.), *Intercultural Encounters with Japan: Communication, contact, and conflict*, Tokyo: Simul Press, pp. 185–92.

Urban, G. (1991) *A Discourse-Centered Approach to Culture: Native South American myths and rituals*. Austin: University of Texas Press.

Urban, G. (1996) *Metaphysical Community: The interplay of the senses and the intellect*. Austin: University of Texas Press.

Ure, J. (1982) Introduction: Approaches to the study of register range. *International Journal of the Sociology of Language*, 35, 5–23.

van Dijk, T. A. (1980) *Macrostructures: An interdisciplinary study of global structures in discourse, interaction, and cognition*. Hillsdale, NJ: Lawrence Erlbaum.

van Dijk, T. A. (1981) Episodes as units of discourse analysis. In D. Tannen (ed.), *Georgetown University Round Table on Languages and Linguistics 1982*, Washington, DC: Georgetown University Press, pp. 177–95.

van Dijk, T. A. (ed.) (1985) *Handbook of Discourse Analysis* (4 vols.). London/ Orlando, FL: Academic Press.

van Dijk, T. A. (1986) News schemata. In C. R. Cooper and S. Greenbaum (eds.), *Studying Writing: Linguistic approaches*, Beverly Hills, CA: Sage, pp. 155–85.

van Dijk, T. A. (1987) *Communicating Racism: Ethnic prejudice in thought and talk.* Newbury Park, CA: Sage.

van Dijk, T. A. (1993a) Principles of critical discourse analysis. *Discourse in Society*, 4, 249–83.

van Dijk, T. A. (1993b) *Discourse and Elite Racism.* London: Sage.

van Dijk, T. A. (ed.) (1997) *Discourse Studies: A multidisciplinary introduction* (2 vols.). London: Sage.

Vande Kopple, W. J. (1986) Given and new information and some aspects of the structures, semantics, and pragmatics of written texts. In C. R. Cooper and S. Greenbaum (eds.), *Studying Writing: Linguistic approaches*, Beverly Hills: Sage, pp. 72–111.

Varenne, H. (1978) Culture as rhetoric: Patterning in the verbal interpretation of interaction between teachers and administrators in an American high school. *American Ethnologist*, 5, 635–50.

Walker, A. G. (1982) *Discourse Rights of Witnesses: Their circumscription in trial.* Sociolinguistic Working Paper, vol. 25. Austin, TX: Southwest Educational Development Laboratory.

Washington, J. M. (ed.) (1986) *A Testament of Hope: The essential writings of Martin Luther King, Jr.* San Francisco: Harper and Row.

Watts, R. J. (2003) *Politeness.* Cambridge: Cambridge University Press.

Webber, B. L. (2001) Computational perspectives on discourse and dialog. In D. Schiffrin, D. Tannen, and H. Hamilton (eds.), *Handbook of Discourse Analysis*, Malden, MA: Blackwell, pp. 798–816.

Webster's Ninth New Collegiate Dictionary (1983). Springfield, MA: Merriam-Webster.

Welty, E. (1984) *One Writer's Beginnings.* Cambridge, MA: Harvard University Press.

Wenger, E. (1998) *Communities of Practice.* Cambridge and New York: Cambridge University Press.

Werry, C. C. (1996) Linguistic and interactional features of Internet relay chat. In S. C. Herring (ed.), *Computer-Mediated Communication: Linguistic, social, and cross-cultural perspectives*, Amsterdam/Philadelphia: John Benjamins, pp. 47–63.

Wharry, C. (2003) Amen and hallelujah preaching: Discourse functions in African American sermons. *Language in Society*, 32, 203–25.

Whorf, B. L. (1941) The relation of habitual thought and behavior to language. In Leslie Spier (ed.), *Language, Culture, and Personality: Essays in memory of Edward Sapir*, Menasha, WI: Sapir Memorial Publication Fund, pp. 75–93.

Wittgenstein, L. (1953) *Philosophical Investigations.* New York: Macmillan.

Wittgenstein, L. (1955) *Tractatus Logico-Philosophicus.* London: Routledge and Kegan Paul.

Wittgenstein, L. (1958) *The Blue and Brown Books.* New York: Harper and Row.

Wodak, R. (1996) *Disorders of Discourse.* London: Longman.

Wolfson, N. (1981) Compliments in cross-cultural perspective. *TESOL Quarterly*, 15, 117–24.

Woodbury, A. C. (1987) Rhetorical structure in a Central Alaskan Yupik Eskimo traditional narrative. In J. Sherzer and A. C. Woodbury (eds.), *Native American Discourse: Poetics and rhetoric*, New York: Cambridge University Press, pp. 176–239.

Wooffitt, R. (2005) *Conversation Analysis and Discourse Analysis: A comparative and critical introduction.* London: Sage.

Wooffitt, R., Fraser, N., Gilbert, N., and McGlashan, S. (1997) *Humans, Computers, and Wizards: Analysing human (simulated) computer interaction.* London: Routledge.

Woolard, K. A., and Schieffelin, B. B. (1994) Language ideology. *Annual Review of Anthropology*, 23, 55–82.

Young, K. G. (1987) *Taleworlds and Storyrealms.* Boston: Martinus Nijhoff.

Young, R. E., Becker, A. L., and Pike, K. L. (1970) *Rhetoric: Discovery and change.* New York: Harcourt, Brace, and World.

Zawodny-Wetzel, D. (1999) Conversing at the citizen police review board meetings: Negotiating group identity and individual discourse expectations. Paper presented at Penn State Rhetoric Conference. University Park, PA, July 4–7.

Zdenek, S. (1999) Rising up from the MUD: Inscribing gender in software design. *Discourse in Society*, 10, 379–409.

Zimmerman, D. H. (1998) Identity, context, and interaction. In C. Antaki and S. Widdicombe (eds.), *Identities in Talk*, London: Sage, pp. 87–106.

Index